Music and German N

Two week loan

Please return on or before the last
date stamped below.
Charges are made for late return.

IS 239/0799

INFORMATION SERVICES PO BOX 430, CARDIFF CF10 3XT

Music and German National Identity

EDITED BY CELIA APPLEGATE AND PAMELA POTTER

The University of Chicago Press / Chicago and London

The University of Chicago Press, Chicago 60637
The University of Chicago Press, Ltd., London
© 2002 by The University of Chicago
All rights reserved. Published 2002
Printed in the United States of America
11 10 09 08 07 06 05 04 03 02   1 2 3 4 5

ISBN: 0-226-02130-0 (cloth)
ISBN: 0-226-02131-9 (paper)

Library of Congress Cataloging-in-Publication Data

Music and German national identity / edited by Celia Applegate and
    Pamela Potter.
      p.   cm.
    Includes bibliographical references and index.
    ISBN 0-226-02130-0 (cloth : alk. paper)—ISBN 0-226-02131-9 (paper :
alk. paper)
      1. Music—Germany—History and criticism. 2. Music—Social
aspects—Germany. I. Applegate, Celia. II. Potter, Pamela Maxine.

ML275 .M933 2002
780'.943—dc21

                                        2001007534

Contents

Acknowledgments

The editors are most indebted to the authors represented in this collection and are especially appreciative of their willingness to meet the challenge of shaping their contributions toward strengthening the volume as a whole. We would also like to express our gratitude to the following for the financial support made available to facilitate collaboration on this project: the William F. Vilas Trust, the Eugenie Mayer Bolz Fellowships, the Institute for Research in the Humanities at the University of Wisconsin-Madison, and faculty research support from the University of Rochester. In addition, we wish to offer our thanks to Eric Jarosinski, Sherri Jones, Ted Rippey, and Sara B. Young for their work on translating the German contributions to this volume (the essays by Bernd Sponheuer, Jost Hermand, and Albrecht Riethmüller), to Anna Nekola for her help in the final preparation of the manuscript, to David Bemelmans for his meticulous copyediting of the text, and to Leslie Keros for shepherding the book through its final stages. A special debt of gratitude also goes to Stewart Weaver, who generously gave his expertise and many hours to assisting with the preparation of the index.

Mary Applegate, Charles Fisher, David Applegate, and Heidi Applegate all graciously provided hospitable meeting places in which our collaboration could flourish, as did (unknown to itself but much appreciated by us) the Annual Meeting of the German Studies Association, where we first learned of each other's work and were able to develop this project over several successive years. Finally, we want to thank Kathleen Hansell of the University of Chicago Press for her patience, encouragement, and support of the project throughout its many stages of development.

Abbreviations

A	Thomas Mann, *Addresses Delivered at the Library of Congress, 1942–1949* (Washington, D.C.: Library of Congress, 1963)
AdJ	Archiv der deutschen Jugendbewegung
AEKR	Archiv der evangelischen Kirche im Rheinland
BA MA Freiburg	Bundesarchiv-Militärarchiv Freiburg
BA Potsdam	Bundesarchiv Potsdam
BNF	Robert Schumann. *Briefe, Neue Folge,* 2d ed., ed. Gustav Jansen (Leipzig: Breitkopf & Härtel, 1904)
CDU	Christian Democratic Union
CSU	Christian Socialist Union
DF	Thomas Mann, *Doctor Faustus,* trans. John E. Woods (New York: Knopf, 1997)
EZA Berlin	Evangelisches Zentralarchiv Berlin
FDJ	Free German Youth (Freie Deutsche Jugend)
FRG	Federal Republic of Germany
GDR	German Democratic Republic (former East Germany)
GW	Thomas Mann, *Gesammelte Werke in dreizehn Bänden* (Frankfurt am Main: S. Fischer, 1990)
HJb	*Hindemith-Jahrbuch*
Int	Interview with former members of the Spielschar and Schilljugend in Germany and Austria
JA-IzJ	Jugendarchiv, Institut für zeitgeschichtliche Jugendforschung

KAG Minden	Kommunalarchiv Minden, Kirchengeschichtliche Arbeitsgemeinschaft
KPD	German Communist Party (Kommunistische Partei Deutschlands)
L	*Letters of Thomas Mann, 1889–1955*, selected and trans. Richard and Clara Winston, intro. Richard Winston (New York: Knopf, 1971)
LKA Bielefeld	Landeskirchenarchiv Bielefeld
LV	Landschaftliche Volkslieder
NA	National Archives
NDW	New German Wave (Neue Deutsche Welle)
NSDAP	National Socialist German Workers' Party (National-sozialistische deutsche Arbeiterpartei)
OW	Österreichische National-Bibliothek, Vienna, Musik-sammlung, F
PCW	Thomas Mann, *Pro and Contra Wagner*, trans. Allan Blunden, intro. Erich Heller (Chicago: University of Chicago Press, 1985)
R	Thomas Mann, *Reflections of a Nonpolitical Man*, trans. and intro. Walter D. Morris (New York: Frederick Ungar, 1983)
SED	Socialist Unity Party (Sozialistische Einheitspartei Deutschlands)
SMAD	Soviet Military Administration in Germany (Sovietische Militäradministration in Deutschland)
SPD	Social Democratic Party (Sozialdemokratische Partei Deutschlands)
TB 1	Robert Schumann. *Tagebücher, Band I: 1827–1838*, ed. Georg Eismann (Leipzig: VEB Deutscher Verlag für Musik, 1971)
TB 2	Robert Schumann. *Tagebücher, Band II: 1836–1854*, ed. Gerd Nauhaus (Leipzig: VEB Deutscher Verlag für Musik, 1987)
TB 3	Robert Schumann. *Tagebücher, Band III: Haushalt-bücher*, pts. 1 (1837–47) and 2 (1847–56), ed. Gerd Nauhaus (Leipzig: VEB Deutscher Verlag für Musik, 1982)
USIA	United States Information Agency
ZfM	*Zeitschrift für Musik*

Germans as the "People of Music": Genealogy of an Identity

CELIA APPLEGATE AND PAMELA POTTER

For musical audiences today, the words "German" and "music" merge so easily into a single concept that their connection is hardly ever questioned. The catechism of the three B's—Bach, Beethoven, and Brahms—reinforces the notion of German leadership in musical developments of the past three hundred years. Even a cursory glance at the repertoires of concert halls throughout the world reveals a preponderance of works from the German-Austrian masters of the eighteenth, nineteenth, and twentieth centuries. These works form the largest share of what we call "classical" or "serious" music, and sustain not only much of concert life but also the classical music recording industry and tourism. Germany and Austria function to this day as the twin centers of classical music, with their multitude of orchestras, opera houses, and conservatories, and have gained renown as home to some of the most influential composers, conductors, educators, and music scholars. When musicologists place Finnish, Czech, Russian, or Spanish musical compositions under the heading of "musical nationalism," they implicitly compare them against a universally accepted German music and presume that other nations tried to distinguish themselves by deviating from the German standard. German music achieved the ultimate in universality when NASA's Voyagers 1 and 2 headed out into space in 1977, each carrying an aluminum-encased, gold-plated phonograph record with generous portions of Bach, Mozart, and Beethoven among its musical offerings from earth to listeners unknown.[1]

---

1. Carl Sagan was largely responsible for this optimistic undertaking. Both Voyager spacecrafts have by now left our solar system and will not encounter another one for about

But how did music come to be so closely associated with Germany or "Germanness"? When and how did Germans come to be regarded as the "people of music," and music regarded as the "most German art"? And what, if anything, distinguishes German music from the music of any other national group? An attempt to answer these questions is not merely an academic exercise. For more than two hundred years, not only academicians have been concerned with the Germanness of music and musicians, and debates far afield from the pages of scholarly journals have raged over the question of just how "German" are these songs, symphonies, sonatas, and operas penned by German and Austrian masters. A preoccupation with music's connection to German identity or character has entered the realms of imaginative literature, philosophy, travel memoirs, private letters and diaries, journalism, and of course music scholarship—ultimately seeping into musical life, influencing musical events, shaping musical organizations, affecting composition, performance, and the music industry, and placing German music in a position of central importance.

The existence of debates, past and contemporary, over how or whether certain music is German reveals the fundamental contribution that music has made to German imaginings of nationhood and collective identity. Paradoxically, however, such connections between music and Germanness were rarely consciously cultivated by the composers themselves. Although at certain points in history people attributed to composers such as Bach, Handel, Mozart, and Beethoven an acute awareness of their own German character and a desire to contribute to German greatness, such attributions were usually made as part of a retrospective search for a distinct German identity and had little, if anything, to do with the actual intentions of these composers. Even the role of Richard Wagner, an outspoken commentator on the meaning of being German, became exaggerated to the extent of rendering him a prophet of Hitler's "thousand-year Reich,"[2] and although early-twentieth-century composers as diverse as Pfitzner, Strauss, and Schoenberg were known to proclaim their own commitment to perpetuating German musical greatness, their works do not necessarily reveal unambiguous German content or character. Rather, as we suggest in this introductory essay and as most of the following essays further explore, the

---

forty thousand years, so the only hope for extraterrestrial enjoyment of Bach's Brandenburg Concerto no. 2 is if some alien spaceship intersected with our nuclear-powered phonograph equipment. For a complete listing of Voyager's music, see the NASA website, http://vraptor.jpl.nasa.gov/voyager.

2. Joachim Köhler, *Wagner's Hitler: The Prophet and His Disciple*, trans. Ronald Taylor (Cambridge: Polity Press, 1999).

links between music and German identity can more often than not be traced
to writers, thinkers, statesmen, educators, impresarios, demagogues, and
audiences, but only occasionally to composers.

How, then, have the links between music and German national identity
been forged? The further back into history one searches, the more elusive
the very notion of a German national identity becomes. Most historians
would agree that the eighteenth century marked the beginning of an emerging consciousness of German identity among certain speakers of German,
as well as accompanying forms of cultural and political activism aimed at
defining a putative national culture and debating the political future of central Europe.[3] Musicians and composers of the eighteenth century, however,
remained largely on the margins of such activism and did not at first consciously contribute to the emergent national culture. Certainly many would
have called themselves German, but for them to have labeled their music
"German" or to consider their work as a contribution to something called a
national culture would have required a stretch of the imagination exceed-
ingly rare for the time. For although literate and often well traveled, the composers and musicians of the eighteenth century practiced their art mainly
within the confines of either the court or the town. The former was cosmopolitan, the latter provincial. Neither was in any meaningful sense national.
     Musical life of the eighteenth century was not, however, wholly with-
out national significance. But this significance was conveyed through the
process of writing about music, not through musical composition. Indeed,
the one nationalizing milieu that existed in central Europe was that of literary culture—in James Sheehan's words, "a culture of readers and writers
for whom print had become the essential means of communication and
printed matter the primary source and subject of cultural activity."[4] German national consciousness began in such circles, emerging from discussions about developing a unity of taste and judgment on literary matters and
eventually spilling over into musical matters. In 1770, Friedrich Nicolai

---

3. The best single account for Germany is Hagen Schulze, *The Course of German Nationalism: From Frederick the Great to Bismarck, 1763–1867* (New York: Cambridge University Press, 1991); also useful and covering a greater time span is Michael Hughes, *Nationalism
and Society: Germany 1800–1950* (Baltimore: E. Arnold, 1988).
     4. Sheehan's chapter on eighteenth-century culture in his *German History 1770–1866*
(New York: Oxford University Press, 1989), esp. 153, provides an account of these cultural
worlds that makes clear the barriers to national–cultural formation.

estimated that there were about twenty thousand people participating in the national debate. The earliest articulation of music's meaning and of its relationship to national identity came from among those twenty thousand—journalists, aesthetic philosophers, scholars and historians of music, writers of fiction and poetry.[5]

Writers about music existed at first on the edge of literary culture, marginalized because "printed matter" was not their primary focus and because their subject seemed to have far less direct relevance to a national identity defined initially in terms of its literature and language. Still, early music periodicals began to suggest the importance at least of opera to national culture. Already in 1722, Johann Mattheson's *Critica musica* and *Der musikalische Patriot* urged greater attention to native German operatic traditions, which were in danger of disappearing altogether in the maelstrom of Italian opera's popularity. Short-lived though these and many subsequent journals proved to be, they did provide an early forum for discussion of the Germanness of music, as Bernd Sponheuer's contribution to this volume shows. Nevertheless, their articulation of a national identity to music was tentative and inconsistent. Writers like Johann Adolf Scheibe retained a strong Enlightenment interest in the universality of music and regarded German-speaking composers as at their best when drawing on a variety of European styles.

By the end of the eighteenth century, however, claims for music's importance to German national culture grew increasingly bold. For instance, Friedrich Rochlitz, the founding editor of the long-running *Allgemeine Musikalische Zeitung* in Leipzig, committed his new journal almost from the outset to articulating the exclusively German character of certain music, as well as its crucial contribution to German national culture. In 1799, he wrote of how important it was for Germans to understand their musical past, not as a succession of achievements of accomplished men, but, in a curious formulation, as part of "the history of the development [*Bildung*] of the nation overall"—or elsewhere, as the history of "the culture of music among contemporary Germans as well as the shaping [*Ausbildung*] of the nation through this art."[6] In 1801, Rochlitz commissioned Johann Karl

5. Mary Sue Morrow, *German Music Criticism in the Late Eighteenth Century: Aesthetic Issues in Instrumental Music* (Cambridge: Cambridge University Press, 1997), 45–60. See also Mary Sue Morrow, "Building a National Identity with Music: A Story from the Eighteenth Century," in *Searching for Common Ground: Diskurse zur deutschen Identität 1750–1871*, ed. Nicholas Vazsonyi (Cologne: Böhlau, 2000), 255–269.

6. Friedrich Rochlitz, "Vorschläge zu Betrachtungen über die neueste Geschichte der Musik," *Allgemeine Musikalische Zeitung* 1 (1798/99).

Friedrich Triest, a pastor in Stettin and as such a member of the nation of readers and writers, to compile such a musical history of the nation. In his "Comments Regarding the Development of Music in Germany in the Eighteenth Century," an article appearing in the *Allgemeine Musikalische Zeitung* in 1801 and discussed in detail in the essay by Bernd Sponheuer, Triest chose to emphasize the importance of recent developments for Germany's musical self-realization and culminated in a paean to J. S. Bach's "German industriousness and national spirit."[7]

Even bolder, however, was the 1802 Bach biography by J. N. Forkel, whose work as musical director at the University of Göttingen and as musical scholar epitomized the new participation of musicians in the intellectual life of the cultural nation. The biography amounted to the first fully realized statement of the existence of a specifically German music. Moreover, Forkel placed music squarely within the nationalizing project of literary culture (just as Rochlitz had done with his journal by associating music with national *Bildung*) by naming Bach the musical counterpart to the Greek and Roman classics so central to the humanistic curricula of the *Gymnasium* and of reformist universities. Bach was "the first classic that ever was, or perhaps ever will be," and thus "an invaluable national patrimony, with which no other nation has anything to be compared."[8] Rochlitz, Triest, and Forkel together forged the link between writing music history and promoting national consciousness. Their work thus contributed to a process we might label "canon formation," by which the notion of a "national patrimony" came increasingly to inform musical listening and performance.

But how did such ideas on music and national patrimony sit with the authorities? What was the role of this national patrimony in the political process of building a nation? In fact, the states of Germany—whether national, Prussian, Austrian, or otherwise—had not always promoted a unified German state or a German culture. To the contrary, the political nationalists from the late eighteenth century on met with considerable state opposition and even repression. Those promoting a nationalist cultural agenda—through journals, celebrations of great Germans like Luther or Bach, folk song collecting, and other such projects—were hardly less suspect in the eyes of bureaucrats and aristocrats committed to the status quo. Nor were such suspicions unfounded, for after 1815, political and cultural

7. Cited in Erich Reimer, "Nationalbewußtsein und Musikgeschichtsschreibung in Deutschland 1800–1850," *Die Musikforschung* 46 (1993): 20–24.

8. J. N. Forkel, *Über Johann Sebastian Bachs Leben, Kunst und Kunstwerke*, ed. Claudia Maria Knispel (1802: Berlin: Henschel Verlag, 2000), 21–22.

agendas within a loosely defined German nationalist movement often reflected an increasingly generalized dissatisfaction with small statism and the fragmentation of public life that it engendered. Moreover, growing literacy rates meant that the market expanded for books and newspapers, bookshops and coffeehouses, all of which contributed to nationalism's force, even as the states of the German Confederation tried through censorship and taxation to slow down the trend. The result, as Hagen Schulze has written, was that "a huge gulf open[ed] up between state and society." [9]

Given the state's initial opposition to the national project, any evidence of state intervention in musical life before 1871, while abundant, should not mislead one into thinking that German politicians exercised a long tradition of manipulating music toward nationalist ends. Still, a number of state and local governments contributed to the signification of music as a national treasure—not, in other words, as merely a pleasant accessory to public ceremonials. The Prussian state's work in this regard was precedent setting, but also highly pragmatic. For instance, the Prussian king's decision in 1809 to include a special music section in the prestigious Academy of Arts reflected his acquiescence to the reformers' agenda of state and social renewal. But this was a nationalist agenda only insofar as its central axiom was that the state, to successfully combat Napoleonic power, had to draw on the moral as well as the physical resources of the people. Musicians, for their part, saw an opportunity here to advance their own agendas. According to the musician who stood behind this particular reformist initiative, Carl Friedrich Zelter of the Berlin *Singakademie*, music had a "communal purpose," and that was *Bildung*, the "activity of inner or spiritual forces, to the end that man realizes his complete existence and becomes nobler." One could argue that music had contributed more than any other art to the "formation of the German nation," understood morally and culturally, that no other art lay so close to the essence of being German, and hence no other art so deserved the state's sponsorship and support. [10]

Such agendas probably had less immediate effect on how Germans of the time heard music than did the more public statements of men like Rochlitz and Forkel. But gradually, as the state involved itself in the training of musicians as well as in the appointment of musical directors and institutional leaders of various sorts, the public became more aware of the state's compelling interest in the excellence of musical culture. In such

9. Schulze, *Course of German Nationalism*, 60.

10. For a fuller discussion of this episode and era, see Celia Applegate, "How German Is It? Nationalism and the Idea of Serious Music in the Early Nineteenth Century," *19th-Century Music* 21 (spring 1998): 274–96.

large public events as the Lower Rhine Music Festivals, local governments
of Rhenish cities—chief among them Düsseldorf—committed themselves
as Prussia had to celebrating music as a national inheritance and treasure.[11]
Even such a fundamentally silly undertaking as Ludwig I of Bavaria's Doric
temple of Valhalla, a monument to German heroes on the banks of the
Danube above Regensburg, included the busts of a few composers among
those of rulers, warriors, and other great men of the German nation.[12] Ludwig, like Friedrich Wilhelm IV of Prussia, shared a general consciousness
of cultural nationhood with the nationalist movement, and while hardly
eager to change the political arrangements of the German Confederation,
both kings sponsored a number of national cultural projects.

By the time Ludwig was building his Valhalla, composers were no longer as
passive in the creation of their own national significance as composers in
the eighteenth century had been. The nineteenth century was, after all, an
extended period of transformation in Europe, and the social status of musicians changed along with that of many other trades organized through
court and guild. The changing social opportunities for musicians condi-
tioned new attitudes, and an unprecedented awareness of one's importance
to national cultures became a defining feature of the modern nineteenth-
century composer. Such changes developed slowly and unevenly, however,
and each composer had different reasons for and different means of responding to the national idea. Mozart, for example, writing in the thick of
what most historians consider the advent of the national idea, was frustrated by his transitional social status as neither servant nor master in the
world of court culture, but he did not imagine any solution to his problems
in dreams of nationhood.[13]

11. Cecelia Porter, "The New Public and the Reordering of the Musical Establishment:
The Lower Rhine Music Festivals, 1816–67," *19th-Century Music* 13 (spring 1980): 211–24.
    12. Albrecht Riethmüller, *Die Walhalla und ihre Musiker* (Laaber: Laaber-Verlag, 1993);
George L. Mosse, *The Nationalization of the Masses* (New York: Howard Fertig Publishers,
1975), 53–56.
    13. Enlightenment maybe, but enlightenment and nationalism exist as much in tension
as in harmony with each other. Mozart's Enlightenment stance is, again, a largely cosmopolitan one, not especially linked to the concerns of figures of the German Enlightenment (Herder,
for instance) with determining the character of various national cultures. See Nicholas Till,
Mozart and the Enlightenment: Truth, Virtue and Beauty in Mozart's Operas (Boston: Faber
& Faber, 1992).

Beethoven had considerably greater interest in the politics of both revolution and restoration, yet one balks at the notion of calling him a nationalist or of suggesting that he ever thought deeply about Germany (of any shape) or Germanness. One can point to a few works, written at various moments during the Napoleonic wars, which reflected a kind of standard-issue patriotism, perhaps even the nationalism of the anti-French backlash among central Europeans. Yet for every one of Beethoven's utterances about laying his work "upon the altar of the Fatherland" or living "German and free," one can find many more tributes to the "bearers of crowns . . . who have saved the people," to the "princes" who with "God's power" have won the victory, to the kaiser, the king, and so on.[14] Just as one should not conclude that Beethoven was a devoted dynasticist, neither can one cast him as a German nationalist. All such political and even cultural concerns seem for him to have been transitory in contrast to his musical, extraordinarily individual preoccupations. To paraphrase his famous letter to Prince Lichnowsky, there would be thousands of nations, but "there is only one Beethoven." As for his perfunctory and occasional displays of national consciousness, however, one must remember that Beethoven was very much a man of his unsettled and contradictory times.

A generation later, a few composers seem to be more consciously engaged but equally ambivalent with regard to politics and its position in their creative musical output. As John Daverio's contribution to this volume shows, Schumann, like Beethoven, poses complications, even though at first glance he appears to have offered a direct musical response to contemporary political events. He is widely known for having established the *Neue Zeitschrift für Musik* in 1834 partly to address his concerns over a decline of standards in German musical life—expressing frustration over the absence of a successor to Beethoven, proposing to wage war against the degraded musical tastes of his country exhibited in the cult of the piano virtuoso, and hoping to use the journal to expose mediocrities in contemporary music, all of which were of foreign origin.[15] But this reputation as a promoter of German musical self-awareness does not always jibe with his actual political engagement, or lack thereof. In the course of examining the handful of compositions inspired by the revolutions of 1848, Daverio reveals that Schumann, both in his choice of texts and musical styles, dis-

14. See David Dennis's admirable summation of Beethoven's muddled political outlook in *Beethoven in German Politics, 1870–1989* (New Haven: Yale University Press, 1996), 24–31.

15. Leon Plantinga, *Schumann as Critic* (New Haven: Yale University Press, 1967), 16–22.

played a rapid about-face from enthusiast to critic with regard to the contemporary political situation.

Other nineteenth-century German composers took considerably more interest in their place within a national culture, but they did so through activities other than composition. We may take Felix Mendelssohn as exemplary. In his convictions, his activities as a music director, and only occasionally his compositions, the German nation palpably existed, never as a political reality or even a political dream, but as a notional cultural unity— indeed as a source of personal identity. To put it most simply, Mendelssohn more consciously felt himself to be German than any composer of an earlier era and with more far-reaching consequences. His sense of German identity comes through clearly in his travel letters, often in the form of a self-consciously German sense of disappointment that the musical life of various places (Paris, London, Rome, to name a few) should fall so short of his expectations and his German-bred standards. That reaction consisted of equal parts of pride and insecurity: in a letter to his former mentor Carl Friedrich Zelter, he rejected the whole idea of political unity (such things "will surely not come, and I also believe that that is a good thing") and wished for an "end to our exaggerated modesty which makes us accept everything that comes from others as good, and which keeps us from appreciating our own until it has first been recognized by others."[16]

As an orchestral and festival director as well as founder of the Leipzig Conservatory, Mendelssohn went on to achieve a large measure of recognition for "our own" by placing the works of German composers in the center of the European concert repertory, where they have remained ever since. Mendelssohn's historicism, which he shared with an entire generation of intellectuals and artists, reflected his sense of national identity and shaped his work as a composer in such works as the *Reformation* Symphony, the *Lobgesang,* and the *St. Paul* and *Elijah* oratorios.[17] But it was more in his role as musician and organizer that Mendelssohn's historicism left its mark on forging the links between music and German national identity. It emerged in part out of his generation's concern for the future of a specifically German musical heritage that Beethoven's death had rendered vulnerable and in need of both preservation and renewal. As his 1829 performance of Bach's

---

16. Felix Mendelssohn to Karl Friedrich Zelter, 15 February 1832, in *Felix Mendelssohn: A Life in Letters,* ed. Rudolf Elvers, trans. Craig Tomlinson (New York: Fromm International, 1986), 172.

17. An excellent example of the how cultural and musical analysis can be combined to re-illuminate Mendelssohn's music is Peter Mercer-Taylor, "Mendelssohn's 'Scottish' Symphony and the Music of German Memory," *19th-Century Music* 19 (summer 1995): 68–82.

St. Matthew Passion in Berlin (and subsequently, under other directors, throughout northern Germany) revealed, the Bach revival involved much more than performing unfamiliar works for skeptical audiences. It was something of a national movement. Large constituencies of the culture-consuming, taste-making classes were drawn into an affirmation of their German identity through attendance at and amateur participation in Bach's works, and a steady flow of publications for the literate public further clarified the national signification of Bach as a German original.

The case of "Georg Friedrich Händel" (a "re-Germanization" of the Englishman-by-choice, George Frideric Handel) was similar, from the writings of critics like Rochlitz and Ludwig Rellstab to the large-scale participation of musical amateurs in the growing choral festivals of the nineteenth century. Even though Handel spent most of his career away from his native Germany, nineteenth-century patriots placed him firmly in the pantheon of great Germans, demonstrating not only the Germanness of his musical style but the efficacy of the past for revealing the truths of collective identity.[18] Musical historicism also colored the reception of the works of nineteenth-century composers and further strengthened the links between music, even or especially new music, and German national culture. A scant generation after Mendelssohn, music critics found a nationally inflected historicism at the heart of what was German about Brahms' *German Requiem:* as Adolf Schubring wrote, it was "as artful and serious as Sebastian Bach, as elevated and powerful as Beethoven's *Missa Solemnis,* [and] saturated in its melody and harmony by Schubert's benevolent influence."[19]

If we compare Mendelssohn, Schumann, and Brahms in terms of their musical response to a sense of national identity, we find very different devices, approaches, and musical means of evoking nationhood, or at least commenting on its state of being. We might be justified in interpreting all of these devices as evidence of nationalism in music or as evidence of a composer's national identity influencing his compositions. We might not be justified, however, in regarding such evidence of national consciousness as either stable or even essential to the composer's work.

18. M. Zenck, "Zur Aneignung Händels in der nationalen Literaturgeschichtsschreibung des 19. Jahrhunderts," *Bericht über den internationalen musikwissenschftlichen Kongreß Stuttgart 1985* (Kassel: Bärenreiter, 1987), 273–80.

19. Cited in Michael Musgrave, *Brahms: A German Requiem* (Cambridge: Cambridge University Press, 1996), 64. A controversial view of the requiem's Germanness as more political than usually acknowledged may be found in Daniel Beller-McKenna, "How deutsch a Requiem? Absolute Music, Universality, and the Reception of Brahms's *Ein deutsches Requiem,* op. 45," *19th-Century Music* 22 (summer 1998): 3–19.

In this context, one cannot overlook the growing significance of folk song in the nineteenth century and its contribution to the forging of a German national music. Ever since Herder claimed to have discovered the genius of a people in their folk poetry and music, sending generations of patriotic German intellectuals on *Volk*-fishing expeditions in countryside and library, the close association of the "national" in music with whatever sounds folksy has been an inevitable, if often unproductive, feature of debates on national styles. The case of Brahms is again germane. His recent biographer, Jan Swafford, refers unaffectedly to Brahms's "connections to song in general" and "German song in particular" as manifesting his "[r]omantic and nationalistic devotion to folk music and to the idea of songfulness, of lyric melody in instrumental music."[20] The eclecticism and lighthandedness of this judgment is revealing, and perhaps appropriate. The use of folk melody meant many things to composers and sometimes nothing at all. Brahms, of course, just as readily inserted Hungarian melody into his instrumental writing, less because he sympathized with the exile nostalgia of his Hungarian friends and more because he liked the sound of it.

Mendelssohn, in contrast, altogether scorned the appeal of folksiness, but for his own aesthetic reasons: "Anything but national music! May ten thousand devils take all folklore! Here I am in Wales, and oh how lovely, a harpist sits in the lobby of every inn of repute playing so-called folk melodies at you—that is to say, dreadful, vulgar, out-of-tune trash and simultaneously a hurdy-gurdy is tooting out melodies, it's enough to drive one crazy, . . . Scottish bagpipes, Swiss cow horns, Welsh harps—all playing the Huntsmen's Chorus with ghastly variations or improvisations. . . . Anyone who, like myself, can't abide Beethoven's *Nationallieder* ought to come to Wales and hear them howled by shrill nasal voices accompanied by doltish bumbling fingers—and then try to hold his tongue."[21]

And that brings us finally to Wagner, Nightwatchmen's horns, and other issues of national or nationalist composition. Wagner's unique status among composers rests on his capacity to write about music while writing music (a practice that Brahms, among others, despised). Our assessments of his national commitments are thus grossly overinformed compared to those of other composers, even before we approach the issue of how people listened to him. According to the legendary image we have inherited, Wagner defined himself in relation to his nationality; he expressed his ambitions explicitly in terms of the national past and national future; he lobbied for

20. Jan Swafford, *Johannes Brahms: A Biography* (New York: Random House, 1997), 97.
21. Felix Mendelssohn to Abraham Mendelssohn, 25 August 1829, in *Life in Letters*, ed. Elvers, 89.

the imprimatur of national leaders; he sought sources for his operas in both the legendary and the historical past of a cultural Germany; he impugned the Germanness of possible rivals. In all these ways, Wagner presumably overwhelmed any would-be competitors for the title of Most German Composer.

The more his national stature grew during and after his lifetime, the more Germanness in music came simply to denote Wagnerism, thus for a time at least eliding a national style with a personal one and providing an all-too-singular answer to the German question in music. Yet after a close examination of this Most German Composer's "most German work," *Die Meistersinger,* Thomas Grey's essay confronts us with a bundle of contradictions: earlier, discarded versions of the *Meistersinger* libretto were actually more overtly nationalistic and militaristic than the considerably milder final product, and contemporary advocates and opponents alike never took note of any chauvinism in the work. But the coincidence of its premiere with the Franco–Prussian War and Ludwig Nohl's subsequent canonization of Wagner as the first worthy successor to Beethoven and the savior of Germanness started a trend of reading more nationalism into his work than Wagner ever would have intended, a trend that intensified and climaxed in the nazification of Bayreuth in the 1930s and 1940s. Thus even in the case of Wagner, the composer and his works became mythologized as symbols of German nationalism primarily at the hands of critics, essayists, propagandists, and statesmen, far exceeding what the composer himself ever could have envisioned. As Grey reminds us, Wagner was by no means solely responsible for the production of his symbolic status; indeed, when he himself mused on the subject of "what is German," he left the question hanging, unresolved, unanswerable.

The consolidation of a German national culture in the nineteenth century must be seen, then, as only partially the project of composers themselves, in or out of national costume, and just as much that of writers, conductors, bureaucrats, organizers, and musical amateurs, making their own creative use of music both new and old. Among the most enduring and least pretentious of these makers of national culture were the many members of the wide variety of singing organizations. The Prussian capital was home to some of the first such organizations—Fasch's *Singakademie* and Zelter's *Liedertafel.* Although the former was dedicated chiefly to the cultivation of sacred music in the German tradition and the latter to a manly and convivial performance of its members' own song compositions, the two together defined a range of collective celebration of national song. Indeed, the lied itself became a widespread genre that was practically by definition German. Goethe had transformed established forms of German verse from trivial ditties into serious poetry that was immediately set to music by many of his contemporaries, with Goethe himself favoring the musical settings of Zelter. The national importance of the lied began with the Goethe-Zelter pair, then intensified as more German composers gave musical expression to a new German literary canon and as countless performances of lieder, both amateur and professional, gave it a more "national" reach than any other musical genre.[22] Yet it was the authors of these texts who became famous, while the musical settings by such great names as Schumann and Liszt had no greater resonance than those of a host of lesser-known composers.[23] Writers on music then exploited the popularity of these politically charged songs and engaged in lively debates on them in the pages of their newly established music periodicals as a way of reaching a broader readership.

Music critics of the nineteenth century continued the work begun in the eighteenth of defining the Germanness of music in their responses to performances and new publications of music, but they approached the task with far more zeal and imagination than their forerunners. The concept of "absolute music," which E. T. A. Hoffmann inaugurated with his ecstatic review of Beethoven's Fifth Symphony in 1813, would go on to become the single most influential aesthetic idea concerning music. It represented a quintessentially romantic and universalist appreciation of instrumental music, oriented to transcendent questions of existence far above the lesser matters of national character. But at the same time, it valorized musical genres like the symphony that not just the Germans but all Europeans associated with German composers—Beethoven, of course, chief among them. The history of the idea of absolute music, as explored in this volume in the essays of Bernd Sponheuer, Albrecht Riethmüller, and Hans Vaget, thus reveals the gradual development of German music's reputation as superior precisely because of its universality and transcendence of national differences. As these essays all point out, however, few of those engaged in this discourse sought to pinpoint what actually made this music superior.

Music criticism gained a new preponderance in the nineteenth century, both as a result of its sheer bulk and institutional weight and because of its

22. For a variety of insights into the lied's national significance, see Friedhelm Brusniak and Dietmar Klenke, eds., "Heil deutschem Wort und Sang": Nationalidentität und Gesangskultur in der deutschen Geschichte, Feuchtwanger Beiträge zur Musikforschung, vol. 1 (Augsburg: Feuchtwanger Verlag, 1995).

23. See Lorie A. Vanchena, "The Rhine Crisis of 1840: Rheinlieder, German Nationalism, and the Masses," in Searching for Common Ground, 239–51.

close association with composers, conductors, and scholars, many of whom
were themselves active critics. The creation of a unified musical canon
could thus be reinforced simultaneously in concert halls, lecture halls, and
the pages of increasingly specialized journals. Composers, notably Robert
Schumann in his *Neue Zeitschrift für Musik* and Wagner in his occasional
writings, legitimated the act of writing about music as an essential aspect
of understanding music. A marked preoccupation with Germany's importance in the European musical world characterized their work, and even
more, the work of their imitators.

Similarly, music scholarship, still in its infancy and likewise carried
out largely by musicians, critics, and composers, also became preoccupied
with German masters of the past and embarked on one of its greatest
achievements in 1851 when the newly founded Bach Gesellschaft inaugurated a massive project—the complete edition of Bach's works. The Bach
edition, a phenomenon in its own right, marked an important event in the
nascent discipline of musicology and resonated throughout the community of composers, critics, and scholars. Brahms, for instance, himself a
part-time musicologist, received the first volume as a Christmas gift from
Clara Schumann in 1855, and thereafter subscribed to the complete series.
Further critical editions of the works of a single "German" composer followed with the complete works of Handel (1858), Mozart (1876), Schubert
(1883), Beethoven (1884), and Lassus (1894).

Many of the critical editions that followed came to be classified as
"monuments" and served as a sonic counterpart to the many statues, some
devoted to musicians, that patriotic burghers erected in town squares and
city parks during the monument frenzy in Germany dating from the 1860s.[24]
The most ambitious editorial projects were the government-sponsored,
multivolume scholarly editions of early music from German-speaking regions, the "monuments" (*Denkmäler*) series. The largest among them dated
back roughly to the last decade of the nineteenth century: *Denkmäler der
Tonkunst in Österreich* began in 1888, *Denkmäler deutscher Tonkunst* in
1889, and *Denkmäler der Tonkunst in Bayern* in 1900. The term *Denkmal*
literally means an occasion for thought, a spur to thinking, a reminder, even

24. Reinhard Alings, author of a tome on German monuments, estimates that there were
literally thousands of national monuments in Germany by 1914—not even counting ones he
considered merely local. In Berlin alone, the number rose from about 20 in 1858 to 232 by
6:00 A.M. on July 1, 1905, commemorating 716 persons and 128 animals (according to a satirical contemporary account.) See Alings, *Monument und Nation: Das Bild vom Nationalstaat
im Medium Denkmal* (Berlin: DeGruyter, 1996), 76–79. See also Rudy Koshar, *From Monuments to Traces: Artifacts of German Memory, 1870–1990* (Berkeley: University of California
Press, 2000).

a warning. The musical *Denkmäler* projects reminded Germans of their musical greatness and implicitly warned against musical superficiality and fashion. The great German tradition so celebrated was for the most part an eminently serious and intellectually demanding one, embracing a "strong concept of art." Its alternative, as Carl Dahlhaus argued most fully in his synthesis *Nineteenth-Century Music,* was coded foreign, non-German, to wit, Italian.[25]

Finally, the state's participation in emphasizing the national signifi-cation of musical life grew steadily during the nineteenth century, taking on dominant proportions after 1871. The increasing importance of the state in shaping national identity reflected the gradual eclipse of popular nationalism by a more official version, in the German case a matter of the Hohenzollern dynasty seizing in awkward embrace a century-long legacy of nation-making among political liberals and romantic intellectuals.[26] The transformation of the Hohenzollern kings from Prussian dynasts to "Number 1" Germans unfolded to the strains of Beethoven symphonies and overtures. The kaiser's or Bismarck's association with the music of Beethoven constituted, moreover, a fundamentally different phenomenon from the mere accompaniment to royal movement represented by, for in-stance, Handel's *Water Music.* As David Dennis has shown, it was Beetho-ven in particular who mattered to politicians of all stripes, especially in his heroic mode.[27] The nationalist moment, then, had arrived when blue bloods linked themselves to commoners merely on the basis of a shared na-tionality. By the 1870s, certain music could usefully demonstrate the Ger-manness of the new state and its kings, and thereby legitimate the new state's particular solution to the question of what was the German father-land. In 1889, the *Denkmäler deutscher Tonkunst* was launched with an edited volume of Frederick the Great's compositions for flute, presented to the reigning heir Wilhelm II as a means to flatter and simultaneously draw attention to the need to preserve musical "treasures" in published edi-tions. This tactic succeeded, as Wilhelm, impressed with the "patriotic and artistic goals" of the undertaking and seeking legitimation himself, pro-vided the necessary funds to secure future volumes. And the state needed

25. Dahlhaus, *Nineteenth-Century Music,* trans. J. Bradford Robinson (Berkeley: Univer-sity of California Press, 1989), esp. 8–15.

26. For a fuller discussion of the meaning of "official nationalism," see Benedict Ander-son, *Imagined Communities: Reflections on the Origin and Spread of Nationalism* (London: Verso, 1983), 80–103; Hugh Seton-Watson, *Nations and States: An Enquiry into the Origins of Nations and the Politics of Nationalism* (Boulder, Colo.: Westview Press, 1977).

27. Dennis, *Beethoven in German Politics,* 19.

such legitimation. For all its nationalistic bombast, imperial Germany oper-
ated from the start with a deficit of national symbols. As Jost Hermand describes in this volume, it never even settled on a national anthem. Potential candidates for the honor, as in the case of Hoffmann von Fallersleben's
"Lied der Deutschen," could not serve precisely because they celebrated a
different German nation from the one achieved in 1871.

It would not be too extravagant to suggest that imperial Germany's
difficulty in finding national symbols arose out of the disjuncture that suddenly appeared in 1871 between the actual German political nation-state
and the imagined cultural nation of generations of German patriots. As
long as there was no German nation-state, the boundaries of political and
cultural nationhood could coincide in their indefiniteness. But the political
entity proclaimed in 1871 could only serve as the actualization of a German cultural community by ignoring or downplaying the importance of all
the cultural Germans left out. To be sure, as Bismarck himself was happy
to remind people, the question of nationhood by 1871 was not a cultural
one, nor even really a political one, but rather was a military, geopolitical
question of "blood and iron."

It was quite appropriate, in any case, that the intellectual leader most
insistent on the Second Reich's legitimacy as a cultural as well as political
expression of the German nation, Heinrich von Treitschke, was almost
completely deaf by 1871. For the new boundaries of German nationhood
quite glaringly failed to make sense of the German musical heritage for
anyone literal-minded enough to ask whether Mozart—or heaven forbid,
Beethoven himself—must now be considered an Austrian musician and
not a German one at all. Indeed, the notable feature of music and German
national identity after 1871 was the continuity of established ways of talk-
ing and thinking about German music across what one might expect to be
a great and momentous divide. People did not trouble themselves with fig-
uring out whether Mozart was German in the 1871 sense of the term. But
more than a reluctance to lose their star attractions explains the absence
of such discussion: the cultural nation that discussions of German music
had done so much to consolidate was not reconfigured by political unification, just as its consolidation had not been precluded by the political fragmentation before 1871. Although we do not know as much as we might
about the differing understandings of the German musical heritage within
the various subcultures of German-speaking Europe—Catholic versus
Protestant, working class versus elite, Swiss versus Hapsburg versus imperial German—what we do know suggests a tremendous amount of commonality and continuity, centered around a canon of musical greatness that is

still recognizable today. As Bruno Nettl's contributed essay suggests, even the German speakers of the Hapsburg Czech lands felt ownership of a German musical heritage that both transcended political borders and was capable of assimilating ethnic Czech traditions. In other words, political unification in 1871 proved initially at least to be irrelevant to the strengthening of the links between music and a broadly defined German identity that embraced a *grossdeutsch* understanding of the cultural nation.

This is not to say, however, that nothing changed in musical-national matters in the latter part of the nineteenth century. The musically attentive German reacted to the death of Wagner in 1883 very much in the same manner as his or her ancestor had to the death of Beethoven in 1827. Beethoven's death left the German musical world sensing that something great had been lost, and unless it could be replaced, Germany's musical life would be left vulnerable to foreign infiltration. Similarly, Wagner's death seemed to mark the end of the great era of German opera. It haunted a new generation of opera composers who either carried on the Wagnerian tradition, pursued the direction of fairy-tale opera (such as Humperdinck), or tried to venture beyond Wagner and explore a new operatic conception (Richard Strauss pursued all of these paths in his first three operas, *Guntram, Feuersnot,* and *Salome*). Exploiting this sense of loss, Wagner's widow Cosima proceeded to enlarge Wagner's legacy into mythological proportions and to lay the foundations for the dynastic tradition at Bayreuth.

While Wagner's mourners feared a crucial break in the chain of German musical greatness and composers contemplated their purpose in the looming shadow of this imposing cultural icon, educators, bureaucrats, and reformers continued to reinforce the reputation of the German people as the "people of music." German musical life in the late nineteenth and early twentieth centuries continued to emphasize the importance of music as a component of *Bildung* and focused increasingly on the cultivation of a specifically German repertoire. From the 1870s on, German amateur music groups devoted to the promotion of German music proliferated.[28] The amateur choral movement was particularly committed to strengthening German identity. The 1862 charter of the German Singers' League

---

28. *Die Musik in Geschichte und Gegenwart: Allgemeine Enzyklopädie der Musik,* 1st ed., s.v. "Gesellschaften und Vereine."

(*Deutscher Sängerbund*) dedicated itself to "the promotion of German feeling [t]hrough the unifying power of German song . . . to preserve and enhance the German national consciousness and a feeling of solidarity among German tribes."[29] Choral singing also increased significantly when it was adopted by the workers' movement as a suitable means to instill a political consciousness. Between 1892 and 1900, membership in the loose federation of workers' singing groups had grown from about ten thousand to nearly one hundred thousand, and in 1908 a national organization known as the German Workers' Singers' League (*Deutsche Arbeiter-Sängerbund*) was founded.[30] Music was also an important activity in the growing youth organizations, and music publishers and instrument makers benefited from a surge of interest in music-making in the home (*Hausmusik*).

Music education was simultaneously undergoing important reforms, not only in the classrooms but also in the concert halls, where conductors such as Hans von Bülow strove to elevate audiences' knowledge of contemporary symphonic repertoire. Von Bülow was especially intent on promoting the music of Brahms through the subscription series of the Berlin Philharmonic Orchestra and on introducing formal recitals as an educational experience.[31] The influence of conductors on shaping Germany's musical life was generally on the rise in the late nineteenth century, a period that not surprisingly also witnessed a shift in the roles of composers from writers to conductors. Whereas nineteenth-century Germans—most notably Schumann and Wagner—had expressed their thoughts on the state of music through the written word, the generation that included Gustav Mahler and Richard Strauss focused more attention on exerting their influence from the podium as orchestral and opera conductors.

Musicology started to come into its own as a distinct academic discipline pursued by full-time scholars at this time as well, and Germans and Austrians took the lead in developing the field into an organized, active, and serious academic pursuit. The University of Vienna was the first to adopt musicology as an academic department with the appointment of music critic Eduard Hanslick as professor of music history and aesthetics in 1861. There followed the establishment of chairs in Strasbourg (1897), Berlin

29. From the introductory paragraph of the 1927 charter, quoted in Leo Kestenberg, *Jahrbuch der deutschen Musikorganisationen 1931* (Berlin: Max Hesse, 1931), 19.

30. See W. L. Guttsman, *Workers' Culture in Weimar Germany: Between Tradition and Commitment* (New York: Berg, 1990), 4, 61, 155–76.

31. A detailed study of Hans von Bülow's impact as a musical reformer is included in Hans Joachim Hinrichsen, *Musikalische Interpretation Hans von Bülow*, Beihefte zum Archiv für Musikwissenschaft 46 (Stuttgart: Steiner, 1999).

(1904), Munich (1909), and Bonn (1915). As the twentieth century approached, German and Austrian scholars together distinguished themselves as pathbreakers in research, methodology, and organization. They set standards for creating catalogues, indexes, and critical editions of musical works.[32] Germans and Austrians also proved themselves to be the prime motivators in organizing the discipline. The first journal dedicated to serious music scholarship was a joint German–Austrian venture, *Vierteljahrsschrift für Musikwissenschaft,* edited by Friedrich Chrysander, Philip Spitta, and Guido Adler (professor in Prague, later Hanslick's successor) from 1885 to 1894. Oskar Fleischer spearheaded the founding of the International Music Society in 1904 and its scholarly journal *Sammelbände der Internationalen Musikgesellschaft.* It is noteworthy, however, that despite the international stamp borne by these initiatives, the scholars involved continued to dedicate most of their efforts to proliferating the works of German and Austrian masters. In addition to the continued production of critical editions of composers' works and the ongoing *Denkmäler* series, pathbreaking publications of thematic catalogues began to appear with Köchel's catalogue of Mozart's works in 1862 and Nottebohm's Beethoven catalogue in 1868.

Yet while choral directors, conductors, and scholars exposed the public to German and Austrian masters past and present, many contemporary composers prior to World War I, by contrast, actually looked beyond the borders of the German-speaking world for inspiration. They became particularly fascinated with developments in the non-German literary world. Mahler, for example, drew upon Chinese poetry for *Das Lied von der Erde;* Schoenberg's groundbreaking atonal composition, *Pierrot lunaire,* was set to the German translation of a French text; and for *Salome,* Strauss's most daring break with German operatic tradition, the composer used Oscar Wilde's play. When the part-German, Italian-born composer Ferruccio Busoni began teaching in Berlin, he encouraged students (who included Kurt Weill) to embrace a wide array of musical influences from all nations in order to achieve a universal musical aesthetic.

32. In addition to German and Austrian musicologists' innovative techniques in compiling critical editions and thematic catalogues, vast amounts of newly discovered source materials for early music were made accessible through Robert Eitner's ten-volume index *Biographisch-bibliographisch Quellen-Lexikon* (1900–1904); Eitner et al., *Bibliographie der Musik-Sammelwerke des XVI. und XVII. Jahrhunderts* (1877); Friedrich Ludwig, *Repertorium organorum recentioris et motetorum vetustissimi stili* (1910); Emil Vogel, *Bibliothek der gedruckten weltlichen Vocalmusik Italiens* (1892); and Johannes Zahn's six-volume *Die Melodien der deutschen evangelischen Kirchenlieder* (1888–93).

Such advocacy of an international brotherhood was anathema to conservatives such as Hans Pfitzner, who witnessed the encroachments of foreign entertainment as slowly poisoning Germany's musical culture. Pfitzner launched an attack on Busoni's pamphlet *Entwurf einer neuen Ästhetik der Tonkunst*, first published in 1907 and reissued during World War I in 1916. In it Busoni had downplayed the importance of German masters in order to foster a more open and less didactic approach to composition. Pfitzner saw this as an affront not only to German music but to the German nation, and in 1917 used his critique of Busoni as a springboard to promote the ideas of German musical superiority: "German music is not just some kind of cerebral sport, but an art we love; and when the spirit of one of our great masters is willing to appear before us, we should receive him accordingly, should call him 'Prince' or 'Father,' and by no means should we try to attack him; otherwise he won't speak to us. Berlioz and Liszt are held by Busoni— and unfortunately by a great many others—to be great composers."[33]

World War I cast a shadow that extended over the years to the end of World War II and that inspired composers and others to express national assertiveness as never before: the pain of "a dark and unhappy age," as Thomas Mann put it, seized "men with its iron fist" and wrung "from them sounds that were formerly alien to them."[34] We might refer to a nationalist phase among German composers that lasted throughout the extraordinary period from 1914 to 1945. Before and since, intense engagement in political nationalism among composers was more the exception than the rule. In this context one reads, for instance, Arnold Schoenberg's surprising declaration that his twelve-tone compositional technique will "secure for German music an ascendancy for the next hundred years."[35] Michael Kater's contribution to this volume, on "Hans Pfitzner the German," draws on previously unknown archival sources to gain insight into the psyche of this musical nationalist, whose attacks on internationalism, bolshevism, and Judaism only intensified after World War I. Pfitzner's obsessive commitment to his own conservative notion of German music deluded him into thinking he deserved the highest accolades once Hitler came to power—an honor that was to pass him by—and held on to his convictions even after

---

33. Marc Weiner, *Undertones of Insurrection: Music, Politics, and the Social Sphere in Modern German Narrative* (Lincoln: University of Nebraska Press, 1993), 35–50, quote on 39.

34. Mann was, of course, himself quoting E. T. A Hoffmann's "Extremely Random Thoughts." See R, 24.

35. Cited in Reimer, "Nationalbewußtsein," 17.

Hitler's defeat. At the end of World War II, Richard Strauss, too, witnessed the "destruction of Germany" with an elegy that was all the more poignant in its declaration that "Germany fulfilled its last and highest cultural achievement with the invention of German music, and with this thought in mind I will gladly wait until I am called to join my gods on Olympus."[36]

World War I marked a crisis in German identity that deeply influenced the discourse on German music while condoning attempts to exploit music for political aims. Military defeat and modernization created a longing for a lost national pride and a nostalgia for simpler times. The German public took a great interest in music of Germany's past, simple instruments like the recorder, and antiquated performance practices. Amateur groups continued to flourish, the youth movement made music-making one of its central activities, and music education rose to a prominent place on the government's agenda and enjoyed sweeping reforms in the 1920s. A proliferation of instrumental music-making in and outside the home demonstrates even further the degree to which music had become part of daily German activity. Indeed, by 1931, choral groups continued to grow by mobilizing as many as 2 million German citizens, and many of these groups provided an activity that transcended political and social boundaries.[37] Acute tensions among social and political factions also inspired many to search for ways to bring Germans together. Music, by virtue of its "community-building powers" (gemeinschaftsbildende Kraft der Musik), was widely promoted as holding the key to healing the wounds of a fractured society and promoting feelings of camaraderie. Bruce Campbell's essay in this collection shows how Gerhard Roßbach embraced this notion by using folk songs and classical music to bring together competing factions of the right wing under the umbrella of a shared musical heritage.

This postwar saturation of German society with musical activity only reinforced the Germans' reputation as the "people of music." Germany had steadily produced some of the world's most influential composers, conductors, and performers. Moreover, it had established conservatories that attracted students from all over the world, and preserved more city and state orchestras and opera houses per capita than any other country. Now it seemed that even World War I could not seriously affect its standing. Hans Joachim Moser reported in 1928 that Germany had managed to maintain state-run institutions despite the war and economic collapse, and boasted

---

36. Richard Strauss to A. Kippenberg, 24 September 1945, quoted in Gerhard Splitt, "Richard Strauss' Idee vom Ende der deutschen Musik 1945," *Musik in Bayern* 41 (1990): 51.

37. Derived from Kestenberg, *Jahrbuch der deutschen Musikorganisationen 1931*.

the preservation of approximately fifty opera houses and "perhaps 150 orchestras of rank." Moser valued this as a clear indication of the high priority Germans placed on music.[38] More than ever, music was coming across as Germany's most important cultural commodity and musical talent as a distinguishing feature of the German nation. It seemed only logical that understanding Germany's musical past and present could lead to a deeper understanding of the German character and help define the German nation. Perhaps such an understanding would even lead to reconciling the quarreling factions that were threatening to break the nation apart.

Musicologists, swept up in the spirit of the times, used all at their disposal to come up with a sound definition of musical Germanness with a new fervor and assertiveness. As Philip Bohlman shows in his essay in this volume, a group of leading folk-song scholars embarked in 1924 on an ambitious project (which would ultimately take forty-eight years to complete) to map the entire landscape of Germany's ethnic musical heritage. Music historian Hugo Riemann had concluded that German musical output could not be identified by specific musical characteristics but rather by a distinctly German approach to composition that could be traced to a long-standing tradition of thorough musical training, particularly among the church musicians of northern Germany.[39] Blind nationalism of the postwar period virtually consumed other scholars, who strove to trace German superiority even further back in history and looked mostly in vain to the music itself for clues to unlocking the essence of Germanness.

These critics and scholars were as incensed as Pfitzner over the open-door policy to foreign culture, regardless of its quality, and the persistence of bourgeois individualism and "art for art's sake" that created an ever-increasing gulf between musicians and the public. These tendencies, for which many now held Jews accountable, were bound to poison a healthy German musical environment, especially when they allowed the spread of such destructive elements as jazz and other American grotesqueries.[40] The conductor, organizer, and part-time musicologist Peter Raabe sounded the

38. ". . . so kann man daraus ablesen, was die Musik im geistigen Haushalt der Nation bedeutet." Hans Joachim Moser, *Geschichte der deutschen Musik*, 2d ed. (Stuttgart: Cotta, 1928), 3:467.

39. Hugo Riemann, *Das Generalbaßzeitalter: Die Monodie des 17. Jahrhunderts und die Weltherrschaft der Italiener*, vol. 2, pt. 2 of *Handbuch der Musikgeschichte*, 2d ed. (Leipzig: Breitkopf & Härtel, 1922), 492. He developed this argument in his discussion of Bach in *Die Musik des 18. und 19. Jahrhunderts: Die großen deutschen Meister*, vol. 2, pt. 3 of *Handbuch der Musikgeschichte*, 2d ed. (Leipzig: Breitkopf & Härtel, 1922), 104–5.

40. Moser, *Geschichte*, pt. 2, 2:501–17; Karl Hasse, "Das Deutschtum in der Musik," *Akademische Monatsblätter* 43 (1928): 49–50.

death knell for German music in 1926, echoing the prewar polemics of Pfitzner in his querulous lamenting that German character was in more danger than ever before: "Negro dance bands" and American films flourished, while German opera and theater languished.[41] (Raabe would rise to prominence in the Third Reich as president of the Reich Music Chamber.)

Political demagogues could also play on the growing centrality of both amateur musical activity and the notion of German musical superiority. Bruce Campbell's essay considers a semiprofessional music and dance group of the Weimar era, known as the "Spielschar Ekkehard," which employed folk and classical repertoire to convey a message of political conservatism and *völkisch* nationalism. It evoked the idea of a German musical tradition for the purpose of demonstrating to its audiences the false and un-German character of the Weimar Republic. Yet the right wing was not the only political faction to exploit Germany's musical heritage for its own ends. Left-wing politicians used the works of Beethoven, Bach, and Handel to promote democracy and solidarity among the German working class. In 1918, shortly after Kurt Eisner became prime minister in Bavaria as the result of a putsch, he organized a revolutionary festival that featured Beethoven's *Leonore Overture* and Handel's *Messiah*, while the communists in their daily newspaper *Die Rote Fahne* adamantly rejected bourgeois characterizations of Beethoven and in 1919 used his music at the funeral of Rosa Luxembourg and Karl Liebknecht.[42]

Handel was also exploited for a variety of political purposes during the Weimar years. On the one hand, his oratorios could serve the socialist and communist goals of bringing high culture to the masses and providing repertoire suitable for the growing choral culture. The oratorios were said to reflect Handel's populism because the people were given a "voice" through the prominent role given to the chorus. There were German Workers' Handel Festivals in 1911, 1926, and 1928, and several oratorios were popularized with fully staged productions for the first time.[43] On the other hand, following Germany's defeat in World War I and the damage to national pride,

41. Peter Raabe, "Deutsches Musikwesen und deutsche Art," *Allgemeine Musikzeitung* 53 (1926): 737–38.

42. Dennis, *Beethoven in German Politics*, 87–90.

43. Michael G. Werner, "'Das Fest unserer Zeit': Händel-Inszenierungen in den 1920er Jahren und ihre Implikationen für das nationalsozialistische Thingspiel," in P. Csobádi et al., eds., *"Und Jedermann erwartet sich ein Fest." Fest, Theater, Festspiele. Gesammelte Vorträge des Salzburger Symposions 1995* (Anif, Salzburg: Müller-Speiser, 1996), 675–87. Göttingen remained a center of Handel cultivation, but its annual festivals noticeably favored the production of operas to the point of neglecting the oratorios up until the 1960s. See Konrad Ameln, "30 Jahre Göttinger Händel-Gesellschaft," in *50 Jahre Göttinger Händel-Festspiele:*

Handel's wide appeal and international stature rendered him a model of German greatness. Just as in the nineteenth century, Handel's exile in Italy and England was glossed over and, by the 1920s, his Germanness was practically a foregone conclusion. Ironically, his prolonged absence from Germany reinforced his image as a German, but as one who left a culturally impoverished Germany expressly to give vent to his German nature.[44] This could serve as a useful allegory for the pessimists of the 1920s, who warned that the current sorry state of German musical culture, overrun with foreign influences, cheap entertainment music, and other perceived degeneracies, might once again carelessly drive away its native sons.[45]

As much as the notion of the "people of music" flourished during the Weimar Republic, the Weimar government lacked not only the financial resources but also the infrastructure to deal with the problems facing musicians and their institutions in the fluctuating economy of the 1920s. The Hitler government, by contrast, paid more attention than its forerunner to creating protection for music professionals and institutions. Thus contrary to what one might assume, the year 1933 does not represent the onset of a terrible era of totalitarian repression and cultural deprivation in German musical life. Although it is difficult to look beyond the devastating effects of the elimination of massive numbers of Jews and other "undesirables" from active participation in musical activities, and assumptions about repressive censorship emanate from some of the more high-profile propaganda campaigns, one of the most far-reaching effects of the Nazi administration on Germany's musical life before and after World War II actually came in the form of raising the social, economic, and professional status of musicians to an unprecedented level and rescuing several musical institutions— opera houses, orchestras, even the Bayreuth festival—from financial ruin.

Festschrift, ed. Walter Meyerhoff (Kassel: Bärenreiter, 1970), 29–39. For a broader overview of the political exploitation of Handel, see Pamela M. Potter, "The Politicization of Handel's Oratorios in the Weimar Republic, the Third Reich, and the Early Years of the GDR," *Musical Quarterly* 85 (2001): 311–41.

44. Rudolf Steglich portrayed Handel as a frustrated German, alienated from his country by its unhealthy craze for foreign music. Handel's Germany was in a state of national dissolution, lacking the sort of national musical consciousness that was so strong in Italy and England. Thus Handel could only be a true German outside Germany. Steglich, "Händel und die Gegenwart," *Zeitschrift für Musik* 92 (1925): 335.

45. This opinion was expressed by Steglich, Arnold Schering, and Joseph Müller-Blattau, among others.

The establishment of the Propaganda Ministry and its Reich Chamber of Culture, the obligatory union for all practicing cultural professionals, offered benefits to those directly or remotely involved in cultural production. The Music Chamber could boast great accomplishments within a relatively short amount of time—the setting of wages for professional musicians, regulations for professional certification and for restricting amateurs from performing for money, the introduction of exams and training courses for private music instructors, and an old-age pension plan—but it ultimately also functioned as a mechanism to exclude Jews and others from Germany's musical life.[46] The overall aim of Nazi cultural policy was to enlist the cooperation of cultural professionals by allaying their fears about threats to their existence and giving in to a number of their demands for financial and professional security, all the time reassuring them that control over such matters would remain in the hands of the cultural professionals themselves. The fact that Richard Strauss agreed to serve as president of the Reich Music Chamber, with conductor Wilhelm Furtwängler as vice president, indicates just how much promise of progress the Nazi programs offered to the musical community. Both Strauss and Furtwängler would soon become disillusioned with the more extreme measures of fanatical Nazi bureaucrats—Strauss after the hounding he endured by working with Jewish librettist Stefan Zweig, Furtwängler in his championing of the targeted Paul Hindemith—but the vast majority of musicians continued to find numerous advantages in the cultural blueprints of the Nazis.

The Nazi government also continued to encourage and even elevate to official status many of the more successful musical trends inherited from the Weimar Republic. The state recognized the importance of music in amateur, ceremonial, and paramilitary activities and drew on their strength by granting official status to such activities and organizing them within divisions of the Reich Music Chamber. Nazi leaders also encouraged research and education in areas of German music, particularly in the special area of folk music. The Institute for German Music Research, resurrected and incorporated into the state in 1935 by the Nazi education minister Bernhard Rust, established a large folk-music department, and the Propaganda Ministry banded with the Hitler Youth and the SS-Ahnenerbe to sponsor editions of folk songs for everyday use. The SS-Ahnenerbe also supported a number of research projects that used folk music and early music to search for evidence of untainted "*urdeutsche* music," giving preference to

46. Alan Steinweis, Art, Ideology, and Economics in Nazi Germany: The Reich Chambers of Music, Theater, and the Visual Arts (Chapel Hill: University of North Carolina Press, 1993), 80–88, 94, 98–102, 110–11.

studies that investigated the folk music of ethnic Germans, the music of prehistoric Germanic tribes, and the alleged strains of Germanness in medieval liturgical chant.[47] Joseph Müller-Blattau's 1938 study, underwritten by the Hitler Youth and the SS-Ahnenerbe, used folk songs, lullabies, and children's songs to derive melodic gestures that could allegedly be found throughout German art music. The author praised the National-Socialist state for its support of the folk-music revival and for showing its respect for German folk song by elevating the "Horst-Wessel Lied" to official status.[48]

Enthusiasm for the Nazis' encouragement of musical life came from likely as well as unlikely sources. Heinrich Schenker's overt nationalism in his theoretical writings of the 1920s and early 1930s are well known, and Schoenberg's student Anton Webern openly expressed his support for the regime.[49] German musicologists proved all too willing to take advantage of the situation: in 1933, Wilibald Gurlitt, who would later lose his academic post because of his partial Jewish lineage and his Jewish wife, acknowledged Hitler's demands to learn the essence of Germanness, and the growing popularity of racial sciences in the 1930s offered musicologists new potential methods for deriving German musical proclivities.[50] But, aside from their jargon, such racial studies revealed nothing new. In addition, as Doris Bergen's contributed essay on German Protestants in the Third Reich reveals, one branch of the church attempted to purge its hymns of all references to Judaism, but found so much resistance among the congregants that it simply had to tolerate the continued use of Hebraisms. In a similar irony, the Reich Culture Chamber also issued explicit permission to perform Handel's oratorios based on Old Testament texts despite their apparent glorification of the ancient Hebrews. They were aware of the importance of these works in the German repertoire and rationalized that such glorification could be understood as an allegory, perhaps even an allusion to the bravery of the Germanic nations.

Composers, for their part, largely pursued their musical independence often with little regard for the "official" pronouncements of Nazi propaganda on music. Thus despite the virulent defamation of jazz, atonality,

47. See Pamela M. Potter, "Did Himmler *Really* Like Gregorian Chant? The SS and Musicological Research," *Modernism/Modernity* 2/3 (1995): 45–68.

48. Joseph Müller-Blattau, *Germanisches Erbe in deutscher Tonkunst* (Berlin: Vieweg, 1938).

49. See, for example, Nicholas Cook, "Schenker's Theory of Music as Ethics," *Journal of Musicology* 7 (1989): 415–39; Michael H. Kater, *The Twisted Muse: Musicians and their Music in the Third Reich* (New York: Oxford University Press, 1997), 72–74.

50. Wilibald Gurlitt, "Vom Deutschtum in der Musik," *Die Kirchenmusik* 14 (1933): 167–69.

and twelve-tone composition as racially inferior and anti-German in the highly publicized "Degenerate Music" exhibit of 1938, composers such as Boris Blacher successfully incorporated jazz elements into concert music performed by the Berlin Philharmonic, and other composers experimenting with the twelve-tone technique received public acclaim.[51] Even one of the most ardent Nazi music critics, Herbert Gerigk, was unwilling to reject atonality outright and claimed that in the right hands, that is to say, in the hands of a composer of pure blood and pure character, even atonality could be an effective means of expression. (Schoenberg, however, apparently even failed to appeal to other Jews in his misguided, destructive attempts, according to Gerigk.)[52] The Nazis' general ambivalence toward music in their official policies is especially well illustrated in the case of opera, discussed in Joy Calico's contribution to this volume. This ambivalence may be interpreted as a lack of expertise or concern, but given the lofty praise heaped on German music in the speeches of Hitler, Goebbels, and Rosenberg, this hands-off approach can be attributed to something else: a deeply internalized respect and admiration for the accomplishments of German composers past and present. Choosing not to tamper with success, Nazi policymakers interfered far less in musical affairs than in the operations of other arts (especially visual arts and film). They perpetuated the belief in the universality of German music and regarded this lofty accomplishment as further evidence of German superiority.

This notion of German music's universality took a curious turn in World War II, as spurious claims of German musical hegemony in surrounding countries served to justify territorial expansion. The annexations and occupations of neighboring territories encouraged a corollary expansion of the definition of "German music" as Germany's boundaries widened. Up to that point, there had been a growing tendency to adopt certain groups or individuals as Germanic kin: the Franco-Flemish composers who dominated the international scene in the fifteenth and sixteenth centuries, especially Heinrich Isaac, and the later "German-blooded" masters Franz Liszt, César Franck, and others. In the course of the war the definition of "German" expanded even more. Investigations of the music of all countries occupied or annexed by German troops aimed to show that a German presence in the music of those areas could be traced back for centuries.

51. See "Dissonance and Deviance," in Kater, *Twisted Muse.* For a complete reconstruction of the "Degenerate Music" and commentaries on its contents and their ramifications, see Albrecht Dümling and Peter Girth, eds., *Entartete Musik. Zur Düsseldorfer Ausstellung von 1938. Eine kommentierte Rekonstruktion* (Düsseldorf: Kleinherne, 1988).

52. Herbert Gerigk, "Eine Lanze für Schönberg," *Die Musik* 27 (1934): 87–91.

This yielded claims that some countries never really had their own musical culture but merely flaunted a cheap imitation of the German product, or that their masters credited with musical advancements could be shown to be German trained, or, in the case of occupied France, even "racially" German.[53] Furthermore, as Philip Bohlman investigates in this volume, what counted as German folk music also expanded beyond Germany's traditional boundaries, as reflected in the publication of the multivolume folksong collection *Landschaftliche Volkslieder*. From its inception in 1924 to its conclusion in 1972, the collection represented a truly idealistic picture of "Großdeutschland" that looked to include the Polish regions of Silesia and Pomerania as well as French Alsace and German-speaking parts of Romania, Slovenia, Ukraine, and Czechoslovakia in volumes that appeared from 1924 to 1934; extended into occupied Poland, Yugoslavia, and Austria in volumes produced during World War II; and even somewhat nostalgically embraced Hungary and Moravia in volumes appearing between 1953 and 1971, while looking ahead hopefully to German reunification by including regions lying in both East and West Germany.

The end of World War II marked a crucial break in the history of German music as well as the history of German identity. The shocking discovery of the Holocaust, the process of denazification, and the need to rebuild without looking to the past and all that it represented penetrated the world of musical composition, production, and reception. As Hans Vaget shows in his essay, the most complex, "passionate and articulate" engagement with questions of musical greatness and national identity came not from a musical scholar or critic, but from a novelist, Thomas Mann. Already in his early works, Mann had acknowledged the power of music for the German people through his fictional characters and hinted allegorically at its devastating as well as elevating effects on the German character. Vaget argues that by the time he wrote his last novel, *Doctor Faustus*, Mann went so far as to connect the German passion for music and conviction of German musical superiority with its decline into National Socialist barbarism.

Even more surprising, perhaps, is the heightened involvement—heightened even in comparison with the Nazi era—of politicians in the shaping of a new German identity through music. As Gesa Kordes's contribution on the West German musical avant-garde shows, postwar composers shunned

53. Pamela M. Potter, "Musicology under Hitler: New Sources in Context," *Journal of the American Musicological Society* 49 (1996): 70–113.

any association, even a stylistic one, with the music of Germany's past that had, in their view, allowed itself to be exploited for overzealous nationalist aims. Severing all ties with the music from German romanticism on, they turned instead to the most symbolic victims of National Socialist musical propaganda, Arnold Schoenberg and his school [Yet this turn to the esoteric realms of serialism and electronic music was not solely a rejection of the past and flight into the realm of purely musical abstraction, but also an indication of the infiltration of Cold War ideology into musical politics] For as West German composers received encouragement in their ventures from American military consultants operating German radio stations, East German composers received a clear message that such forays into avant-garde "formalism" would not be tolerated in the new socialist state. Joy Calico's revealing essay on the East German conception of a new genre of "National Opera" shows how composers in East Germany were directed by the state to pursue [a new form of German music that would be accessible to the public and would set an example for the morally dissolute West] This solution, however, harbored unmistakable similarities to the unifying national agendas of nineteenth-century proponents of a "national opera" and emphasized its function as a vehicle for the eventual cultural unification of the "temporarily" divided German nation.

Meanwhile, as musical production and consumption in the postwar era came to be dominated by new technologies, radio and recording were making a much wider variety of music accessible to everyone. The resulting burgeoning of the popular music industry, with its core of American jazz and pop, confronted Germans with a new musical idiom and with the challenge to understand its role within their own culture. Thus, as Uta Poiger shows in her essay, music critics and even politicians in both East and West Germany embraced American jazz as appropriate for the new Germanys, albeit for widely diverse reasons. That German critics and statesmen even bothered with this exercise is telling: there seemed to be a profound need to come to terms politically with current musical practices and understand their meaning for the German state and the German people. West German music critics strove to highlight the "absolute music" features of bebop and took note of Bix Beiderbecke's German ancestry. Even the likes of conservative leader Franz-Josef Strauß invoked the old adage of music's "community-building powers" in linking jazz with the West German military, and Willy Brandt exploited jazz's image by posing for photographs with Louis Armstrong.

The sweep of British and American jazz, rock, and pop and the growing importance of the popular music industry in the global economy also had some very curious ramifications for the ever-complex relationship between

German music and German identity. The centrality of music to defining who and what is German seems to have lingered as an issue of great importance even into the postwar world of multiculturalism and globalization. Edward Larkey's essay shows that as the popular music industry took on a life of its own, there occurred an almost dialectical process in which nostalgic, folksy *Schlager* and *volkstümlich* music survived any possible rejection they might have suffered on account of their Nazi blood-and-soil associations. At the same time, the American and British occupation fostered an all-consuming craze for Anglo-American pop of the 1950s and 1960s throughout West Germany (East German officials tried to suppress the infiltration of Western pop, but without lasting success). In subsequent years, however, German artists developed a fusion of distinctly German and globally popular idioms, creating, for example, a German adaptation of new wave (termed *Neue Deutsche Welle*) and hip-hop (*Sprechgesang*).

By 1945, in the rest of the world as in Germany, German music of the past had acquired certain nationalist associations. It would suffer a worldwide backlash against anything that seemed a reflection or a product of German nationalism. To this day, the composers Richard Wagner and Richard Strauss remain so closely associated with the Nazi regime, justly or not, that the perceived Germanness especially in Wagner's music can still constitute an unacceptable marker of nationalistic aggression: Zubin Mehta, an ardent promoter of Wagner and Strauss and the conductor of the Israel Philharmonic, said recently, "Music is something that transports you, and they [Holocaust survivors] do not wish to be transported back." Wagner's and Strauss's position are highly unusual in this regard, and there have been signs that even this is changing. In 1998, in an explanation that itself reflects the universality of German music's appeal, David Shallon of the Jerusalem Symphony said, apropos of his orchestra's first performance of *Till Eulenspiegel*, "Now we schedule Strauss just like any other important symphonic composer—Mozart, Beethoven, you name it."[54] And Shallon is certainly not alone in his choices.[55]

54. All quotes from Emanuel Krasovsky, "Music Once Banned, Now Business as Usual," *New York Times*, 18 January 1998, 33.

55. In the fall of 2000, despite court challenges to the performance, the Israel Symphony Orchestra performed Wagner's *Siegfried Idyll* (Suzanne Goldenberg, "Is Israel Ready for Wagner?" *Guardian*, 27 October 2000). In July 2001, Daniel Barenboim conducted the Prelude to *Tristan und Isolde* with the Berliner Staatskapelle in Jerusalem, allowing those who might be

To be sure, the concert and opera repertoire in Germany and Austria never rid itself of the standard fare of classical and romantic works by German and Austrian composers. Moreover, the serious music scene around the world still preserves this core of German and Austrian masterworks past and present, perpetuating music as the identifying marker of German culture. Contemporary German composers, too, seem to have overcome the initial aversion against the German past that they felt in the 1950s and are more willing to embrace their own past and find a place for their works in the continuum of Germany's esteemed musical traditions. In describing Hans Werner Henze's Ninth Symphony, music critic Paul Griffiths stated: "Germany is inscribed in the memories on which the symphony is based, the Germany in which Mr. Henze grew up and in whose army he had to serve, as a radio operator and propaganda film extra, in the last year and a half of [World War II]. Germanic, too, is his music's heritage: Bach, Beethoven, Wagner, Mahler, Schoenberg."[56]

Little wonder then that over the years, German—and to a lesser extent Austrian—statesmen have taken this identification so seriously that they have come to regard the health of music-making as a reflection of the health of the nation. From the era of Prussian reform to the formation of today's republic, governments have reinforced the links between music and Germanness. The state's interest in music is still far more pronounced in German-speaking lands than anywhere else in the Western world. It comes into question as part of the heightened awareness of national identity as a live issue in German public life. This only became more intense since the unification of the two postwar German states in 1990 and most recently in the context of the on-going debates about how to bring immigrants into the dominant "German culture."[57]

It may very well be, though, that the parallel emergence of the German nation and the universally acknowledged masterworks of music was nothing more than a coincidence in chronology after all. As we have seen, the course of the German national movement swept up any number of musical writers and eventually composers in its gathering momentum. Simultaneously, the national movement and creation of a national culture were sustained by the vitality and diversity of musical life in German-speaking

---

offended to leave the concert hall. Although most of the audience applauded the end of the "Wagner ban," the Israeli government urged a boycott of Barenboim unless he apologized (Anthony Tommasini, "A Cultural Disconnect on Wagner," *New York Times*, 5 August 2001).

56. "Facing Challenges of Greatness and Mortality," *New York Times*, 18 February 2001.

57. See, for instance, Peter Finn, "Debate Over 'Defining Culture' Roils in Germany," *Washington Post*, 2 November 2000.

regions. The parallel growth of these two movements—the national and
the musical—may have constituted a historical accident, but their interaction developed into an interdependence over the last two centuries. The
preservation of a vast number of court orchestras and theaters attracted
talented musicians from all over Europe, encouraged the creation of rival
middle-class and later working-class musical venues, and fed into the remarkable growth of choral societies, amateur orchestras, and *Hausmusik*
within German society. These were consciously linked with *Bildung* as a
cultural and a national ideal and persevered in the promotion of music education in the formal sense, as well as "music as education" in a more general sense. From the late eighteenth century, music had come to constitute
an essential aspect of a specifically German self-cultivation and led to the
institutionalization of music education. Composers and music publishers
responded to these demands by developing new genres of instrumental and
vocal music appropriate for musicians of all levels, including such exclusively German phenomena as the lied.

And yet, for all the richness of musical culture in central Europe, the
more insistently one poses the question of what is German music or what
makes music German, the more elusive are the answers. The essays in this
volume, for the most part arranged chronologically as well as thematically,
approach the various intersections of music and identity from the perspectives of musicologists, ethnomusicologists, historians, and Germanists (all
translations of quotes are by the individual authors or their translators, unless otherwise indicated). In the first essay, Bernd Sponheuer reveals that
since the eighteenth century, writers have pondered out loud the nature of
German musical distinctiveness and have even managed to adhere to some
vague generalities without ever coming up with a fully persuasive definition. The subsequent essays by John Daverio and Thomas Grey consider
the works of Schumann and Wagner, two composers on equal footing with
the "three B's" as symbols of Germanness, only to find that the composers'
own nationalist convictions were far less consistent than has been ascribed
them by later commentators.

Philip Bohlman's contribution unveils the idealistic pursuits of folk-
song collectors from the 1920s on to draw and redraw the map of Germany
by identifying certain folk music traditions as emanating from a "German"
landscape. Bruce Cambell and Doris Bergen then provide evidence of how,
during the Weimar and Nazi years, the performance of folk songs and hymns
had seeped into everyday musical practice to the extent of drowning out
the political and ideological messages they were meant to enhance. The essays of Hans Vaget and Michael Kater then look at the very different strug-

gles of two contemporaries, Hans Pfitzner and Thomas Mann, each with his own perceived role as spokesman for German music and German identity: Pfitzner using his defense of "true" German music as a vehicle for self-promotion in the Third Reich, and Mann reflecting on Germany's preoccupation with music as the source of its ultimate self-destruction. The following four essays turn to postwar Germany and the conflicting but also overlapping agendas of East and West Germany to forge a new German musical identity, challenged by the burden of the Holocaust and the pressures of the Cold War. Joy Calico and Gesa Kordes examine the missions of East and West German composers and their interactions with state officials in defining German identity through music, while Uta Poiger and Edward Larkey analyze the various ways of embracing and even "Germanizing" American and British popular music once it became impossible to stem the tide of their infusion into German culture.

The last three essays each take on a much broader historical sweep to reflect on larger questions of music and identity. By tracing the fate of one patriotic song over the course of three centuries, Jost Hermand illustrates the erasure of liberal nationalism and its replacement by an aggressive doctrine of national superiority, the echoes of which, he fears, still ring today in the national anthem of the Federal Republic of Germany. Bruno Nettl and Albrecht Riethmüller integrate historical evidence with personal anecdotes to further limn the problems concerning the notion of "German music": Nettl, who spent his boyhood among the German-speaking and German-cultured Jewish community in Prague, uses history and personal recollections to show how a concept of German music in the Czech lands emerged as a minority mentality but always displayed a distinctly hybrid character. Riethmüller similarly draws together historical references and personal experiences to call attention to the persistent failure in Germany and Austria to reflect on seemingly indestructible notions of German musical superiority. The Germanness question remains in limbo, while, as Riethmüller so persuasively demonstrates, the legend of Germans as the "people of music" lives on.

In 1878, thirteen years after drafting the original essay "What Is German?," Wagner added a postscript, posing the question again and answering: "I have come up against this question with more and more confusion . . . it is impossible to answer." The essays that follow do not attempt to answer the question either, but instead direct our attention to a wide range of questions about cultural context, political consequence, and musical meaning in the era of nation-states, nationalism, and globalization. Rather than scrutinizing the music itself to unlock the "secrets" of Germanness, an exercise that has already proved futile on numerous occasions, the authors of the essays that make up this volume examine the centuries-long process by which the idea of musical Germanness has survived and undergone change. They provide a glimpse into the eclectic nature of the intersection of music with German identity, showing that this preoccupation is not exclusively a musical project but far more a complex of ideas and agendas originating from a wide range of players in German cultural and political life. Together these essays constitute an overview of the problem of German music, that is, the problem of how national identity and musical language have come together in history and continue to influence our contemporary perceptions of music.

Guide to Further Reading

Anderson, Benedict. *Imagined Communities: Reflections on the Origin and Spread of Nationalism.* London: Verso, 1983.

Applegate, Celia. "How German Is It? Nationalism and the Idea of Serious Music in the Early Nineteenth Century." *19th-Century Music* 21 (spring 1998): 274–96.

Beller-McKenna, Daniel. "How deutsch a Requiem? Absolute Music, Universality, and the Reception of Brahms's *Ein deutsches Requiem,* op. 45." *19th-Century Music* 22 (summer 1998): 3–19.

Blackbourn, David. *The Long Nineteenth Century: A History of Germany, 1780–1918.* New York: Oxford University Press, 1998.

Dahlhaus, Carl. *Nineteenth-Century Music.* Trans. J. Bradford Robinson. Berkeley: University of California Press, 1989.

Dennis, David. *Beethoven in German Politics, 1870–1989.* New Haven: Yale University Press, 1996.

Dümling, Albrecht, and Peter Girth, eds. *Entartete Musik. Zur Düsseldorfer Ausstellung von 1938. Eine kommentierte Rekonstruktion.* Düsseldorf: Kleinherne, 1988.

Hinrichsen, Hans Joachim. *Musikalische Interpretation Hans von Bülow.* Beihefte zum Archiv für Musikwissenschaft 46. Stuttgart: Steiner, 1999.

Hughes, Michael. *Nationalism and Society: Germany 1800–1950.* Baltimore: E. Arnold, 1988.

Kater, Michael H. *The Twisted Muse: Musicians and their Music in the Third Reich.* New York: Oxford University Press, 1997.

Köhler, Joachim. *Wagner's Hitler: The Prophet and His Disciple.* Trans. Ronald Taylor. Cambridge: Polity Press, 1999.

Koshar, Rudy. *From Monuments to Traces: Artifacts of German Memory, 1870–1990.* Berkeley: University of California Press, 2000.

Mann, Thomas. *Reflections of a Non-Political Man.* Trans. Walter D. Morris. New
    York: Frederick Ungar, 1983.
Mercer-Taylor, Peter. "Mendelssohn's 'Scottish' Symphony and the Music of German
    Memory." *19th-Century Music* 19 (summer 1995): 68–82.
Morrow, Mary Sue. *German Music Criticism in the Late Eighteenth Century: Aes-
    thetic Issues in Instrumental Music.* Cambridge: Cambridge University Press,
    1997.
Mosse, George L. *The Nationalization of the Masses.* New York: Howard Fertig, 1975.
Pedersen, Sanna. "A. B. Marx, Berlin Concert Life, and German National Identity."
    19th-Century Music 18 (fall 1994): 87–107.
Porter, Cecelia. "The New Public and the Reordering of the Musical Establishment:
    The Lower Rhine Music Festivals, 1816–67." *19th-Century Music* 13 (spring
    1980): 211–24.
Potter, Pamela M. *Most German of the Arts: Musicology and Society from the Weimar
    Republic to the End of Hitler's Reich.* New Haven: Yale University Press, 1998.
Reimer, Erich. "Nationalbewußtsein und Musikgeschichtsschreibung in Deutsch-
    land 1800–1850." *Die Musikforschung* 46 (1993): 20–24.
Riethmüller, Albrecht. *Die Walhalla und ihre Musiker.* Laaber: Laaber-Verlag, 1993.
Rumph, Stephen. "A Kingdom Not of This World: The Political Context of E. T. A.
    Hoffmann's Beethoven Criticism." *19th-Century Music* 19 (summer 1995):
    50–67.
Schulze, Hagen. *The Course of German Nationalism: From Frederick the Great to
    Bismarck, 1763–1867.* Trans. Sarah Hanbury-Tenison. New York: Cambridge
    University Press, 1991.
Seton-Watson, Hugh. *Nations and States: An Enquiry into the Origins of Nations
    and the Politics of Nationalism.* Boulder, Colo.: Westview Press, 1977.
Sheehan, James. *German History 1770–1866.* New York: Oxford University Press,
    1989.
Steinweis, Alan. *Art, Ideology, and Economics in Nazi Germany: The Reich Cham-
    bers of Music, Theater, and the Visual Arts.* Chapel Hill: University of North
    Carolina Press, 1993.
Vazsonyi, Nicholas, ed. *Searching for Common Ground: Diskurse zur deutschen
    Identität 1750–1871.* Cologne: Böhlau, 2000.
Weiner, Marc. *Undertones of Insurrection: Music, Politics, and the Social Sphere in
    Modern German Narrative.* Lincoln: University of Nebraska Press, 1993.

Reconstructing Ideal Types of the "German" in Music

BERND SPONHEUER

> It is characteristic of the Germans that the question "What is German?"
> never dies out among them.
> —Friedrich Nietzsche, *Beyond Good and Evil*

From Forkel to Adorno, or Time That Stood Still

Nietzsche's proclamation quoted above points to the "deficit of self-confidence" often ascribed to the Germans.[1] If this is accurate, then it is surprising to see the relative constancy of a notion of the "German" in music over the last two hundred years. Among all other proverbial *"incertitudes allemandes,"* this touchstone for German identity has remained remarkably unchanged over the years. Indeed, the zealousness with which a specifically "German quality" in music has been asserted often leaves one to question its actual existence.

Three examples from highly diverse authors of different periods illustrate this constancy. In 1937, a short journalistic article by Wilhelm Zentner, "German and American Conceptions of Music: Meandering Thoughts at a Concert by Jack Hylton," appeared in the journal *Zeitschrift für Musik*.[2] Although reporting on a rather modest musical event (Jack Hylton's "jazz orchestra" was a kind of sophisticated pop music, influenced by Paul Whiteman), Zentner used the opportunity to make some fundamental assertions about the difference between German and American approaches to music. Employing stereotypes and sensationalist imagery, he characterized Ger-

---

1. Dieter Henrich, *Nach dem Ende der Teilung: Über Identitäten und Intellektualität in Deutschland* (Frankfurt am Main: Suhrkamp, 1993), 26 ff., 30.

2. Wilhelm Zentner, "Deutsche und amerikanische Musikauffassung: Schweifende Gedanken bei einem Konzert Jack Hyltons," *Zeitschrift für Musik* 104 (1937): 425–27.

man music with phrases such as the "immortal beloved," a "child of the gods," and an "echo of a higher world," which, with its "flowers of heavenly beauty," transforms the German listener into a "metaphysician" who mystically experiences the "certainty of the highest world order." American music is "moody and impatient" and does "not wander through life as a chaste goddess." This is "music as sport," music of a "vacuous worldliness," which "speaks to our nerves but not our heart," and, through its "perfectly functioning mechanics," belongs to "the everyday world, to civilization." The two approaches to music represented for Zentner the differences between external and internal, between physical and metaphysical, and between music as reality-based entertainment and music as a message from a higher world.

Such an assessment might be taken to merely reflect the anti-Western spirit of the Nazi era in Germany. A good twenty years later, however, the same understanding would appear nearly unchanged in the words of an author from whom one would not have expected such blatantly undialectical crassness, namely, Theodor Adorno, in his 1958 radio lecture on Toscanini (which he chose to include in his *Musikalische Schriften*). Adorno unconsciously elevated the same concepts to a higher theoretical plane and adapted the language accordingly. The "vacuous worldliness" figures here as "the present, merely abstracted"; the "music as sport" as "physically nimble precision"; and the "perfectly functioning mechanics" as "rattling off," "streamlining," and "hollow functioning" associated with the "reified" spirit of the "culture industry." Zentner's "machine heart" or "music motor" returns in Adorno's text as an "orchestra machine," and both criticize a circus-like performance of isolated auditory stimuli and an absence of "transcendence" as well as retreat from the "spiritual abyss." Adorno's resentful lecture depicted Toscanini, the "Settembrini of music," as Furtwängler's antipope. He concluded by quoting an "equally smart and incorruptible female musician of Latin origins" who described Toscanini's interpretation of the scherzo from Mendelssohn's music for *A Midsummer Night's Dream* as "very wonderful, yet rather as if Italian goats had eaten up the German forest." The "ideal maestro" Toscanini is also described as the embodiment of the "Platonic idea of the military band leader" and ultimately condemned for his "technocratic hostility against the intellect."[3]

3. Theodor Adorno, "Die Meisterschaft des Maestro," in *Musikalische Schriften I–III*, vol. 16 of *Gesammelte Schriften* (Frankfurt am Main: Suhrkamp, 1978), 52–67. Originally a radio broadcast for NDR (1958), it was first published in the journal *Merkur* (12 [1958]: 924ff.) and then appeared in Theodor Adorno, *Klangfiguren: Musikalische Schriften I* (Frankfurt am

In 1779, one hundred and eighty years before Adorno, Johann Nikolaus
Forkel wrote an extensive review of Burney's general history of music, at-
tributing Burney's failure adequately to describe the German in music to
"certain national prejudices." The writing style differs, but the argument
prefigured that which was to follow nearly two centuries later. Forkel's
criticism was sparked by Burney's definition of music: "What is Music? An
innocent luxury, unnecessary, indeed, to our existence, but a great improvement and gratification of the sense of hearing." Forkel dismissed this definition as an "unworthy" reduction of music to the physical and superficial
realms. "Has Mr. B., then, never seen or heard any works of art other than
those whose creators have only fornicated with the muses, given that he
appears to be so convinced that the muses . . . only exist to amuse us . . . ?"
Forkel found those "elevated ideas" that were missing in Burney in the art
theory of Sulzer, "one of our first philosophers in this subject." Here music's essence goes beyond "empty entertainment for the ears" and becomes
instead something for the "soul," the "ultimate purpose" of which was to
create a "moral feeling." Forkel contended that Burney had dismissed German musicians as "dwarves, or even . . . musical ogres" because "they did
not skip and dance before his eyes in a dainty and charming manner." He
ought rather to have seen them "as giants."[4]

Though vastly different in origin, format, and historical context, the
texts of Zentner, Forkel, and Adorno represent a variation on the same
theme. The substance of their argument reflects a configuration that pervaded the entire discourse of the history of German music between the late
eighteenth and the mid-twentieth centuries. As if time stood still between
Forkel and Adorno, the discourse of the German in music adheres to essentially the same modes of thought and motifs, despite extensive changes
in the history of music from Beethoven to Schoenberg.

Main: Suhrkamp, 1959). Furtwängler's own notes about Toscanini show a strong affinity to
Adorno's ideas. See Wilhelm Furtwängler, "Toscanini in Deutschland: Ein Beitrag zur wahren
Situation des deutschen Musizierens im Jahr 1930," in Aufzeichnungen 1924–1954, ed. Elisa-
beth Furtwängler and Günter Birkner (Wiesbaden: Brockhaus, 1980), 69–80. Adorno similarly
belittled Toscanini's "somewhat haphazard" use of "applause-happy Verdiesque strettos" in
German symphonies and flatly denied him any ability to interpret Beethoven. See Adorno,
"Meisterschaft," 58, 62f. Furtwängler used similar arguments. See also his dictum (Aufzeichnungen, 64): "a true symphony has never once been written by non-Germans."
    4. Johann Nicolaus Forkel, review of A General History of Music, by Charles Burney,
Musikalisch-Kritische Bibliothek 3 (1779): 117 ff. For more on Burney and the difficulties of
the German Burney reception , see the detailed description by Eberhardt Klemm in the foreword to his edition of Burney's travel diary: Eberhardt Klemm, ed., Charles Burney: Tagebuch
einer musikalischen Reise . . . 1770–1772 (Wilhelmshaven: Heinrichshofen, 1985), 5–15.

In order to reconstruct this discourse, it is necessary to construct ideal types. Following the distinction made by Carl Dahlhaus, the German in music is understood here not as a substantive but as a a functional term.[5] The "German" is accordingly not an empirically demonstrable musical trait derived from style criticism. All attempts in this direction can be considered failures.[6] Rather it is a property "which emerges in a historical process," "through a confused web of events, circumstances, decisions, and intentions," in which aesthetic and sociopolitical concerns intermingle and often become indistinguishable from one another.[7] Similar to Max Weber's concept of the nation, the "German in music" also represents a normative concept, that is, an idealized form of self-description sanctioned by the elite and disseminated through education.[8] Itself a product of history, it has also had a significant influence on the history of German music with its idealized notions of the past and of the future.

5. Compare to this ideal type approach (following Max Weber) the explanations of Carl Dahlhaus about structural history in his *Foundations of Music History*, trans. J. B. Robinson (Cambridge: Cambridge University Press, 1983), 129–49. See especially idem, *Nineteenth-Century Music*, trans. J. Bradford Robinson (Berkeley: University of California Press, 1989), 35–41; idem, "Nationalism and Music," in *Between Romanticism and Modernism: Four Studies in the Music of the Later Nineteenth Century*, trans. Mary Whittall (Berkeley: University of California Press, 1980), 79–101; idem, "Die Musikgeschichte Österreichs und die Idee der deutschen Musik," in *Deutschland und Österreich*, ed. Robert A. Kann and Friedrich E. Prinz (Vienna: Jugend und Volk, 1980), 322–49; idem, "Nationale und übernationale Musikgeschichtsschreibung," in *Europäische Musik zwischen Nationalismus und Exotismus*, Forum Musicologicum, vol. 4 (Winterthur: Amadeus, 1984), 9–32.

6. In addition to numerous pseudoscientific utterances, particularly from the era of National Socialism, the most extensive representation of this sort to date is probably Hans Joachim Moser's three-volume work, *Geschichte der deutschen Musik* (Stuttgart: Cotta, 1920–24). For critiques of such attempts, see Hans Engel, "Das Deutsche in der Musik," in *Deutsche Musikkultur* 3 (1938/39): 185–205. Engel wrote that "[a]ttempts to find certain details, for example the different national rhythms, . . . almost always allow for an example that could prove the opposite!" (205) An interesting curiosity is Robert Pessenlehner's *Vom Wesen der deutschen Musik* (Regensburg: Bosse, 1937), which using measures 12 and 13 of Beethoven's "Freude, schöner Götterfunke," attempts to claim the syncopation as unmistakably German. A more modest attempt can be found in the twelfth edition of the *Riemann Musiklexikon* (Mainz: Schott, 1967), in Heinrich Besseler's article "Deutsche Musik."

7. Dahlhaus, *Nineteenth-Century Music*, 38–39; Henrich, *Nach dem Ende der Teilung*, 78.

8. See Max Weber, *Economy and Society*, 2 vols., ed. Guenther Roth and Claus Wittich, trans. Ephraim Fischoff et al. (Berkeley: University of California Press, 1978), 2:921–26; Henrich, *Nach dem Ende der Teilung*, 69–124, especially 77 ff.; Norbert Elias, *The Germans: Power Struggles and the Development of Habitus in the Nineteenth and Twentieth Centuries*, ed. Michael Schröter, trans. Eric Dunning and Stephen Mennel (New York: Columbia University Press), 158–62.

Two Ideal Types of the "German" in Music

"Do the Germans have a national character in their music, and of what does it consist?"[9] Any ideal type put forward as an answer to this question must be both flexible enough to accommodate real disparities in German music and cohesive enough to serve as a "unified concept."[10] A few basic patterns emerge in searching for such an answer in the writings of the eighteenth, nineteenth, and twentieth centuries and basically come down to two concepts. The first ideal type of the German in music focuses on the specifically German, which differs from non-German in its "depth, hard work and thoroughness" (*Tiefsinn, Arbeit, Gründlichkeit*). It is exclusive, denying to the non-German any of the qualities claimed to be German, and it can be applied to various epochs and musical genres. A chain of binary opposites arises, all revolving around sensuality (*Sinnlichkeit*) versus intellect (*Geist*). Examples of such opposites include melody versus harmony, *galant* versus learned, nature versus art, beauty versus character, prosaic versus poetic, physical versus metaphysical, mechanical versus organic, sequence versus development, civilization (Western *civilisation*) versus culture (German *Kultur*), and entertainment versus ideas.[11] The second ideal type conceives of the German in music as something "mixed" (relying on the famous definition of Johann Joachim Quantz), that is, "universal" and synthetic. The German manifests itself in the fusion of things otherwise separated, for example Italian and French, form and expression, horizontal and vertical. In short, it is "music for the world" that brings the "purely human" to its fullest expression.[12]

9. Carl Friedrich Cramer, *Magazin der Musik* 1 (1783): 348.

10. Max Weber, "Die 'Objektivität' sozialwissenschaftlicher und sozialpolitischer Erkenntnis," in *Gesammelte Aufsätze zur Wissenschaftslehre*, 7th ed. (Tübingen: Mohr, 1988), 191.

11. See also Fritz Reckow, "Die 'Schwülstigkeit' Johann Sebastian Bachs oder 'Melodie' versus 'Harmonie': Ein musiktheoretischer Prinzipienstreit der europäischen Aufklärung und seine kompositions- und sozialgeschichtlichen Implikationen," in *Aufbruch aus dem Ancien régime: Beiträge zur Geschichte des 18. Jahrhunderts*, ed. Helmut Neuhaus (Cologne: Böhlau, 1993), 211–43; Bernd Sponheuer, *Musik als Kunst und Nicht-Kunst. Untersuchungen zur Dichotomie von 'hoher' und 'niederer' Musik im musikästhetischen Denken zwischen Kant und Hanslick* (Kassel: Bärenreiter, 1987). On parallels in German literary history, see Jürgen Link, "Die mythische Konvergenz Goethe-Schiller als diskurskonstitutives Prinzip deutscher Literaturgeschichtsschreibung im 19. Jahrhundert," in *Der Diskurs der Literatur- und Sprachhistorie*, ed. Bernhard Cerquiglini and Hans Ulrich Gumbrecht (Frankfurt am Main: Suhrkamp, 1983), 225–42.

12. Franz Brendel, *Geschichte der Musik in Italien, Deutschland und Frankreich*, 6th ed. (Leipzig: Matthes, 1878), 129; Richard Wagner, "What is German?" in *Richard Wagner's Prose Works*, 8 vols., trans William Ashton Ellis (New York: Broude Bros., 1966), 4:151–69.

These two concepts of the "German"—the exclusivist and the universalist—can parallel one another or share various relationships with one another. The first, exclusivist type can appear as a positive expression of the German in music, as a negative expression of the German in music (for example, in the writings of Enlightenment thinkers or non-German critics), or as an integrated part of the other, universalist type. The negative interpretation has most to do with the paradigm of German instrumental music or "absolute music," which arose out of a conflict between the music aesthetics of the Enlightenment and the early-nineteenth-century reception of Bach and Beethoven. When integrated with the universalist type, the notion of German exclusivity always prevails: the German in music might be presented as a single element among others of equal importance, but an implicit hierarchy always informs such discussions and assigns a decisive role to the German as the "intellectual." [13]

The universalist concept of the German in music promotes the idea that German music is either universally understood or superior to that of all other nations. The universalist concept as an expression of a purely "human" and supranational quality can hardly be separated from claims of German musical superiority (the Germans as "homines maxime homines"). [14] Wagner's infamous words—that "to be German" means "to do something for its own sake"—has at its core the idea that free and unfettered art makes life worth living. Schiller expressed the same idea when he said that a person is "only fully a human being when he plays." [15] Wagner meant to identify this human capacity with the German.

13. See Brendel, *Geschichte der Musik*, 129 f., 287 ff.

14. Helmut Kuhn, "Die Vollendung der klassischen deutschen Ästhetik durch Hegel," in *Schriften zur Ästhetik*, ed. W. Henckmann (Munich: Kösel, 1966), 74. Kuhn's formulation refers to Schiller's view of the Greeks in the sixth letter "On the Aesthetic Education of Man." In reference to Mozart and the "Viennese" as the "true universal language of music," Adorno once said that, "[t]he humane is the reconcilement with nature by virtue of nonviolent spiritualization." Theodor W. Adorno, *Introduction to the Sociology of Music*, trans. E. B. Ashton (New York: Continuum, 1988), 161.

15. Georg Büchmann, *Geflügelte Worte. Neue Ausgabe* (Munich: Droemer,1959), 195; Friedrich Schiller, "Letters on the Aesthetic Education of Man: Fifteenth Letter," in *Essays*, ed. Walter Hinderer and Daniel O. Dahlstrom, The German Library, vol. 17 (New York: Continuum, 1993), 127–32. Wagner's original formulation reads as follows: "Here came to consciousness and received its plain expression, what *German* is: to wit, the thing one does for its own sake, for very joy of doing it; whereas Utilitarianism, namely the principle whereby a thing is done for sake of some personal end, ulterior to the thing itself, was shewn [sic] to be un-German. The German virtue herein expressed thus coincided with the highest principle of aesthetics, through it perceived, according to which the 'objectless' alone is beautiful. . . ." Wagner, "German Art and German Policy," in *Prose Works*, 4:107. A similar formulation can

The two ideal types of the German in music, the exclusivist and the universalist, seem at first glance to represent opposite tendencies, but they are frequently interconnected in the same text, representing different paths to identity: the exclusivist type is narrow, inward-looking, and relies on the past, while the universalist is open and looks toward the future. Both reinforce Nietzsche's classic pronouncement about the German in music in his essay on the prelude to *Meistersinger:* "This kind of music best expresses what I consider true of the Germans: they are of the day before yesterday and the day after tomorrow—*they have as yet no today.*"[16] Yet whether identity is achieved through exclusion and demonization of others, or through an ambivalent notion of universality in which insecurity and overconfidence go hand in hand, both types reflect the notion of a distinct German path or *Sonderweg* in music history. Music historians have used this notion to legitimate a history based as much on myth as on empirical evidence.[17] As with the ideal types themselves, the notion of a German *Sonderweg* arose in the eighteenth century. Although historians no longer favor it, the *Sonderweg* concept may still be a useful term in cultural history. It is, moreover, not surprising that it characterized musical discourse so early, since few nations have articulated their self-understanding through music as much as have the Germans.[18]

The following sections focus on a few important historical moments in the discourse of the German in music. The development of the two ideal types was essentially completed by the 1850s or 1860s, and nothing substantial has developed since then. Over the ensuing one hundred years (the year 1945 marks a conceptual break), music critics and writers simply further refined the distinctions between the two types. Especially after 1870, in step with growing nationalism, the distinctions became increasingly

---

be found already in 1820 by Carl Maria von Weber in an essay about Ludwig Hellwig's opera *Die Bergknappen:* "[T]he chief virtue of the German artist is his genuine enthusiasm for his art for its own sake." Carl Maria von Weber, *Writings on Music,* trans. Martin Cooper (Cambridge: Cambridge University Press, 1981), 292.

16. Nietzsche, *Beyond Good and Evil,* 152. For an examination of the way in which performances of *Meistersinger* mirrored contemporary views of national identity, see Thomas Grey's essay in this volume.

17. Dahlhaus, "Musikgeschichte Österreichs," 344. For general information about the category of the German *Sonderweg,* see Bernhard Faulenbach, "'Deutscher Sonderweg': Zur Geschichte und Problematik einer zentralen Kategorie des deutschen geschichtlichen Bewußtseins," *Aus Politik und Zeitgeschichte* B33 (1981): 3–21; Kurt Sontheimer, "Ein deutscher Sonderweg?" in *Die Identität der Deutschen,* ed. Werner Weidenfeld (Bonn: Bundeszentrale für politische Bildung, 1983), 324–35.

18. See Helmuth Plessner, *Die verspätete Nation. Über die politische Verführbarkeit bürgerlichen Geistes,* 4th ed. (Frankfurt am Main: Suhrkamp, 1992), 14.

crude, monodimensional expressions of cultural chauvinism. This culminated in the militaristic "Spirit of 1914" (represented by Thomas Mann's *Reflections of a Nonpolitical Man*, a classic text in art and culture with substantial discussion of music) and in the theories of race that later prevailed.[19]

Beginnings in the Eighteenth Century

Discussing the German in music in its eighteenth-century context is tricky. Clearly the conceptual ground for subsequent discursive developments was laid in these early years of modern musical culture, yet one has to be careful not to rely on hindsight in reconstructing the intellectual and cultural milieu. Difficulties arise primarily from three interrelated constellations. First, bourgeois emancipation (as described by Norbert Elias) was both a social movement in opposition to the aristocracy as well as a national movement in opposition to foreign influences. Second, Germany's relative lateness in becoming a nation led to its obsession to compensate culturally. Third, the opposition of northern Germany's Protestantism and southern Germany's Catholicism made it impossible to speak of any single "German" music in the eighteenth century.[20] In addition, new nationalist and bourgeois principles often conflicted with more deeply rooted musical-aesthetic principles. Despite the criticism of Italian music, designated as "courtly-aristocratic" and "sensual," even German musicians of the eighteenth century agreed that, in the end, the "true source and irrefutable training ground of all music"—the "fatherland of music"—was

19. Mann wrote, "Can one be a musician without being German?" (R, 74). For more general material, see also the analysis, which includes a large collection of materials, by Heinz Lemmermann, *Kriegserziehung im Kaiserreich: Studien zur politischen Funktion von Schule und Schulmusik, 1890–1918*, 2 vols. (Lilienthal/Bremen: Eres, 1984). For an overview of this development since 1870, see Heinrich August Winkler, ed., *Nationalismus* (Königstein: Athenäum-Verlag, 1978), 5–46. For more on developments after 1945, see Sven Papcke, "Gibt es eine kulturelle Identität der Deutschen?" in *Die Identität der Deutschen*, 248–73. With regard to race theories, one should not forget that more elevated ideas also perpetuated the ideal types during the Nazi era, such as Friedrich Blume's *Wesen und Werden deutscher Musik*, which highlighted the "tension between the sensory and the supersensory," the metaphysical "notion of service" and the "striving for the universal." Friedrich Blume, *Wesen und Werden deutscher Musik* (Kassel: Bärenreiter-Verlag, 1944), 22. For further discussion of Mann's views on music, see the essay in this volume by Hans Vaget.

20. Norbert Elias, *The Civilizing Process: The History of Manners*, trans. Edmund Jephcott (New York: Urizen Books, 1978), 1–50; idem, *The Germans*, 154–70; Dahlhaus, "Nationale und übernationale Musikgeschichtsschreibung"; idem, "Die Musikgeschichte Österreichs."

Italy.[21] Italian music, an antagonist from a national and social perspective, figured aesthetically as a sort of universal language that formed the compositional and technical foundation for other national styles. In an age in which music was basically understood as vocal music in general and opera in particular, Italian music, seen as the incarnation of the melodic and the vocal, represented precisely the most universally valid kind of music.[22] The one-sided national interpretations of Mozart's "anti-foreign" statements, as well as the notorious belittling of the dominant Italian court culture of the eighteenth century in the writings of later bourgeois music historians, fail to acknowledge this essential historical fact.[23]

The ever-changing borders between the social, the national, and the musical-aesthetic realms in the eighteenth century constitute a fluid set of circumstances, making simple classifications and differentiation impossible. Two relatively stable concepts of the German in music did develop, however, that on the one hand responded to the specific historical situation of the eighteenth century, and on the other hand represented the genesis of both the exclusivist and the universalist ideal types.

According to Arno Forchert's provocative thesis, the concepts of German music in the eighteenth century followed one of two paths. Either the German musicians were seen as somehow better at being Italian or French than the Italians or French themselves, or "thoroughness, uprightness, technical solidity and depth of thought as specific values . . . of German music" were compared with "the foreign thoughtlessness, shallowness and cheap showmanship."[24] Eighteenth-century writers thereby reinterpreted Germany's historical and cultural backwardness, especially evident in its dependence on Italian musical culture, as a superior trait. This polemical maneuver compensated for Germany's lack of self-sufficiency. Johann Adolph

---

21. The quoted words are from Johann Mattheson, *Critica Musica* (1722–23), 67, in the early years of the eighteenth century and, at century's end, from Johann Karl Friedrich Triest, "Bemerkungen über die Ausbildung der Tonkunst in Deutschland im achtzehnten Jahrhundert," *Allgemeine Musikalische Zeitung* 3 (1800–1801), 275.

22. For more on this aspect of universalizing the national, see Wilhelm Seidel, "Nation und Musik. Anmerkungen zur Ästhetik und Ideologie ihrer Relationen," in *Nationaler Stil und europäische Dimension in der Musik der Jahrhundertwende*, ed. Helga de la Motte-Haber (Darmstadt: Wissenschaftliche Buchgesellschaft, 1991) 5–19.

23. See the famous letter to Anton Klein dated May 21, 1785, with his emphasis on the "German," in *Briefe und Aufzeichnungen*, ed. A. Bauer and O. E. Deutsch, 7 vols. (Kassel: Bärenreiter, 1962–75), 3:393.

24. Arno Forchert, "Von Bach zu Mendelssohn: Vortrag bei den Bach-Tagen Berlin 1979," in *Bachtage Berlin: Vorträge 1970 bis 1981*, ed. Günther Wagner (Neuhausen-Stuttgart: Hänssler, 1985), 211–23.

Scheibe succinctly formulated both ideas in 1737 in the fifteenth issue of the *Critischer Musicus*, in which he initiated a long discourse about the German in music. In a skillful dual strategy, Scheibe attempted to transform the reproach against mere imitation of a foreign model into something positive, and simultaneously to lay claim to something inalienably German. "German music is primarily borrowed from foreigners, and it differentiates itself only through hard work, regularity of phrases, and deep sensitivity of the harmony." These qualities, in conjunction with the special role of Protestant church music and instrumental (particularly keyboard) music, would shape later discourse of the German in music.[25] The word "only" in Scheibe's introductory statement does not adequately prepare the reader for his conclusion that such "secondary" merits allow German music to assume a leadership role. It is these characteristics—"particularly" its "imitation" and "untiring diligence"—

> which we have to thank for the improvement of the Italian and French styles of music, and through which we, more than anyone else, have given the former a more impressive form than any Italian has ever achieved. And who can be sure that the so-called Italian music, as we now know it in the works of our greatest German composers, is not itself of German heritage, and that it otherwise would never have achieved the prestige which it now enjoys. Yes, we have finally found good taste in music, such as Italy has not yet shown us in its entire beauty. The creation of good taste in music has therefore been the work of the German spirit, and no other nation can pride itself on this distinction.[26]

A short but steep path from lack of originality to superiority.

25. Peter Schleuning has collected a number of relevant original sources in the third chapter of *Das 18. Jahrhundert: Der Bürger erhebt sich* (Reinbek: Rowohlt, 1984), 293 ff. Goethe's article "Musik," part of his commentary to his 1805 translation of Diderot's *Rameau's Nephew*, contains a retrospective summary of the ideas of the eighteenth century: see Günter Metken, ed., *Denis Diderot, Rameaus Neffe. Ein Dialog. Aus dem Ms. übersetzt von Johann Wolfgang Goethe* (Stuttgart: Reclam, 1967), 110–13. In comments regarding national styles from the eighteenth century, French music together with German music often formed the counterpart to Italian music. See, for example, the argument between Marpurg and Agricola in Marpurg's *Des Critischen Musicus an der Spree*, excerpted with commentary in *Der Critische Musicus an der Spree: Berliner Musikschrifttum von 1748 bis 1799, Eine Dokumentation*, ed. Hans-Günter Ottenberg (Leipzig: Reclam, 1983), 83–106.

26. Johann Adolph Scheibe, *Critischer Musicus. Neue, vermehrte und verbesserte Auflage* (1745; reprint, Hildesheim: Olms, 1970), 148 f.

Yet Scheibe did not hesitate to identify a shortcoming in the one-sided cultivation of German characteristics: the tendency "toward pompousness," of which he had accused Johann Sebastian Bach just a few months before. In this respect, Bach was, in a way, too German, and it becomes clear that for Scheibe a strictly exclusive concept of German music (with no interaction with the musical style of other nations) held little promise. According to Scheibe, only by engaging and overtaking the foreign could Germans demonstrate their leading role (as the "better Italians," and so forth). Thus Bach took on a dual function for Scheibe. On the one hand he was a positive example of an outstanding composer of instrumental music, "with whom we can most certainly defy the foreigners." On the other hand he was a negative example, most of all as a composer of vocal music, who lost himself in an entirely too-German style that was dark and confused.[27] The specifically German aspects of depth, hard work, and thoroughness could thus be judged as an asset or a detriment, depending on the context.

One sees in Scheibe a merging of the exclusivist and universalist tendencies, not unusual for musical discourse of the German Enlightenment. His writing hinted at patriotic exclusiveness but still emphasized the universalist, European aspects of German music (for example, the "Italian" tinged priority of melody and vocal music, mentioned above). However, one cannot deny that Scheibe subscribed to the notion of a hegemonic German *Sonderweg*, albeit mitigated by Enlightenment cautiousness. Equally prophetic, if also compromised, is the special position accorded to Bach. A simple correction of Scheibe's conception of Bach had the potential to turn the negative "all too German" into a completely positive concept. His view of Bach thus foreshadowed a crucial development in the discourse of "Germanness" in the second half of the eighteenth century.

The cosmopolitan and universalist components behind Scheibe's hegemonic conception emerge more clearly in Johann Joachim Quantz's notion of "mixed taste" (*vermischter Geschmack*). Quantz started from premises similar to Scheibe's—German music lacked "an individual style entirely different from that of other nations" and tended toward full-voiced harmony and craftsmanship rather than the melodic and the pleasing. Quantz, however, saw that Germans might take advantage of "the good things in all types of foreign music," especially Italian and French. He suggested that

27. Ibid., 62, 637 (in reference to the *Italian Concerto*, BMV 971); see also Friedhelm Krummacher, "Bach als Zeitgenosse: Zum historischen und aktuellen Verständnis von Bachs Musik," *Archiv für Musikwissenschaft* 48 (1991): 64–83; Reckow, "Die 'Schwülstigkeit' Johann Sebastian Bachs."

they develop a "mixed taste that without overstepping the bounds of modesty, could well be called *the German style*. [Calling this style "German" is appropriate] not only because the Germans came upon it first, but because it has already been established at different places in Germany for many years, flourishes still, and displeases in neither Italy nor France, nor in other lands."[28] In Carl Dahlhaus's words, this was the chance to "become universal by bypassing the national, instead of remaining provincial."[29] The emphasis was on the mixed, not the purely German—on the synthetic, enlightened, cosmopolitan "general good taste in music," which brings together "the best" of the various nations (which in their "pure" national form would remain "peculiar"). "For a style of music," Quantz wrote in the conclusion of his essay, "that is received and approved by many peoples, and not just by a single land, a single province, or a particular nation . . . , must, if it is also founded on sound judgment and healthy feeling, be the very best."[30]

The difference between Quantz and Scheibe is clear. Even given his somewhat restrained pride in the special role of the Germans, Quantz's main goal was a great synthesis, a somewhat unreal and idealistic paradigm of a universal language of music that would do away with the differences between national languages. Quantz thus inaugurated a conceptual model that basically remained intact in subsequent discussions of the German in music. One finds his conceptual model of a harmonious synthesis created out of complex reality first in Triest's account of the history of eighteenth-century German music as a dialectical process of integration, a movement from the "harmonic-rational" to the "melodic-sensual," leading to their synthesis in the poetic ideal. It recurs in Brendel's representation of German music as a "music for the world," blending the French and Italian styles with its own. It characterizes German musicology's long-held consensus that the Viennese classicists synthesized learned style with *galant* style, as well as Alban Berg's formulation of a music that is "German, and

28. Johann Joachim Quantz, *On Playing the Flute*, trans. Edward R. Reilly (London: Faber and Faber, 1966), 335–36, 338, 341.

29. Carl Dahlhaus, ed., *Die Musik des 18. Jahrhunderts*, Neues Handbuch der Musikwissenschaft, vol. 5 (Laaber: Laaber Verlag, 1985), 21.

30. Quantz, *On Playing the Flute*, 335–36, 341–42. A similar if more reserved perspective is evident in Goethe's comment about "music" that he added to his translation of Diderot's *Rameau's Nephew*. He contrasted Italian and German (or French) music—the "pleasant" and the "meaningful"—as the two complementary "main branches" of "modern music," stating that they come together in a synthesis only in the "best works of the best masters," but then they represent a complete concept of music (Diderot, *Rameaus Neffe*, 110–12).

therefore uniquely universal.[31] The nature of this complex reality oscil-
lates peculiarly between a cosmopolitan tolerance and an imperialist notion of totality. The latter does not seem to play a role in Quantz's thinking, although he may well have considered the "German" as the most
important component in the synthesis.

Bach, the Gothic, and the "German"

Although both ideal types arose during the eighteenth century, the dual assessment of Bach prevented a full embracing of the German traits of depth,
hard work, and thoroughness. It might seem counterintuitive that the
same characteristics that helped German music achieve its hegemony simultaneously threw it back into the "Gothic age of dark contrapuntal music."[32] This irony makes sense, however, in light of a fundamental change in
the definition of music in the second half of the eighteenth century. Writers on musical matters began to move outside of an Italian paradigm of vocal music (associated with opera, the court, and the "melodic-sensual"),
adopting instead the paradigm of German instrumental music (associated
with "pure music," the bourgeoisie, and the "challenging and profound").
We find, in other words, the shift from Enlightenment aesthetics to an aesthetic trend that would culminate in the romantic "idea of absolute music."
The change is exemplified by the transformation of the term "Gothic"
from a pejorative in the first half of the eighteenth century to a quality of
wonder around 1800. This transformation provided the broader cultural
context in which the German in Bach could be accepted as a kind of musical Gothic because of its "mixture of depth, mystery and pedantry."[33]
    Enlightenment aesthetics rested on a strictly formulaic system of an-

---

31. See Triest, "Bemerkungen," and also Carl Dahlhaus, "Zur Entstehung der roman-
tischen Bach-Deutung," Bach-Jahrbuch 64 (1978): 192–210; Brendel, Geschichte der Musik,
192 f. (Brendel exemplifies this with Mozart, as does Wagner in "Über deutsches Musikwesen"
in Gesammelte Schriften, 1:161); Alfred Einstein, Mozart: Sein Charakter—Sein Werk (Frankfurt am Main: Fischer Taschenbuch Verlag, 1978), 128 ff.; Rosemary Hilmar, ed., Alban Berg
1885–1935: Ausstellung der Österreichischen Nationalbibliothek 1985, Katalog (Vienna:
Österreichische Nationalbibliothek, 1985), 188; Constantin Floros, "Die Wiener Schule und
das Problem der 'deutschen Musik'," in Die Wiener Schule und das Hakenkreuz, ed. O. Kol-
leritsch (Vienna: Universal Edition, 1990), 35–50.
    32. Ernst Ludwig Gerber, Historisch-biographisches Lexicon der Tonkünstler (Leipzig:
Breitkopf, 1790), I: col. 610.
    33. See Carl Dahlhaus, The Idea of Absolute Music, trans. Roger Lustig (Chicago: Uni-
versity of Chicago Press, 1989); idem, Nineteenth-Century Music, 38–39.

titheses. The contrasts that were drawn between such concepts as "harmony" and "melody," "learned style" and "*galant* style," "pure" and "applied" music can all be traced back to a model in the philosophy of art that poses reason against feeling (*raison* and *sentiment*). With the help of this model, the natural and the singable were polemically disassociated from the "barbaric taste" of baroque counterpoint. The category of the "Gothic," for which we have Rousseau's 1768 *Dictionnaire de Musique* to thank (the "century's most influential book about music"), became a negative collective term. The "confused," "pompous," "calculated," and "dark" (referring to works of complex structure and ambiguous affect) together create a "deformed, bristly monster" from the dark and distant past. German Enlightenment aestheticians had to look to the flip-side of the Gothic, German thoroughness, to reclaim Germany's hegemony in the realm of good—that is, non-Gothic—taste. In Scheibe's view, Bach's Gothic had two sides: the unacceptably "pompous" and a "thoroughness" acceptable only in combination with the "Italian" and "French" styles.[34]

The classic text for this reinterpretation of the Gothic is Goethe's "hymn to the Strasbourg Cathedral" of 1772, which had a musical parallel in Reichardt's 1782 paean to Bach and Handel.[35] These two texts cannot be seen in isolation; rather they are part of larger currents in the second half of the eighteenth century that challenged normative, classical traits of the Enlightenment and that, in a complicated, contradictory process, led to the

34. Scheibe, *Critischer Musicus*, 756f.: "We know of composers, who see it as an honor to be able to compose incomprehensible and unnatural music. They pile up musical figures. They make unusual embellishments. . . . Are these not truly musical Goths?" It cannot be proven that Scheibe is referring to Bach, but compare this to similar reproaches he makes in his polemic against Bach (Scheibe, *Critischer Musicus*, 62). See also Dahlhaus, "Bach-Deutung"; Reckow, "Die 'Schwülstigkeit' Johann Sebastian Bachs"; Triest, "Bemerkungen," 242f., 300; Jean Jacques Rousseau, *Dictionnaire de Musique* (Paris, 1768), s.v. "Harmony"; idem, "Lettre sur la musique françoise," in *Ecrits sur la musique*, preface by Catherine Kintzler (Paris: Stock, 1979), 288f. On the use of Gothic in Germany, which began even before Rousseau, see, for example, Scheibe, *Critischer Musicus*, preface, 756f.; Friedrich Wilhelm Marpurg, *Des Critischen Musicus an der Spree* (1749–50; reprint, Hildesheim: Olms, 1970), I:4; Johann Georg Sulzer, s.v. "Gotisch," *Allgemeine Theorie der schönen Künst* (Leipzig: Weidemann, 1792–99; reprinted, Hildesheim: Olms, 1967). On the Gothic in a broader context, see Josef Haslag, *"Gothic" im siebzehnten und achtzehnten Jahrhundert: Eine wort- und ideengeschichtliche Untersuchung*, Anglistische Studien, vol. 1 (Cologne: Böhlau, 1963).

35. Goethe's account is to be found in "On German Architecture," in *Essays on Art and Literature*, ed. John Geary, trans. Ellen von Nardroff and Ernest H. von Nardroff, *Goethe's Collected Works*, 12 vols. (Princeton: Princeton University Press, 1986), 3:3–9. Referring to Goethe's text, see Dahlhaus, *Nineteenth-Century Music*, 30–31; see also Johann Friedrich Reichardt, "Johann Sebastian Bach," *Musikalisches Kunstmagazin* 1 (Berlin, 1782): 196–202.

classic-romantic age.[36] Goethe's view of the Strasbourg cathedral represents a new experience of monumental greatness, of the sublime, and of
revolutionary genius, as opposed to the *galant* style, sentimentality, and
aesthetic regularity. While Reichardt applied this approach to Bach's music, albeit still with some reservations, Bach first came into his own with
Reichardt's student, E. T. A. Hoffmann.[37]

> There are many arguments today as to who is superior, our Sebastian
> Bach or the old Italians. And my ingenious friend said, "Sebastian Bach's
> music is to the music of the Italians as the cathedral in Strasbourg is to
> St. Peter's in Rome." How moved I was by this apt, vivid image! In Bach's
> motet for eight voices, I see the bold and wonderful, romantic cathedral
> with all of its fantastic embellishments, which, artistically swept up
> into a whole, proudly and magnificently rise into the air. . . .[38]

Hoffmann's linking of Bach's music with Gothic architecture comes from
his "Kreisleriana," the centerpiece of which deals with Beethoven's instrumental music, a fundamental document of romantic musical aesthetics.[39]
The romantic metaphysics of instrumental music—in which music (analogous to Goethe's Strasbourg experience) turns from the beautiful to the
sublime, abandons all that is empirical or utilitarian, and is free to express
the meta-empirical or absolute—forms the framework of Hoffmann's understanding of both Bach and Beethoven. Despite the mention of the
motets, Hoffmann and his contemporaries were more interested in the instrumental composer Bach.[40] The "mysterious shudder" and "inner horror" evoked by the "mystical rules of counterpoint" in Bach's music belong
to the same "infinite spiritual realm" that Hoffmann hears in Beethoven's
symphonies.[41] And just as in Goethe's "Hymn," the constellation of Bach

36. Dahlhaus, *Die Musik des 18. Jahrhunderts*, 1–70.
37. Reichardt appears to be referring directly to Scheibe's anti-Bach formulations of
1737 when he says things such as "so natural and unconfusing." Reichardt, "Johann Sebastian
Bach," 97.
38. E. T. A. Hoffmann, in *E. T. A. Hoffman's Musical Writings: "Kreisleriana," "The
Poet and the Composer," Music Criticism*, ed. David Charlton, trans. Martyn Clarke (New
York: Cambridge University Press, 1989), 104.
39. Hoffmann, "Beethoven's Instrumental Music," in *E. T. A. Hoffman's Musical Writings*, ed. Charlton, 96–103.
40. See also Dahlhaus, "Bach-Deutung," 192–27; Bernd Sponheuer, "Das Bach-Bild
Hans Georg Nägelis und die Entstehung der musikalischen Autonomieästhetik," *Die Musikforschung* 39 (1986): 107–23.
41. Hoffmann, "Fantasiestücke," 52, 66.

and Beethoven as symbols of absolute music (hardly justifiable in terms of music history) is a mythical construction of the German in music: an "aesthetic reality" taken on faith.[42]

The paradigm shift for the Gothic could hardly have been more abrupt. The Enlightenment accusations against Gothic music acquire a positive meaning. Instead of being criticized for its lack of words, affect, and subject and its calculated, pondering, confusing nature, the Gothic benefits from a preference for the meta-empirical, mysterious, deeply felt, and unutterable (*Unsagbare*). The idea of musical Gothic in the German reception of Bach from the time of Weber to Wagner also has to be seen in the context of events such as the renovation of the Cologne cathedral and the "rediscovery" of the *St. Matthew Passion*.[43] Musical Gothic combined a number of ideas. First it embodied the idea of art as a religion, as in the metaphor of the "Gothic cathedral dedicated to the arts." It also encompassed a historical and national impulse to overlook Italian and French music and to consider Bach the profound, contrapuntal "patriarch of German music," influencing Beethoven and beyond. Finally, it made an aesthetic distinction between the sublime and the merely beautiful and pleasing (connoted by the Italian and the French styles).[44]

Thus began a national cultural myth that developed in the first half of the nineteenth century: the formation of an imaginary "spiritual realm" of

42. Thomas Nipperdey, "Der Mythos im Zeitalter der Revolution," in *Wege des Mythos in der Moderne: Richard Wagner "Der Ring des Nibelungen,"* ed. D. Borchmeyer (Munich: Deutscher Taschenbuch-Verlag, 1987), 109.

43. See, for example, Carl Maria von Weber's article "Bach," in *Allgemeine Enzyklopädie der Wissenschaften und Künste,* ed. J. S. Ersch and J. G. Gruber (1821), included in Weber, *Writings on Music,* 296–99; Hans Georg Nägeli, *Vorlesungen über Musik mit Berücksichtigung der Dilettanten* (1826; reprint, Hildesheim: Olms, 1980), 46; A. B. Marx, "Bach," in *Encyclopädie der gesammten musikalischen Wissenschaften oder Universal-Lexicon der Tonkunst,* ed. G. Schilling (Stuttgart, 1835), 1:374; Robert Schumann, *Music and Musicians: Essays and Criticisms,* trans. Fanny Raymond Ritter (London: Reeves, n.d.), 1:129; Wilhelm Heinrich Riehl, "Bach und Mendelssohn aus dem sozialen Gesichtspunkte," in *Musikalische Charakterköpfe,* 8th ed. (Stuttgart: Cotta, 1899), 1:61; Eduard Hanslick, "The *St. Matthew Passion,*" in *Music Criticisms 1846–99,* trans. Henry Pleasants (Baltimore: Penguin, 1950), 96–97; and on Wagner, see Martin Geck, "Richard Wagner und die ältere Musik," in *Die Ausbreitung des Historismus über die Musik,* ed. Walter Wiora (Regensburg: Bosse Verlag, 1969), 123–46. See also Martin Geck, *Die Wiederentdeckung der Matthäuspassion im 19. Jahrhundert: Die zeitgenössischen Dokumente und ihre ideengeschichtliche Deutung* (Regensburg: Bosse Verlag, 1967).

44. Weber, "Bach," 297 (the cathedral metaphor can also be found in A. B. Marx, Riehl, Hanslick, and Wagner); Johann Friedrich Rochlitz, *Allgemeine Musikalische Zeitung* 1 (1798–99): col. 117 (Rochlitz reports here about the performance of the motet *Singet dem Herrn ein neues Lied* in honor of Mozart's visit to Leipzig in 1789); Goethe, "Baukunst," 402.

German music in which absolute music retroactively furnishes a meaningful identity. In cases where no historical continuity existed, either in the form of a nation or a state, or in the form of music or culture, an aesthetic, historical, and philosophical idea synthetically was needed to create such a continuity. This task became especially urgent in light of the modern conception of a nation that arose in the wake of the French Revolution.

The idea of the German as musical Gothic was the first completely positive concept of the German in music. It also diverged from the European concept of music in the eighteenth century with its orientation toward vocal music and the beautiful. The question, to use Hanslick's words, of whether music should "be beautiful" or "have a profound meaning" became a division that from the German perspective separated the German from the non-German in more than just musical terms.[45] Hence the thesis of German music's special role in history arose and was immediately substantiated within a historical-philosophical framework.

Constructions of History and the German Sonderweg

Since the notion of Bach as the Gothic foundation of an age of German, which is to say absolute, music seemed limited to a specific moment in early-nineteenth-century Bach reception, it required validation in a broader musical and historical context. Johann Karl Friedrich Triest, a theologian from Stettin, accomplished this in a comprehensive treatise that appeared anonymously in the *Allgemeine Musikzeitung* in 1801. With the unprepossessing title "Comments Regarding the Development of Music in Germany in the Eighteenth Century," Triest started with Enlightenment antitheses and carried them through a historical process to culminate in a synthesis. Behind this historical process lay an idea, apparently from Kant and Schiller, of a humanity, the essence of which was communicated aesthetically. Humanity, for Triest, was a harmonious balance, a never-ending "free interplay" of two human "forces of mood": sensuality and understanding.[46]

This abstract model became more meaningful when applied to concrete historical developments. In relation to "pure music" (*reine Musik*) in the eighteenth century (Triest's term for instrumental, specifically Ger-

---

45. Hanslick, *The Beautiful in Music*, trans. Gustav Cohen (Indianapolis: Bobbs-Merrill, 1957), 68 f., footnote.

46. Triest, "Bemerkungen," 227–30, 442–45 (Triest refers to the "standard for culture for individual people, as well as for entire eras and peoples"); see also Immanuel Kant, *Kritik der Urteilskraft*, ed. Karl Vorländer (1790; reprint, Hamburg: Meiner, 1959), sec. 49, p. 167.

man music), this model appeared as a dialectical development, combining the extremes of the "learned style" with the "*galant* style" to form a synthesis of the "poetic." The initial predominance of the learned style and harmony from 1700 to 1750 (with Bach as the "greatest, most profound harmonist of all times") missed the true "aesthetic spirit" because of its concentration on the inner "logic" of the music. The later predominance of the sensual and pleasing in the second stage of development (1750–80) imported the "bright spring" of melodic beauty to Germany through the "warming rays" from Italy and France, but suffered from "melodic vacuousness." Far from hopeless, however, both proved necessary for the subsequent synthesis into the "poetic" (1780–1800), which combined the rational with the sensual ("Italy's tender loveliness and France's energy with German thoroughness"). Only by temporarily conceding to the forces of "applied music" (*angewandte Musik*) did "pure music" realize its "poetic" expression of "aesthetic ideas" in the music of the Viennese classicists.[47]

Although Triest's approach differed from that of Quantz, the two shared a tendency toward imbuing humanism and cosmopolitanism with a patriotic and national flavor (Triest, as a man of the eighteenth century, firmly believed in the preeminence of vocal music, even counter to his own theory). Triest's philosophical model of history, which linked Bach to the Viennese classicists more convincingly than Hoffmann would, gained wide acceptance in the nineteenth century. Others adopted his acceptance of Bach as the founder of an age of German music, his identification of German with pure or absolute music, and his dialectical argument. The evolution of Triest's model took shape especially in the constellation of Bach and Beethoven.[48] Ever since Schumann offered his utopian vision of a "new poetic era" merging (in Dahlhaus's words) "the profundity of Bach with the sublimity of Beethoven" (the fugue with the sonata), the idea of a synthetic

---

47. Triest, "Bemerkungen," 227; his footnote to this passage is obviously based on Kant, *Kritik der Urteilskraft*, sec. 53, p. 185; see also, Triest, "Bemerkungen," 233–34, 242, 244, 258, 259, 264, 299. Reichardt, "Johann Sebastian Bach," 51, used similar superlatives to describe Bach as the "greatest harmonist of all times and of all peoples." A. B. Marx later described the *St. Matthew Passion* as "the greatest and most holy piece of music of all peoples" (*Berliner Allgemeine Musikalische Zeitung* 5 [1828]: 132).

48. See Triest, "Bemerkungen," 276 f., 408: here Haydn and Mozart are more important for Triest; Beethoven is only casually mentioned, as a young composer for the piano, who "could, perhaps, when the wild enthusiasm has quieted down somewhat," "challenge the status of the other two." After Hoffmann, Triest, and Nägeli, Schumann, Wagner, Nietzsche, Halm, Bloch, and Webern became in turn the most important exponents of this model. See Nägeli, "Geschichte der Instrumentalmusik," in *Vorlesungen*, 106–96; Dahlhaus, *Idea of Absolute Music*, 117–27.

"third music culture" (Halm) became an idée fixe of German musical discourse.[49] Realized also in composers' reception of Bach and Beethoven in their composition, this idea received both philosophical and aesthetic sanction through the idea of absolute music, which, as in the case of Wagner, could also hold vocal music to the same high standards.[50] Moreover, the awesome constellation of Bach and Beethoven, which sometimes expanded to include Brahms, Wagner, Bruckner, or the Second Viennese School, formed the nucleus of the "myth of German music." Idealizing both the past and the future, this myth worked most importantly to give German music its predominant place in world history.

Franz Brendel's music history, which laid the groundwork for the German *Sonderweg* in music, first appeared in 1852 and had a considerable influence on the musical consciousness of the educated public. Working with Hegelian categories, Brendel gave German music a unique position in world history. He relied on a "combination of interpretations of the past, orientations to the present and expectations for the future" that was characteristic of notions of a German *Sonderweg*. German *Kultur*, as opposed to Western *civilisation*, took on paramount meaning in this context. Brendel's elevation of the "intellectual and cultural" over the "political and social" naturally gave preference to music as the art of introspection. This "most German art," as designated by Johann Gustav Droysen in 1846 and by Thomas Mann a century later, thus had special significance for theorists of a German *Sonderweg*, perhaps even forming its nucleus.[51]

Without going into further detail, it is still important to note that Brendel's construction of history, generally oriented toward Hegel, resembled Triest's in employing both the exclusivist and universalist ideal types and relating them to one another.[52] Brendel maintained the basic opposi-

49. Schumann, *The Musical World of Robert Schumann: A Selection from His Own Writings*, trans. Henry Pleasants (London: Gollancz, 1965), 28; Dahlhaus, *Idea of Absolute Music*, 119; August Halm, *Von zwei Kulturen der Musik*, 3d ed. (1913; reprint, Stuttgart: Cotta, 1947), 253.

50. See Dahlhaus, *Idea of Absolute Music*, 128ff.

51. Johann Gustav Droysen, *Vorlesungen über die Freiheitskriege* (Kiel: Univ.-Buchhandlung, 1846), 1:112; Thomas Mann, *Doktor Faustus: Die Entstehung des Doktor Faustus* (Frankfurt am Main: S. Fischer, 1967), 763. See also Faulenbach, "Deutscher Sonderweg," 20; Elias, *The Civilizing Process*, 1–50; Werner Friedrich Kümmel, *Geschichte und Musikgeschichte: Die Musik der Neuzeit in Geschichtsschreibung und Geschichtsauffassung des deutschen Kulturbereichs von der Aufklärung bis zu J.G. Droysen und Jacob Burckhardt*, Marburger Beiträge zur Musikforschung, 1 (Marburg, 1967), 132f., 178, 199, 200, 203ff., 258, 283.

52. See Kümmel, *Geschichte und Musikgeschichte* 196–207; Bernd Sponheuer, "Zur ästhetischen Dichotomie als Denkform in der ersten Hälfte des 19. Jahrhunderts: Eine historische Skizze am Beispiel Schumanns, Brendels und Hanslicks," *Archiv für Musikwis-*

tion of intellect versus sensuality (which appears in Triest as the opposition of the *galant* and learned styles), and he also proposed synthesis as the ultimate goal. Yet Brendel's historical context differed, as did his effort to elevate the intellectual element. While Triest restricted his discussion to the eighteenth century, Brendel, borrowing from Hegel's philosophy of history, encompassed a larger historical sweep. The Enlightenment opposition of *galant* versus learned styles became in Brendel's account the opposition of Germanic versus Latin or German versus Italian, also described in terms of "elevated counterpoint" versus "melodic principle," "intellect" versus "sensuality," or "formal development" versus "characterization." Similarly geared toward synthesis, Brendel's "pinnacle of art" exhibited "the depth of German character combined with the magic of Italian beauty," and was exemplified in the "universal music" of the "world's composer" Mozart.

A hint of classical-idealist universalism still lingered here, but it vanished when Brendel contended in the same context that the "historical responsibility of Germany" was to "collect all the other peoples around the throne of Germany's universal monarchy." The "highest" of all, he asserted, was the "predominantly intellectual nature of Germany." This intellectualism, he believed, could be attributed to Protestant individualism, a "principle" that originated in Germany and constituted the deciding principle of the modern age. Observing that music was the modern art of "subjective introspection" and could flourish only in an era of subjectivity, Brendel concluded that German music achieved its hegemony with Beethoven. "Beethoven," he wrote, "was the first in the modern era to counter the commonly held idea that art is only and exclusively intended for pleasure, and awoke people to the idea that the artist is entrusted with revealing the highest meaning of humanity." Although the German as an exclusivist type still had to be complemented by the sensuality and beauty of the Italian, it retained its place of privilege in "world history" through this universalist connection.[53] Brendel combined conciliatory and cosmopolitan motifs with exclusive and hegemonic ones. His successors, however, reduced his liberal notions to a one-way street paved with the "idea of a

---

senschaft 37 (1980): 10–22; Peter Ramroth, *Robert Schumann und Richard Wagner im geschichtsphilosophischen Urteil von Franz Brendel* (Frankfurt am Main: Lang, 1991).

53. Brendel, *Geschichte der Musik*, 127–30. Compare Amadeus Wendt's argument about Mozart, which follows a similar path, in "Gedanken über die neuere Tonkunst, und van Beethovens Musik, namentlich dessen Fidelio," *Allgemeine Musikalische Zeitung* 17 (1815), 345 ff.; as well as that of Adorno in *Introduction to the Sociology of Music*, 160–70. For more on the location of music in the Hegelian framework of world history, see Kümmel, *Geschichte und Musikgeschichte*, 187–294.

musical mission of the German people in history."[54] Thus began the German *Sonderweg*.

Conclusion: "In Praise of Diversity"

As outlined here, the idea of the German in music constitutes little more than a sketch of ideal types, ever vulnerable to excessive reduction. But basic strands of thought at least are discernible in a discourse that has remained relatively stable throughout history, even up to recent times. This holds true for the National Socialist era, in which the same path was followed but with reductionist emphasis on the biological and racial underpinnings of art. National Socialism, too, proved to be a suitable agent for reception and rearticulation of these existing concepts.[55]

The continuity—or rather, the limitations—of the German in music is striking. An underlying dichotomy persists, best expressed by Hanslick's "being beautiful" versus "having a profound meaning," with its series of oppositions: melody versus harmony, beautiful versus sublime, music as listening enjoyment versus music as the representation of ideas, and so on. In almost every case, writers have sought to identify the pure German to the exclusion of all others. Rarely, however, does one find a "tolerance for ambiguity" (Else Frenkel-Brunswik), that is, an acceptance of contradictions, lack of clarity, or "impurity."[56] In a similar way, French philosopher Jean-Luc Nancy argued that the "unity and uniqueness of a culture . . . are one and unique precisely because of a blending or a mingling"—a postmodern insight that, of course, had different meanings in 1993 from those of the eighteenth and nineteenth centuries. One needs to understand that the rational core of the universalist type lies in the realization that such di-

---

54. Kümmel, *Geschichte und Musikgeschichte*, 63.

55. Richard Eichenauer, *Polyphonie—die ewige Sprache der deutschen Seele*, Schriften zur musikalischen Volks- und Rassenkunde, vol. 2 (Wolfenbüttel/Berlin: Kallmeyer, 1938); Wilibald Gurlitt, "Vom Deutschtum in der Musik," *Musik im Zeitbewußtsein* 1 (1933): 1f.; Friedrich W. Herzog, "Was ist deutsche Musik? Erkenntnisse und Folgerungen," *Die Musik* 26 (1934): 801–6; Hans Joachim Moser, "Über die Eigentümlichkeit der deutschen Musikbegabung," *Jahrbuch der Musikbibliothek Peters* 30 (1924): 35–45; Joseph Müller-Blattau, "Das Deutsche in der Musik," *Singgemeinde* 5 (1928/29): 145–54, 188–94; Walter Vetter, "Zur Erforschung des Deutschen in der Musik," *Deutsche Musikkultur* 4 (1939/49): 101–7. See also Bernd Sponheuer, "Musik, Faschismus, Ideologie: Heuristische Überlegungen," *Die Musikforschung* 46 (1993): 241 ff.

56. On this subject see also Papcke, "Gibt es eine kulturelle Identität der Deutschen?" in *Die Identität der Deutschen*.

chotomies can be carried to absurdity for any work of art that defies a clear differentiation between "sign" and "meaning." Thus unresolved difficulties in the concept of art itself bedevil the dichotomous and exclusive model. Such incoherence might suggest that the dichotomies are inherently false and cannot justify the existence of any pure identity of German music. It would be rash, however, to conclude that there is therefore no German identity in music. To quote Nancy once more:

> A "culture" is a certain "one." The fact and the rights of this "one" may not be ignored, and definitely not denied, in the name of essentializing the "mixture." Yet, as distinctly and clearly as this "one" may distinguish itself, it is still by no means its own, "pure" foundation. Not confusing diversity with foundation is without doubt the most important point—philosophically, ethically and politically—when one concerns oneself with the question of "identities" or "subjects" of any type.[57]

Guide to Further Reading

Adorno, Theodor. *Beethoven: The Philosophy of Music, Fragments and Texts.* Ed. Rolf Tiedemann. Trans. Edmund Jephcott. Stanford: Stanford University Press, 1998.

———. *In Search of Wagner.* Trans. Rodney Livingstone. New York: Verso, 1991.

———. *Introduction to the Sociology of Music.* Trans. E. B. Ashton. New York: Seabury Press, 1976.

Burney, Charles. *The Present State of Music in Germany, the Netherlands and United Provinces.* London: T. Beckett, 1775.

Charlton, David, ed. *E. T. A. Hoffmann's Musical Writings: "Kreisleriana," "The Poet and the Composer," Music Criticism.* Trans. Martyn Clarke. Cambridge: Cambridge University Press, 1989.

Dahlhaus, Carl. *Between Romanticism and Modernism: Four Studies in the Music of the Later Nineteenth Century.* Trans. Mary Whittall. Berkeley: University of California Press, 1980.

———. *The Idea of Absolute Music.* Trans. Roger Lustig. Chicago: University of Chicago Press, 1989.

———. *Nineteenth-Century Music.* Trans. J. Bradford Robinson. Berkeley: University of California Press, 1989.

57. Jean-Luc Nancy, "Lob der Vermischung," *Lettre International* 21 (1993): 4–7. On this aspect of "mixing," see Rudolf Stephan, Ludwig Finscher, Andreas Jaschinski, and Klaus Mehner's entry "Deutschland" in *Die Musik in Geschichte und Gegenwart,* 2d ed.

David, Hans T., Arthur Mendel, and Christoph Wolff, eds. *The New Bach Reader: A Life of Johann Sebastian Bach in Letters and Documents.* New York: Norton, 1998.

Elias, Norbert. *The Civilizing Process: The History of Manners.* Trans. Edmund Jephcott. New York: Urizen Books, 1978.

———. *The Germans: Power Struggles and the Development of Habitus in the Nineteeth and Twentieth Centuries.* Trans. Eric Dunning and Stephen Mennell. New York: Columbia University Press, 1996.

Forkel, Johann Nikolaus. *Johann Sebastian Bach: His Life, Art, and Work.* Trans. Charles Sanford Terry. New York: Harcourt Brace, 1920.

Hanslick, Eduard. *Music Criticisms: 1846–99.* Ed. and trans. Henry Pleasants. Baltimore: Penguin Books, 1963.

Mann, Thomas. *Reflections of a Non-Political Man.* Trans. Walter D. Morris. New York: Frederick Ungar, 1983.

Quantz, Johann Joachim. *On Playing the Flute.* Trans. Edward R. Reilly. London: Faber and Faber, 1966.

Schumann, Robert. *On Music and Musicians.* Ed. Konrad Wolff. Trans. Paul Rosenfeld. Berkeley: University of California Press, 1983.

Reimer, Erich. "National Consciousness and Music Historiography in Germany, 1800–1850." *History of European Ideas* 16 (1993): 721–28.

Sponheuer, Bernd. *Musik als Kunst und Nicht-Kunst: Untersuchungen zur Dichotomie von 'hoher' und 'niederer' Musik im musikästhetischen Denken zwischen Kant und Hanslick.* Kassel: Bärenreiter Verlag, 1987.

Wagner, Richard. *Richard Wagner's Prose Works.* Vol. 4, *Art and Politics.* Trans. William Ashton Ellis. New York: Broude Brothers, 1966.

Weber, Carl Maria von. *Writings on Music.* Ed. John Warrack. Trans. Martin Cooper. New York: Cambridge University Press, 1981.

Einheit—Freiheit—Vaterland: Intimations of Utopia in Robert Schumann's Late Choral Music

JOHN DAVERIO

"Schumann, fleeing into the 'Saxon Switzerland' of his soul, half like Werther, half like Jean Paul, certainly not like Beethoven, certainly not like Byron . . . Schumann with his taste which was basically a *small* taste . . . constantly walking off to withdraw shyly and retire, a noble tender-heart who wallowed in all sorts of anonymous bliss and woe . . . this Schumann was already a merely *German* event in music, no longer a European one, as Beethoven was and, to a still greater extent, Mozart. With him German music was threatened by its greatest danger: losing *the voice for the soul of Europe* and descending to mere fatherlandishness."[1]

Thus spake Friedrich Nietzsche in 1886, in a section from *Beyond Good and Evil* that issues a harsh indictment against the ennervating effect of romanticism on nineteenth-century music. While Nietzsche's argument as a whole is not without validity, both of his principal points regarding Schumann—whom he portrayed as the epitome of the distracted, unengaged artist, and whose music he characterized as a descent into "mere fatherlandishness"—are open to question. In the first place, Nietzsche's use of the qualifying adverb "merely" in the phrase "this Schumann was already a merely *German* event in music" belittles the composer's efforts to promote that blend of culture, education, and self-formation that the Germans call *Bildung*. According to Reinhard Kapp, one of the most astute interpreters of the later phase of Schumann's career, it was precisely during the

---

1. Friedrich Nietzsche, *Beyond Good and Evil*, trans. Walter Kaufmann (New York: Vintage, 1966), 181–82.

late 1840s and early 1850s that the composer became a veritable "music-master to the German people," a *Praeceptor Germaniae*.[2] Acting in this capacity, he published maxims for fledgling musicians (*Musikalische Haus-und Lebensregeln*), prepared a collected edition of his writings on music, offered advice to aspiring young composers, took an active part in the found-ing of the Bach Gesellschaft, and, in his choice of repertoire for the concerts of his orchestra and chorus in Düsseldorf, promoted the formation of a Ger-man musical canon. The same concern for *Bildung* informed his musical settings based on monuments of German literature such as Goethe's *Faust* and *Wilhelm Meister*, his plans to write an oratorio on the life of Martin Luther, and his desire to compose a *Deutsches Requiem* on texts by Fried-rich Rückert.

The other element in Nietzsche's view of Schumann—the image of a withdrawn, inwardly turned figure, oblivious to the world around him—is still alive today. There are anecdotes aplenty to support this outlook. Per-haps the best known, a tale that will bring us to our central topic, involves Schumann's behavior during the clash between republican and royalist forces that broke out in Dresden early in May 1849. Afraid that he might be forcibly enlisted into a civic security brigade (*Sicherheitswache*), Schu-mann departed by the back gate of his townhouse, pausing only long enough to collect his wife Clara and their oldest daughter Marie. Soon thereafter it was Clara alone, then seven months pregnant, who fetched the three re-maining children and led them to the Schumanns' safe haven in the coun-tryside. While Richard Wagner, then a Kapellmeister at the Dresden Opera, ordered the printing of banners, arranged for their distribution to the in-surgents, and warded off sniper fire from his lookout atop the tower of the Kreuzkirche in Dresden, Schumann enjoyed a pleasant idyll with his fam-ily in the resort village of Bad Kreischa.[3]

Of course, it would be unfair to compare Schumann's behavior during the Dresden uprising only with Wagner's. If Schumann was cowardly, then so too was his entire circle of friends, all of whom, though they considered themselves freethinking liberals, either hunkered down in their homes or sought refuge outside the city. Indeed, it is likely that Schumann and his Dresden circle looked on the activism of the banner-waving, pamphleteer-ing Kapellmeister as an ill-advised—if not downright batty—reaction to

2. Reinhard Kapp, "Schumann nach der Revolution: Vorüberlegungen, Statements, Hin-weise, Materielen, Fragen," in *Schumann in Düsseldorf: Werke—Texte—Interpretationen*, vol. 3 of *Schumann Forschungen*, ed. Bernhard R. Appel (Mainz: Schott, 1993), 337.

3. For more on Wagner's revolutionary activities, see Thomas Grey's essay in this volume.

the current situation. To quote Kapp, "We should not expect Schumann to have taken up a bayonet . . . even if many musicologists today take it amiss that he did not." [4]

Schumann's less than heroic deportment during the Dresden revolt should not blind us to the fact that the European revolutions of 1848 and 1849 were of central importance for him as man and artist. Writing to the publisher Friedrich Kistner on 9 December 1847, in response to the recent defeat of reactionary Catholic forces in Switzerland, Schumann asked, "Whose heart could not have been moved by the victory of dear old free Switzerland?" [5] During the tumultuous late winter and spring of 1848, he tracked the fortunes of the liberal cause, making careful note in his household account books of the upheavals in Paris, Vienna, Berlin, Schleswig-Holstein, and Milan. [6] Almost immediately after settling in Bad Kreischa in May 1849, he ordered a subscription to the *Augsburger Allgemeine Zeitung* so that he and Clara could keep abreast of the breaking news of rebellion in Dresden and the Rhineland. [7] Even though Schumann never took to the barricades, he was keenly interested in the plight of those who did.

These observations raise two questions: first, what was the nature of Schumann's political views, and second, what effect, if any, did they have on his creativity? Unfortunately, the documentary evidence pertinent to Schumann's political outlook is meager. In a diary entry from 1827, he wrote that "political freedom is perhaps the wet-nurse of poetry . . . real poetry can never thrive in a country where serfdom and slavery prevail," and in all likelihood this conviction developed over the next twenty years into genuine sympathy for the republican cause. [8] In a letter of 17 June 1849 to the publisher Friedrich Whistling, Schumann described his recently completed *IV Märsche* for piano, op. 76, as "republican" (*republicanische*) in spirit, noting further that "I knew of no better way to express my delight [in the upsurge of republicanism]—the marches were conceived with ardent zeal (*Feuerseifer*)." [9] Of course, republicanism cut a broad swath in the volatile political scene at midcentury. While some republicans were willing to compromise with the moderate liberals, who supported a constitutional monarchy of some sort, those on the extreme Left lobbied for the

---

4. Kapp, "Schumann nach der Revolution," 320.

5. *BNF*, 451–52.

6. See *TB* 3:454–56, 460.

7. See Berthold Litzmann, *Clara Schumann: Ein Künstlerleben*, vol. 2 (Leipzig: Breitkopf & Härtel, 1927), 191.

8. *TB* 1:77.

9. *BNF*, 461.

62   JOHN DAVERIO

elimination of absolutist regimes and the establishment of genuinely democratic governments. From what we know of Schumann's political discussions with his friend the painter Eduard Bendemann (a supporter of the
moderate liberal position), it can be surmised that his politics tended to be
left of center.[10]

Determining the relationship between Schumann's politics and his
artistry proves to be no easy task. Although he wrote to Franz Brendel in
June 1849, "Ah yes, to tell in music of the sorrows and joys that motivate
the times, this, I feel, has fallen to me more than to many others," it is
difficult to establish with precision the scope, form, and content of his musical narrative of turbulent times.[11] If early writers on Schumann were all
but silent on the political dimension of his music, then revisionists such as
Kapp go too far in portraying him as a "political author" whose later works
represent a "running commentary" on the revolutions.[12] This sort of blan-
ket politicization of Schumann's compositional output between 1848 and
1853 only clouds what ideally should stand out in bold relief.

In short, we will probably come closer to understanding the political
character of Schumann's art by limiting ourselves to those works either directly inspired by the midcentury revolutions or clearly bound up with revolutionary themes. Only a handful of compositions belong to the former category, and not surprisingly, most of them were conceived for *Männerchor*,
a musical institution that had served as an outlet for liberal sentiments in
Germany since the Wars of Liberation earlier in the nineteenth century.
Schumann's first two sets of pieces written in response to the events of late
1847 and 1848—the *Drei Gesänge*, op. 62, and the three *Freiheitsgesänge*,
WoO 13–15—were meant as vehicles for his Dresden *Liedertafel* (men's
chorus). As Schumann noted in a letter to Kistner, the *Drei Gesänge*—he
called them his "patriotic songs" (*patriotischen Lieder*)—owed their existence to the November 1847 victory of the Swiss federalists.[13] The *Freiheitsgesänge*, conceived like the *Drei Gesänge* for male chorus in its customary
format (tenors I and II, basses I and II), date from early April 1848, a period

10. See TB 3:458; Litzmann, *Clara Schumann*, 2:178. According to Clara, Bendemann and
her husband quarreled over the deployment of Prussian royalist troops in Schleswig-Holstein.
Schumann is also supposed to have made an unequivocal statement of his political sentiments to a Count Baudissin, who, like Bendemann, favored constitutional monarchy: "'The
republic remains the best form of government!'" Quoted from Richard Batka, *Schumann*
(Leipzig, 1891), in Georg Eismann, *Robert Schumann: Ein Quellenwerk über sein Leben und
Schaffen*, vol. 1 (Leipzig: Breitkopf & Härtel, 1956), 15.
11. *BNF*, 306.
12. Kapp, "Schumann nach der Revolution," 327, 329.
13. Letter to Friedrich Kistner, 9 December 1847; in *BNF* 451–52.

when Schumann and his Dresden friends were keeping close tabs on Schleswig's demands for independence from Denmark.[14] The second part-song's connection with the spirit of the 1848–49 revolutions could hardly be more direct. Entitled "Schwarz, Rot, Gold" ("Black, Red, Gold"), it apostrophizes the tricolor adopted by moderates and radicals alike as an emblem for popular sovereignty and national unity. Far more ambitious in scope than the part-songs for *Männerchor* is the motet (or "religiöser Gesang," as Schumann called it) for double men's chorus, *Verzweifle nicht im Schmerzensthal*, drafted May 1849 in Kreischa "in response to the world events without."[15] The text, taken from Friedrich Rückert's *Makamen des Hariri*, projects the hopeful conceit that present woes may be a potential source of future joys.[16] Similarly, the four "republican" marches for piano (*IV Märsche*), composed after the Schumanns had returned to Dresden in June 1849, suggest that the revolutionary spirit had survived in spite of Prussian royalist victories in Saxony and the Rhineland.

Schumann also drew on the poetry of Rückert for two cantata-like works on revolutionary themes: the *Adventlied*, op. 71 (drafted November–December 1848) and the *Neujahrslied*, op. 144 (completed January 1850), both of which employ Christian imagery as the basis for allegories of enlightened rule. Revolutionary themes assume an even more prominent role in the impressive cycle of four ballades for solo voices, chorus, and orchestra that Schumann composed in Düsseldorf between April 1851 and March 1853: *Der Königssohn*, op. 116, *Des Sängers Fluch*, op. 139, *Vom Pagen und der Königstochter*, op. 140, and *Das Glück von Edenhall*, op. 143.[17] The verses of Ludwig Uhland, the poetic voice of the Wars of Liberation in Germany and an outspoken advocate of the leftist agenda during the mid-century revolutions, served as the point of departure for the texts of all but one of the ballades, *Vom Pagen und der Königstochter*.[18] Decked out with

---

14. *TB* 3:457.

15. See Wilhelm Joseph von Wasielewski, *Robert Schumann: Eine Biographie*, enl. ed. (Leipzig: Breitkopf & Härtel, 1906), 403; Litzmann, *Clara Schumann*, 2:192. Schumann provided the composition with an *ad libitum* organ part in June 1850. While working on his *Requiem*, op. 148, in May 1852, he drafted an orchestral accompaniment for the motet.

16. Rückert's *Makamen* were free translations of the *maqames*, or essays, of the Arabic poet Hariri (1054–1122). Schumann's *Bilder aus Osten*, op. 66, for piano four hands (composed December 1848) were also inspired by Rückert's *Makamen*.

17. On Schumann's correspondence concerning a possible fifth ballade with Hermann Rollett, a writer of political verses known for his republican sympathies, see Kapp, "Schumann nach der Revolution," 396.

18. Uhland served enthusiastically as a delegate to the Frankfurt National Assembly. Even after the group began to disband, its draft constitution having failed to win the support of the

all the fanciful trappings so dear to the hearts of German romantic poets—
fire-breathing dragons, frolicking mermaids, harp-strumming minstrels,
magical goblets—the texts of the ballades can also be construed as allegories for several of the political issues that fueled the revolutions of 1848–
49: the question of a monarch's divine right to rule (*Der Königssohn*), tensions between populist demands and monarchical prerogatives (*Des
Sängers Fluch*), conflicts between bourgeois and aristocratic classes (*Vom
Pagen und der Königstochter*), and the eternal return of repressive regimes
(*Das Glück von Edenhall*).

A thorough analysis of the political ramifications of all of these works
could easily fill the pages of a lengthy monograph. My aim here is considerably more modest. What I propose is a consideration of Schumann's musical
response to the slogan that encapsulated the hopes and dreams of the revolutionaries of 1848–49: "Einheit und Freiheit des deutschen Vaterlandes"
("Freedom and Unity for the German Fatherland"). A rallying cry for the
Reichsverfassungskampagne—the campaign to adopt the federal constitution drafted by the German National Assembly that convened in Frankfurt
in May 1848—this slogan was surely on the lips of every republican in each
of the thirty-eight German states. (It became the motto of the insurgents
whose establishment of a short-lived provisional government in Dresden
occasioned the Schumanns' flight from the city.) While some might read
the slogan as an ominous prefiguration of the horrific ideologies that over-
took Germany in the 1930s, it would be a grave error to do so. For Schumann
and his generation, the call for "Einheit" and "Freiheit" was not a portent
but rather an echo, a German equivalent of the ideals of the French Revolution: *liberté, egalité,* and *fraternité*.

The ideology embodied in the slogan—unity for the disparate German
states, but freedom in the form of basic human and civil rights for their citizens—is never far from the surface of Schumann's "revolutionary" works.
While the texted compositions from this repertory are rich in both literal
and metaphoric references to the key terms in the slogan, the slogan itself
assumes palpable form in one work more than any other. In *Des Sängers
Fluch*, the second stanza of the *Freiheitslied* (a duo with chorus involving
an aged harper and his companion, a young Minnesinger) begins with a

---

most powerful German princes, Uhland stuck it out to the bitter end as a member of the
"rump parliament" convened in Stuttgart. That group was forcibly dissolved on 18 June 1849.

The text of *Vom Pagen und der Königstochter* derives from a ballad-cycle by Emanuel
Geibel. On the genesis of the texts of Schumann's choral-orchestral ballades, see Michael Jar-
czyk, *Die Chorballade im 19. Jahrhundert: Studien zu ihrer Form, Entstehung und Verbrei-
tung* (Munich: Katzbichler, 1978), 40–58, 85–88.

clear echo of the revolutionary motto: "Wenn 'Freiheit! Vaterland!' ring-sum erschallet" ("When Freedom! Fatherland! resounds far and wide").[19] An examination of Schumann's reaction to this conceit in his revolution-inspired works of the late 1840s and early 1850s will allow us to sketch a kind of musical-political portrait of the composer, or more precisely, a se-ries of portraits, for as we shall see, Schumann's political profile as mani-fested in his works underwent a marked transformation over a relatively brief span of time. While in the part-songs for male chorus of 1847 and 1848 he adopted the manner of a "patriot," that is, an enthusiastic advocate of the republican agenda, his larger-scale semireligious works on Rückert texts show him to have been something of a "priest," at least in the secu-lar sense in which the German romantics understood the term.[20] Finally, in the cycle of ballades for vocal forces and orchestra, Schumann adopted the more detached, objective stance of a historian, specifically, of a musi-cal chronicler of the "joys and sorrows" that motivated the age. Although the utopia Schumann envisioned in several of the works from the revolu-tionary years was not totally shattered in the early 1850s, it was undoubt-edly compromised.

Schumann made his debut as a musical patriot well before the midcentury revolutions. Already in late 1840 he joined the small army of German com-posers who set Nikolaus Becker's *Der deutsche Rhein*, an aesthetically undistinguished poem that nonetheless managed to trigger a tidal wave of nationalist fervor in the wake of French threats to renew their ancient claims for territories along the Rhine. Schumann's setting of the Becker poem for solo voice, chorus, and piano caused something of a sensation, and indeed, its commercial success was such that Schumann soon arranged the original version for four-part men's chorus, and also for mixed chorus

19. This moment also speaks powerfully to the transfer of French revolutionary ideals into a mid-nineteenth-century German context. In fashioning the text of the *Freiheitslied*, Schumann and his librettist Richard Pohl drew on Uhland's *Sänger und Krieg*, a poem dense in references to the upheavals of the Napoleonic period.

20. For Friedrich Schlegel and Novalis, artists were priests insofar as they acted as medi-ators between the divine and the human. As Schlegel put it in one of the fragments from his *Ideen* (1799): "You can immediately feel, or immediately think, nature or the universe, but not therefore divinity. . . . To mediate, and to be mediated, is the whole higher life of man, and every artist is a mediator for all others." Quoted in *The Early Political Writings of the Ger-man Romantics*, ed. and trans. Frederick C. Beiser (Cambridge: Cambridge University Press, 1996), 128–29.

and orchestra.[21] Clara put her finger on the reasons for the immediate appeal of this music: it was at once *volkstümlich* (folkish or popular in tone) and *eingänglich* (accessible).[22]

The same features reappear as agencies of patriotic sentiment in Schumann's revolution-inspired music for men's chorus. The rough-and-ready enthusiasm of the choral part-songs reflects not only the feelings of the bourgeois-liberal public for which it was intended, but also the convictions of the composer himself. The rhetoric of Schumann's terse commentary on the tumultuous incidents of March and April 1848, duly recorded in his household account books, speaks vividly to an emotional response made up of ardor, zeal, and trepidation as well: witness his references to "the *awesome* events of the times" (2 March 1848), "*enormous* political excitement" (5 March 1848), "reports from Vienna and Berlin—*great* times" (16 March 1848), and "*colossal* political agitation" (23 April 1848).[23] The same sort of high drama is implicit in the tempo and expressive indications that Schumann regularly employed in his part-songs for men's chorus: *Mit Begeisterung* (With enthusiasm), *Sehr kräftig* (With utmost vigor), *Feurig* (Ardently).[24]

On the whole, the texts of these pieces circle around the two great revolutionary themes: *Einheit* and *Freiheit*, unity and freedom, though the latter probably has the edge. In the second of the *Drei Gesänge* (*Freiheitslied*; text by Rückert), freedom appears in the guise of a great thought "that in awakening ruffles its feathers," no doubt an allusion to the mighty German eagle that soars heavenward in the *Freiheitsgesang*, WoO 15, a setting of J. Fürst's "Der Sieg ist dein! mein Heldenvolk." Drawing further on the imagery of renewal and ascent, Titus Ulrich's "Zu den Waffen" (*Freiheitsgesang*, WoO 14) presents freedom as "the spirit, in league with the newly dawning day, [that] arises from the tomb." The concept of unity appears in the guise of the "mighty fortress" in "Der Eidgenossen Nachtwache" (op. 62, no. 1; text by Eichendorff),[25] and the heroic folk in "Der Sieg is dein!

---

21. See *TB* 2:126–27, 129; *TB* 3:168. Both later versions are now lost. For a comprehensive discussion of Becker's *Rheinlied* and the musical settings it inspired, see Cecelia Hopkins Porter, *The Rhine as Musical Metaphor: Cultural Identity in German Romantic Music* (Boston: Northeastern University Press, 1996), 45–73, 129–35.

22. *TB* 2:126–27. See Porter, *The Rhine as Musical Metaphor*, 124–68, on the role of *Volkstümlichkeit* in musical settings of Rhine-related poetry.

23. See *TB* 3:454–55, 458. The emphasis in the quotations is added.

24. Similar indications appear in the *IV Märsche*: *Mit größter Energie* (no. 1), *Sehr kräftig* (no. 2), *Mit Feuer und Kraft* (no. 4).

25. The title alludes to the Swiss Confederation, or *Eidgenossenschaft*. An *Eidgenosse* was a Swiss confederate.

mein Heldenvolk." Freedom and unity come together in the image of the tricolor, the emblem glorified by Ferdinand Freiligrath—Rhenish poet and champion of a "'second,' republican revolution"—in "Schwarz, Rot, Gold" (*Freiheitsgesang*, WoO 13).[26]

Schumann responded to these textual conceits with a more-or-less conventional but effective body of musical gestures, textures, and techniques: figures geared to project the poetic message with the utmost clarity and force. In this, they functioned much like the emblems and slogans through which the ideals of the 1848–49 revolutions were communicated to the masses. As the historian Jonathan Sperber shrewdly observed, an image such as the black-red-gold tricolor was crucial to the political significance of a mass meeting, rally, or demonstration, since without amplification, a crowd could not follow the precise line of argument of the speeches given on such occasions. Furthermore, the content of the speech itself, in Sperber's view, "was less important to the meaning of these large events than the nonverbal symbols displayed at them."[27] Similarly, the precise meaning of Schumann's texts was of less significance than the broad meaning conveyed by a small repertory of musical-rhetorical figures.

In the part-songs for men's chorus, these figures include sharply profiled melodic lines, dotted rhythmic patterns, rapidly ascending triadic figures evocative of brass fanfares, gradually accelerating tempi, and sudden, dramatic interjections—all of which function as signifiers for the freedom proclaimed in the texts. In addition, the male-choral medium itself provides a ready-made emblem for unity, for the ensemble can be readily taken to represent a community of citizens united against the exercise of arbitrary force and oppression. (We should keep in mind that the citizens of the hoped-for republic were men: the universal suffrage demanded by midcentury radicals generally extended to the male population only.) When the whole ensemble proceeds in rhythmic unison and block-chordal style, the favored texture in these pieces, the representation of unity is complete. And when one voice is pitted against the mass to create a call-and-response effect—as at the words "will geflügelt dir entflieh'n" ("[the great thought, that is, freedom] struggles to take flight and escape from within") in the *Freiheitslied*, op. 62, no. 2—the result is a musical emblem for the perfect accord between the individual citizen and the community of which he is a

---

26. In Freiligrath's view, the revolutionary uprisings of 1848 had not fully realized the goal of popular sovereignty, hence his call for a "second" revolution. See Jonathan Sperber, *Rhineland Radicals: The Democratic Movement and the Revolution of 1848–1849* (Princeton: Princeton University Press, 1991), 295.

27. Ibid., 219.

part. Finally, since the technical demands of the part-songs are relatively
few, every citizen with a modicum of musical ability could participate in
performing them. In this sense, Schumann's music for *Männerchor* constitutes a genuinely "democratic" repertory.

Many of the musical emblems for freedom in Schumann's part-songs
of 1847–48 (march-like melodies; propulsive, rhythmically dotted figures;
fanfares) impart an unmistakably militaristic tone to these pieces. Re-
minders that freedom must be fought for, they are especially prominent in
the three *Freiheitsgesänge,* WoO 13–15, and also determine the musical
character of the cycle of "republican" marches for piano (*IV Märsche,*
op. 76) that Schumann composed in June 1849. To ensure the listener's and
the player's apprehension of the republican message in a context where
words are obviously lacking, Schumann deftly interwove an allusion to the
Marseillaise into the central interlude of the fourth march.[28] Composed
over a month after the suppression of the republican uprising in Dresden,
the *IV Märsche* thus held out more than a glimmer of hope that *liberté,
egalité,* and *fraternité* would ultimately prevail.

Several of the revolution-inspired works I have considered thus far display an unusual blend of militarism and religiosity. In "Der Eidgenossen
Nachtwache," for instance, the textual reference to a heavenly force whose
"golden hosts protect the pious" brings with it an evocation of the chorale.
Hymnic moments such as this also occur in the *IV Märsche,* especially in
the lyrical, trio-like sections of the second and fourth pieces. The mixture
of martial and religious elements in Schumann's "revolutionary" music is
a sounding metaphor for the intertwining of politics and religion in the

28. Schumann was anxious to project the "revolutionary" content of the *IV Märsche* not
only aurally, but visually as well. Writing to the publisher Friedrich Whistling on 17 June 1849,
he insisted that the marches be printed with large noteheads and that the date, 1849, appear
in bold type on the title page. Whistling complied with both requests. When he sent Liszt a
copy of the published marches in August, Schumann again emphasized the importance of the
year 1849: "The date affixed to these pieces has genuine significance, as you will easily see.
O times—O princes—O folk!" ["O Zeit—o Fürsten—o Volk!"]. See *BNF,* 310, 462.

The *Marseillaise* turns up in a number of Schumann's pieces dating from both before
and after the 1848-49 revolutions. It makes its first appearance in the opening movement of
the *Faschingsschwank aus Wien,* Op. 26 (composed 1839), where Schumann assimilates it to
the rhythms of a whirling dance. An extended quotation of the tune underpins the speech of the
dying French soldier in Schumann's setting of Heine's *Die beiden Grenadiere,* op. 49 no. 1
(composed 1840). In addition, references to the French anthem play a key part in the Overture
to Goethe's *Hermann und Dorothea,* op. 136, composed in 1851 during Schumann's tenure
as municipal music director in Düsseldorf. Set in the Rhineland during the reign of terror,
Goethe's pastoral epic would have struck a powerful chord with Schumann's Düsseldorf
audience.

German romantic outlook on society as a whole. Of course, the "religion" imagined by Friedrich Schleiermacher, Novalis, and Friedrich Schlegel was devoid of the sort of doctrinal framework that characterized Catholicism, Protestantism, or any other organized religion. At once ecumenical, pantheistic, and egalitarian, the religion of the early romantics had less to do with the tenets of a specific faith than with the *idea* of religious faith itself.[29] And since the religion of the romantics was neither more nor less than "an original way of looking at infinity," its high priests were those individuals who had the uncanny ability to embody the infinite in finite forms, that is, creative artists.[30] This was Schumann's outlook as well (already in 1830 he characterized himself as "religious but without religion"), and it manifested itself with striking clarity in the cycle of choral-orchestral works on Rückert texts that date from during and just after the midcentury revolutions.[31] In these pieces—the *Adventlied, Verzweifle nicht im Schmerzensthal,* and the *Neujahrslied*—the secular priest takes the place of the republican patriot.

While metaphors for freedom have the upper hand over those for unity in the texts of Schumann's part-songs for men's chorus, the balance tips toward unity in the Rückert trilogy. Taking as its point of departure Christ's greeting by the palm-bearing populace of Jerusalem, the *Adventlied* celebrates the Christian Lord as the founder of a "neues Bund" (new confederation). An allegory for the renewal occasioned by the accession of a liberal monarch, the *Neujahrslied* culminates in an emphatic statement of unity: "Stets laßt uns in Bunde vereinigt sein" ("May our alliance endure forever"). Both works thus proclaim the arrival of an age in which rulers and their

29. As Novalis put it in his manifesto of the romantic religiopolitical philosophy, *Christenheit oder Europa* (1799): "Christianity has three forms. One is the creative element of religion, the joy in all religion. Another is mediation in general. . . . Yet a third is the belief in Christ. . . . Choose whichever you like. Choose all three. It makes no difference." Translation (slightly modified) quoted from Beiser, *The Early Political Writings of the German Romantics,* 78. Friedrich Schlegel argued for essentially the same inclusivity in one of his *Athenäum* fragments: "Religion is quite simply as vast as nature, and even the best priest has only a little piece of it. There are infinite varieties of religion which nonetheless seem to fall of themselves under a few main headings." Translation quoted from *Friedrich Schlegel's Lucinde and the Fragments,* trans. Peter Firchow (Minneapolis: University of Minnesota Press, 1971), 210–11.

30. Friedrich Schlegel, *Ideen,* fragment 13; translation quoted from *Friedrich Schlegel's Lucinde and the Fragments,* 242.

31. *TB* 1:243. Schumann held to this position in his later years as well. According to his Düsseldorf concertmaster, and eventually biographer, Wilhelm J. von Wasielewski, the composer had "genuine religious feeling," but as a " 'free-thinking spirit' " he remained aloof from all specific church dogmas. See Wasielewski, *Robert Schumann,* 404.

subjects together form a brotherhood, an ideal community founded on mutual trust and shared beliefs. Not surprisingly, Schumann often projects this utopian vision with music that possesses the melodic and textural qualities of the chorale. In fact, the *Neujahrslied* culminates in a block-chordal statement of an actual Lutheran hymn, "Nun danket alle Gott."

Strictly speaking, the textual theme of the motet for double men's chorus *Verzweifle nicht im Schmerzensthal* is not unity, but rather the consoling thought that pain suffered in the present is often a harbinger of happier times, or, to quote the opening lines of the text: "Verzweifle nicht im Schmerzensthal, wo manche Wonne quillt aus Qual" ("Do not despair in this valley of woe, for many a joy may spring from torment"). Clearly, the dialectic between "Wonne" and "Qual" must have struck Schumann as a particularly apt reflection of the situation that inspired the composition in the first place: the suppression of radical republicanism in Dresden in May 1849. The motet features two chief musical styles. First, in place of the martial tone frequently encountered in the part-songs of 1847–48, Schumann adopted a genuinely monumental idiom—no doubt borne of his close study of Handel's oratorios—in which freely imitative textures give way to broad, rhythmically incisive tuttis.[32] Second, many passages evoke the devotional idiom of the Protestant chorale. The alternation of full choral and soloistic textures provides a further layer of stylistic contrast, and it is here, in the interplay between motivic design and texture, that we may discern a musical commentary on the "revolutionary" themes of unity and freedom.

Schumann imparts a degree of melodic coherence to the five-movement motet through the recall and transformation of its opening idea, an upwardly striving chromatic line initially linked with the words "Verzweifle nicht im Schmerzensthal." While in the first and fourth movements this idea is the exclusive property of the full chorus, in the fifth movement it passes to the solo group, which is then gradually absorbed into the choral mass. In other words, the thematic and textural design suggests a utopian scenario in which the claims of the individual (as voiced by the soloists) and

---

32. Several entries from Schumann's *Lektürebüchlein* for the year 1847 attest to a preoccupation with Handel and his music. Under the heading "Musikalische Studien" he listed all of Handel's major English oratorios with the exception of *The Triumph of Time and Truth*; moreover, Schumann's readings during this period included Mattheson's 1761 rendering of Mainwaring's biography of Handel (*Georg Friedrich Händels Lebensbeschreibung*) and a German translation of Burney's account of the Handel Commemoration Festival held in Westminster Abbey in 1784. See Gerd Nauhaus, "Schumann's *Lektürebüchlein*," in *Robert Schumann und die Dichter: Ein Musiker als Leser*, ed. Bernhard R. Appel and Inge Hermstrüwer (Düsseldorf: Droste Verlag, 1991), 71, 85.

the demands of the collective are in harmonious accord. Furthermore, the motet culminates in what, given the makeup of Schumann's world of musical symbols, was clearly intended as an emblem for redemption. Repeated twice for good measure, the passage is comprised of a slowly descending chromatic line in the uppermost voice part that leads into a solemn but uplifting tutti. These gestures echo the triumphant conclusion of the oratorio *Das Paradies und die Peri* (composed 1843), where after several failed attempts, the heroine, descended from a fallen angel, is finally admitted into paradise. In evoking the peroration of the oratorio in the final passage of *Verzweifle nicht im Schmerzensthal,* Schumann boldly proclaims that in spite of the setbacks it has suffered, the community of stalwart republicans may look forward to a similar moment of redemption.

Over the course of the next several years, Schumann would grow somewhat less optimistic. Already in the weeks before composing *Verzweifle nicht im Schmerzensthal* he expressed his abhorrence of the devastation wrought by the uprising in Dresden. "Bild einer schauerlichen Revolution" ("the image of a horrible revolution"), he wrote in his household account books on 10 May 1849 in response to the awful sights he and Clara observed at first hand as they walked through the city: bullet-pocked houses, crumbling walls, heaps of rubble, and ashes where the opera house once stood.[33] Gone were the "great times" Schumann had hailed in March 1848; in their stead he alluded to "troubled times" in the description of the revolutions entered into the *Erinnerungsbüchelchen* (*Little Book of Memories*) he kept for his children.[34]

While Schumann's first (and last) direct encounter with the devastating effects of the revolution struck a deeply personal chord, it was some time before this experience made its mark on his artistry. When it did so in the early 1850s, the confidently republican and redemptive stances of the previous years were displaced by a more sober perspective. This is not to say, as some writers have, that the new outlook was essentially pessimistic, that it signaled the composer's resigned attitude to the collapse of the revolutionary effort.[35] The distinctive tone of Schumann's politically charged compositions of the early 1850s is less a function of resignation

33. See *TB* 3:491; Litzmann, *Clara Schumann,* 2:190.

34. See Eugenie Schumann, *Memoirs* (London: Eulenburg Books, 1925), 216.

35. See, e.g., Arnfried Edler, *Robert Schumann und seine Zeit* (Laaber: Laaber Verlag, 1982), 105. This view rests on an innaccurate premise. As Jonathan Sperber has recently argued, the traditional account of a "failed" revolution, while not totally false, is one-sided, for it minimizes the extent to which the upheavals of 1848–49 represented a "remarkable mass movement." See Sperber, *Rhineland Radicals,* 3–4, 489–93.

than of reflection. In these works, the four ballades for vocal and orchestral forces conceived during Schumann's tenure as municipal music director in Düsseldorf, the composer assumes the objective manner of a historian.

As we have already observed, these musical tales of fantasy and adventure may also be interpreted as pointed commentaries on a variety of hotly debated political topics ranging from the limits of aristocratic privilege to the proper and improper uses of military force. In all likelihood the political subtext of the ballades was not lost on Schumann's Düsseldorf audiences. After all, the capital of the Prussian Rhine Province had been a veritable hotbed of radical republicanism both before and during the revolutions of 1848–49. Given the republican profile of its Democratic Club and People's Club (the combined membership of which extended to nearly half of the city's adult male population) and the left-wing character of its Sharpshooters' Society, Carnival Society, and civic guard (all of which were controlled by a leading radical, the merchant Lorenz Contador), Düsseldorf more than earned its reputation as a democratic stronghold on the lower Rhine.[36]

The republican fervor in Düsseldorf had certainly cooled by the early 1850s, but it is hard to imagine that it had been totally extinguished. When King Friedrich Wilhelm IV of Prussia paid a visit to the city in August 1848, he was met by an angry mob that bombarded the royal person with horse manure. His brother, Prince Wilhelm (the future emperor of a united Germany), was accorded a more cordial welcome when he passed through Düsseldorf in late April 1851, but within days of the prince's arrival, Schumann began drafting the first of his choral-orchestral ballades, Der Königssohn, a work that in its own way is informed by the same subversive spirit that animated the angry crowd in August 1848. Before he can claim his new kingdom, the title character of the ballade must undergo a series of trials in which he demonstrates his valor, his virtue, and his worthiness to rule. Only after taming a wild horse and subduing a fire-spewing dragon is he hailed as "unser König" by a grateful populace. The message is clear: the only genuine rulers are those who have earned the right to exercise political power.[37]

36. See Sperber, Rhineland Radicals, 94–101, 180, 194–97.
37. The principle of divine right was particularly dear to the heart of Friedrich Wilhelm IV. While he was deeply irritated by the debates surrounding the attempts of the Prussian National Assembly (Landtag) to draft a constitution for the realm, nothing upset him more than the Assembly's intention to drop the phrase "King by the grace of God" from the draft document. See Hajo Holborn, A History of Modern Germany: 1840–1945 (Princeton: Princeton University Press, 1969), 76–77.

At a deeper level, all of the ballades in one way or another touch on the relationship between freedom and unity, a relationship that by the early 1850s had been recognized as a highly problematic one. Although the revolutionary movement had been suppressed above all by the military might of Prussia and her allies, it could not have helped matters that the movement itself was wracked by inner turmoil, by divisions between moderate liberals and radical democrats, between bourgeois and artisan classes, between supporters of the "großdeutsch" and "kleindeutsch" positions, and perhaps most important, between those who valued freedom and unity in unequal measure.[38] As the historian Friedrich Dahlmann put it to the Frankfurt Assembly in January 1849: "[I]t is not only freedom that [some] Germans have in mind . . . they are primarily craving for power, which has been denied to them until now."[39] The mediation of freedom and unity had been a pressing concern among political thinkers since the early years of the nineteenth century, but whereas a philosopher such as Friedrich Schlegel was able to resolve the conflict with a dialectical flick of the wrist, by invoking the principle of equality,[40] the mid-nineteenth-century revolutionaries discovered that the task was not so easily accomplished.

Schumann's late ballades reflect a subliminal awareness of these fundamental political realities—and of the difficulties inherent in mediating them. For Schumann, the combination of instrumental and vocal forces on a large scale offered an ideal medium for the resolution of the tensions between freedom and unity, since, as he once put it: "Chorus and orchestra lift us beyond ourselves."[41] Moreover, the choral-orchestral ballades were conceived for the grand music festivals that by midcentury had become a staple of German musical life, events that symbolized both bourgeois identity (given their administration by committees of prominent burghers who recruited star conductors and soloists) and national unity (in

38. Adherents of the "großdeutsch" cause campaigned for the absorption of the Habsburg empire into the new German federal state, while the "kleindeutsch" group argued against including the Austrians.

39. Quoted in Holborn, *History of Modern Germany*, 103.

40. Schlegel addressed the problem in his *Lectures on Transcendental Philosophy* (1800–1801): "We now have to seek the *categories of society*. In the concept of society lies immediately the concept *community* and the concept *freedom*. Society is unity in multiplicity and multiplicity in unity. But if freedom were absolute there could be no community, and vice versa. We therefore must seek a mediating concept that unites both concepts and makes them possible. This is the *concept of equality*." Quoted from Beiser, *Early Political Writings of the German Romantics*, 145.

41. Letter of 28 December 1853 to Carl Meinardus, in *BNF*, 388.

that the festivals gathered massive forces for the express purpose of celebrating the cultural monuments of the fatherland). One might even say
that the choral-orchestral ballade, as a genre, represents a kind of music
festival in microcosm.[42] In any case, the interplay between individual and
communal modes of utterance is indelibly imprinted on the generic and
stylistic constitution of the works themselves. While the operatic decla-
mation and expressive lyricism of the soloists allow free rein for the expression of individual feelings, the folkish, ceremonial, and celebratory
choruses in which the ballades abound may be viewed as musical emblems
of unity. The interplay between these contrasting genres and styles proves
to be particularly decisive for the articulation of the political themes of the
first two ballades: *Der Königssohn* and *Des Sängers Fluch.*

In *Der Königssohn,* Schumann seems to resolve the tension between
subjective and communal modes at the very end of the work, where an aging minstrel, his sight miraculously restored, celebrates the Königssohn's
accession to the throne with a *volkstümlicher Lied* that is promptly taken
up by the chorus. Culminating with the minstrel and the populace united
in their acclamation of the new ruler, the ballade thus strikes a frankly
utopian note. Yet there is something oddly unsatisfying about this musical-
dramatic representation of utopia. Touted by the minstrel as his "schönstes
Lied" (most beautiful song), the closing paean to the new king and his queen
rings hollow. Rigidly foursquare, melodically uninteresting, pompous and
overblown, this intentionally banal music sets in relief the far "schöner"
music that precedes it: a suave and expressive *Kunstlied* (art song) presented
first by the alto *Erzählerin* (narrator), who tells of the exultant atmosphere
at the new king's court, and then repeated almost note for note by the old
minstrel. Of all the voices in *Der Königssohn,* these are by far the most eloquent, and it is significant that they do not belong to the active participants
in the drama, but rather to commentators who must of necessity maintain
a certain distance from the unfolding events. In other words, the ballade is
less a celebration of individuals or nations than of the narrative or bardic
voice that keeps them alive in memory. Hence, the central figure of *Der
Königssohn* is neither an enlightened monarch nor a contented populace,
but rather a historian, represented here by the figure to whom all historians trace their lineage: the bard.[43]

42. Consider Schumann's remarks on his first ballade in a letter of 23 July 1853 to Johann Verhulst: "*Der Königssohn* is well suited to massed performance [*Massenaufführung*],
for it consists largely of folk choruses [*Volkschöre*]." Quoted in Kapp, "Schumann nach der
Revolution," 400.

43. Schumann, with the help of his textual collaborator Moritz Horn, underscored this

Des Sängers Fluch offers an even more explicit critique of the utopian order envisioned by some of the mid-nineteenth-century revolutionaries. Two minstrels, an aged harper and a young Minnesinger, have been summoned to entertain a royal couple and their courtiers. Fearful that the minstrels' songs of love and war might incite his subjects to revolt—and worse yet, that they might cast a seductive spell on his queen—the king murders the younger of the pair, an act that precipitates the harper's utterance of a spine-chilling curse on the monarch and his realm: "May your name be forgotten, consumed by eternal night, croaked out like a death-rattle in the void!" ("Dein Name sei vergessen, in ew'ge Nacht getaucht, sei wie ein letztes Röcheln in leere Luft verhaucht!"). The third of the minstrels' lieder, a rousing duet with chorus on a text loosely based on Uhland's poem *Sänger und Krieg*, is of particular interest in this context. Heroic in tone, proceeding with an irresistible melodic surge, and bathed in the cascading arpeggios of the harp (the instrument traditionally associated with the bard), this *Freiheitslied* builds toward two stirring climaxes. The first, signaled by the minstrels' invocation "Freiheit! Vaterland," is as powerful a statement of the individual's demand for liberty as one might imagine. The second, ushered in as the minstrels and chorus jointly hail the *Volk* that hearkens to their song, asserts the oneness of the earlier demand with the communal will.[44] Yet this image of utopia is brutally destroyed when, just as minstrels and populace together are about to bring their song round to its final cadence, the king bursts in with an angry rejoinder: "Did you come here only to foment rebellion in our kingdom with your songs?" ("Kamt ihr hier her, mit euren Lieder Aufruhr zu bringen unserm Thron?"). While this gesture calls into question the possibility of attaining an ideal condition in which the claims for both freedom and unity have been perfectly reconciled, the king's murder of the younger minstrel, at the height of the latter's impassioned *Minnelied*, is a no less potent critique of an idea dear to the hearts of the early romantics—namely, that the new order will be founded on the rule of love, not law.[45]

---

point through a telling alteration in the original poem. Whereas Uhland's minstrel expires after regaining his sight, the minstrel in Schumann's ballade lives.

44. This climactic moment, the text of which was supplied by Schumann and Pohl, represents a realization in sound of the young Schumann's conviction that "[t]he actual times of poetry are those when poets and people form themselves into a unity, a whole." Entry of early 1827 in *TB* 1:77.

45. Novalis was an eloquent proponent of this notion, which he put forward in a collection of fragments entitled *Glauben und Liebe* (*Faith and Love*) of 1798. The collection appears in translation in Beiser, *Early Political Writings of the German Romantics*, 33–49.

Des Sängers Fluch has been interpreted as an allegory for the revolutionary potential of art, as indeed it is.[46] At the same time, it might also be viewed as a statement of the conviction that artists fulfill their highest calling when they engage in acts of reflection. For Schumann, these two outlooks on art were complementary, not contradictory. Although he never consciously attempted to resolve the antinomy between art as revolution and art as reflection, he probably would have done so by asserting that art is most revolutionary when it is most reflective. This, at least, is the impression conveyed by the final tableau of *Des Sängers Fluch*. The chorus has the last word, narrating in melancholy tones the fulfillment of the harper's prophecy. Just as a barren wasteland now lies where the king's palace once stood, so his name—obliterated, forgotten ("Versunken und vergessen")—has disappeared from the annals of history. And that, the chorus reports, *that* is the singer's curse ("Das ist des Sängers Fluch"). The voice that delivers this message, though emanating from the chorus, is not the voice of the masses. Disembodied, detached, it exudes an aura of epic distance. It suggests that the republican of 1848–49 had lost faith in political slogans. We observe him engaging in an act of historical reflection, and the issues that consume him extend well beyond "mere fatherlandishness." His bardic voice and Nietzsche's "voice for the soul of Europe" draw breath from the same source.

Guide to Further Reading

Beiser, Frederick C., ed. and trans. *The Early Political Writings of the German Romantics*. Cambridge: Cambridge University Press, 1996.

Daverio, John. "Schumann's Ossianic Manner." *19th-Century Music* 21 (spring 1998): 247–73.

———."Sounds without the Gate: Schumann and the Dresden Revolution." *Il Saggiatore Musicale* 4 (1997): 87–112.

Finson, Jon W. "Schumann's Mature Style and the 'Album of Songs for the Young.'" *Journal of Musicology* 8 (1990): 227–50.

Kapp, Reinhard. "Schumann nach der Revolution: Vorüberlegungen, Statements, Hinweise, Materielen, Fragen." *Schumann Forschungen*, vol. 3, *Schumann in Düsseldorf: Werke—Texte—Interpretationen*. Ed. Bernhard R. Appel. Mainz: Schott, 1993. Pp. 315–415.

Mahlert, Ulrich. *Fortschritt und Kunstlied: Späte Lieder Robert Schumanns im Licht der liedästhetischen Diskussion ab 1848*. Munich: Katzbichler, 1983.

Sheehan, James J. *German History 1770–1866*. Oxford: Clarendon Press, 1989.

46. See Kapp, "Schumann nach der Revolution," 401–2.

Sperber, Jonathan. *Rhineland Radicals: The Democratic Movement and the Revolution of 1848–1849*. Princeton: Princeton University Press, 1991.

———. *The European Revolutions, 1848–1851*. Cambridge: Cambridge University Press, 1994.

Struck, Michael. "Kunstwerk-Anspruch und Popularitätsstrebungen—Ursachen ohne Wirkung? Bermerkungen zum *Glück von Edenhall* op. 143 und zur *Fest-Ouvertüre* op. 123." *Schumann Forschungen*, vol. 3, *Schumann in Düsseldorf: Werke—Texte—Interpretationen*. Ed. by Bernhard R. Appel. Mainz: Schott, 1993. Pp. 265–311.

Wagner's *Die Meistersinger* as National Opera (1868–1945)

THOMAS S. GREY

Was ist deutsch? Wagner posed this question in an eponymous essay published in the *Bayreuther Blätter* in 1878. Most of the essay derives from a series of journal entries written back in 1865, aiming to instruct the young King Ludwig II of Bavaria in matters relating to art, politics, and society in the emerging German nation and Wagner's own conception of the "German spirit." In readying the text for publication, Wagner appended a brief afterword in which he revisited the titular question ("What is German?") from the perspective of 1878, conceding that it had only become more of a puzzle to him.[1] In this afterword he suggested (in a characteristically elliptical way) that it was the failure of the new German Reich to adopt him more wholeheartedly as its official cultural standard-bearer that disillusioned him on the subject of national identity. But, along with the original text, the afterword also reminds us that the status of Wagner and his works as symbols of a consciously *national* German culture has never been quite as straightforward as we tend to suppose.

At the time he first drafted the text of this essay, Wagner was engaged in the composition of the work most closely identified with the thematics of German cultural and national identity, *Die Meistersinger von Nürnberg*. If Wagner equivocated in answering the question about "Germanness" in his prose essay, it would seem that he meant to offer a more definitive, tangible answer in this operatic tribute to his cultural patrimony. In 1865

---

1. "The question puzzled me more and more." Richard Wagner, "What Is German?" in *Richard Wagner's Prose Works*, 8 vols., trans. William Ashton Ellis (New York: Broude Bros., 1966), 4:167.

Wagner had been repatriated after more than a dozen years in exile, and the unification of the German states was already an imminent prospect. The topic Wagner had first envisioned in July of 1845 as a light-hearted "satyr play" to the drama of Tannhäuser and the singing contest of the Wartburg had become in the meantime rife with possibilities as a "national opera." Late-medieval and early-modern Nuremberg, no less than the Wartburg, had acquired an iconic status in the context of early-nineteenth-century German national aspirations.[2] Certainly the bourgeois artist-craftsman Hans Sachs was a more appropriate model for the new German nation's musical poet laureate—as Wagner aspired to be—than the morally conflicted knightly *Minnesänger*, Tannhäuser.

Did *Die Meistersinger* become, in Wagner's own mind, a celebration of the emerging German nation, a touchstone for the still-problematic definition of what is German? Was it received as such by Wagner's contemporaries? Was it a "national opera" by authorial design, or rather by popular and critical acclamation (to invoke a distinction drawn by Carl Dahlhaus with respect to works or repertoires understood as representative of national cultures)?[3] Or did these two factors, authorial design and popular acclaim, merge in a natural, harmonious accord? Was the contribution of *Die Meistersinger* to the fateful trajectory of German nationalism in the first half of the twentieth century consistent with Wagner's own ideas about German art and the German state? Or did the National Socialists merely exploit Wagner's utopian vision of a harmonious national *Kulturstaat* as another bit of cultural propaganda, masking their ruthlessly political aims? A brief survey of the career of *Die Meistersinger* as an icon of national cultural identity, from the time of its premiere through the end of the Third Reich, may help to illuminate—if not definitively resolve—some of these questions.

2. The symbolic value of historical Nuremberg in nineteenth-century discussions of German national and cultural identity is examined in Arthur Groos, "Constructing Nuremberg: Typological and Proleptic Communities in *Die Meistersinger*," *19th-Century Music* 16 (summer 1992): 18–34; Stewart Spencer, "Wagner's Nuremberg," *Cambridge Opera Journal* 4 (1992): 21–41; Peter Uwe Hohendahl, "Reworking History: Wagner's German Myth of Nuremberg," in *Re-reading Wagner*, ed. R. Grimm and J. Hermand (Madison: University of Wisconsin Press, 1993), 39–60. Sixteenth-century Nuremberg was, as Groos puts it, "a locus for contemporary discourse about 'Germanness,' a cultural unity projected backward onto the period of the Reformation by the middle-class intelligentsia and intended to figure as a model and inspiration for both present and future." Groos, "Constructing Nuremberg," 20.

3. Carl Dahlhaus, *Nineteenth-Century Music*, trans. J. Bradford Robinson (Berkeley: University of California Press, 1989), 38. See also the section on "The Idea of National Opera," ibid., 217–26.

German Art or German Politics? The "National Idea" in the Genesis of Die Meistersinger

When in July 1845 Wagner first sketched the idea of a comedy on the subject of Hans Sachs and the Nuremberg mastersingers' guild, he had not yet developed a sense of himself as cultural representative—or indeed savior—of the German nation. While many political intellectuals of the 1848 generation were concerned with the question of a modernized, unified German state, Wagner's own involvement with the revolutionary movement was not much informed by patriotic or nationalistic motives. According to the 1851 *Communication to My Friends*, Wagner's first approach to the subject of Sachs and the mastersingers was in response to "the well-intentioned advice of some good friends" who believed he would sooner find access to the repertoire of German theaters with a light-hearted comedy (presumably in the manner of Albert Lortzing, who had ventured a comic opera on the subject of Hans Sachs five years earlier) than with his ambitious adaptations of German legend and mythology.[4] Yet, while Wagner had not yet begun to hold forth in print about the relation of his creative work to the future of German art and the German nation, the 1845 sketch for the *Meistersinger* project is in fact more heavily inflected by nationalist cultural rhetoric than the 1861 prose draft (existing in two fairly similar redactions) that immediately preceded the full libretto. What would eventually become Sachs's so-called *Wahn* monologue, for example, is conceived in the 1845 sketch as a meditation—repeatedly interrupted by amorous flirtations between David and Magdalene—on the preservation of German culture. "Is it really over with now, the art of poetry?" he asks himself. "Am I, a cobbler, the last to draw inspiration from the realm of the great German past?"[5] Later in act 3, when Sachs coaches the young knight (here still unnamed) on the art of poetry and song, he starts to exhort him—with the bellicose nationalistic rhetoric of the *Burschenschaften* or Körner's *Leyer und Schwert*—to take up arms in defense of German culture, to preserve the line from "Walther, Wolfram, and the *Heldenlieder*" through Hans Sachs himself and on into

4. Richard Wagner, "Eine Mittheilung an meine Freunde," in *Sämtliche Schriften und Dichtungen* (Leipzig: Breitkopf & Härtel, 1911–16), 4:284–86. Lortzing's *Hans Sachs*, to a libretto by Philipp Reger after a play by J. L. F. Deinhardstein, premiered in Leipzig in 1840, but had also been successfully revived in Mannheim on 25 May 1845, just two months before Wagner sketched his version of a Sachs comedy.

5. "—Sachs im Nachdenken: 'So ginge es wirklich zu Ende mit der schönen Dichtkunst? Ich, ein Schuster, wäre noch der einzige, der im Reiche der großen deutschen Vergangenheit atmete?'" "Die Meistersinger von Nürnberg. Komische Oper in drei Akten" (prose draft, 1845), in *Sämtliche Schriften und Dichtungen*, 11:351.

the distant national future. "Go back to your [ancestral] castle, study what Ulrich von Hutten and the Wittemberger [Martin Luther] have written, and should it prove necessary, so defend what you've learned with the sword!" All three of the prose drafts (the 1845 and both 1861 versions) conclude with the same preliminary text of the couplet honoring the legacy of "German Art" that ends the opera. In the drafts, the couplet reads:

> Zerging' das heil'ge röm'sche Reich in Dunst,
> Uns bliebe doch die heil'ge deutsche Kunst.

> [And should the Holy Roman Empire collapse in smoke,
> there will remain for us holy German art.]

This motto—to the effect of *ars longa, vita brevis*—seems to have been felt to convey the central "philosophy" of his work from its earliest conception, and (as has often been pointed out in defense of an "a-political" Wagner) it appears to place a higher premium on the continuity of artistic achievement than on that of a unified nation-state. (That leaves open the question, however, of how Wagner or his fictional mastersingers would evaluate the status of the Holy Roman Empire as against some potential future *German* empire, apart from the spiritual "empire" of German art.)

What *was* eliminated, however, was the note of irony that originally accompanied his "Lob der Meistersingerzunft" at the end of the opera (originally to be delivered "halb ironisch, halb ernst")—what became the *Schlußansprache* or closing address in defense of national culture and its institutions. (This note of irony had already been deleted from the two 1861 prose drafts.) Sachs himself, however, does not entirely lose his sense of ironic detachment from his simpler, less reflective fellow burghers in the completed opera. But that this tone should be expunged from his closing address is significant—the one place in the opera (as opposed to the earlier prose drafts) where Sachs puts the art of song in the perspective of an explicitly national culture, and where the assorted burghers, guildsmen, apprentices, and other townsfolk are assembled as a microcosm of the nation, their massed choral voice becoming the massed voice of the *Volk*.

"Was deutsch und echt . . .": The Closing Address of Hans Sachs

If Wagner seemed to know from the earliest conception of *Die Meistersinger* that the work would end with a paean to "holy German art," he remained uncertain up to the last minute of his work on the composition as to the rhetorical strategy by which the central figure of Hans Sachs should

incite the people to their rousing *Kunsthymnus*. The earliest full draft of
the libretto (1862) contained a couplet exhorting Walther (et al.) to "honor
the German warrior, whether victorious or vanquished," alongside the exhortation to "honor your German [guild] masters."[6] The line about warriors, however, was later left out—it was somewhat out of place here, in fact,
following the essentially pacifistic sentiments of the lines that preceded it
(these not deleted from the text, but not finally set to music either):

> Welkt manche Sitt' und mancher Brauch,
> zerfällt in Schutt, vergeht in Rauch,—
> laßt ab vom Kampf!
> Nicht Donnerbüchs' noch Pulverdampf
> macht wieder dicht was nur noch Hauch!
>
> [Customs and mores will fade,
> collapse in rubble and smoke,—
> so cease to fight!
> Muskets' thunder and clouds of gunpowder
> will not revive what's just thin air!]

As in the opera's closing "motto," Wagner stresses the enduring "spiritual"
legacy of art over and against the temporal aims of government and politics.
Some further uncomposed lines from this first draft of the libretto spoke to
past conflicts between the old feudal lords (like Walther's ancestors) and
the enterprising burghers of the new German city-states (like Nuremberg),
but also to the frequent spats arising between the burghers and their guilds.
The art of song, says Sachs, has always been the best means of achieving
civic harmony—hence the special honor due to the mastersingers among
all the guilds. Wagner's ideal state is an aesthetic one, in which private and
public life alike are subject to the beneficent rule of art.

When he got around to composing the third act in 1867, however, Wagner was ready to scrap the whole of this hortatory address on the value of
artistic tradition and institutions, and to conclude the opera with Walther's
victorious "Prize Song." (Presumably in this case he would have linked the

---

6. These original lines read: "Rühme der deutsche Krieger [*recte:* dem deutschen??], /
Besiegter oder Sieger; / Ehrt ihr die deutschen Meister / dann werd' ihr Herr der Geister."
See John Warrack, "Sources and Genesis of the Text," in *Richard Wagner: Die Meistersinger
von Nürnberg* (Cambridge: Cambridge University Press, 1996) 29, 157–58. The second of these
couplets became "Ehrt eure deutschen Meister, dann bannt ihr gute Geister."

choral acclamation of Walther's song, "Reich ihm das Reis, sein sei der Preis," with a choral-ensemble setting of the "motto" about holy German art outliving the Holy Roman Empire.) But just on the point of completing the full composition draft, on 27–28 January 1867, Wagner let himself be persuaded by Cosima (according to her testimony to King Ludwig) to retain an abbreviated version of the address. As finally composed, twenty-three of the original lines were replaced by eight lines that resonate distinctly with the cultural-political concerns of Wagner's prose essays of the 1860s, "What Is German?" and "German Art and German Politics," namely, the importance of a spiritual bond between political leaders and the *Volk* (which art could provide, in Wagner's view), and the continual threat of cultural domination and "contamination" of Germany by France:

> Habt acht! / Uns dräuen üble Streich':—
> zerfällt erst deutsches Volk und Reich,
> in falscher wälscher Majestät
> kein Fürst bald mehr sein Volk versteht;
> und wälschem Dunst mit wälschem Tand
> sie pflanzen uns in deutsches Land;
> was deutsch und echt, wüßt keiner mehr,
> lebt's nicht in deutscher Meister Ehr.

> [Beware! / We're threatened by an evil blow:
> if German people and empire collapse,
> if in false foreign (Latin) majesty
> no prince understands his people any more;
> if foreign (Latin) airs and foreign vanities
> should infiltrate our German land;
> then none would know what's German and true,
> were it not to survive through the honor of German masters.]

These defensively chauvinistic lines lead into the closing exhortation to "honor your German masters," whose efforts will preserve the legacy of German art against the vagaries of political and social change. The troublesome resonance the added lines have acquired in the wake of the two world wars in the twentieth century overshadows their significance in the 1860s. Yet with the Franco–Prussian War only two years off in 1868, the original significance of the lines is not finally unrelated to that later resonance.

The notion that German art and culture needed to be defended against corrosive foreign influences (specifically French, from without, but also

"Jewish," from within) was indeed a major new component of Wagner's thought in the 1860s and 1870s and represents a significant departure from the traditional universalist view of German culture that had dominated the later Enlightenment and early romantic eras, including Wagner's own views through at least the 1840s, when he first conceived the *Meistersinger* plan. In this universalizing view, German culture was distinguished by its propensity to adopt and refine or "deepen" the best traits of other classical and modern cultures, grafting them onto whatever traits might be considered native Teutonic ones.[7] In the gendered terms of Wagner's operatic critique in *Opera and Drama*, this traditional view cast German culture in a "feminine" role, receiving and nurturing some fertilizing germ provided by an outside "source" culture. (In *Opera and Drama* the model applies to music as "fertilized" by the external, conceptual "poetic intent.") While the expression of explicitly chauvinistic sentiments in *Die Meistersinger* is limited to those few lines inserted in 1867, it is possible to see here the germination, as it were, of a new "masculine" model of German culture that would come to dominate the later nineteenth and, of course, the early twentieth centuries, at least among the most vocal, self-conscious nationalists. If German art had reached a new stage of independence and maturity (with Wagner, as he would suggest), it also assumed a new role in actively defending the integrity, even purity, of a German culture whose eclectic, cosmopolitan roots had gone deep underground. The old model of German culture assimilating and refining diverse national sources was uncomfortably close to Wagner's own influential view of "Jewish" eclecticism and its "parasitic" adaptation of authentic national identities, and hence needed to be replaced by a new insistence on a cohesive and perfected German tradition. Even apart from the brief insertion of antiforeign rhetoric into Sachs's closing address, *Die Meistersinger* provided a significant model for the construction of such a pure, cohesive national tradition.[8]

7. For an exploration of "ideal types" of Germanness in music, see Bernd Sponheuer's essay included in this volume.

8. In a lengthy essay on *Die Meistersinger*, for example, written in the wake of the Munich premiere, the staunchly nationalistic Ludwig Nohl identified the universalizing, assimilationist phrase of German culture as nearing completion, and pointed to a new turn toward an individualized, more concretely national sense of German culture. *Die Meistersinger*, for Nohl, was an important manifestation of this newly self-sufficient, even self-regarding perspective on German cultural identity. Ludwig Nohl, "R. Wagner's Meistersinger von Nürnberg," in *Neues Skizzenbuch: Zur Kenntnis der deutschen, namentlich der Münchener Musik- und Opernzustände der Gegenwart* (Munich: Carl Merhoff's Verlag, 1869), 309–460, here, 400–401.

*National Identity as a Theme in the Early Reception
of* Die Meistersinger

Die Meistersinger entered the repertoire of German opera houses at the time of the Franco–Prussian War and the consolidation of the new German empire under Bismarck and Wilhelm I. Under these circumstances, the work's appeal to an emerging cultural identity at once progressive and rooted in long tradition is not difficult to fathom. Even a Wagnerian of Jewish descent such as Heinrich Porges had no compunction about extolling the "German" virtues of the work, and even at the expense of foreign, non-German cultures. Wagner, he wrote, chose to set his drama in a period when "the German spirit was ruled by a collective unity" that has scarcely been recovered since.[9] His depiction of these early German burghers illustrates the qualities that have given present-day Germany her "pre-eminence among all nations in the arts and sciences." "For that reason," Porges continued, in a manner that closely approximates that of Joseph Goebbels's radio broadcast from Bayreuth in 1933, "it is un-German when the spirit of freedom is enslaved by the powers of sensuality, or when the German is expected to regulate his life according to some foreign, external authority rather than looking inside himself. . . . It is this innermost core of the German nature that Wagner has represented in his work."[10] Though as yet unpublished, the text of Wagner's essay "What Is German?" was surely familiar to Porges, and that text, along with the series on "German Art and German Politics," provided the obvious blueprint for Porges's remarks, as it does for Sachs's final address exhorting the German "princes and people" to defend the integrity of German art against the incursions of foreign and philistine (French/Jewish) influences.

There is no shortage of similar responses to the exemplary Germanness of *Die Meistersinger* from the period of its first traversal of German stages and the founding of the new Reich. A series of essays by the Wagner disciple Peter Cornelius and the ardently patriotic Ludwig Nohl published

9. ". . . wie W. mit Nothwendigkeit dazu gedrängt wurde, die Handlung seines Dramas in eine Epoche zu verlegen, wo im deutschen Volke ein Geist der Gemeinsamkeit herrschte, wie er seitdem in gleicher Weise sich noch nicht wieder wirksam erwiesen hat." Heinrich Porges, "Richard Wagner's 'Meistersinger von Nürnberg,'" *Neue Zeitschrift für Musik* 46, no. 30 (1868): 254.

10. "Darum ist es undeutsch, wenn die Mächte der Sinnlichkeit die Freiheit des Geistes in Banden schlagen, oder wenn der Deutsche das Gesetz für sein Leben erst von einer fremden, äußeren Autorität empfangen soll und es nicht in seinem eigenen Innern sucht. . . . Diesen innersten Kern des deutschen Wesens hat W. in seinem Werke zur Darstellung gebracht." Ibid.

in the context of the opera's Munich premiere immediately canonized *Die Meistersinger* as the definitive touchstone of German music and "national" culture. For Cornelius, the "poetic Genius of our *Volk*" had found at last a proper refuge in this new opera, after a generation of mediocre artistic production in all genres. "Here we have the eternal idea of Germanness, the glorious, world-conquering *deutsche Michel* represented in a concrete portrait of German cultural life," and the worthy heir, in a new genre, to Bach's fugues, Beethoven's symphonies, or the overture to Mozart's *Magic Flute*.[11] If in the past Hamlet was seen to represent the German "in times of political despondency," in these days of unification and progress toward Germany's proper standing in the world, Cornelius maintained, "we can heartily welcome Wagner's Hans Sachs as a substitute for the melancholy Dane."

Ludwig Nohl's *Meistersinger* essays are, even more than those of Cornelius, a veritable panegyric to the national character and significance of the piece. He begins by observing a spiritual parallel between the opera's premiere and a Luther festival being celebrated concurrently in Worms. "Both events," he writes, represent "the deed of the fully-awakened spirit of the German nation," which now, "after an epoch of servitude to a foreign pseudo-civilization"—evidently the French, as Ernest Newman observed—is emerging into a clear consciousness of itself and its "mission." Alluding to the political ascendancy of Prussia in the wake of its recent conflict with Austria, Nohl discerned a significant parallel to "this latest battle within the sphere of art, . . . proof enough that there is a general instinctive . . . connection between the two things."[12] The apparent salute to the growing hegemony of Prussia in German politics seems scarcely tactful in view of the deep-seated resistance of Bavaria and of Wagner's patron, King Ludwig, to assimilation into a Prussian-dominated Reich. But Nohl's remarks leave no doubt that Wagner's supporters saw his latest, most conspicuously German opera as a signal, even symbolic event in the emergence of a contemporary German national consciousness. He located this national significance in the musical idiom, too, as well as in the subject matter: "[I]n this new work of Wagner's, whose special tendency was above all

11. "Hier ist in einem konkreten Bilde deutschen Kulturlebens die ewige Idee des Deutschtums, der glorreiche, weltüberwindende deutsche Michel hingestellt . . . . " Peter Cornelius, "Richard Wagners 'Meistersinger' in München," *Die Tonhalle* (Leipzig), 7 September 1868; reprinted in *Literarische Werke*, vol. 3, ed. Edgar Istel (Leipzig: Breitkopf & Härtel, 1904), 173–87; here, 180.

12. Quoted in Ernest Newman, *The Life of Richard Wagner*, 4 vols. (New York: Knopf, 1933–46), 4:146–47. The remarks come from the introduction (309–29) to the series of early articles on *Die Meistersinger* republished in the *Neues Skizzenbuch*, 309–460.

the glorification of German art and German life," Nohl maintains, we knew that "the music itself would be speaking German."[13]

While Nohl acknowledged that the still incomplete dramatic cycle, *The Ring of the Nibelung*, would ultimately provide the great German *Nationaltragödie* ("which will embody in sensible form the final goal of our national striving"), he called *Die Meistersinger*, in a review of the 1870 Vienna production, the "first true German national comedy" ("das erste wahre deutsche Nationallustspiel und Volkslebensbild").[14] And at the close of his long encomium to *Die Meistersinger*, with an eye also to the promise of the *Ring*, Nohl explicitly lauds Wagner's works for contributing to a new awareness of national identity: "interpreting the nature of the nation according to its fundamental components and needs" and "bringing the nation to a complete consciousness of itself and its deepest inner coherence."[15] Though emanating from an enthusiastic acolyte, these reactions to Wagner's role as beacon of national culture at the time of *Die Meistersinger* and the founding of the new Reich (likewise of the Bayreuth project) are not atypical. When Cornelius published his essay on "German Art and Richard Wagner" in the Viennese *Deutsche Zeitung* at the end of 1871, for example, the editor accompanied it with the lapidary assertion: "[H]enceforth the Wagner matter is inseparable from the German matter."[16]

Appreciation—and exaggeration—of the national character or spirit of *Die Meistersinger* may have intensified to some degree around 1914 or through

13. "So wußte man, daß in dem neuen Werke Wagners, dessen spezielle Tendenz es obendrein war, deutsche Kunst und deutsches Leben zu verherrlichen, auch innerhalb der Musik vor allem *deutsch* geredet werden würde." Nohl, *Neues Skizzenbuch*, 419.

14. Ibid., 459; Ludwig Nohl, "Die 'Meistersinger' in Wien," *Neue Zeitschrift für Musik* 66, no. 11 (11 March 1870): 105. Nohl found the Viennese production "too theatrically coquettish," in the manner of a French *opéra comique*, for a work that "discloses even in the truthfulness and simplicity of the German nature its great inwardness and sublimity." This review, incidentally, confirms a report mentioned in Cosima Wagner's diaries from this time (14 March 1870) that the Viennese performances had been disrupted by the rumor that Beckmesser's serenade in act 2 was based on "a Jewish melody, chosen by the composer in order mock the Jews and their music." Ibid., 104. Nohl explicitly denied the truth of this rumor—very likely inspired by the recent republication of *Das Judenthum in der Musik*, as were some other protests against early performances of the opera.

15. "Dieses Wesen der Nation aber nach seinen Urbestandtheilen und Grundbedürfnisse zu deuten . . . "; "er hälfe der Nation das Vollbewußtsein ihrer selbst und der tiefinnersten Zusammengehörigkeit zueinander . . . erwecken." Nohl, *Neues Skizzenbuch*, 458, 459.

16. Cornelius, *Literarische Werke*, 3:187; also quoted in Newman, *Life of Wagner*, 4:145

the 1930s and 1940s in Germany, but the terms in which it is expressed do
not change markedly from the time of the work's premiere or the early years
of the new Reich. Even those who rejected Wagner before the turn of the
century were not primarily opposed to a perceived national or chauvinist
content to his works, however clearly such a content manifested itself in
his writings and cultural persona. Before World War I, Wagnerism and anti-
Wagnerism alike tended to be cosmopolitan phenomena. Earlier opponents
of Wagner did not differentiate between an overtly political, national persona in the composer-librettist of *Die Meistersinger* and the *Ring*, on one
hand, and a more apolitical Wagner, the pioneer of psychological, aesthetic,
and compositional modernism in *Tristan* or in *Parsifal*. They resisted Wagner altogether, as a modern cultural anarchist. Nationalists in other countries who *did* oppose Wagner as a figurehead of aggressive Pan-German politics and culture, on the other hand, did not often distinguish among
different tendencies within the artistic oeuvre. To them, it was all equally
and indelibly German.

Thus Wagner's celebrated nemesis Eduard Hanslick—in his own way
just as devout a believer in the "holy German art" of music as Wagner—felt
no need to accommodate the "national" character of the opera within his
critique of it as a musical drama. Hanslick admired the general treatment
of local and historical color, atmospheric setting, and so forth, such as the
Nightwatchman's horn in act 2, or the "animated, genuine historical tableau" presented by the closing scene. (He also made a point of keeping his
critical distance from the parody of Wagner's own critics so overtly inscribed
in Beckmesser's role.) The "realistic" historical setting, with its "lively historical picture of German popular and burgher-life from the middle ages" is
appraised as a distinct improvement over the mythical bombast of the other
music dramas.[17] But at the same time, Hanslick was sensitive to precisely
those aspects of the opera that to us might seem to anticipate the later excesses of German nationalism, objecting to an element of "brutality" in
the action as well as the music. He judged the prelude to be a "piece of labo-
rious artifice and downright brutal effect" ("ein Musikstück von peinlicher
Künstelei und geradezu brutaler Wirkung"). While he had hoped to be fa-
vorably impressed by the immensely complex dramatic-vocal polyphony of
the pugilistic ensemble-finale to act 2, Hanslick complained that the effect
in performance was merely a "brutal screaming and shouting" ("ein brutales

---

17. Eduard Hanslick, *Die moderne Oper: Kritiken und Studien* (Berlin: Hofmann, 1875),
298–99.

Schreien und Lärmen").[18] And perhaps he could not help identifying with Beckmesser, if only tacitly, as a victim of Wagner's aggressive, vengeful "humor": both Sachs's little game with him during the abortive serenade in act 2 and the ensuing street brawl left Hanslick feeling uneasy, not amused. Sachs's closing address he mentioned not at all.[19]

Outside of Germany even pro-Wagnerian critics were understandably less interested in *Die Meistersinger* as a talisman of the German psyche or a tribute to the creative spirit of that specific *Volk*. As a Frenchman, for example, Julien Tiersot had obvious motives for downplaying the "national" element in his otherwise enthusiastic *Étude sur les Maîtres-Chanteurs de Nuremberg de Richard Wagner* of 1899. For Tiersot, the leading "idea" of the opera is simply "art" and the glorification thereof (see his chapter 7). "We French might prefer that the word 'art' be employed in a more universal way, and not tied to a too-restrictive adjective," he admitted with reference to Sachs's closing address and the final "motto." Art itself, he argued, is what really mattered to Wagner, and what is "destined to survive national identities themselves." To this end Tiersot cited the closing epigraph cleansed of its national modifiers, as if simply willing them away.[20] Henry T. Finck, an American music critic of German extraction (hence with less reason to shy away from the work's nationalistic overtones), omitted any mention of the closing address within an otherwise detailed précis of the action.[21] He had no more to say about the "national character" or significance of the work than did Hanslick or Tiersot. (With the exception, perhaps, of a suggestive anecdote about the last dress rehearsal in Munich. After congratulating and embracing the singers, Finck reported, Wagner turned to the pit and announced, "To you I have nothing further to say. We

---

18. Ibid., 293, 297; cf. 301–2. In later life Hanslick regretted that his first response to the opera may have been hasty and intemperate. Knowing as he did that his own name was likely to be immortalized in that of the "marker," he had reason enough to approach it in a less than sympathetic frame of mind. He was not alone in this (see note 22 below)—and his first impressions count for something.

19. This may in fact have been cut from the Viennese performances Hanslick attended in 1870 and later, but he would have known it from the original Munich production and, of course, from the printed libretto and score.

20. " 'L'Empire peut se dissoudre en poussière: mai que du moins l'Art nous reste!'— Tels sont les derniers mots des *Maîtres-Chanteurs*." Julien Tiersot, *Étude sur les Maîtres-Chanteurs de Nuremberg de Richard Wagner* (Paris: Fischbacher, 1899), 103.

21. Henry T. Finck, *Wagner and His Works: The Story of His Life, with Critical Comments*, 2 vols. (New York: Charles Scribner's Sons, 1897), 2:211–41. The lacuna appears (so to speak) when he summarizes the action of the final scene (223).

are German musicians; we understand each other without words."[22] Thus Wagner, the music-dramatist, pays homage to the romantic exaltation of "pure music" and its incarnation in a German musical culture, transcending thought and language.)

Other late-nineteenth- and early-twentieth-century writers on Wagner from France (Maurice Kufferath, Catulle Mendès, Albert Lavignac, Eduard Schuré), from the United States (Henry Krehbiel, William J. Henderson, James Huneker), and from England (William Ashton Ellis, Edward Evans, Ernest Newman) dealt with the nationalistic element in *Die Meistersinger*— and in Wagner's thought more generally—in a similar way. They made no special efforts to deny or resist it, but tended simply to leave it alone. Their motives in doing so may have been various, but presumably they felt this nationalistic component was a matter that concerned the Germans, not themselves. Cultural nationalism was accepted as a self-evidently positive value even in artistic production; yet there seems to have been a tacit agreement that it could be checked at the border when such works were exported. Those outside of Germany who were susceptible to the nationalist rhetoric of Wagner and his works, such as Houston Stewart Chamberlain, went to Germany to practice their Wagnerism.

Even within Germany, as I have suggested, a certain ambivalence toward this face of Wagner and Wagnerism can be found, though it was only seldom articulated until after 1918. Such an ambivalence might be faintly detected, for example, in Guido Adler's lectures on Wagner at the University of Vienna (1904), at least if we compare it with the nationalistic swooning of someone like Ludwig Nohl. Adler at one point does mention *Die Meistersinger* as "the real festival opera of the Germans" ("die eigentliche Festoper der deutschen"). But this statement does not appear in the context of a discussion of distinctively "German" traits or how these might celebrate a communal understanding of German cultural identity. Instead, it is dropped as a complete non sequitur within an appreciation of the opera's artful deployment of motives, polyphony, and other constructive parame-

22. Ibid., 216. Finck probably took this anecdote from Nohl's essay in the 1869 *Neues Skizzenbuch*, where it is found on p. 372. A selection of "Beckmesser criticisms"—dissenting voices on the value of Wagner's *Meistersinger*—are cited as examples of critical error. Several of these echo Hanslick's response to the "brutal" undercurrent (musical and representational) of the would-be merry comedy. In addition to citing Hanslick himself on the "brutality" of the prelude, Finck mentions Otto Gumprecht's description of its "vicious kind of polyphony, poisoned counterpoint," its "ugly rioting of dissonances that make one's hair stand on end," and the "brutal terrorism of the brass," as well as Heinrich Dorn's description of the "brutal" effect of the riot-scene in act 2 (237–38).

ters in the service of an overall organic "harmony."[23] Like Tiersot and others, Adler preferred to see *Die Meistersinger* as a celebration of art *tout court* and a demonstration of Wagnerian aesthetic principles. No doubt Adler, like Hanslick before him, was firmly enough convinced of the hegemonic position of German-Austrian music from Bach to the present. Like Paul Bekker and others of their generation, he was ready to grant Wagner a preeminent place in the line of great German masters, even to demonstrate why that place was deserved. But as a Jew by birth, living and working in the socially volatile context of early 1900s Vienna, Adler had good reason to resist the use of Wagner and *Die Meistersinger* as symbols of a militant cultural patriotism.

The Twentieth-Century Afterlife of Die Meistersinger *as "National Opera"*

It is because of the history of the German nation itself in the first half of the twentieth century, of course, that we now regard the "national" element of *Die Meistersinger* as problematic, in a way that requires confrontation rather than a discreet aversion of the critical eye (as seems to have been the practice of non-German critics before 1914). In particular, the history of *Die Meistersinger* in the twentieth century becomes a focus for the larger question of how and to what extent works of art acquire a social, cultural, and historical agency that continues to operate after the artist is gone and the works have passed from the status of topical novelty to become part of a canon of "national" masterpieces. The history of *Die Meistersinger* in the twentieth century is thus a focus for the larger "Wagner question," the question of his vexed legacy in Germany between the founding of the "Second" Reich and the collapse of the Third.

Critics and audiences in Wagner's own time paid most attention to the universal theme of the opera—the confrontation between Walther and the mastersingers, between artistic innovation and tradition—with its obvious allusion to the debates over Wagner's alleged *Zukunftsmusik* versus the musical legacy of the German "masters" back to Bach and beyond. (As a mediating figure, Sachs represents the mature Wagner who wanted recognition of his own deep roots in that classical legacy.) Of course, this "universal" theme is given a distinctly German ambiance in Wagner's opera, and its specific relevance to German music of the modern era transposes

23. Guido Adler, *Richard Wagner*, 2d ed. (Munich: Drei Masken Verlag, 1923), 312.

the theme into a distinctly national key. A preoccupation with "naturalism" in historical representation, characteristic of the nineteenth century,
had benefited the reception of *Die Meistersinger* from the outset; in this
sense, the opera offered something like a grandiose musical diorama of Renaissance Nuremberg. While historical Nuremberg had been a symbol of
German national culture for almost a century, Wagner's operatic recreation
of its style and customs had been as much a point of interest to Frenchmen
like Tiersot or Americans like Henry Krehbiehl as it was to German critics.
All of them delighted in demonstrating how the opera faithfully brought to
life the Nuremberg of Hans Sachs, as described in Wagenseil's *Buch von der
Meister-Singer Holdseligen Kunst, Anfang, Fortübung, Nutzbarkeiten, und
Lehr-Sätzen* (a vernacular appendix to his 1697 Latin chronicle of old Nuremberg), with all the means at the disposal of this most modern of opera
composers—a kind of protocinematic historical spectacle.

   This celebratory reenactment of the German past continued to constitute the opera's main claim to national status into the twentieth century.
Paradoxically, in light of the protocinematic quality I have ascribed to the
work, a silent-film version in 1927 provoked a "cultural protest" in the
Münchener Neueste Nachrichten (6 October 1927), with twenty signatories representing diverse Nuremberg civic organizations. The film was denounced as abusing "the most German work of Richard Wagner . . . in the
most unscrupulous manner. . . . [T]he city of Nuremberg with its great historical past has been debased before the entire *Volk* by being thus dragged
down into a low atmosphere."[24] One is reminded of the contemporaneous
outrage provoked by Eduard Dülberg's abstract constructivist staging of
Der fliegende Holländer at the Berlin Krolloper, or the statement published
in that same *Neueste Nachrichten* just a few years later (with similarly "respectable" signatories) protesting Thomas Mann's "debasement" of Wagner in his lecture "Leiden und Grösse Richard Wagners."

   We might find it puzzling, today, how a silent film of *Die Meistersinger*
or Mann's nuanced but deeply respectful appreciation of his great idol
could be perceived as serious injuries to national pride and dignity. In the
former case, the offense evidently lay in transposing Wagner's and Sachs's
Nuremberg into the "lowly atmosphere" of modern urban mass entertainment. (The fact that a silent film would have necessitated processing Wag-

24. ". . . vor dem ganzen Volk in eine niedrige Atmosphäre gebracht wird." Quoted in
*Richard Wagner und die Meistersinger: die Rezeptionsgeschichte einer Oper von 1868 bis
heute,* exhibition catalogue, ed. Gerhard Bott (Munich: Germanisches Nationalmuseum,
1981), 321.

ner's magisterial score as a string of musical "highlights" for small theater orchestra or organ was apparently not a factor in this protest.) In Mann's case, one offending point was surely his claim, toward the end of the essay, that the German national character in Wagner's works is informed by a wider, cosmopolitan (and eminently modern) sensibility. Despite the element of brazen, almost caricatured Teutonism that, as Mann wrote, elicits a kind of "horrified curiosity" from a foreign audience ("Ah, ça c'est bien allemand, par exemple!"), Wagner's oeuvre involves a self-conscious, reflective "representation" of Germanness:

> [T]his Germanness is refracted and fragmented in the modern mode, is decorative, analytical, and intellectual—hence its powerful fascination, its innate capacity for cosmopolitan, not to say planetary influence. Wagner's art is the most sensational self-portrayal and self-critique of the German character that could possibly be imagined. . . . [His] nationalism is steeped in a European artistry to a degree that renders it profoundly unsusceptible to any simplification—especially of the simple-minded variety.[25]

This last remark leaves little doubt as to the target of Mann's own covert protest against the wholesale appropriation of Wagner and Bayreuth by the newly ascendant Nazi regime. However "simple-minded" the aesthetic doctrines of that regime, it could hardly fail to register the snub.

Much as we may want to sympathize with Mann's more nuanced view of Wagner's representation of the German "national character" in artistic terms, it would be naïve (not to say "simple-minded") to be surprised at the Nazi annexation of Bayreuth and appropriation of Wagner's oeuvre. The process entailed nothing like the manipulation and selective blindness required by the nazification of many other intellectual figures, such as Nietzsche. Bayreuth fixtures like Hans von Wolzogen and Houston Stewart Chamberlain had been grooming the institution for this annexation for decades. Winifred Wagner's eagerness to play hostess to Hitler may not, in itself, reflect directly on her "posthumous" father-in-law, who had died fourteen years before she was born. But there is no question that the Bayreuth establishment had become a breeding ground for conservative-chauvinistic nationalism and all manner of specious racial and cultural theorizing since

25. PCW, 145.

well before World War I, and that at least *some* of this was easily traceable
to Richard Wagner's amply documented *Weltanschauung*.[26]

Wagner's written and unwritten "teachings" apart, what did *Die Meistersinger* offer to the cultural agenda of the National Socialist regime? Above
all, it offered the perfect national "festival opera," an established masterpiece that was still relatively new but no longer offensively "modern." It
assumed this capacity already on the "Day of Potsdam" (21 March 1933),
the official inauguration of the new regime, when it was given a special
state-sponsored production at the Berlin State Opera. In November of the
same year, it reopened the Deutsches Opernhaus in Berlin (with a poster
quoting "Was deutsch und echt" and adorned with a swastika); and it soon
made its inevitable debut as part of the the the Nuremberg party rallies in
1935, the "Parteitag der Freiheit."

Leni Riefenstahl had already co-opted *Die Meistersinger* for the previous party rally in 1934 by using excerpts in the soundtrack to her famous
documentary *Triumph of the Will*. Since Riefenstahl's footage already included ample military band music and other *völkisch* musical effusions,
she eschewed the more obviously festive, boisterous aspects of the opera,
and turned instead to the meditative act 3 prelude, heard as her camera scans
the tranquil streets and rooftops of old Nuremberg at the break of day. Riefenstahl—or whoever advised her on the music—realized that the Nazi
Party could make better use of Wagner to express the tender, inner soul of
the *Heimat*. The brash, aggressive side of the national spirit, which was so
often perceived as characteristically Wagnerian—as, for example, by the
"curious and horrified" foreign audiences postulated by Thomas Mann—
found adequate expression in the military parades and state-sponsored populist festivities that pervaded the everyday public image of the Nazi regime.
Parallels between the acclamation of art by and for the German people in
Die Meistersinger and National Socialist celebrations of the *Volk* (and the
state) were by no means ignored, however. To cite just one well-known in-

26. Paul Bekker, for example, accused the Bayreuth establishment in 1921 (while the
festival was still suspended) of propagating "political reaction, bad Teutonism, religious hypocrisy [*Frömmelei*], racial hatred, and narrow-minded nationalism." Oswald G. Bauer, *Richard
Wagner—Die Bühnenwerke von der Uraufführung bis heute* (Frankfurt am Main: Propyläen,
1982), 176. On the receptivity of the Bayreuth "circle" to the nascent Nazi ideology between
the wars, see also Frederic Spotts, *Bayreuth: A History of the Festival* (New Haven: Yale University Press, 1994), 156–57.

stance, Benno von Arent's staging of the final scene for the 1935 Nuremberg production (later produced in Berlin, Munich, Weimar, and Bayreuth)
famously transposed the vast "alley of banners" (*Fahnenreihe*) of the party
celebrations, in miniature, to the festival meadow of Wagner's finale (even
though the military precision of the image is quite at odds with the lively
confusion that reigned in Wagner's own staging, to judge by Michael Ech-
ter's illustrations of the first Munich performances).

As mentioned, Bayreuth had already prepared the way for the Nazi
appropriation of *Die Meistersinger*, as well as of the Wagnerian *Weltanschauung* and Wagner as symbol of German culture. At the reopening of the
festival in 1924, following its closure during and after World War I, Sachs's
address and the final motto on the durability of German art inspired the
public (or some part of it) to a collective outbreak of the "Deutschland
Lied." The next year Siegfried Wagner exhorted the audience to "suppress
any singing, however well-intentioned—*hier gilt's der Kunst!*" [27] Nonetheless, nationalistic fervor won the upper hand again. Starting immediately
with the 1933 Bayreuth festival, Joseph Goebbels consecrated *Die Meistersinger* as the official opera of the Nazi regime in an intermission address
during a radio broadcast, taking his cue from Sachs's own final speech but
substituting, naturally, the modern *Meister* Richard Wagner for those of
old. Goebbels underlined the opera's relevance to "our time and its spiritual and intellectual tensions":

> How often in years past has its rousing mass chorus "Awake! Soon will
> dawn the day" been [heard] by an ardently longing, believing German
> people [as] a palpable symbol of the reawkening of the German nation
> from the deep political and spiritual narcosis of November 1918? [28]

"Of all [Wagner's] music dramas," he continued, "*Die Meistersinger* stands
out as the most German. It is simply the incarnation of our national identity." Goebbels supported this observation with some sentimental clichés

27. As quoted, for example, in Dieter Mack, "Die Bayreuther Inszenierungen der 'Meistersinger,'" in *Richard Wagner: Die Meistersinger von Nürnberg. Texte, Materialen, Kommentare*, ed. Attila Csampai and Dieter Holland (Reinbek/Hamburg: Rowohlt, 1981), 163.
Ironically, Hitler likewise requested Bayreuth audiences to suppress any "manifestations"
(*Kundgebungen*) not directly related to the work of Richard Wagner during *Meistesinger* performances at the first festival under the Nazi regime in July 1933. This measure, taken in the
name of good taste and the dignity of "holy German art," did not of course preclude such
"manifestations" outside of the festival theater, which were abundant.

28. Quoted in Spotts, *Bayreuth*, 173. The original text is reproduced in *Richard Wagner:
Die Meistersinger von Nürnberg*, ed. Csampai and Holland, 194–99.

about the German *Kulturseele*, its propensity for romantic melancholy and bittersweet humor, but also its industry and national pride. Not surprisingly, Goebbels closed his address by citing the opera's final lines, although in doing so he only underscored the discrepancy between Wagner's historically imagined utopia of art and the present Nazi state, where a work like *Die Meistersinger* was essentially reduced to the status of a propagandistic façade.

By 1943 and 1944, this "façade" was all that was left of the Bayreuth Festival. These officially designated "wartime festivals" (*Kriegsfestpiele*) featured only this one work, offered as a kind of symbolic cultural bulwark in defense of Germany's beleaguered state.[29] Selected officers and soldiers, especially those wounded in service, were invited through the "Kraft durch Freude" program to attend performances of *Die Meistersinger* and thereby refresh their souls at this great source of German art—even as the German Reich was collapsing in ruins around them, like the Holy Roman Empire in the opera's closing motto. Surely few of them would have had much interest in Wagner's work even under the best of circumstances. Still, these wartime festivals represented a natural culmination of Hitler's desire to bring Wagner to the *Volk* as well as to the party faithful—a desire that was consistently frustrated (as Frederic Spotts has pointed out), achieving at best a superficial cooperation under the pressure of the Führer's official command.[30]

Dr. Richard Wilhelm Stock's pamphlet, *Richard Wagner und seine Meistersinger*, originally published in conjunction with Benno von Arent's production for the Nuremberg party rallies in the later 1930s, was reissued as a commemoration of the Bayreuth *Kriegsfestspiel* of 1943 with a new description of the production and a kind of "mail bag," excerpting letters from grateful attendees and intended to demonstrate the success of this effort to instill the troops with loving respect for the culture they were called to defend. Whether genuine or not, these responses only exposed the forced and artificial character of the whole enterprise. In addition to rehashing all the familiar clichés about *Die Meistersinger* as portrait of the German "soul" and the sound artistic instincts of the *Volk*, Stock's pamphlet in-

---

29. The performances were led by Furtwängler with two casts, including such leading Nazi-era Bayreuth regulars as Jaro Prohaska, Maria Müller, and Max Lorenz. The stage design was an early effort by Wieland Wagner, largely preserving the traditional settings from Cosima's time.

30. Spotts, *Bayreuth*, 165. Spotts also points out (169) how attendance at Bayreuth suffered significantly with the sudden exclusion of much of the Jewish audience after 1933, soon exacerbated by the loss of most of the international audience as well.

cluded extracts from "Jewish critics [*Kritikaster*] on Wagner's *Meister-singer*" and an introduction detailing the early resistance to Wagner and his opera as the natural result of the "Jewish-democratic spirit" that had "infected the bourgeoisie" of that era.[31] Stock mainly chided Wagner's Jewish critics for their effrontery in taking offense at the Master's vocal anti-semitism. Many of the "offending" comments cited are merely innocuous (such as the observation that a new work of Wagner's "always stirs up a lot of commotion"), and many are cited without attribution, as if their negative tone and journalistic origin were enough to brand them as "Jewish," following the same circular reasoning of Wagner's own anti-Jewish tirades. Conspicuously absent in Stock's own commentary on the opera is any reference to the possibility that the role of Beckmesser might be intended as a send-up of Jewish musicians or critics, or indeed of Jews at all. Stock's is clearly not a subtle mind, nor a particularly educated one (despite the ubiquitous doctorate). But it is surprising, in light of more recent speculation on a possible layer of anti-Jewish caricature in the role, that no mention of such a reading of Beckmesser is to be found here, in a context where it would be unreservedly sanctioned.[32] Stock, or at least some considerable

---

31. Stock refers in particular to the failure of Nuremberg to pursue Wagner's offer of producing the premiere of the opera in that city (not a plan Wagner himself showed much interest in, actually), and the building of a synagogue "in the purest oriental style" within arm's length of the Hans Sachs monument. The latter detail had been observed by Wagner with some indignation in his 1879 essay "Wollen wir hoffen?" (*Sämtliche Schriften und Dichtungen*, 10:120). "Diese Kulturschande des damaligen durch den jüdisch-demokratischen Geist verseuchten Bürgertums auszulöschen," Stock writes, "und das dem großen deutschen Genius zugefügte Unrecht wieder gutzumachen, blieb Adolf Hitler vorbehalten." Richard W. Stock, *Richard Wagner und seine Meistersinger—Eine Erinnerungsausgabe zu den Bayreuther Kriegsfestspielen 1943* (Nuremberg: Karl Ulrich, 1938, 1943), 7.

32. Theodor Adorno's intuition that Beckmesser was conceived, in some part, as a caricature of negative "Jewish" traits has been developed by Paul Lawrence Rose, Barry Millington, and Marc Weiner, among others (see "Guide to Further Reading" at the end of this essay). While each makes a reasonably persuasive case for the possibility of reading Beckmesser as an embodiment or allegory of such stereotypical traits, as defined by Wagner and contemporary antisemitic rhetoric, there remains a surprising dearth of evidence for such a reading having been articulated publicly or even privately from Wagner's time through the Nazi era. Wilhelm Stock cites a reference in the *Berliner Montagszeitung* of 28 August 1872 to a "recently published brochure entitled *Hepp! Hepp! oder die Meistersinger von Nürnberg*," described as "decidedly one of the most witty and humorous parodies of the eponymous *Prügelopus*." Stock would have recognized, of course, the title phrase "Hepp! Hepp!" as long associated with the practice of hazing or baiting Jews, though he made no comment on it. And in fact, allusions to Wagner's antisemitism in this and a number of other parodies of *Die Meistersinger* documented in Andrea Schneider's extremely interesting (and amusing) study of Wagner parodies from the 1850s to World War I (*Die parodierten Musikdramen Richard Wagners: Geschichte*

portion of Nazi-era writers, critics, and directors, must have been well
aware of the tradition connecting Beckmesser with Eduard Hanslick (going
back to Wagner's own prose drafts of 1862, with the Marker named "Veit
Hanslich") and the fact that Wagner considered Hanslick to be Jewish. Yet
even with the factors of such an equation so readily available, no one seems
to have formulated it explicitly, either in writing or on stage. Most of the
evidence suggests that Beckmesser continued to be presented as a foppish
pedant, a German cousin to the Bolognese "learned doctor" and the lech-
erous or money-grubbing, superannuated bachelors of the opera buffa,
commedia dell'arte, and other popular comic traditions. Complaints about
tendencies for heavy-handed exaggeration of Beckmesser's buffoonery were
occasionally voiced by German critics earlier in the century (Richard Rote
in 1910 and Otto Neitzel in 1920, for instance). Yet there is little to suggest
that then, or even after 1933, such buffoonery was enlisted to reveal a latent
antisemitic caricature, waiting to be detected by a generation more fully
sympathetic to this Wagnerian cause.[33] That does not mean that Wagner

---

und Dokumentation [Anif/Salzburg: Müller-Speiser, 1996]) suggest that, like other allusions
to the topic clustering around the early performances of the opera, they were inspired by the
highly publicized 1869 reissue of Das Judenthum in der Musik, with a new and lengthy preface by the author. In the 1872 Hepp! Hepp! as well as in Robert Weil's Die Meistersinger von
Ottakring (Vienna, 1917), it is the Walther von Stolzing character who is (sardonically) portrayed as Jewish—analogous to the pictorial caricatures of a "Jewish" Wagner in circulation
from around this same time. In the latter parody Beckmesser is given the name Simon Beck-
Messer, and identified as a "raschsüchtiger Schnittwarencommis aus dem Warenhaus Gern-
gros, Plüschabteilung," seemingly a Jewish figure, although in the play he tries to keep
Walther ("Walther Isidor Goldzink, Vertreter der Firma Goldzink & Sohn, Gänsefett en gros")
out of the local Gesangsverein: ". . . denn jener Goldzink ist a Jud! . . . Daitsch bleibt und rein
der Sangsverein!" (Schneider, Die parodierten Musikdramen, 380). In the earliest of these parodies, Franz Bittong's Die Meistersinger oder Das Judentum in der Musik (Berlin, 1870/71),
Walther represents Wagner himself ("Richard von Wahnsing") who competes against a band
of thinly disguised Jewish musicians: Jacob Meyerbach, Jacob Offenbeer, Jacob Haltevieh
[=Halévy], and Felix Mandelbaum. Interestingly, however, the role of Beckmesser is not portrayed by any of these Jewish musicians, but by another figure ("Werda") whose foreign-
accented pidgin German is suspiciously laced with Italianisms: thus Giuseppe Verdi. (The
idea seems to be that the Italian composer represents the conservative standard of operatic
melody.) The whole text of Bittong's parody can be found in Jens Malte Fischer's useful essay-
edition-anthology, Richard Wagners "Das Judentum in der Musik." Eine kritische Dokumentation als Beitrag zur Geschichte des Antisemitismus (Frankfurt: Insel Verlag, 2000), 329–52.
    33. Joachim Köhler gives the impression that an antisemitic reading of the opera was in-
deed current in the Nazi era, but this is based only on Köhler's own citation of Marc Weiner,
who does not address the history of Wagner or his operas in the twentieth century at all. See
Köhler, "Life under the Mastersingers," chap. 15 in Wagner's Hitler, trans. Ronald Taylor
(Cambridge: Polity Press, 1999), 242–68, esp. 256–60. Köhler also blurs the distinction between his own "Jewish" reading of Beckmesser and statements from Hitler's Mein Kampf,

himself might not have imbued the character with traits of his "Jewish" adversaries, as he imagined them—both the traits and the adversaries, that is.[34] But if so, it is perhaps (ironically) another case where the subtleties of Wagner's creative imagination were lost on his fascist admirers.

". . . uns bliebe gleich die heil'ge deutsche Kunst"

Exactly one hundred years after Wagner first sketched out his idea for a comic opera on the subject of Hans Sachs and the Nuremberg mastersingers in the summer of 1845, Nuremberg lay in ruins along with Hitler's "thousand-year Reich," which had collapsed several months earlier. Sachs's dictum about German art outliving German empire had proven all too true. Was that dictum, the original kernel of the *Meistersinger* plan, a self-fulfilling prophecy, thanks to the maniacal hubris of Wagner, and his conception of the German nation and its mission? How much of this conception was inherited by Hitler, and how much distorted in his "execution" of it (to borrow Joachim Köhler's double-edged term)? How much of Hitler's nationalist megalomania—*Größenwahn*—descends from the *Wahn* of Sachs and Wagner?

The general question has been endlessly discussed, and I cannot expect to resolve it here. One answer would be to distinguish Sachs's (and Wagner's?) "apolitical," cultural nationalism from Hitler's unscrupulous and criminal *Machtpolitik* that demoted German art to propagandistic window

---

giving the impression that the latter refer specifically to the former (371). For Rote and Neitzel, see Bott, *Die Meistersinger und Richard Wagner*, 318–20.

34. The negative evidence regarding Nazi-era interpretation and performance of Beckmesser's role would seem to support Dieter Borchmeyer's defense of the ideological "purity" of Wagner's works against the "Jewish" reading of Beckmesser ("Beckmesser—der Jude im Dorn?" in the 1996 Bayreuth Festival program book, 89–99; Borchmeyer's argument is directed primarily against the reading of an allusion to the Grimm brothers' tale of the "Jew in the Brambles" as first suggested by Adorno—an allusion that is merely incidental, however, to those interpretations mentioned in note 32). The fact that Beckmesser's character embodies stock attributes of the comic pedant and aging suitor, or that his role was clearly conceived already in the 1845 prose sketch (before Wagner's published attacks on the Jews and his feud with Hanslick) says nothing about how the characterization might be inflected by details of the final libretto and score; certainly these must count for something if we take Wagner seriously as a dramatist and a composer. The possibility remains that a strain of antisemitic "coding" of characters such as Beckmesser, Mime, or Alberich was part of Wagner's intent, but at a subtextual level—neither a fully consistent component of the roles nor one available to the general public, but reserved for initiates. Even so, one might expect a long-lived intimate of the original Bayreuth circle such as Hans von Wolzogen to have passed along such information to later generations, especially in the 1930s.

dressing. However valid this distinction, it necessarily begs further questions about the problematic nature of the "apolitical," especially in German cultural history of the last two centuries, as well as about the fascist
aestheticization of politics (in Walter Benjamin's diagnosis)—both of which
could be traced through Wagner. The history of Die Meistersinger distills
the larger question of Wagner's legacy in early twentieth-century German
nationalism, and fascism in particular.

In Die Meistersinger Wagner constructed a parable about the great tradition of German art—principally music, or "song"—and its renewal. The
aesthetic parable of tradition and renewal is placed in a historical setting,
sixteenth-century Nuremberg, already possessing strong symbolic resonance for the development of a national cultural consciousness in modern-
day Germany. Wagner artfully imbued his score with appropriate musical
resonances: the counterpoint of J. S. Bach (symbolic of the reconciliation of
musical "craftsmanship" and poetic inspiration) and the Lutheran chorale,
the latter mediating between the artifice of Bach, or Wagner, and a popular
historical "spirit."[35] At the same time, the skillful formal elaboration of his
materials and their sumptuous, "state-of-the-art" orchestration provided a
testament to the present and future progress of German music. Wagner's
cultural chauvinism—his antagonism toward the French and the Jews,
grounded in a paranoid persecution complex—leaves only a faint imprint
on the work, thought it can be easily traced to the contemporaneous essays
"What Is German?" and "German Art and Politics." Thus Wagner left to
subsequent generations a legitimate operatic masterpiece that paid conscious tribute to the cultural past and future of the nation, and one that—
for all its artistic merit and the warmth and humanity of its characters (by
and large)—was perfectly suited to serve as the festival opera of National
Socialism, for which it seemed to provide an impeccable cultural pedigree.[36]

Die Meistersinger is the product of a national consciousness directly
antecedent to National Socialism, yet no more or less so than a work like
Brahms's Triumphlied. Neither is it, in itself, a direct or necessary contrib-

35. Carl Dahlhaus discusses Bach's symbolic value as the foundation of a German "na-
tional music" in the nineteenth century in the section "Nationalism and Universality" in
Nineteenth-Century Music, trans. J. Bradford Robinson (Berkeley: University of California
Press, 1989), 35–40. See also Ludwig Finscher, "Über den Kontrapunkt der Meistersinger," in
Das Drama Richard Wagners als musikalisches Kunstwerk, ed. Carl Dahlhaus (Regensburg:
Bosse Verlag, 1970), 303–12.

36. As Arthur Groos says of Sachs's Schlußansprache, its "final series of gestures out-
fitted Die Meistersinger with a predisposition toward future appropriations [with] the Volk
approvingly echoing whatever their prescient spokesman can be made to represent or oppose." Groos, "Constructing Nuremberg," 33.

uting cause to twentieth-century fascism. As an iconic "happy face" pasted on the Nazi Party rallies, *Die Meistersinger* is not necessarily more compromised than is the melody of Haydn's imperial hymn for being adopted as the national anthem. One might doubt the propriety of the continued use of the opera as a festival piece in the postwar years, often consecrating the reopening of opera houses ruined by the war (or in the case of Bayreuth, "spiritually ruined"). But the fact that little aside from Sachs's few lines about *welsche Dunst* and *falsche welsche Majestät* seemed to be a cause for concern after 1945 does point up the lack of any direct, obvious correlation between the opera and the fascist national ideology it had been used to celebrate. In musical terms, it is even more difficult to assign a moral culpability to elements that might be thought to appeal to a "Nazi" sensibility (such as the admixture of folkish *Gemütlichkeit* and ceremonial grandeur), simply on the grounds of that appeal. Richard's son Siegfried, for example, mined similar veins of a national romantic sensibility in his operas, and in the context of the 1910s and 1920s their conscious rejection of modernist styles might well seem to implicate them in the nascent Nazi ideology. Yet Siegfried (unlike his wife Winifred) remained wholly unsympathetic to the emerging Nazi Party up until his death in 1930.

To label the Nazi regime a "*Meistersinger* state" (as Joachim Köhler does in his recent contribution to the Wagner-and-Hitler literature) is to capitulate to the Nazis' own flattening appropriation of Wagner. Without denying the sustenance Hitler could draw from Wagner's musical, dramatic, and literary oeuvre, it is only fair to keep in mind that a quite different state might have evolved from a still more literal reading of that combined oeuvre: for example, a pacifistic, vegetarian regime dedicated foremost to the patronage of the arts. It is no surprise that an aesthetic utopia of this sort never developed in Germany or elsewhere. But that has everything to do with social, economic, and political realities (along with Wagner's relative alienation from these), and little to do with the example of Wagner's "teachings" or his works.

The question remains how to approach the "national character" of Wagner's *Meistersinger* today. In the 1960s, when the opera was still undergoing a process of denazification, Adorno expressed a typical postwar skepticism toward the "discomforting, Spitzweg-like" nostalgia of the second-act setting, which nonetheless remained "a functional part of the work, part of the almost irresistible, yet poisoned attempt to simulate a mythologized recent past of the German people, with which it was able to intoxicate itself."[37]

---

37. "Noch das peinlich Spitzwegsche des zweiten *Meistersinger*-Akts ist funktionell in der Sache, gehört zu dem fast unwiderstehlichen, aber vergifteten Versuch, eine mythologische

He allowed for the viability of surrealist and/or "alienating" productions, but also advocated an attitude we would describe now as postmodern or deconstructionist: "Since whatever one tries to do with Wagner today will likely ring false, the best thing would be to make a point of this very falseness, of the fissures and the contradictions, instead of smoothing these over and trying to manufacture a kind of harmony that is essentially at odds with Wagner's own being."[38] Adorno was still too close to Wagner (let alone Hitler's Germany) to contemplate the simpler alternative of reading or producing *Die Meistersinger* "straight," in which case it becomes a document of the nationalistic cultural consciousness that gave it birth, leaving the reader/listener/viewer to reflect on the causes and effects of that phenomenon. Even this way it doesn't cease to be a meaningful work of art, however. Whatever approach one takes—modernist, postmodernist, or premodernist—it is important to respond to the piece both as a work of art *and* as a historical artifact. *Die Meistersinger* is more than an object lesson in nineteenth-century historicist and nationalist culture, of course. But more than any other opera, perhaps, its own history has become an indelible part of the work, adding to the comedy yet a further serious layer that far exceeds the author's original intentions—at least, we can only hope so.

Guide to Further Reading

Adorno, Theodor. *In Search of Wagner.* Trans. Rodney Livingstone. Manchster (UK): NLB, 1981.

Bermbach, Udo. "*Die Meistersinger von Nürnberg.* Politische Gehalt einer Künstleroper," in *Deutsche Meister—böse Geister? Nationale Selbstfindung in der Musik,* ed. Hermann Danuser and Herfried Münkler. Schliengen: Edition Argus, 2001. Pp. 274–85.

Borchmeyer, Dieter. "Beckmesser—der Jude im Dorn?" In 1996 Bayreuth Festival Program Book. Pp. 89–99.

Borchmeyer, Dieter. "Nürnberg als Reich des schönen Scheins. Metamorphosen eines Künstlerdramas." In *Deutsche Meister—böse Geister? Nationale Selbstfindung in der Musik,* ed. Hermann Danuser and Herfried Münkler. Schliengen: Edition Argus, 2001. Pp. 286–302.

Jüngstvergangenheit des deutschen Volkes zu fingieren, an der es sich dann hat berauschen können." Theodor Adorno, "Wagners Aktualität," in *Richard Wagner,* ed. Csampai and Holland, 186.

38. "Gilt schon Wagner gegenüber, daß man, wie man es macht, es falsch mache, so hilft man am ehesten, wenn man das Falsche, Brüchige, Antinomische selbst zur Erscheinung zwingt, anstatt es zu glätten und eine Art von Harmonie herzustellen, der das Tiefste an Wagner widerstreitet." Ibid.

Bott, Gerhard, ed. *Die Meistersinger und Richard Wagner: die Rezeptionsgeschichte einer Oper von 1868 bis heute*. Germanisches Nationalmuseum, 1981 (exhibition catalogue).

Cornelius, Peter. "Die Meistersinger von Richard Wagner" (1868); "Richard Wagners Meistersinger in München" (1868); "Deutsche Kunst und Richard Wagner" (1871). Reprinted in Cornelius, *Literarische Werke*, vol. 3, *Aufsätze über Musik und Kunst*. Ed. Edgar Istel. Leipzig: Breitkopf & Härtel, 1904.

Csampai, Attila, and Dieter Holland, eds. *Richard Wagner: Die Meistersinger von Nürnberg (Texte, Materialien, Kommentare)*. Reinbek/Hamburg: Rowohlt, 1981.

Fischer, Jens Malte. *Richard Wagners "Das Judentum in der Musik." Eine kritische Dokumentation als Beitrag zur Geschichte des Antisemitismus*. Frankfurt: Insel Verlag, 2000.

Grey, Thomas. "Selbstbehauptung oder Fremdmißbrauch? Zur Rezeptionsgeschichte von Wagners *Meistersingern*." In *Deutsche Meister-böse Geister? Nationale Selbstfindung in der Musik*. Ed. Hermann Danuser and Herfried Münkler. Schliengen: Edition Argus, 2001. Pp. 303–25.

Groos, Arthur. "Constructing Nuremberg: Typological and Proleptic Communities in *Die Meistersinger*." *19th-Century Music* 16 (summer 1992): 18–34.

Hohendahl, Peter Uwe. "Reworking History: Wagner's German Myth of Nuremberg." In *Re-reading Wagner*. Ed. R. Grimm and J. Hermand. Madison: University of Wisconsin Press, 1993. Pp. 39–60.

Köhler, Joachim. *Wagner's Hitler: The Prophet and His Disciple*. Trans. Ronald Taylor. Cambridge: Polity Press, 1999.

Kolland, Hubert. "Wagner und der deutsche Faschismus." In *Musik und Musikpolitik im faschistischen Deutschland*. Ed. H.-W. Heister and H.-G. Klein. Frankfurt am Main: Fischer Verlag, 1984. Pp. 126–35.

Millington, Barry. "Nuremberg Trial: Is there Anti-Semitism in *Die Meistersinger?*" *Cambridge Opera Journal* 3 (1991): 247–60.

Münkler, Herfried. "Kunst und Kultur als Stifter politischer Identität. Webers *Freischütz* und Wagners *Meistersinger*." In *Deutsche Meister—böse Geister? Nationale Selbstfindung in der Musik*, ed. Hermann Danuser and Herfried Münkler. Schliengen: Edition Argus, 2001. Pp. 45–60.

Nohl, Ludwig. "R. Wagners Meistersinger von Nürnberg" [three essays]. In *Neues Skizzenbuch. Zur Kenntniß der deutschen, namentlich der Münchener Musik- und Opernzustände der Gegenwart*. Munich: Carl Merhoff's Verlag, 1869. Pp. 309–460.

Raabe, Peter. "Wagners 'Meistersinger' und unsere Zeit." In *Die Musik im dritten Reich: Kulturpolitische Reden und Aufsätze*. Regensburg: Bosse Verlag, 1936. Pp. 68–72.

Rose, Paul Lawrence. *Richard Wagner: Race and Revolution*. New Haven: Yale University Press, 1992.

104THOMAS S. GREY

Salmi, Hannu. *Imagined Germany: Richard Wagner's National Utopia.* New York: P. Lang, 1999.

Schneider, Andrea. *Die parodierten Musikdramen Richard Wagners. Geschichte und Dokumentation Wagnerscher Opernparodien im deutschsprachigen Raum von der Mitte des 19. Jahnhunderts bis zum Ende des Ersten Weltkriegs.* Anif/Salzburg: Verlag Müller-Speiser, 1996.

Schulze, Hagen. *The Course of German Nationalism from Frederick the Great to Bismarck, 1763–1867.* Trans. Sarah Hanbury-Tenison. New York: Cambridge University Press, 1991.

Spencer, Stewart. "Wagner's Nuremberg." *Cambridge Opera Journal* 4 (1992): 21–41.

Spotts, Frederic. *Bayreuth: A History of the Wagner Festival.* New Haven: Yale University Press, 1994.

Vaget, Hans Rudolf. "The 'Metapolitics' of *Die Meistersinger:* Wagner's Nuremberg as Imagined Community." In *Searching for Common Ground: Diskurse zur deutschen Identität 1750–1871.* Ed. Nicholas Vazsonyi. Cologne: Böhlau Verlag, 2000. Pp. 269–82.

Warrack, John, ed. *Richard Wagner: Die Meistersinger von Nürnberg.* Cambridge: Cambridge University Press, 1994.

Weiner, Marc. *Richard Wagner and the Anti-Semitic Imagination.* Lincoln: University of Nebraska Press, 1995.

Wessling, Berndt W., ed. *Bayreuth im Dritten Reich. Richard Wagners politische Erben–eine Dokumentation.* Weinheim: Beltz Verlag, 1983.

Landscape—Region—Nation—Reich: German Folk Song in the Nexus of National Identity

PHILIP V. BOHLMAN

Das schönste Land in Deutschlands Gau'n,
das ist mein Badner Land,
es ist so herrlich anzuschau'n
und ruht in Gottes Hand.

Zu Haslach gräbt man Silbererz,
Bei Freiburg wächst der Wein,
Im Schwarzwald schöne Mädchen;
Ein Badner möcht' ich sein.

[The most beautiful among Germany's regions,
it is my own land, Baden,
it is so beautiful just to see,
and it rests in the hand of God.

At Haslach one mines for silver,
vineyards grow near Freiburg,
in the Black Forest there are pretty girls;
I want to be from Baden.]
—"Das Badner Land," song 1, vol. 2 (1925)

Everything and nothing is left to the listener's imagination in "Das Badner Land," the *Landeshymne*, or provincial hymn, that opens the second volume of the forty-four-volume series *Landschaftliche Volkslieder* (henceforth LV), whose publication was stewarded over the course of a half-century by the German Folk-Song Archive (*Deutsches Volksliedarchiv*) in Freiburg im Breisgau. The song unfolds as a catalogue of place names in Baden, which stretches along the eastern bank of the Rhine from Mannheim in the north to Lörrach in the south. "Das Badner Land" is quite literally a *landschaftliches Volkslied*, a "folk song" representing its "landscape," for it symbolically maps out that landscape, moving from Haslach to Freiburg into the Black Forest already in the second verse, charting the southern sector of Baden.

The LV project was established in 1924 with the official sanction of the

Association of German Folklore Societies (*Verband deutscher Vereine für Volkskunde*) and the labors of the German Folk-Song Archive by Germany's leading folk-song scholars Johannes Bolte, Max Friedländer, and John Meier. The project would move from region to region, and within regions from village to village, as if to set aside regional differences and to weave the geographical parts of a complete German folk-song landscape together as a national identity. Including "Das Badner Land" in an early volume of the LV project, however, was not without the same paradoxes that would characterize the larger German national identity charted by the LV volumes over the next forty-eight years. Was "Das Badner Land" a folk song, or a provincial anthem, a *Landeshymne*? Who really sang the song, and in what versions and contexts? Why is the text of a regional song national (High German) rather than regional (dialect)?

For those who conceived of the LV project and set it in motion, it was not of primary concern to represent the diversity of folk-music repertoires but rather to create a unified text that would be a musical simulacrum for national identity. The founders of the LV project conceived it as a whole, but it was eventually completed during a period of forty-eight years fraught with events that in many ways belied that goal: the rise of Nazism, World War II, the Holocaust, and the Cold War. The meaning of German unity shifted constantly during the course of the LV project, at times implicit in military expansion, and at other times explicit in German unification.

Bringing questions to bear on the wholeness of the LV project is crucial to this essay, not least because the project's insistence of wholeness laid bare the fissures and paradoxes in German national identity. Such paradoxes ranged from the early and significant role of Max Friedländer, one of Germany's most distinguished folk-song scholars, who was Jewish, to the changing guises of science and scientific method throughout the project. The parts that made up the whole were more often than not contradictory. Despite paradox and internal contradictions, the LV project, begun in 1924, reached its final stage of completion in 1972.

The volumes themselves embody an historical dynamic at once independent from and implicated in the historical moments during which the volumes appeared—Weimar and Nazi Germany, and then the divided Germany of the Cold War. The internal dynamic is evident in the way individual volumes reflect a tension between "self" and "other." Genres and songs at the center—from a region in Germany itself—contrast with the otherness confronted at the peripheries—in settlements beyond the borders of German-speaking Central Europe, such as those in Romania or Ukraine. There is also an historical dynamic between folk songs without historical references (for example, ballads) and those that are explicitly historical (for

Figure 1. Series cover for *Landschaftliche Volkslieder*

example, soldiers' songs). At each stage, moreover, there is a dynamic between the conscious reference to the past and a social relevance for the contemporary user. Folk music is thus made meaningful and it makes national
identity meaningful.

Even though each volume had its own editors, illustrators, and arrang-
ers, a single format was deliberately used so the volumes would look alike
(see fig. 1). This was true even when a regional press, in the interests of en-
hancing local connections, was chosen to publish a particular volume, for
the regional presses unfailingly maintained the series format. Continuity is
evident at every stage of the project's planning and execution, for example
in the role of the German Folk-Song Archive, whose staff contributed advice from the first to the last volume.[1]

1. Otto Holzapfel, *Das Deutsche Volksliedarchiv Freiburg i. Br.*, Studien zur Volksliedforschung, vol. 3 (Bern: Peter Lang, 1989).

Despite the distinctive landscapes that each volume was meant to demonstrate, and despite the dramatic historical changes over the project's half-
century of publication, the historical processes represented by individual
volumes and songs undergird a unity that we can understand as German
national identity. In this essay I am concerned with establishing patterns
within and throughout the entire LV project, and I map these on modern
German history. I look beyond the fragments of individual songs to the un-
settling dynamic of a national identity that fuses the fragments together,
connecting past, present, and future.

On Folk Song's "Germanness"

> Es wohnt' ein Graf wohl an dem Rhein,
> der hatt' drei schöne Töchterlein.
> Die erste wohnt' in Pommerland,
> Die zweite auch nicht weit davon.
>
> [A count lived on the Rhine,
> and he had three beautiful daughters.
> The first lived in Pomerania,
> the second also not very far away.]
> —"Des Grafen Töchterlein," song 1, vol. 11 (1927) (see fig. 2)

German folk song has never been just German. Imagined during the late
eighteenth-century *Aufklärung*, the German Enlightenment, and invented
during the romanticism of the early nineteenth century, German folk song
became a visible player in the struggle to construct German nationalism.
"Germanness" accrued to folk song as it accompanied the spread of the *Aufklärung*'s constituent parts: *Bildung* (the heightened belief in the achievements possible through education and culture), modernity, and nationalism. By coining the term *Volkslied*, or folk song, in the 1770s, Johann
Gottfried Herder consciously engaged in an act of naming a previously unnamed quality of Germanness. From its Enlightenment beginnings, folk
song served to connect language to place. The folk songs of Herder's seminal
volumes, *"Stimmen der Völker in Liedern"* (1778) and *Volkslieder* (1779),
gave shape to a cultural atlas of Europe, for they were songs that came from
throughout the continent and beyond, that is, from Europe's colonies.[2]

---

2. Johann Gottfried Herder, *"Stimmen der Völker in Liedern"* and *Volkslieder* (Leipzig:
Weygandsche Buchhandlung, 1778–79).

Figure 2. "Es wohnt' ein Graf wohl an dem Rhein." Illustration and
first system of music (vol. 11, p. 3)

Characteristically, it was the philologists and folklorists, intellectuals and
writers—Goethe, the Brothers Grimm, Achim von Arnim, and Clemens
Brentano—who determined that folk songs helped to define regional differences in language.

Folk song's German landscape became ever more complex in the course
of the nineteenth century. Its forms and genres of folk song proliferated,
becoming richer and more profound in their representation of Germanness.
On the one hand, folk songs demonstrated the capacity to embody a local or

regional landscape by mapping dialects on local and regional versions. On the other hand, the voluminous anthologies of "German folk songs" published by Ludwig Uhland (1844–45), Ludwig Erk (1893–94), and Franz Magnus Böhme (1877) depended on a shared sense of national identity.

German folk songs did not simply represent German national identity, they were agents participating in its formation and implementation. For one thing, the music and text could be printed and hence used to standardize folk-song repertories for student and military organizations, for church and occupational groups, and for singing societies throughout the world.[3] The editors of folk-song anthologies, moreover, came increasingly to depend on the false assumption that German national identity in folk song had been orally transmitted in High German. German ballads especially could unify Germans throughout Central Europe, at the European peripheries, or in immigrant cultures. The language of the songs was the same, even if the dialects spoken by the singers were not.[4]

The delicate balance between oral and written traditions began to shift in the twentieth century. The written began to dominate the oral, as the notion of uniformity reinforced by publishing folk songs in High German outweighed the reality of variation existing in regional practices. This ideal of unity even proved more durable than the political empire that it had come to represent. As the nation-state collapsed in World War I, folk song gave new meaning to Germanness by rewriting its history under the pretense of documenting tradition. It was the potential to document this "history" that so attracted the Association of German Folklore Societies and inspired them to carry out this mission on a large, unified scale in the *Landschaftliche Volkslieder*.

Folk Songs, Their Landscapes, and the Place of the Nation

> Es liegt ein Schloß in Österreich,
> ganz wunderschön gebauet
> von Silber und von rotem Gold,
> mit Marmorstein gemauert.
>
> [There stands a castle in Austria,
> that is marvelously built,

---

3. Heinrich W. Schwab, "Das Vereinslied des 19. Jahrhunderts," in *Handbuch des Volksliedes*, ed. Rolf Wilhelm Brednich et al. (Munich: Wilhelm Fink, 1973), 1:863–98.

4. Erich Seemann, "Die europäische Volksballade," in *Handbuch des Volksliedes*, ed. Brednich et al., 1:37–56.

from silver and from red gold,
its walls made of marble.]
—"Das Schloß in Österreich," song 49, vol. 3 (1925)

Another striking feature of the LV project as a whole is the ubiquity of references to landscapes and regions in the songs. Each text contains specific references to place, whether a symbolic reference to a river, forest, or mountain range, or a deliberate connection to a city or political boundary. In addition, the songs often evoke a sense of travel across the regional landscape, as does the "portable" small format of the volumes. It is hardly surprising that the LV volumes were published in the familiar format of the *Wandervögel* (lit., wandering birds) and the widely distributed *Zupfgeigenhansel* (1908) that were used to accompany hiking trips arranged by the Wandervögel.

At the same time, while each volume is intended to represent a specific region, each contains items that connect it to "Germany" as a whole through references to some common location, whether it belongs to that region or not. In folk songs throughout the series, for example, the Rhine may possess different political, military, and historical meanings, or no explicitly nationalistic meanings at all, as in the song "Christinchen im Garten," one of the most frequently occurring songs in the LV, in which Christine resolves her sadness over a broken engagement by drowning in the Rhine. There is no reason she must drown in the Rhine as opposed to other rivers, but even as narrative stereotype the Rhine locates a particular landscape in Germany. There are several other songs that appear in many or most of the volumes, as if to connect the folk-song landscapes. The most common of these is the ballad known most generally as "Das Schloß in Österreich" ("The Castle in Austria") (fig. 3), regarded as one of the oldest of all ballads and having actually very little to do with Austria (even when the final strophe includes a reference to Vienna; indeed, in volume 12, *Folk Songs from Schleswig-Holstein* (1927), "Schleswig" is substituted for "Österreich," though without any other substantial changes other than the accompanying depiction of a very North German–looking castle). There are also songs that appear in the volumes in significantly different versions, while nevertheless unifying the project. In *Bergmann* (mining) and *Jäger* (hunting) songs, for example, the texts in distinctive variants speak to local traditions and institutions (for example, the mining songs in volume 44, dedicated to the Harz, a mining region in eastern Germany), whereas in other volumes they are more general in their signification of German identity.

Less crucial to the unifying ideal but also significant are the songs that attempt to identify the "other." Especially in the songs marked as "old,"

Figure 3. "Das Schloß in Österreich." Musical setting framed by the two illustrations for the song (vol. 3, pp. 108, 110–11)

foreign landscapes are used to represent exotic otherness. Lovers come from exotic, foreign landscapes, and soldiers march off into them, that is, *"ins Fremde."* Foreignness assumes various orientalized guises, ranging from "Turkish wars" in military songs to the lands that German farmers cultivate in the volumes devoted to East European German settlements. Some foreign landscapes are fixed by genre, as in the case of *Dreikönigslieder,* songs of the three kings sung for Epiphany. In contrast, there is a noticeable absence of *Spottlieder,* songs used to insult or make fun of others, even though they might have served racist ends in volumes produced during the Nazi period. The well-known ballad "Die Jüdin" ("The Jewish Woman"; DVldr 158), appears only in volume 16, from East Prussia (1927: 31), where it stands as the only explicit reference to Jews or Jewishness in all forty-four of the LV volumes. Even in this single appearance, "Die Jüdin" does not focus on otherness or express prejudice. The mockery that *Spottlieder* would engender might have undermined the pristine, timeless character of the individual landscapes, a character essential to imagining a more capacious German national identity.

Folk Song in Twentieth-Century Germany:
Modern History and the LV Project

The LV project unfolded across three distinct periods in twentieth-century German history, and the series as a whole falls into three phases: (1) 1924 to about 1930, roughly the Weimar period; (2) the early 1930s through World War II; and (3) post–World War II and the Cold War. Just as German national identity must be interpreted as extraordinarily complex during each of the three periods, so too does it assume strikingly complex forms during each phase of the LV's publication. The rupture between each historical period, moreover, is clearly present in the series, not only because of the clear shift in approach to folk song, but because of the changing guard of scholars and publishers responsible for the volumes. All in all, the forty-four volumes in the LV project offer historical documentation of the changing attitudes toward German national identity from the early 1920s until the early 1970s.

The initial phase of the LV project spans the history of the Weimar Republic, with planning for the early volumes beginning soon after the German defeat in World War I and concluding at the end of the 1920s. The first volume, devoted to Silesia in southwestern Poland, appeared in 1924, and the final volumes of this phase appeared in 1929 and 1930. Roughly twenty volumes were produced during this period, though volumes 17–25 represent a transitional group. Even though this phase begins with a volume devoted to a region in Poland and concludes with one devoted to the Gottschee region of Slovenia, the great majority of volumes include songs from regions within Germany's borders. For the most part, even the areas outside of Germany (for example, Silesia and Alsace) were geographically contiguous with Germany. The volumes of this first phase, therefore, represent Weimar Germany as geographically reduced, indeed, collapsed and consolidated to form a set of folk-song landscapes unified according to the nineteenth-century canon of German song collections (for instance, in the predominance of ballads).

With the onset of a new historical phase in 1933 a fairly dramatic transformation of the LV volumes was already underway. In the early 1930s, volumes anthologizing songs from eastern and southeastern Europe (for example, Siebenbürgen, volume 20, and the Volga colonies, volume 25) had begun to appear, but these included songs from more "traditional" German speech islands and drew upon earlier anthologies. The real "expansion" of the LV into Eastern Europe began in 1934, with volumes 26 and 27, which were devoted to the Mazur region of Poland and the Sudetenland in Czechoslovakia. The Mazur region was significant because it had long symbolized the cultural distinctiveness of Poland (for example, with the mazurka), and the Sudetenland, with its many German-speaking towns and cities, had long been coveted by Germany. The symbolic expansion of these volumes, therefore, anticipated the military or political expansion that would follow in the coming years (the invasion of Poland and the plebiscite to give the Sudetenland to Germany) and echoed the intensified expansionist propaganda of the 1930s.

Of the fourteen volumes to appear between 1934 and 1944 only two represent regions in the modern Federal Republic of Germany, Saxony (volume 30) and the Lower Rhine (volume 39) (it is not clear that the Lower Rhine volume ever appeared—publication was scheduled for 1944—but it is significant that it would have included the Low Countries as well as Germany). Whereas some volumes in the second phase demonstrate more traditional connections to historical folk-music research (Lorraine in eastern France, volume 31, for example, and the Lower Danube, or Austria, volume 38), others were possible only because of the ideology of expansionism that accompanied the rise of Nazism. Several remapped Europe as German (for example, Bukovina, volume 32), and at least one anthology, Central Poland, volume 35, was the direct result of fieldwork accompanying military occupation.

In no other phase is the representation of German national identity by LV volumes as difficult to understand as in the final group of five volumes, which began to appear eight years after World War II and concluded with two pairs of publications in the 1960s and 1970s. At least one motivating factor for publishing the volumes in the final phase was to complete the LV project, utilizing materials already gathered earlier. For this reason, three of the five volumes represent German-speaking areas ceded by Germany in 1945 (volumes 40, 41, and 43). The other two volumes cover landscapes in both East and West Germany: Hohenlohe in the west, and the Harz Mountains in the east. From a scientific perspective, all five volumes are the products of ethnographic landscapes whose boundaries are distinctive and relatively impermeable. And this is precisely the unifying factor: the final five volumes are the products of a new scholarship, on its surface stripped of nationalistic rhetoric and free of political ideology, but nevertheless pursuing the ideals of Germany that defined the project from the outset. The scholarly framework set forth in the critical prefaces of the final five volumes is the most extensive, and they dispense with the illustrations and instrumental or choral arrangements included in volumes from the earlier phases. These are museumized, even ahistorical folk-song landscapes that gather traces from the past and present it as evidence for a new Germany. Such "objective nationalism," of course, is especially problematic in the postwar period. These volumes demonstrate an almost anachronistic adherence to past goals of the project, validated now by their new academic and scholarly format.

Three Groups of Folk-Song Landscapes—Three National Identities

> Wir reisen nun zum Tor hinaus, ade!
> Feinsliebchen schaut zum Fenster 'raus.
> Ade, ade, ade!

> [We're leaving from the gate, farewell!
> Look out of the window, my love.
> Farewell, farewell, farewell!]
> —"Wir reisen nun zum Tor hinaus," song 28, vol. 33 (1938)

Despite the larger historical discourses each volume reflected, individual volume editors and illustrators portrayed their folk-music landscapes as distinctively as possible. The uniqueness of each volume contrasted with the larger historical discourses, creating a tension, or historical dynamic, between that volume and the whole project. In this section I examine individual volumes to reveal the historical dynamic to which their contents contribute. From each of the historical periods I have chosen several volumes, not so much because they represent the period itself but rather because they reveal a salient characteristic of its historical dynamic and inherent contradictions.

The first two volumes of the LV represent regions lying both within and outside modern Germany's borders. Volume 1, *Schlesische Volkslieder* (1924), contains songs from Silesia in southwestern Poland, a region with an historically multicultural and multireligious population, and with economic, cultural, and educational institutions that had long served both the German- and Polish-speaking populations. Silesia was not a speech island, but rather a *Grenzlandschaft*, a border landscape, and accordingly volume 1 serves as a prototype for other border-landscape volumes that would follow, such as Alsace. Neither of the first two volumes established an overtly political agenda for the LV, but rather each served as models for the format and operation of the series. Both appear in publishing houses in their region; volume 1 from Silesia was published by the Bergstadtverlag in Breslau (Wrocław), and volume 2 from Baden was published by G. Braun Verlag in Karlsruhe. The volumes draw attention to the distinctiveness of their folk-song landscapes in quite different ways. Dialect songs, for example, achieve this end for Theodor Siebs and Max Schneider in their Silesian collection.

The volumes appearing during the Nazi Period were increasingly direct in linking folk songs to explicit symbols of German military expansion. The illustration reproduced here as figure 4, for example, appears in the 1938 Upper Silesian volume; on the facing page is the song "Wir reisen nun zum Tor hinaus." That this volume of songs from the northern Czech lands should actually presage the first German military incursions beyond its borders is remarkable but by no means coincidental. The rhetoric of German expansion was fully articulated in the LV volumes of the 1930s that appeared before World War II, for example in Edmund Neumann's preface to volume 32, a collection of songs from the Bukovina, for which he deliberately used a Germanified name, "Buchenland" ("Land of Beech Trees"), that had no currency in Germany or in Austria, which had administered the Bukovina as part of the Habsburg Empire until World War I:

> They came from the Palatinate, from the forests of Bohemia, and from the Zips [a German speech island in northern Slovakia]—farmers, lumbermen, and miners—for whom the old homeland offered too little space and freedom. . . . They had to struggle with the soil before they were able to create a new homeland from the land destroyed by war. Even more difficult was the struggle for Germanness. Through their persistence, however, and through their struggle for language, customs and culture, song and dance, they showed an unshakable loyalty that they are prepared to remain bound to their Germanness. (LV 1938: 5)

Whereas the volumes of 1938 look forward to a "struggle in the future," that struggle is reified through the pages of the volumes appearing in the 1940s. The language of the volumes undergoes an ideological nazification: designations such as "Landschaft" are supplanted by *Gau*, and the folklorists willingly thank the *Gauleiter*, or regional Nazi Party leaders, with whom they collaborate in assembling the collection. Editors also make mention of their own military service, even writing their prefaces from the front lines. The editors, however, were not contributing to the LV as ideologues per se, but rather as folk-song scholars.

The editors of volumes 35 (Central Poland) and 38 (Lower Danube) were Karl Horak and Leopold Schmidt, who would later join the ranks of the most distinguished Austrian scholars of their generation after World War II. Their volumes use folk song to project German national identity in quite different ways. Publishing the collection from Central Poland in 1940, Horak was working in the midst of the Eastern front. His rhetoric and the songs he drew from earlier collections (for example, those of Robert Klatt, his deceased coeditor) imagine a world of German peasants toiling to cultivate the

Figure 4. "Abschied des Soldaten." Illustration
accompanying "Wir reisen nun zum Tor hinaus"
(vol. 33, p. 41)

soil, singing calendric songs, and living in a world of ritual bound to the soil.
In effect, Horak excavated a region of Poland to expose a German cultural
landscape. Horak, who enjoyed a highly successful career under the Nazis,
exploited the opportunity to work on the Reich's expanding landscapes; his
collections in South Tyrol in northern Italy are even more notable, and
even today provide the basis for Tyrolian folk-music collections.[5]

If Karl Horak had explicit motivations for using folk-song collections
for political ends and for building his own career, Leopold Schmidt seemed
to have been motivated by strangely mixed ideologies. The songs in the
Lower Danube volume come not from the edges of an expanding Reich but
from its musically secure center, indeed, from the "core of the *Ostmark*

5. Walter Deutsch, Harald Dreo, Gerlinde Haid, and Karl Horak, eds., *Volksmusik in Österreich* (Vienna: Österreichischer Bundesverlag, 1984).

[that is, Austria], a classical land for the folk song and its research."[6] According to his own account, Schmidt had served in the army since the outbreak of the war, and it was only through the support and assurances from John Meier, director of the German Folk-Song Archive, that he was able to publish this volume in 1944 (he had already prepared it in 1939). Emanating from the Lower Danube volume, however, is a form of nostalgia in which folk song is used to secure life in a world that is rapidly deteriorating. On one hand, the folk songs were representative of the traditional Austrian practice of distinguishing its repertories from those of Germany; on the other, Schmidt connected these with suggestive images of a world devastated by war. Though he did not camouflage his own service in the war, Schmidt used the volume to give closure to the second period, signaling a return to the safe haven of the Austrian folk-song repertory.[7]

The five volumes in the third historical period extend the process of closure, and their sporadic publication over twenty-seven years following World War II demonstrates the difficulty of achieving a sense of completion for the LV project. The final two volumes, devoted to southern Moravia (vol. 43) and the Harz Mountains (vol. 44), meet the challenge in different ways, and the final volume actually poses new questions about German identity. The songs from southern Moravia were collected before World War II, during "song weeks" from 1929 to 1939. Whereas the editor, Wenzel Max, made it clear that southern Moravia was fully Czech in 1971, he stressed the historical connections to northern Austria through the network of rivers flowing across Upper and Lower Austria into the Danube. Volume 43, therefore, memorializes an era of multiculturalism in the Habsburg monarchy.

The Harz volume does not conclude the LV by reflecting on the past. Quite the contrary, a new ideological agenda becomes evident: reunification. The folk songs in volume 44 should "dutifully make available to the people of the Harz, in both East and West, a songbook binding hearts together."[8] The Harz folk-song landscape had remained largely unexplored during much of the history of German folk-music research, and the editors of volume 44 announced their intent to redress that situation. To do so,

6. Leopold Schmidt, ed., *Volkslieder aus Niederdonau mit Bildern und Weisen*, Landschaftliche Volkslieder, vol. 38 (Kassel: Bärenreiter, 1944), 73.

7. Thomas Nußbaumer, "Das Ostmärkische Volksliedunternehmen und die ostmärkischen Gauausschüsse für Volksmusik: Ein Beitrag zur Geschichte des Österreichischen Volksliedwerkes," in *Volksmusik—Wandel und Deutung: Festschrift Walter Deutsch zum 75. Geburtstag*, ed. Gerlinde Haid, Ursula Hemetek, and Rudolf Pietsch, Schriften zur Volksmusik, vol. 19 (Vienna: Böhlau, 2000), 149–72.

8. Louis Wille and Hellmut Ludwig, eds., *Lieder aus dem Harz*, Landschaftliche Volkslieder, vol. 44 (Wolfenbüttel: Möseler Verlag, 1972), 3.

they relied in part on some post–World War I collections, but the primary source for their songs were the organizations devoted to the revival of folk costumes (*Trachtenvereine*) and to folk-music cultivation and preservation (*Volksmusikpflege*) in both East and West Germany, as well as Harz refugee organizations in West Germany. The editors, Louis Wille and Hellmut Ludwig, turned to the German Folk-Song Archive for assistance, as did the previous LV editors, but it was a new generation of scholars in Freiburg, Rolf Wilhelm Brednich and Otto Holzapfel, whose advice proved helpful in assembling this edition. The process of closure that the volumes in the third historical period might have effected, had that really been the goal of the editors, was subtly, but unequivocally, arrested. A new problem of German national identity loomed on the horizon of the German folk-song landscape, the problem of reunification, which the LV, in a final gesture, incorporated into its complex representation of German national identity.

The Persistence of German National Identity

> O Straßburg, O Straßburg,
> du wunderschöne Stadt,
> darinnen liegt begraben
> so mancher Soldat.
>
> [O Strasbourg, O Strasbourg,
> you wonderful city,
> many soldiers lie
> buried within your walls.]
> —"O, Straßburg," vol. 3 (1925), pp. 75–76

The Germany that emerges from the forty-four LV volumes is hardly distinguishable from any other Germany portrayed by the art, folk, folklike, and popular songs of the past two centuries. In fact, there is little that sticks out as extraordinary from a series that stretches across the most extraordinary periods of modern German history. The historical dynamic of the series was generated from within, and it responded to the events of twentieth-century German history by circumventing them, that is, by surviving World War II and the Cold War. Survival ensured continuity, and continuity secured a unified, historical identity of Germanness.

    If one analyzes the genres and topoi that form a unifying fabric for the LV, they too yield very few surprises. All the usual folk-song genres are present in volume after volume: songs of the homeland or *Heimat*; historical songs; religious songs; songs about hunters, peasants, and soldiers;

songs about the nobility and the landowners; songs about monuments and memory. Given the historical moments in which these songs were published, it would be reasonable to expect some recognition of modernity and the modern dilemmas facing German national identity, but these are almost entirely absent in the volumes, and they are indeed entirely absent in the songs themselves (see fig. 5). There are no songs about cities and their problems; among the occupational songs, there is no hint of the oppressive role of industry, or of the in-migration of ethnic and minority groups from the peripheries after the collapse of German and Austrian empires in World War I; there is little sense of self-reflection or historical reevaluation, or, in the post–World War II volumes, *Vergangenheitsbewältigung*, reassessing Germany's questionable military past and the human trauma of the Holocaust.

The folk songs of the LV project are secure, even frozen, in a timeless, mythological world, and to a quite remarkable degree they reflect that complex of myths that Christian Graf von Krockow has associated with German national identity.[9] Such myths not only provide a network of interrelated symbols and a pattern for distinguishing "self" from "other," but they do so by relying on the temporal stasis of myth. Whereas history and historicism are everywhere, they also contain a certain autonomy, at least in the historical imagination that connects modern German identity to its pasts. Time is also everywhere in the songs, but its omnipresence marks timelessness; its immediacy lies in its constant yearning to recover the unrecoverable past—that, for example, of the "Dorfstraße in Gottschee" illustrated in figure 6, which had little chance to survive German occupation of Yugoslavia in World War II.

The mythological world of the LV project is a direct outgrowth of the landscapes themselves. The places the songs evoke, even when they are named and seemingly connected to real historical events, contribute to the historical imagination but fail to acknowledge modernity. We then ask ourselves which is more real, modernity or the historical imagination? And does German national identity become more discernible through myth or through history? The LV project does not answer these questions, but their relevance does not diminish over the course of the project's history, despite its stubborn adherence to uniformity. If most songs were more historicist than historical, they also revealed that music complicated the boundaries between the landscapes shaped by history and those shaped by myth. If the volumes at each historical stage responded to the reality of the moment in

9. Christian Graf von Krockow, *Von deutschen Mythen* (Stuttgart: Deutsche Verlags-Anstalt, 1995).

Figure 5. "O Straßburg." Musical setting of verse 1

different ways, they force us to understand that myth is rarely separable from history. As we encounter each new folk-song landscape, it changes, and so too does any German national identity it projects.

Postcards and Postunification

Today, in the early years of the twenty-first century, it is possible to purchase the postcard reproduced as figure 7 at just about any kiosk or gift shop in southwestern Germany. Called the "Lied der Badener" ("Song of the People of Baden"), it is the same song as "Das Badner Land" in figure 1. The contemporary postcard version lacks the lute accompaniment of the LV

Figure 6. "Dorfstraße in Gottschee." Illustration from
the Gottschee Colonies (vol. 24, p. 9)

version, it is set a half-step higher, and the image of the Baden countryside
has been replaced with the region's shield, but in many other ways the
songs bear striking similarities. The texts in both are printed in atavistic
gothic fonts, and despite the seeming popularity their print versions would
suggest, neither the earlier song nor the later seems to be a part of the oral
tradition of its day. My own informal poll of friends and colleagues in
Baden—in Mannheim and Freiburg—turned up no one who knew the song
or even knew it existed.

"Das Badner Land" and "Lied der Badener" are both about a cultural and
historical landscape instantiated through song. They are about the same region, though we wonder whether that region had the same meaning to the
founders of the LV project as to the publishers of postcards for tourists at
the beginning of a new century. Postcards with musical representations of
specific regions are hardly a postmodern innovation, and they have historically contributed to creating local identities through music, the same historical process to which the LV editors were contributing. The more difficult question, I believe, is why Baden? Or why Styria in Austria, where such
cards are also common? Or how do we account for revived interest in local
and regional culture in Europe today?

Since the events marking the transition to the New Europe—the fall of

Figure 7. "Lied der Badener." Common postcard in southwestern Germany (1990s)

the Berlin Wall in 1989, German reunification in 1990, revolutions, velvet
and otherwise, in the communist states of Eastern Europe during 1990, and
the civil war in the former Yugoslavia beginning in 1991 and intensifying in
Bosnia in the mid-1990s and in Kosovo in 1999—regions have acquired a renewed importance as antidotes to the spread of nationalism. This is evident
from the fact that regional cultural projects receive international funding,
especially in boundary regions, and the most pervasive encouragement
comes from the cultural departments of the European Union. Suddenly,
folk-song landscapes are becoming visible again, for example, in the two
CD series ("Tondokumente zur Volksmusik in Österreich" and "Musik der
Regionen") and the musical-monument series ("Corpus musicae popularis
austriacae") published in Austria. The German Folk-Song Archive itself
had already sponsored a retrospective subseries devoted to folk-song landscapes in the previous decade.[10] The regional series often remix the sounds
of their respective folk-music landscapes, devoting special volumes to ethnic minorities, for instance, but they also rely extensively on regional publication projects that went before.

The LV project establishes continuity not because of *what* it represents, but because of *how* it historicizes the representational power of folk
song. As the nations of the New Europe struggle to understand just what

10. Petra Farwick, *Deutsche Volksliedlandschaften: Landschaftliches Register der
Aufzeichnungen im Deutschen Volksliedarchiv*, 3 vols. (Berne: Peter Lang, 1983–86).

national identity was, is, or might be, the voices of its regions and folk-song landscapes offer a wealth of alternatives. These tendencies are not without contradictions: Do they unify or fragment national identity? Do they respond to shifting patterns of ethnic and cultural diversity, or do they confuse an idealized and imaginary past with its modern memorialization? And what if this revival of regionalism implicitly leads to armed intervention pretending to restore fractured unity? These paradoxes at the beginning of the twenty-first century have an increasing familiarity, for they resound with the dilemmas encountered by the *Landschaftliche Volkslieder* project as it passed through different stages of German history and both implicitly and complicitly mirrored German national identity at every moment, all the while negotiating the tensions between regional identity, German identity, and the constantly changing implications of each. It may well be the case that the national identities revealed by German folk-song landscapes are not distant reflections of mythical pasts but trenchant images of contemporary realities.

Guide to Further Reading

Arnim, Achim von, and Clemens Brentano. *Des Knaben Wunderhorn: Alte deutsche Lieder.* 2 vols. 1806, 1808. Munich: Winkler, 1957.

Bohlman, Philip V. *Central European Folk Music: An Annotated Bibliography of Sources in German.* Garland Library of Music Ethnology, vol. 3. New York: Garland, 1996.

Brednich, Rolf Wilhelm, Lutz Röhrich, and Wolfgang Suppan, eds. *Handbuch des Volksliedes.* Vol. 1, *Die Gattungen des Volksliedes.* Vol. 2, *Historisches und Systematisches—Interethnische Beziehungen—Musikethnologie.* Munich: Wilhelm Fink, 1973, 1975.

Brednich, Rolf Wilhelm, Zmaga Kumer, and Wolfgang Suppan, eds. *Gottscheer Volkslieder.* 3 vols. Mainz: B. Schott's Söhne, 1969–84.

Deutsch, Walter, Harald Dreo, Gerlinde Haid, and Karl Horak, eds. *Volksmusik in Österreich.* Vienna: Österreichischer Bundesverlag, 1984.

Deutsches Volksliedarchiv, ed. *Deutsche Volkslieder mit ihren Melodien.* 10 vols. Berlin: Walter de Gruyter et al., 1935–96.

Farwick, Petra. *Deutsche Volksliedlandschaften: Landschaftliches Register der Aufzeichnungen im Deutschen Volksliedarchiv.* 3 vols. Bern: Peter Lang, 1983–86.

Herder, Johann Gottfried. *"Stimmen der Völker in Liedern"* and *Volkslieder.* Leipzig: Weygandsche Buchhandlung, 1778–79.

Holzapfel, Otto. *Das Deutsche Volksliedarchiv Freiburg i. Br.* Studien zur Volksliedforschung, vol. 3. Bern: Peter Lang, 1989.

Holzapfel, Otto, and Wiegand Stief, eds. *Deutsche Volkslieder mit ihren Melodien: Balladen.* Vol. 10. Bern: Peter Lang, 1996.

Klusen, Ernst. *Volkslied: Fund und Erfindung.* Cologne: Hans Gerig, 1969.

Klusen, Ernst, comp. *Deutsche Lieder.* Frankfurt am Main: Insel, 1980.

von Krockow, Christian Graf. *Von deutschen Mythen.* Stuttgart: Deutsche Verlags-Anstalt, 1995.

Kurzke, Hermann. *Hymnen und Lieder der Deutschen.* Mainz: Dietrich'sche Verlags-buchhandlung, 1990.

Röhrich, Lutz. "'. . . und das ist Badens Glück'—Heimatlieder und Regionalhymnen im deutschen Südwesten: Auf der Suche nach Identität." *Jahrbuch für Volks-liedforschung* 35 (1990): 13–25.

Schmidt, Leopold. *Volksgesang und Volkslied: Proben und Probleme.* Berlin: Erich Schmidt, 1970.

Steinitz, Wolfgang. *Deutsche Volkslieder demokratischen Charakters aus sechs Jahrhunderten.* Berlin: Akademie-Verlag, 1978.

Volumes of the Landschaftliche Volkslieder *Discussed in This Essay*

Vol. 1. *Schlesische Volkslieder mit Bildern und Weisen.* Ed. Theodor Siebs and Max Schneider. Breslau: Bergstadtverlag., 1924.

Vol. 2. *Badische Volkslieder mit Bildern und Weisen.* Ed. Deutsches Volksliedarchiv. Karlsruhe: G. Braun, 1925.

Vol. 3. *Anhaltliche Volkslieder mit Bildern und Weisen.* Ed. Alfred Wirth. Dessau: C. Dünnhaupt, 1925.

Vol. 11. *Hannoversche Volkslieder mit Bildern und Weisen.* Ed. Paul Alpers. Frankfurt am Main: Moritz Diesterweg, 1927.

Vol. 12. *Schleswig-Holsteinische Volkslieder mit Bildern und Weisen.* Ed. Gustav Fr. Meyer. Altona: Hans Ruhe, 1927.

Vol. 16. *Ostpreußische Volkslieder mit Bildern und Weisen.* Ed. Karl Plenzat. Leipzig: Hermann Eichblatt, 1927.

Vol. 24. *Gottscheer Volkslieder mit Bildern und Weisen.* Ed. Deutsches Volksliedarchiv. Berlin: Walter de Gruyter, 1930.

Vol. 32. *Volkslieder aus dem Buchenland mit Bildern und Weisen.* Ed. Edmund Neumann. Cassel: Bärenreiter, 1938.

Vol. 33. *Oberschlesische Volkslieder mit Bildern und Weisen.* Ed. Grete Schmedes. Cassel: Bärenreiter, 1938.

Vol. 35. *Deutsche Volkslieder aus Mittelpolen mit Bildern und Weisen.* Ed. Robert Klatt and Karl Horak. Cassel: Bärenreiter, 1940.

Vol. 38. *Volkslieder aus Niederdonau mit Bildern und Weisen.* Ed. Leopold Schmidt. Cassel: Bärenreiter, 1944.

Vol. 43. *Deutsche Volksweisen aus Südmähren.* Ed. Wenzel Max. Cassel: Bärenreiter, 1971.

Vol. 44. *Lieder aus dem Harz.* Ed. Louis Wille and Hellmut Ludwig. Wolfenbüttel: Möseler Verlag, 1972.

Appendix: The Folk-Song Landscapes

Volume Number	Landscape	Date of Publication
1	Silesia (southwestern Poland)	1924
2	Baden	1925
3	Anhalt	1925
4	Alsace (eastern France)	1926
5	Central Rhine region	1926
6	Eifel	1929
7	Mosel and Saarland	1926
8	Nassau	1929
9	Westphalia	1928
10	Low German folk songs from Schleswig-Holstein and the Hanseatic Cities	1928
11	Hannover	1927
12	Schleswig-Holstein	1927
13	Silesia: Graffschaft Glatz	1926
14	Pomerania (northeastern Germany, northwestern Poland)	1927
15	Palatinate	1927
16	East Prussia (northeastern Poland, southern Baltic area)	1927
17	Thuringia	1933
18	Franconia	1933
19	Württemberg	1929
20	Mecklenburg	1933
21	Siebenbürgen (German speech island in Romania)	1932
22	Egerland (western Czech Republic)	1932
23	Upper Bavaria	1930
24	Gottschee (German speech island in Slovenia)	1930
25	German colonies on the Volga River (Ukraine)	1932
26	Mazur (Poland)	1934

Volume Number	Landscape	Date of Publication
27	Sudetenland (northwestern Czech Republic)	1934
28	Romanian Banat (German speech island)	1935
29	Luxemburg	1936
30	Saxony	1937
31	Lorraine (eastern France)	1937
32	Bukovina (largely western Ukraine, with some border regions from Slovakia, Romania, and Poland)	1938
33	Upper Silesia (northern Czech Republic)	1938
34	Bavarian Ostmark (northeastern Bavaria and Czech border region)	1938
35	Central Poland	1940
36	Trier region and Luxemburg	1940
37	Yugoslav Batschka (Serbia)	1941
38	Lower Danube (Austria)	1944
39	Lower Rhine	(in preparation in 1944)
40	Old Swabian folk songs from Sathmar (Hungary)	1953
41	Swabian Turkey (central Hungary)	1960
42	Hohenlohe	1962
43	South Moravia (Czech Republic)	1971
44	Harz (German Democratic Republic)	1972

Kein schöner Land: The Spielschar Ekkehard and the Struggle to Define German National Identity in the Weimar Republic

BRUCE CAMPBELL

Kein schöner Land in dieser Zeit
Als hier das unsere weit und breit
Wo wir uns finden, wohl unter Linden
zur Abendzeit.[1]

[No prettier land these times betide
as here our own, far and wide
Where we dwell, under linden trees well
at even tide.]

A song or group of songs can be as revealing of one's identity as a résumé or a manifesto of political beliefs, though the exact significance is almost always harder to pin down than a text of words alone. In this essay I examine just such a collection of songs sung during the Weimar Republic by the "Spielschar Ekkehard," an amateur music and dance group that grew out of the German youth movement and that was led by Gerhard Roßbach, a well-known political and military figure.[2] The seemingly innocuous performances of these young people were actually a carefully crafted attack on the Republic and an effort to redefine German identity in a conservative and *völkisch* direction. They serve to show in a particularly concentrated way how music was an explicit element in the struggle for national identity in the Weimar Republic.

Though Roßbach was eventually overshadowed by the larger and better-organized Nazi movement, the power of his cultural message should not be measured by his modest political success alone. The Nazi movement suc-

---

1. The song was first published in 1840, with a traditional melody and words by W. V. Zuccalmaglio. It was republished in the *Preußisches Soldatenliederbuch* in 1844, and was popular with the youth movement around 1918. See Ernst Klusen, ed., *Deutsche Lieder*, 2d ed. (Frankfurt am Main: Insel Verlag, 1988).

2. See Arnolt Bronnen, *Roßbach* (Berlin: Rowolt, 1930); Gerhard Roßbach, *Mein Weg durch die Zeit* (Weilburg am Lahn: Vereinigte Weilburger Buchdruckereien, 1950).

ceeded not only because of the attractiveness of its promises but also because by the early 1930s there were too few Germans left who had a stake
in defending the Republic. Between 1919 and 1933, an anti-Republican majority consensus was created in Germany—a consensus the Nazis worked
mightily to bring about; but so did countless others, and the eventual defeat of the Republic was their common effort. Roßbach was one of these
many participants in the slow undermining of support for the Republic, and
this discussion of the Spielschar should leave no doubt that it was not an innocent excursion to the land of the blue blossom and linden tree. Roßbach
himself may not have succeeded in imposing his definition of German
identity on his contemporaries, but the larger movement of which he was
a part did undermine support for the Republic and prepare (often unwittingly) the way for the success of National Socialism.

From its beginnings in the late nineteenth century, the German youth
movement had always given music a place of fundamental importance. Its
integration into daily life became a key element in the movement's pre-
and postwar self-definition and mission.[3] The experience of World War I
gave its preoccupation with reforming society a new intensity and a more
explicitly political coloration that mirrored larger national debates over
the future and identity of Germany.[4] Music was a central part of the language of this debate on every level. Accurately or not, members of the youth
movement identified the Weimar Republic with new movements in the
arts and attempts to change prewar German culture. Those opposing the
Republic generally opposed modernism in the arts as well, often as a means
of expressing their antirepublicanism. Though the youth movement encompassed a broad spectrum of opinion, the strength of its commitment to
traditional and "authentic" German culture generally placed it to the right
of center in the "cultural wars" of the Weimar era.
    The Spielschar Ekkehard, in its short but frenetically active career as
a performing youth group, represented one of the clearest examples of this
kind of intertwining of cultural and political conservatism. Its founder and

---

3. Basic works on the German youth movement include Walter Z. Laqueur, *Young Germany: A History of the German Youth Movement* (New York: Basic Books, 1962); Peter D.
Stachura, *The German Youth Movement 1900–1945* (New York: St. Martin's, 1981). On the
music of the German youth movement, see in particular Hilmar Höckner, *Die Musik in der
deutschen Jugendbewegung* (Wolfenbüttel: Georg Kallmeyer Verlag, 1927).
    4. See Stachura, *German Youth Movement*, chaps. 2, 4.

leader Gerhard Roßbach himself had been the commander of a Free Corps
and a leading activist in the putschist underground that flourished immediately after the end of World War I. He remained a well-known public
personality and a kind of a symbol for conservatives until World War II.
Though he was close to the Nationalsozialistische Deutsche Arbeiter-
partei (NSDAP) in 1922 and 1923, he became critical of it after the failure
of the Hitler Putsch. Roßbach's orientation was always antirepublican, antidemocratic, promilitary, and *völkisch,* though he was never a rabid anti-
semite. Still very close to the ideals of the NSDAP in 1925 or 1926, by the
early 1930s he had become a vocal supporter of the man who became
Hitler's nemesis and victim, General von Schleicher.[5]

Nevertheless, Roßbach was much more than a military adventurer, and
believed deeply in the importance of culture in shaping German identity. He
had grown up in a musical family and remained close to the arts throughout his life.[6] After the failure of the Hitler Putsch in 1923, he decided that
the era of armed action to overthrow German democracy was over, and
therefore sought new ways to attain the same goal. He recognized that to
influence the political shape of Germany, one would first have to reshape
its cultural self-definition on an intimate, grassroots level.[7] The Spielschar
reflected his notion of the transformative potential inherent in amateur
musical performance. Out of what was originally just a group of Schilljugend members on a hiking trip, he created a nonprofessional, full-time
group of young men and women who would perform music, songs, dances,
and small plays.[8] In terms of skill, popularity, and number of performances,

5. For 1926, see Felix Wankel, "Gerhard Roßbach—Schilljugend und Felix Wankel—
Großdeutsche Jugendwehr (GIW Heidelberg). Einzelauszüge der Felix-Wankel-Tagebücher,"
ms. n.d., entries for 23–24 February 1926 in Archiv der deutschen Jugendbewegung (AdJ). For
the early 1930s, see Gerhard Roßbach, ed., *Lagebericht* no. 15, 19 May 1932, and no. 16,
6 June 1932, in Bundesarchiv Koblenz, Nachlaß Wegener/10.

6. Roßbach's mother had been a professional singer, and he himself had always loved
music and had even formed a choir within his company during World War I. He was an accomplished musician, playing the piano and even arranging and writing music. Roßbach, *Mein
Weg,* 48, 50; Int, Oehningen, 1991.

7. Dr. Georg Richter, "Der Weg zur Seele der Jugend," *Mecklenburger Warte* (Beilage),
21 September 1924, in Stadtarchiv Wismar. "Georg Richter" was a pseudonym used by Roßbach during his exile in Austria in 1924.

8. The Schilljugend (Bund Ekkehard) was a German–Austrian youth group in the *völk-
isch* wing of the *Bündische Jugend* founded in 1924. Der Bundesführer, "Nachtrag," *Der
Flamberg* no. 1 (Brachmond, 1925), 16; Gerhard Roßbach, "Die Spielschar Ekkehard," *Der
Flamberg* (Sonderdruck, [1927]), 62 (note that this original *Flamberg* is different from the one
published in the 1970s and 1980s); Int, Salzburg, 1989. See generally Martin Winckler, "die
Spielschar Ekkehard," *Flamberg,* n.s., no. 17 (March 1991).

the Spielschar became one of the most successful amateur (really semi-professional) musical groups during the Weimar Republic and gave an astounding two thousand performances from the time of its founding in 1926 until its last concert on 21 April 1934.[9]

Roßbach pursued several simultaneous goals with the Spielschar. First, he wanted to emphasize and revive the German cultural heritage he saw rejected in his time, and in the process to capture and claim it for the forces of political conservatism. In this way he could combat modernism, foreign influences, and liberal values all at once. Second, the Spielschar was designed to define and shape a particular vision of German identity and present it as legitimate and effective, to the exclusion of other, competing identities. More immediately, Roßbach hoped to use his version of German cultural identity to unite the chronically divided anti-Republican and conservative forces in Germany. In Roßbach's mind, those who would not yet unite around a common political program could still perhaps be held together by Beethoven and Bach.[10] Finally, Roßbach's version of German identity was specifically calculated to include Germany's Germanic neighbors and to draw them into a single blood-based community.[11] All activities of the Spielschar were consciously structured to attain these ends or to support Roßbach's other political initiatives.[12]

The most important activity of the group was, of course, its public performances, with which it could reach the largest number of people. Roßbach had learned that open political statements and appeals often did not

9. "Spielfolge der 2000 und letzten Volkskunststunde der Ekkehardspiele e.V.", in the private archive of the journal *Flamberg, Zeitschrift des Freundeskreises R*, Heidenheim, Federal Republic of Germany, henceforth cited as *"Flamberg* archive"; Int, Detmold, 1989; Int, Aalen, 1989; Int, Waldbröl, 1990.

10. The call for unity in the conservative camp was widely made in the early and mid-1920s. See, for example, the extended discussion initiated in 1926 in *Der Standarte*, a publication of the large veteran's organization, the *Stahlhelm*. The series began with Ernst Jünger, "Schließt Euch zusammen!" *Der Standarte* (3 June 1926): 222–26. Roßbach was aware of this discussion and reprinted Jünger's original article, together with his own response, in *Flamberg* 2, no. 6 ("Brachet," 1926), 67–71.

11. The Spielschar made several trips to the Netherlands, Denmark, and Sweden. The Schilljugend engaged in parallel activities.

12. The individual members of the Spielschar were intended to serve as cultural ambassadors, a goal made easier by the fact that they were always lodged in private homes while on tour. Int, Detmold, 1989; Int, Waldbröl, 1990; Int, Aalen, 1989. Roßbach used the information he collected while traveling with the Spielschar to publish a private political newsletter he entitled *Lagebericht*, and at times published special newsletters to be used in conjunction with Spielschar tours overseas. *Lageberichte* in Bundesarchiv, Nachlaß Wegener/10. See also *Ekkehard Courant* ("Ende Oktober" 1929), in AdJ.

work, so he used a more long-term and subtle strategy to influence the public. He cleverly designed the performances of the Spielschar to appear as innocent and apolitical as possible, and yet to project a certain image of society and of German culture in opposition to the Republic and prorepublican, modernist political and cultural forces. The performances consisted of a mix of classical instrumental music, folk songs sung either solo or in chorus with musical accompaniment, folk dances, short plays (both comical and religious), vocal choruses, and "living tableaus." Of all these elements, the music made up the largest part of any performance and best described the German identity supported by Roßbach.

The Spielschar combined instrumental classical music from the traditional canon of great German composers with folk songs sung either in chorus or solo.[13] Some sixty-eight pieces of classical music are found in the surviving play lists of the Spielschar.[14] All but two of the works originated from or before the time of Schubert (1797–1828). Only two more modern composers were represented, and each with only one composition in a single play list.[15] In fact, 44 percent of all the classical music performed by the Spielschar was written by Bach, Beethoven, and Mozart, and if Handel and Haydn are added, the five composers make up just under 65 percent. Clearly, this was not music intended to shock, confuse, or offend a public raised on the accepted canon of German classical music. There was nothing offensively modern, nothing by identifiably Jewish composers, and

13. Of course, much of the traditional canon of German classical music was technically Austrian, but it was considered to be a part of a greater (pan-) German culture. See Celia Applegate, "What Is German Music? Reflections on the Role of Art in the Creation of the Nation," *German Studies Review* 15 (winter 1992): 21–32.

14. This analysis of the Spielschar's music is drawn from the following yearly repertoires of the Spielschar: 2. und 3. Spieljahr 1928/1929; 4. Spieljahr 1929; 5. Spieljahr 1930; 8. Spieljahr 1933; and a number of programs for individual performances, all in the *Flamberg* archive. Play lists from the years 1926, 1931, and 1932 are missing, but the latter two are partially compensated for with programs from individual performances. The music used by the Spielschar remained within a fairly narrow spectrum, and the missing play lists should not influence the overall impression of the Spielschar's music. Not included under classical music are two works by Roßbach himself ("Klagende Weise für Flöte und Laute," and a musical version of the Lord's Prayer) and a third work written by Marc Roland for the film *Fredericus Rex*.

15. The first was Max Reger (1873–1916), with his Duo No. 2 for Two Violins, Opus 132b, No. 2, a piece based on themes from Mozart (Horst Weber, ed., *Metzler Komponisten Lexikon* [Stuttgart: Verlag J. B. Metzler, 1992], 621–27). The second was Richard Wagner (1813–83), represented by a short selection from *Lohengrin*. Roßbach and the Spielschar were actually quite close to the Wagner family, and even performed at the funeral of Richard Wagner's son Siegfried, so that the lack of more music by Wagner is likely due to the artistic limitations of the Spielschar rather than any ideological reason.

very little that was foreign.[16] Instead, the Spielschar's choice of classical music validated the audiences' own conservative musical taste and allowed them to celebrate, as Christopher Small has argued about classical music in general, their own middle-class identity.[17] The legitimating presence of well-known classics thus prepared the audience to receive the message conveyed by the folk music and represented visually by the appearance of the Spielschar. It reminded the audience of the success of the great German tradition of music and its enormous contribution to world culture. Finally, the exclusion of the modern, the dissonant, and the controversial and the emphasis on a seemingly eternal and unchanging canon of "great works" were particularly welcome at a time when traditional values and tastes seemed to be under attack.

The folk music also reflected identifiable choices. Approximately one hundred folk songs figured in the repertoire of the Spielschar.[18] Whether traditional or contemporary, the folk songs, like the classical music, were overwhelmingly German and Germanic.[19] Much of the folk music performed by the Spielschar came more or less directly out of the musical tradition of the youth movement, of which the Spielschar was certainly a part.[20] Thus, some 28 percent of the folk songs performed by the Spielschar may be found in the contemporary version of the *Zupfgeigenhansl*, the

16. Only seven non-German composers were represented on the play lists of the Spielschar, with nine compositions (13 percent of the total). They were Corelli, Giulini, and Pettoletti (Italian); Field (Irish); Gossec (Belgian); Purcell (English); and Rameau (French). None of them were represented in play lists after 1930.

17. Christopher Small, "Performance as Ritual: Sketch for an Enquiry into the True Nature of a Symphony Concert," in *Lost in Music: Culture, Style and the Musical Event,* ed. Avron L. White, Sociological Review Monograph 34 (London: Routledge & Kegan Paul, 1987), 6–32.

18. The term "folk song" is not always easy to define, since it shades off into historical music on the one hand and, on the other, into modern popular music. While many of the folk songs sung by the Spielschar were "modern folk songs," none were "popular music" in the sense of music hall or show tunes. For more on the German understanding of folk song, especially in the interwar period, see Philip Bohlman's essay included in this volume.

19. Only five of the folk songs performed by the Spielschar were not German. Two were Finnish, something of a fad in the youth movement, one was from Flanders, and a fourth from the Faroe Islands. The only non-Germanic folk song ever sung by the Spielschar was the "Wolgalied" ("Volga Boatman"), a song made popular by the Don Cossacks, a professional company emulated by the Spielschar. Int, Salzburg, 1989; Int, Detmold, 1989; Int, Minden, 1990.

20. The value of both folk songs and dance was taught to Roßbach by the early close association between the Schilljugend and another *völkisch-bündisch* youth group, the Adler und Falken. Hugo Haase, "Dokumentation über den Bund Ekkehard e.V.," ms. (1973), 5, and Gerhard Roßbach to Walter Pudelko of 5. Julmond 1925, both in the AdJ. On the Adler und

most famous and widely used of the song books identified with the youth movement.[21] Others were musical settings of the works of such well-known German poets as Theodor Storm, Ludwig Uhland, and Johann Wolfgang von Goethe.[22] Still other songs were drawn from or inspired by the age of religious wars, many of them militantly Protestant. Not only did this music coincide with Roßbach's own Protestantism and suspicion of political Catholicism, but its linked themes of sorrow over present suffering, faith in eventual redemption, and militant defense of the faith could not fail to have a poignant resonance in post-Versailles Germany.[23]

Other folk songs sung by the Spielschar were less typical of the youth movement, less innocent, and more indicative of Roßbach's cultural-political agenda. These were contemporary, *völkisch* folk songs that had begun to infiltrate the youth movement by 1913.[24] What distinguised them from the more traditional folk songs often was subtle; rarely were they openly antisemitic or overtly chauvinistic. Yet this class of folk song was a contemporary creation specifically intended to transmit values of "true Germanness." They were generally either musical settings of poems by *völkisch* authors such as Hermann Löns or else completely new compositions.[25] Depending on how they are defined, *völkisch* folk songs made up between 15 and 40 percent of the folk song repertoire of the Spielschar, though the lower figure is perhaps closer to the truth.[26]

The importance of the *völkisch* music lay less in the sheer number of such songs than in the way in which they were carefully combined with

Falken, see Günther Ehrenthal, *Die Deutschen Jugendbünde: Ein Handbuch ihrer Organisation und ihrer Bestrebungen* (Berlin: Zentral-Verlag, 1927), 49–51.

21. Hans Breuer, *Der Zupfgeigenhansl*, 30th ed. (Leipzig: Friedrich Hofmeister, 1927).

Four are also from the *Jenaer Liedheften* and one from the *Geißener Liederblatt*, folk song collections arising within the youth movement. Höckner, *Musik in der deutschen Jugendbewegung*, 34–40, 111–114.

22. Storm: "Over de stillen Stratten"; Uhland: "Ich hätt einen Kamerad"; Goethe: "Die Schneidercourage."

23. See, for example, *Lagebericht* no. 11, 1 January 1932; *Lagebericht* no. 19, 22 July 1932. Examples include Luther's "Ein feste Burg ist Unser Gott" and "Wenn alle untreu werden."

24. Höckner, *Musik in der deutschen Jugendbewegung*, 100–104.

25. Löns began to become popular in the youth movement around 1913. An example of completely new compositions would be Roßbach's own "Die Speere Empor" ("Raise Up the Spears").

26. These include six songs with words by Hermann Löns, seven by Walther Hensel, three by Hans Saddey, and one by Gerhard Roßbach. This does not include many more traditional songs collected or arranged by Hensel and Saddey, nor does it include other arrangements by Roßbach. None of these songs were included in the 1927 edition of the *Zupfgeigenhansl* used as a benchmark for this study.

classical and traditional folk songs. A typical performance of the Spielschar, an evening concert in Copenhagen on 3 February 1932, provides a good example.[27] It began with a traditional folk song ("Es blus en Jäger"), after which came a Hermann Löns poem set to music by Hermann Koch ("Rote Husaren"). This was followed by a selection from the "Nibelungenlied" set to music by the Spielschar itself ("Volkers Nachtlied"). Then came the performances of a minuet by Handel and Haydn's Adagio from the D-Minor Quartet. The first half of the performance was completed with a medieval mystery play "Gevatter Tod, en Spiel der Liebe," arranged by Rudolf Mirbt. After the intermission (with tea) came a modern *Sprech- und Bewegungschor* (chorus with movement) by Erich Calberg entitled "Der Morgen."[28] This was followed in chorus with the song "Wenn alle untreu werden."[29] This very dramatic and serious portion of the performance was lightened by the four folk dances that followed.[30] The evening's performance then closed with the singing of a song long favored by the prewar German youth movement, "Kein schöner Land."[31]

This brief description shows how the combination of elements in a performance could make a German nationalist and even *völkisch* statement. The traditional folk song at the onset announced the performance and anchored it in German tradition and history. The performance that followed of a *völkisch* and martial modern folk song with words by Hermann Löns effectively linked these values to the musical and cultural tradition

27. "Ekkehard Spiele. Ein deutscher Volkskunst-Abend der neuen idealistischen Jugend" (Performance Program), Copenhagen, 29 January 1932, in *Flamberg* Archive.

28. The program notes identify this as an adaptation of a theater piece originally written for the "Sozialistische Arbeiterbühne." The message, as summarized in the program, is still quite acceptable to *völkisch* nationalists: "Der Kontrast der Unfähigen, Schwachen, Verzweifelten gegenüber der starken Lebensfreude der Schaffenden, die immer den Morgen sehen und das werdende Licht.—Eine Hymne auf das Schöpferische, auf das Siegfried-Schicksal des deutschen Volkes, das immer in tiefer Not das Heldische, das Lichte zu finden weiss.—So durch Sprache und Rythmus in dauernder Steigung bis zu dem Glaubensbekenntnis der Ekkehard-Schar: 'Aus sehnendem Hoffen wird Deutschland, wird Tat!'" ("The contrast between the incapable, weak and desperate person and the powerful joy of the creative man, who always sees the dawn and the coming light.—A hymn to the creative principle, to the Siegfried fate of the German people, which always knows in its hour of need how to find the heroic, the pure.— In this fashion, in rising tension, through speech and rhythm down to the final statement of faith of the Ekkehard band: 'From hopeful yearning will come Germany, will come action!'")

29. This song was very popular in ultranationalist circles in Germany after the World War I, and was much admired by National Socialists, particularly in the SA and SS. It was an adaptation of a Dutch hymn "Wilhelmus von Nassauen" dating from the sixteenth century.

30. "Jungmöhl" from northern Germany, "Jan Pierewiet" from Holland, "Watschenplattler" from Bavaria, and "Schwedisch-Schottisch."

31. See text at note 1.

just announced. With just two songs, Roßbach's version of German identity had already taken shape. "Volkers Nachtlied" then continued in this same vein, with its evocation of a heroic Germanic past (and a common tradition with Germanic Denmark.)

The classical music served as a counterpoint to the folk music. It evoked the great and lasting contribution of the German musical heritage, stimulating national pride and a common bond among those in the audience. It also worked to legitimate both the earlier folk music and the coming vignettes and music. In effect, the classical music was intended to make clear that all of the folk music (both traditional and *völkisch*), the play, and the *Bewegungschor* were together part of a single German tradition, indeed, that they were *the* German tradition.

The mystery play then gave a religious, mystic aura to the performance, further linking it to the deep mists of German tradition. It touched on profound ideas of life, death, and spirit, telling the audience that matters of faith were still relevant today, and implicitly adding a secular, national faith to the original religious one by juxtaposing the Germanic Middle Ages with the present day. It also prepared the audience for the *Bewegungschor* that followed, demonstrating that the use of theater to make a political statement was marked by tradition and therefore need not necessarily be objectionable as modernist political theater might have been.

"Der Morgen" then went to the heart of Roßbach's message, showing a Germany beset by problems but capable of resolving them through hard work and faith in the future based on the proper set of values. The exact shape of that future was purposely left vague, but in the context of the entire performance there could be no doubt that the way to a brighter future consisted in returning to the German traditions that had just been asserted. Just in case the message had not quite sunk in, the singing in chorus of "Wenn alle untreu werden" reinforced it. Its emphasis on loyalty in adversity and faith in Germany precisely fit Roßbach's desire to unify conservative forces behind a project of political and cultural renewal: "Ihr Sterne seid uns Zeugen, die ruhig niederschaun: Wenn alle Brüder schweigen und falschen Götzen traun, wir wollen das Wort nicht brechen, nicht Buben werden gleich, wolln predigen und sprechen vom heiligen deutschen Reich."[32]

---

32. "Wenn alle untreu werden," fourth verse, words by Max von Schenkendorf, tune 1578. Words and music reprinted in *Flamberg,* n.s., no. 15 (May 1989), 518. "You stars shall be our witness, who calmly shine below: When all our brothers are silent, and false gods do follow, we will not break the word, will not soon become knaves, will preach and speak of the holy German kingdom."

After the dramatic seriousness of the two plays, the lightness of the following folk dances provided welcome relief, though they too reinforced the basic message of the other performances. As folk dances, they were a part of living *Volk* tradition. Moreover, the performance of dances drawn not only from different parts of Germany but also from other Germanic cultures stressed in a subtle way the fundamental unity of all Germanic peoples.[33] They also provided models of functioning hierarchy, because the dance works only if everyone works together, and only if everyone follows the rules. In a sense, then, the folk dances performed by the Spielschar were an example of a properly functioning German society, where all worked hard with real inner commitment, but kept in their place.[34]

The performance then ended with a final folk song that repeated the message of national pride and the values of solidarity and community. Again, the political content was there, derived as much from the context of the entire performance as from the words themslves. Just as clearly, this political message on its face was subtle and nonpartisan, cleverly geared to provide a maximum of elements that would provoke agreement and a minimum of concrete political statements that might provoke dissent. While clearly favoring an (artificial) historical and idealized vision of German tradition and calling for German renewal based on these values, the performance was not a simplistic version of antimodernism. While it did focus on the idealized past presented in the folk songs and tied to the greatness of German classical music, the use of a modernist play like "Der Morgen" made the message appear up to date and realistic. The emotional impact of the almost expressionist staging of the piece could be used to reinforce the basically traditionalist and *völkisch* message of the rest of the performance as a whole.[35]

The vision of Germany Roßbach presented was thus firmly anchored in both the "ancient" German tradition of folk song and in the greatness of German classical music. Yet it was meant to be taken as forward looking, and combined *völkisch* racial unity with an emotional vitalism and idealism that was part youth movement and part expressionism. In it all worked together willingly for German greatness, and everyone stayed in his or her

33. On the social significance of dance, see, for example, Peter Parkes, "Personal and Collective Identity in Kalasha Song Performance," in *Ethnicity, Identity and Music: The Musical Construction of Place*, ed. Martin Stokes (Providence, R.I.: Berg, 1994), 47.

34. Surviving Spielschar members often comment on how much they enjoyed the folk dances, even if they were often quite difficult. Int, Salzburg, 1989; Int, Detmold, 1989.

35. A photograph of a Spielschar performance of "Der Morgen" may be found in *Flamberg*, n.s., no. 42 (August 1978).

appointed role. It was a world where democracy, class conflict, and any
modernism not rooted in an appreciation for the past had no place.

Gerhard Roßbach never succeeded in imposing his definition of German
identity on his contemporaries and was never able to overthrow the Weimar Republic, either as right-wing putschist or cultural impresario—that
success went to others. But one thing Roßbach did accomplish was im-
printing the members of the Spielschar with a lifelong love of German folk
music that would subsequently help them construct and reconstruct a
sense of personal and national identity throughout their lives despite the
twists and turns of German history. This is properly the subject of another
paper, but it is worth a moment to show the power of Roßbach's message
and the lasting way in which music remained central to the German identity of these former Spielschar members.

Surprisingly, an association of former followers and associates of Gerhard Roßbach—called the *Freundeskreis "R"*—still exists in the Federal
Republic of Germany. Though open to anyone formerly associated with
Roßbach, most members today (or their husbands or wives) are former members of the Schilljugend or the Spielschar. Music and singing still make up
a central part of their identity. Their yearly meetings all involve solo and
group singing, as do other informal meetings between individual members.[36] Their journal, *Der Flamberg,* often contains the words and music of
folk songs, generally from "the old days," but sometimes from more recent
sources.[37] In short, the experience of the Spielschar or Schilljugend, including most specifically the music of that period, continue to be the defining elements in their lives. While some tried to carry the *bündische Jugend*
and its music into the postwar era,[38] the majority were content to get on
with their lives after the war and pursue other interests. And yet the music was always there and, particularly in the dark and uncertain days of the
war and the immediate postwar period, often provided an anchor for their
sense of themselves and their nation when other symbols and signs were

36. Int, Hamburg, 1989; Int, Lengreis, 1989; Int, Heidenheim, 1989; Int, Aalen, 1989; Int,
Waldbröl, 1990. See also, for example, "Traueransprache für Hugo Haase 15.8.1977," in *Flamberg,* n.s., no. 1 (November 1977), 25–26; "Erinnerungen an Bayreuth," in ibid., 21–22; "Unser
Treffen in Michelbach vom 3. bis 5.10.1980," in *Flamberg,* n.s., no. 5 (May 1981), 168–69.
37. See, for example, *Flamberg,* n.s., no. 1 (August 1978); *Flamberg,* n.s., no. 3
(March 1979); *Flamberg,* n.s., no. 10 (December 1985); *Flamberg,* n.s., no. 17 (March 1991).
38. Int, Heidenheim, 1989; Int, Berlin, 1990.

lacking or objectionable.[39] Even after the *Wirtschaftswunder* began and the German economy regained its momentum, the music of their youth continued to be important. Roßbach himself, as businessman and insurance salesman, often used the piano to charm his clients and business associates, and he was a leading supporter of the Bayreuth Wagner Festival.[40] Several of the former members of the Spielschar have remarked on the importance of songs like "Kein schöner Land" and the special feelings they provoke.[41] A part of that feeling is an identity as a German that has endured unsuccessful democracy, economic chaos, fascism, war, and now successful democracy.

Guide to Further Reading

Campbell, Bruce. "Gerhard Roßbach, the Spielschar Ekkehard, and the Cultural Attack on the Weimar Republic." In *Weimar 1930. Politik und Kultur im Vorfeld der NS-Diktatur*. Ed. Lothar Ehrlich and Jürgen John. Köln: Böhlau, 1998. Pp. 243–49.

————. "The Schilljugend: From Wehrjugend to Luftschutz." In *Politische Jugend in der Weimarer Republik*. Ed. Wolfgang R. Krabbe. Bochum: Brockmeyer, 1993. Pp. 183–201.

Klusen, Ernst, ed. *Deutsche Lieder*. Frankfurt am Main: Insel Verlag, 1980, 1988.

Laqueur, Walter Z. *Young Germany: A History of the German Youth Movement*. New York: Basic Books, 1962.

Raab, Felix. *Die Bündische Jugend: Ein Beitrag zur Geschichte der Weimarer Republik*. Stuttgart: Bretano Verlag, 1961.

Roßbach, Gerhard. *Mein Weg durch die Zeit*. Weilburg am Lahn: Vereinigte Weilburger Buchdruckereien, 1950.

Stachura, Peter D. *The German Youth Movement 1900–1945*. New York: St. Martin's, 1981.

Stokes, Martin, ed. *Ethnicity, Identity and Music: The Musical Construction of Place*. Oxford: Berg, 1994.

White, Avron L., ed. *Lost in Music: Culture, Style and the Musical Event*. Sociological Review Monograph 34. London: Routledge & Kegan Paul, 1987.

39. Int, Hamburg, 1989; Int, Waldbröl, 1990; Int, Minden, 1991.
40. Int, Oehningen, 1990; Int, Oehningen, 1991.
41. For example, Int, Aalen, 1989.

Hosanna or "Hilf, O Herr Uns": National Identity, the German Christian Movement, and the "Dejudaization" of Sacred Music in the Third Reich

DORIS L. BERGEN

In April 1938 the German Foreign Office hosted an evening with entertainment for international diplomats in Berlin. The final item on the program was a performance by a renowned male vocalist of Handel's setting of Psalm 106, which ends with the words: "Oh give thanks¹ unto Jehovah, to Him that divided the Red Sea in sunder and made Israel to pass through the midst of it." Present for the occasion was German high-society columnist Bella Fromm, who described the event in her diary. "The startled guests gasped," she wrote, when they heard what the man sang instead: "Oh give thanks unto Jehovah, He that united the German people in one mighty Reich!" According to Fromm, "the last verse was absolutely drowned out in the hilarious laughter of the foreigners. The Germans were furious." When asked why he had changed the words, the musician replied, "I couldn't very well sing the original text!" [1]

This episode is telling for a number of reasons. For such a high-profile event involving guests from abroad, much thought certainly went into selecting a musical program that would convey the greatness of German cultural and national achievements. Handel was a significant choice; a composer of international renown in his own day, he had been reclaimed in recent years as a consummate German. The selection of a sacred piece is also important. Not only did it come from the relatively limited number of Handel's works that use a German text—in contrast to his far more numer-

1. Bella Fromm, *Blood and Banquets: A Berlin Social Diary* (New York: Harper & Brothers, 1942), 269.

ous Italian operas and English oratorios—but it also indicates an acknowl-
edgment that sacred music represented the German essence. Most revealing, of course, is the alteration of the words and the guests' reaction. The
Nazis' extreme antisemitism prompted a purge of any references to Israel,
but such tampering with a familiar text went too far, verging on the absurd.
The result could not be taken seriously by the guests, nor—as we shall
see—by many Germans themselves.

This incident illustrates the tensions surrounding the place of sacred
music in the Third Reich. By 1938, Hitler had been in power for five years.
Since 1933, Jews had been barred from the civil service; the Nuremberg
Laws of 1935 stripped most people defined as Jews of the rights of German
citizens. The vocalist's revision of Handel's text mirrors the vicious antisemitism of 1930s Germany and reveals how deeply such ideas had penetrated. Even if sung, a reference to ancient Israel had political connotations,
the performer realized; it might be taken to suggest an insufficient commitment to National Socialist racial policy. At the same time, however, the
situation of sacred music was both less consistent and more complex than
a cursory reading of Bella Fromm's account might suggest. As late as 1938,
Foreign Office representatives—servants of the Nazi state—could still regard performance of an Old Testament text as an appropriate example of
German culture so long as it came in a musical form, set by one of the most
famous German composers. That this was possible given the political climate of the day points up the long-standing connection between sacred
music and German identity.

Although music critics and propagandists might have put forward the
symphonies of Beethoven and the operas of Wagner as crowning achievements of the German nation, "ordinary Germans" arguably felt a more intimate connection to church music as an expression of their national identity. Hymns, especially Protestant hymns, came to mind—and often to the
lips—in moments of patriotic sentiment, in spontaneous demonstrations
of national unity, and in promoting common causes among Christians of
various kinds.

Campaigns to "dejudaize" and "Germanize" sacred music tended to
focus on the texts rather than the music itself. Nevertheless, even such
relatively modest schemes foundered on the loyalties of Christians in Germany to their musical traditions, and attempts at altering texts construed
as philosemitic often encountered opposition. In at least a few cases, similar protectiveness was evident in isolated efforts to retain "non-Aryan"
church musicians whose congregations valued them for their musical talent and years of service. For many Germans of the 1930s and 1940s, sacred

music was such an integral part of cultural practice that they intended to preserve it all costs and would tolerate little alteration for political or ideological causes.

Chorales and Christmas Carols: Sacred Music and the Essence of Germanness

Although Catholics in Germany had their own musical traditions (some unique, others shared with Protestants), it was primarily Protestant contributions—the oratorios and chorales of J. S. Bach and others, hymns from Martin Luther and the Pietists, sentimental Christmas carols—that captured the public imagination as specifically German music. The powerful political, social, and cultural position of German Protestants and Protestantism in the nineteenth century explains at least in part this predilection, since the numbers alone do not necessarily account for the Protestants' overwhelming influence.[2]

By the early twentieth century, sacred music from the Protestant tradition had become both an expression of and a force in shaping a particular understanding of "Germanness." Even in Hitler's Third Reich, where ideologues preferred pagan forms of ritual to Christian ones, sacred music was a crucial part of at least three central notions of what it meant to be German. First, Germans used sacred music to express their self-image as a people of God and a *Volk* unified militarily at arms. Secondly, sacred music was a way to voice the concept of a nation that extended beyond its physical borders, its people allegedly rent asunder by cruel international forces. And finally, sacred music helped project the image of a Germany whose intense spiritual unity soared above historical divisions of religious confession. I examine each of these intersections of sacred music and national identity in turn.

A connection between sacred music and the German military stretched back at least to World War I. Indeed, German Protestant hymnals of the 1930s included songs associated with wars of the previous four centuries. Particularly popular in the Nazi years were musical settings of poems by the nationalist Ernst Moritz Arndt, written during the so-called Wars of Liberation against Napoleon. In the summer of 1914 and long afterward, religious writers symbolized the mythical "Burgfrieden"—peace within For-

---

2. In the late 1930s, Protestants made up close to 60 percent of Germany's population; Catholics accounted for around 40 percent. Jews constituted about 1 percent. Even after years of antichurch propaganda by the Nazi Party and state, those who were unaffiliated with an established church never amounted to more than a percent or two.

tress Germany—with the image of a unified nation marching to war singing Luther's hymn: "Ein feste Burg ist unser Gott" ("A Mighty Fortress Is Our God").[3] Stormtroopers and SS units in the early 1930s accompanied their street violence against homosexuals, communists, and Jews with a folksy musical repertoire that included many hymns. Special favorites were the "Niederlander Dankgebet," "Wir treten zum beten" (the Netherlander prayer of thanks; the melody "Kremser" is familiar in English with the words "We Gather Together to Ask the Lord's Blessing"), and "Nun danket alle Gott" ("Now Thank We All Our God").

In the service of the nation at arms, lines between sacred and secular music could become quite blurred, and not only in Germany. But World War II further consolidated the bond between German militarism and sacred music. Germans at home and at the front sometimes responded to news of military victories with spontaneous renditions of "Lobe den Herren, den Mächtigen König der Erde" ("Praise to the Lord, the Almighty, the King of Creation"). Protestant military chaplains stressed the unifying force of musical tradition for the troops. Catholics may have had their Eucharist, those chaplains conceded, but Protestants had the hymnal. Indeed, military authorities issued a new Protestant soldiers' songbook just weeks before the attack on Poland in September 1939. Throughout the war chaplains clamored for copies, convinced that singing together boosted morale for fighting together. When hostile Nazi functionaries tried to replace the Christian Christmas for the armed forces with a neopagan celebration of the winter solstice, chaplains advised one another to remain calm. The men would not tolerate Christmas without "Stille Nacht" ("Silent Night"), they told themselves. And they were right. Even SS men, infamous for their aggressively anti-Christian paganism, were known to mark 25 December in what they considered uniquely German ways: by singing Christmas hymns familiar from their childhood.

A second area where intimate ties between German Protestant musical traditions and national identity were evident was among the *Volksdeutschen* or ethnic Germans, members of the so-called German diaspora

---

3. Where possible in this essay I have given the English-language titles or first lines of hymns. In those cases the English words of the titles are capitalized. Where I could not locate an English-language version, I have translated the German titles and left the English words in lower case. See John Julian, ed., *A Dictionary of Hymnology* (London: John Murray, 1908); Erik Routley, *A Panorama of Christian Hymnology* (Collegeville, Minn.: Liturgical Press, 1979); Catherine Winkworth, ed., *Lyra Germanica: Hymns for the Sundays and Chief Festivals of the Christian Year* (London: Longman, Brown, Green, Longmans, and Roberts, 1858).

living outside the borders of the Reich. From Romania to Ukraine, Argentina, and Canada, centuries of German emigration had produced communities of people who in the 1930s considered themselves culturally German. For many of them participation in a musical tradition was essential to that identity. German folk songs and hymns helped sustain their connection to the "motherland," even in cases where those links were largely nineteenth-century romantic inventions. Germans at home, for their part, similarly imagined their kinship with these communities in terms of a shared musical heritage. In the 1920s and 1930s, missionaries and church officials from Germany often carried with them hymnals for their hosts when visiting ethnic German communities abroad, and musicians and choir directors were among the most frequent travelers between the core and the diaspora societies.

Between 1914 and 1918, as German forces overran large parts of the Russian Empire, they found settlements of ethnic German Lutherans, Baptists, and Mennonites, some of whom greeted the soldiers with familiar hymns. Just over twenty years later, when Hitler's Wehrmacht invaded and occupied the same territories, its men found comfort in the companionship of loyal *Volksdeutschen* and often used music as a kind of litmus test for determining who was a German. Did the locals know "Gott ist die Liebe" (God is love) and "Stille Nacht," the invaders might ask? If so, the two groups consolidated ties by singing together. Some *Volksdeutschen* would later recall that they felt close to the German soldiers because the soldiers worshipped with them and came to their homes to sing Christmas carols.[4] For soldiers and civilians alike that familiar music provided solace. It conjured memories of childhood and evoked a shared past (no matter how fictitious) and a common future (however illusory).

A third illustration of links between sacred music and German identity is related to confessional (dis)unity. Germany in the 1930s and early 1940s was the largest European country in which the established Protestant and Catholic churches were nearly equal in size. Confessional rivalries and hostilities ran deep; mutual suspicions shaped social, political, even economic interactions. Nevertheless the Third Reich propagated its own myth of a unified *Volksgemeinschaft*, the racially pure community of blood where confessional divisions had lost all relevance. Sacred music played an important role in that context. For many Protestants it represented a sphere of religious activity in which all Christians in Germany, regardless of confession, could unite.

4. Based on interviews and conversations with *Volksdeutschen* from the former Soviet Union, in Espelkamp and Porta Westfalica, June 1998.

This Protestant vision of a unified, Christian Germany ignored Catholic practices. Chauvinistically and rather unrealistically, proponents of confessional unity offered the hymns of Martin Luther as common ground on which all Germans could rally. Other enthusiasts pointed to the music of Bach. According to one 1938 publication, Bach transcended "all theological and church political conflict to reach a place untouched by the confessional and ideological struggles of our day."[5] Still others offered recent compositions, Christian marching songs, as a means to unite the Volk as brothers. Jews disappeared from this imagined Volk, because the notion of church music as a unifying moment for "true Germans" echoed the legal assumption that only Christians were Aryans, and only Aryans were Germans.[6] In each case, sacred music constituted an expression of what it meant to be German, a concrete assertion in a world of abstractions. The myth of the undefeatable German nation that transcended geographic boundaries and confessional differences found voice in the music of the Christian church.

Hallelujah or "Lobgesungen"? Purging Echoes of Judaism

Precisely because music occupied such a key place in German national self-understandings, Nazi fears that it might be tainted extended to popular hymns, the music hymnologist Erik Routley has called "the folk songs of the Christian faith."[7] But because sacred music was so deeply rooted in church as well as secular music traditions, attempts to tamper with it met stubborn opposition. As Nazi purists would learn, sacred music had become such an integral part of standard musical fare that most Germans would not tolerate changes to its content or compromises of its quality, even when that meant retaining texts replete with hebraisms and, in some cases, employing "non-Aryan" church musicians.

5. Untitled piece in *Die Nationalkirche* 45 (7 Nov. 1937): 358, in Landeskirchenarchiv Bielefeld (hereafter LKA Bielefeld) 5,1/292,1. See also Pastor Georg Schneider, "Viele Konfessionskirchen oder Eine Volkskirche?," reprint from *Deutscher Sonntag* 38–40 (20 Sept., 27 Sept., and 4 Oct. 1936): 3, in LKA Bielefeld 5,1/291,1. Translations are my own unless otherwise specified.

6. Nazi law, purportedly racial, in fact used religious criteria to define Jews within Germany. Under the Nuremberg Laws of 1935 it was the religion of one's grandparents, not some physical or biological attributes, that determined who counted as "Aryan" and who did not. Raul Hilberg discusses development of a definition of "Jews" in Nazi Germany in *The Destruction of the European Jews*, rev. ed., vol. 1 (New York: Holmes & Meier, 1985), 65–80.

7. See Erik Routley, *Hymns and Human Life* (Grand Rapids: Eerdmans, 1959), and *Church Music and the Christian Faith* (Carol Stream, Ill.: Agape, 1978).

The assault on sacred music came from two directions: on the one hand, from anti-Christian, often neopagan, Nazi "true believers" who attacked Christianity as a devious, enfeebling form of Judaism; on the other hand, from pro–National Socialist elements within the Protestant church who rushed to defend the traditions they held dear from charges of complicity in Judaism. That defensive posture in turn produced a preemptive dejudaizing zeal designed to prove not only that Christians could be good antisemites, but that they were the original and ultimate opponents of Jews.

German neopagans, who considered Christianity a disguised form of Judaism, complained when songs with Jewish associations, such as "Jerusalem du hochgebaute Stadt" ("Jerusalem Thou City High and Fair"), were played at ceremonies to honor the war dead. Specialists in "Gruppe Seelsorge," the army's pastoral division, discreetly purged names of Old Testament figures—Abraham, Jesse, David—from the World War II soldiers' songbooks. But the most concerted, broad-based efforts to dejudaize what was sung and played in churches across Germany came from a group known as the "Glaubensbewegung Deutsche Christen" (Faith Movement of German Christians).

The German Christians, as adherents of the movement came to be known, existed within the official Protestant church. Throughout the 1930s and until the collapse of the Nazi regime, the approximately six hundred thousand lay and clerical members agitated for a synthesis of National Socialist ideology with Christian theology and urged creation of a people's church defined by blood and "race." The German Christians' influence far outstripped their numbers: they controlled the governments of all but three of Germany's twenty-eight regional Protestant churches and dominated faculties of theology in universities across Germany. As the most outspoken proponents of an anti-Jewish Christian practice, the German Christian movement led the charge on liturgical music in Nazi Germany.

The most famous statement of German Christian intentions came in November 1933 at a rally in Berlin's Sports Palace. There a high-school religion teacher named Reinhold Krause delivered one of the most explosive speeches in the history of German Protestantism. Before an audience of twenty thousand, Krause demanded a radical revision of Christianity to remove all evidence of its Jewish roots. In order to win the Nazi masses over to full participation in the church, he insisted, it was necessary to purge everything "un-German" from the worship service: to expunge the Old Testament, that "book of cattletraders and pimps," and to pray and sing only in German, "for only in the German mother tongue can humanity express its prayers, praise, and thanks in the most profound way." If "we National

Socialists are ashamed to buy even a tie from a Jew," Krause shouted to thunderous applause, "how much more should we refuse to accept something that speaks to our very soul!" [8]

Initially the German Christians, like their Berlin leader Krause, concentrated their purgative efforts on the texts of hymns, where purported offenses were most evident and easiest to address. Publicists and spokespeople railed against the "language of Canaan": references to "Abraham's seed," "Zion," or "Jerusalem." Such "Hebrew vocabulary," they claimed, drove genuine antisemites away from the church. The terms in which they expressed their distaste, however, indicate that words and music were not always so clearly separated. For example, one irate German Christian likened "Jewishisms"—words such as "Hallelujah," "Hosanna," or "Immanuel"—to the "equally reprehensible American hits" with their "Negro beat." [9]

By the fall of 1935, when the Nazi Party rally in Nuremberg became the site of sweeping public denunciation of all that was identified as Jewish, the German Christians had stepped up their attack on hebraisms in church music. They used the weight of officially sanctioned antisemitism to castigate rival clergy for promoting hymns particularly riddled with Old Testament references; they produced instructions for congregations to make pertinent adjustments. "Hallelujah," German Christian liturgists proposed, could be replaced by "Lobgesungen" (praise sung) or by "Lobet den Herrn" (praise the Lord). "Hosanna," they suggested, could be rendered "Hilf, O Herr uns" (Help us, O Lord), and the "Herr Zabaoth" (Lord Sabaoth) in Luther's "Mighty Fortress" could become simply "unser Gott" (our God). If left unchanged, one German Christian warned, such Judaisms would "provide grist for the mills of those who claim that Christianity is a Jewish religion." [10]

On closer inspection German Christians found that a concerted assault on all that smacked of Jewishness in church music could not stop at

8. "Rede des Gauobmannes der Glaubensbewegung 'Deutsche Christen' in Groß-Berlin. Dr. Krause. Gehalten im Sportpalast am 13. November 1933" (Berlin 1933) 9, in LKA Bielefeld 5,1/289,2.

9. Ernst Lot, "Judeleien," *Evangelium und Jugend—Mitteilungen für die evangelischen Gemeindejugend aus dem Reichsjugendpfarramt* 6/7 (Oct. 1934): 24, Bundesarchiv Potsdam (BA Potsdam) DC-I 1933–1935. These materials have since been recatalogued and relocated within the German Federal Archive system.

10. No author, "Gesangbuchnot," *Nachrichtenblatt der Evangelischen Gemeinde Oberhausen I* (10 Nov. 1935), Archiv der evangelischen Kirche im Rheinland, Düsseldorf (AEKR Düsseldorf), Nachlaß Schmidt 18.

words alone, so they broadened their attack to include melodies. Clearly composers with Jewish ancestry, such as Mendelssohn, were out of the question. But the German Christians and their fellow travelers went further still. In 1934, a professor of music from Dresden complained bitterly that skittish choir directors were avoiding his new composition because it incorporated an old Hebrew melody. Furious, the man defended his work by showing other cases where "Jewish music" had infiltrated the German canon. The much-touted Gregorian chants, he countercharged, were full of old Hebrew melodies for psalms and lamentations. Moreover, he maintained, one of the favorite hymns of Stormtroopers and the SS, "Großer Gott wir loben dich" ("Holy God, We Praise Thy Name") bore a striking similarity to the Jewish tune "En Kelohena" [sic]. On top of all that, he charged, the words of the popular "Wir treten zum beten" ("We Gather Together") had been penned "for Zionist purposes by the Jew Weyl." [11] His insistence and evidence notwithstanding, none of the man's accusations really took root. To the contrary, both of the hymns he identified as somehow "Jewish" remained popular with Germans inside and outside the church.

Some German Christians worried about an alienating, ponderous musical style that they claimed originated in the synagogue and weakened the Christian fighting spirit. Those complaints too found limited resonance. More problematic, in the view of many eager opponents of Judaism, were beloved melodies so deeply associated with offensive lyrics that they were effectively unusuable in an antisemitic setting. "Jerusalem Thou City High and Fair," for example, did not have to be sung to draw fire; instrumental renditions likewise infuriated critics of the Jewish influence in Christianity. "Hallelujahs," "Hosannas," and other hebraisms, it seemed, could resonate as loudly in their absence as in their presence, as long as familiar melodies evoked them in the minds of listeners.

Finally there were the musicians themselves. What good did it do to purge the music, German Christians asked rhetorically, if "non-Aryan" choir directors, singers, and organists continued to perform in German churches? Sometimes Nazi cultural authorities removed church musicians deemed "non-Aryan" from their posts; in other cases such initiatives came from within the church itself. The number of people affected was very small: in 1935, an enormous hue and cry about "non-Aryan" organists in Protestant churches managed to locate only three such individuals, attesting to a long-standing practice of exclusion. As mainstream Protestant

11. Otto Richter, "Ich bitte ums Wort," *Deutsches Pfarrerblatt* 3 (16 Jan. 1934): 37, in LKA Bielefeld 5,1/289,1. The German text "Wir treten zum beten" is by Josef Weyl (1821–95).

church officials boasted, even before 1933, sacred music had already been noticeably "free of Jewish influence."[12]

Increasingly the German Christians proposed to solve what they considered the "Jewish problem" in sacred music by creating their own new material, melodies and texts. Most of the hymns they published in the 1930s and early 1940s featured "manly" martial rhythms and lyrics about "blood fresh as the soil," "dead soldiers," "Germany's Heil," "holy war," and the like.[13] A glance at hymnals published in Germany between 1933 and 1945 suggests that well over half of them included at least some of the new German Christian "songs of struggle." The poets and musicians who created these hymns intended them to be the voice of a new, anti-Jewish, Germanic Christianity, a religion for the racially pure community of blood.

The German Amen: Cultural Loyalties to Familiar Church Music

To the surprise and dismay of the dejudaizing crusaders, encroachments on familiar sacred music were anything but welcome, even within the ranks of the extremist German Christians. Such hesitation on the part of the group in turn reveals a great deal about Germans' cultural priorities, as the following examples illustrate.

Bremen's Protestant bishop, an outspoken German Christian named Heinz Weidemann, was one of the most vociferous enemies of Jews and Judaism in the movement. In 1936 he published a "Germanized" version of the gospels that reduced Jesus's message to the most vile anti-Jewish portions from the Gospel of John. Weidemann also changed the names of churches if he found them "too Jewish"—Bethel, Zion, and the like—and tried to christen two new buildings in his jurisdiction the "Hindenburg" and "Horst Wessel" churches. In 1939 he led an initiative by regional church governments to proclaim themselves "free of Jews," that is, to terminate the membership of anyone defined as "non-Aryan" under Nazi law.

When it came to sacred music, however, Weidemann was surprisingly moderate. Three years after the appearance of his vitriolic *Evangelium*

12. Oskar Söhngen, "Vermerk," Berlin-Charlottenburg, 5 Feb. 1941, Evangelisches Zentralarchiv Berlin (EZA Berlin) 1/C3/131; see also Hans Prolingheuer, *Ausgetan aus dem Land der Lebendigen* (Neukirchen-Vluyn, 1983).

13. See, for examples, "Liedblatt Nr. 1," with twelve hymns, attached to flyer, "Wille und Ziel der 'Deutschen Christen' (Nationalkirchliche Bewegung) e.V.," Berlin, March 1938, in LKA Bielefeld 5,1/293; also "Deutsches Volk feiert Advent," 1934, in LKA Bielefeld 5,1/290,2; see also Wilhelm Bauer, *Feierstunden Deutscher Christen* (Weimar: Verlag Deutscher Christen, 1935), 22–31.

Johannes deutsch! (Gospel of John in German!), Weidemann produced a volume of hymns called *Lieder der kommenden Kirche (Songs of the Coming Church)*. Aside from the inclusion of some new, German Christian compositions, it was a rather traditional hymnal that contained much familiar material and no calls to hatred toward Jews.[14] It sold tens of thousands of copies.

Weidemann's position was typical of many Germans, including those in the German Christian movement. At first glance their attention to sacred music seems to have matched their wider efforts to expunge all echoes of Judaism from Christianity. They used the Old Testament both as a scapegoat for Jewish influence in Christianity and as a source for anti-Jewish images. The New Testament became their marching orders for an anti-Jewish faith, its Jesus the arch-antisemite, the god whose death "at the hands of Jews" proved his eternal enmity toward them. But with regard to church music, even the German Christians—the most extreme voices for an anti-Jewish church—never made the same transition from dejudaizing fervor to an overt assault on Judaism and Jews. Among the hundreds of hymns they penned, I have found only one that mentioned Jews explicitly, in a call to follow Luther's condemnation of their "diabolical work."[15] There is no evidence that it was ever sung.

The reasons for such reticence were not theological but cultural. Members of the German Christian movement too felt loyalty to a musical tradition that they associated with their own sense of who they were, both as Christians and as Germans. Musical habits and notions of appropriateness, it seems, provided a more effective brake on anti-Jewish zeal in the church than did doctrinal or ethical considerations. In the words of Wilhelm Bauer, the most promient German Christian liturgist, it was in "bad taste" to sing rabble-rousing, fighting, or even folksy songs in the church because they "clashed" with the solemn tones of the organ and violated the "hallowed stillness" of the house of God.[16]

Thus Reinhold Krause and those others who demanded a total revamping of church music remained frustrated even within the German Christian ranks. An examination of programs for German Christian events

14. *Das Evangelium Johannes deutsch*, foreword by Heinz Weidemann (Bremen: H.M. Hauschild, 1936), Kommunalarchiv Minden, Kirchengeschichtliche Arbeitsgemeinschaft (uncatalogued collection of the "working group on church history," hereafter KAG Minden); *Lieder der kommenden Kirche*, foreword by Heinz Weidemann (Bremen: Verlag "Kommende Kirche," 1939), KAG Minden.

15. Hans Falck to Reich Bishop Ludwig Müller, including text of new "Kampflied," 15 October 1934, EZA Berlin 1/A4/93.

16. Bauer, *Feierstunden*, 44.

indicates that certainly in the first two years of Nazi rule, from 1933 to 1935, the movement remained more or less immune to calls for musical reform. German Christians continued to sing the old favorites, often complete with Old Testament references. Programs in subsequent years show a mix of traditional hymns with new German Christian compositions. It was not so difficult to salvage most of the old hymns; problematic stanzas could simply be left out or new verses with nationalist sentiments tacked onto the end. In this regard the German Christians differed little from their more mainstream Protestant counterparts.

Even the new hymnal produced in 1941, by the Institute for Study and Eradication of Jewish Influence in German Church Life, reflected such restraint. According to a 1939 survey by that institute, traditional hymns were so rife with hebraisms that only 4.4 percent of the content of the current hymnals could be kept in the present form. Nevertheless, most of the 339 hymns in the institute's 1941 collection were standard fare from which the most obvious references to the Old Testament had been excised; the new nationalist, sentimental songs were only supplements. Even the title of the hymnal, *Großer Gott, wir loben dich!* (*Holy God, We Praise Thy Name*) referred to a popular old hymn rather than flaunting a more overtly nationalistic theme.[17]

Meanwhile, years after Reinhold Krause's denunciation of "judaized" sacred music, neopagans and the more radical German Christians continued to decry the presence of hebraisms in almost exactly the same words that Krause had used in 1933, but to little avail.[18] Obstructions to the project of dejudaizing sacred music persisted. For one thing, too many well-known hymns were "corrupted" by hebraisms, and churchgoers were simply not willing to part with all those beloved songs. Proposed substitutions often seemed cumbersome and unlyrical, exemplified by the recommendation to replace "Hallelujah" in Handel's famous chorus from the *Messiah* with the clumsy and lengthy phrase "Gelobet sei Gott" (praised be God). As for the new songs, they were unfamiliar, and very few people enjoyed singing them.

Through the upheavals of the early twentieth century, many Germans held to their Christian traditions out of a desire for security in the face of change. Familiar music was an essential part of the comfort people sought in church, even if they went only a few times a year. Tinkering with the old

17. *Großer Gott, wir loben dich!* (Weimar: Der neue Dom, 1941), KAG Minden.
18. Bell, "David, Abraham und Jakob im hanoverschen Gesangbuch," *Die National-kirche, Briefe an deutsche Christen* 6 (Worms, 5 February 1939): 57–58, in LKA Bielefeld 5,1/293.

hymns or generating new ones defeated that purpose. Even minor changes
in texts could not go unnoticed and often caused a stir. Hence the 1939 Protestant soldiers' songbook retained the "Hallelujah" in the second stanza
of "Stille Nacht," since its absence would have seemed strange to many of
the men.[19] It was one thing, German Christian reformers discovered, to
make theological decisions about scripture: many ordinary Christians had
little idea where the Old Testament left off and the New began. It was quite
another matter to change or eliminate hymns, part of a musical tradition
that Germans, particularly Protestants, considered their patrimony.

The security offered by sacred music could also influence churches to
resist tampering with their musical personnel, a response that even extended into the German Christian movement. In at least two cases, such
allegiance actually induced German Christians to show some, albeit very
limited, solidarity with individual "non-Aryan"musicians. As a movement, the German Christians were adamantly opposed to the presence of
so-called non-Aryans—converts from Judaism, children, and even grand-
children of converts—in the Christian churches. It was German Christians
in 1933 who initiated the move to adopt an "Aryan Paragraph" excluding
anyone defined as non-Aryan from the Protestant clergy. Six years later, it
was also German Christians who revoked the church membership of "non-
Aryans" in those regional churches they controlled. Nevertheless, in 1934,
German Christians in Reich Bishop Ludwig Müller's office intervened (un-
successfully) with the Reich Music Chamber in favor of allowing a "non-
Aryan" choir director to perform with his group in Zittau (Saxony). A year
later, German Christians in Bremen supported a "non-Aryan" church organist in opposition to Nazi cultural experts who targeted him for dis-
missal. The man had served his congregation loyally, the German Christians argued, and anyway, the church desperately needed an organist.[20]

This is not to say that occasional tolerance toward vestiges of Judaism
in traditional church music practices promoted compassion toward Jews or
mitigated participation in Nazi antisemitism. Admittedly, in France and
the Netherlands, some conservative Calvinists translated a passionate at-
tachment to the Old Testament into efforts to rescue Jews. The Huguenots
of Le Chambon-sur-Lignon actually referred to the Jews they harbored as

19. *Evangelisches Feldgesangbuch* (Berlin: E. S. Mittler & Son, [1939]) 59, Bundesarchiv-
Militärarchiv Freiburg (BA-MA Freiburg).
20. See materials in EZA Berlin 1/C3/131, including Reich Music Chamber, signed Kar-
rasch, to German Protestant Church, 22 Oct. 1934; "Liste der nichtarischen Organisten,"
2 September 1935; President of the Bremen Protestant Church to Reich Church Committee,
7 December 1935.

"Old Testaments."[21] In the German case, however, loyalties to familar hymns and even to isolated individual musicians seem to have been cultural only; their proponents never made their case in doctrinal or ethical terms nor did they draw broader conclusions about Nazi racial policies. To the contrary, German Christians and those like-minded church people defended their position by claiming that the hebraisms they considered indispensable—most notably "Amen"—had nothing whatsoever to do with Judaism or modern-day Jews. Through long association, they contended, such words had in fact become German.

Sacred music entered even the sites of the most extreme desperation in the Third Reich. In 1943, inmates of the Theresienstadt camp performed Verdi's *Requiem* for an audience of German guards and camp functionaries. No doubt the listeners enjoyed both the musical beauty of the event and the sadistic irony of having some of Europe's top Jewish musicians sing their own mass for the dead before they were sent to Auschwitz to be murdered. There is no record of those privileged auditors objecting that the performers they heard were Jews and the composer of the work Italian. Antisemites in the audience also managed to overlook the fact that the text of the "Dies Irae," the Day of Wrath, was largely derived from the Old Testament, in particular the Book of Daniel:

> Lo the book exactly worded,
> Wherein all hath been recorded,
> Thence shall judgment be awarded.[22]

One cannot know how the Germans present experienced the event. Did they observe with discomfort the degradation of their nation—the self-proclaimed "people of music"—or feel reinvigorated by the excellence of the musical performance? Either way, the scene expressed in the starkest possible terms the clash of interests between the inclusive and exclusive functions of sacred music in the Third Reich. On the one hand a force for unity and source of commonality, sacred music represented a cultural home that many Germans valued enough to protect, even if it meant compromising Nazi ideology. On the other hand, however, in the Nazi system, sacred music itself became a means of torment and a site of battle, where

---

21. See the 1989 film by Pierre Sauvage, *Weapons of the Spirit*.

22. See Joža Karas, *Music in Terezín, 1941–45* (New York: Beaufort Books, 1985). Biblical allusions include Daniel chapter 7, especially verse 10; Zephaniah 1:15, and Psalms 96:13, 97:3, and 11:6.

artificial claims of purity obscured a legacy of coexistence and shared suffering—between Christians and Jews, Catholics and Protestants, and Germans and their neighbors.

Guide to Further Reading

Bergen, Doris. *Twisted Cross: The German Christian Movement in the Third Reich.* Chapel Hill: University of North Carolina Press, 1996.

Conway, John S. *The Nazi Persecution of the Churches, 1933–45.* New York: Basic, 1968.

Dümling, Albrecht, and Peter Girth, eds. *Entartete Musik. Zur Düsseldorfer Ausstellung von 1938. Eine kommentierte Rekonstruktion.* Düsseldorf: Kleinherne, 1988.

Friedländer, Saul. *Nazi Germany and the Jews.* Vol. 1. *The Years of Persecution, 1933–1939.* New York: HarperCollins, 1997.

Heister, Hanns-Werner, and Hans Günter Klein, eds. *Musik und Musikpolitik im faschistischen Deutschland.* Frankfurt am Main: Fischer Taschenbuch, 1984.

Heschel, Susannah. "Nazifying Christian Theology: Walter Grundmann and the Institute for the Study and Eradication of Jewish Influence in German Church Life." *Church History* 63, no. 4 (Dec. 1994): 587–605.

Levi, Erik. *Music in the Third Reich.* New York: St. Martin's, 1994.

Mahrenholz, Christhard, et al., eds. *Handbuch zum Evangelischen Kirchengesangbuch.* Multiple volumes. Göttingen: Vandenhoeck & Ruprecht, 1953–1990.

Meyer, Michael. *The Politics of Music in the Third Reich.* New York: Peter Lang, 1991.

Müller, Karl Ferdinand, and Walter Blankenburg, eds. *Leiturgia: Handbuch des Evangelischen Gottesdienstes.* Vol. 4. *Die Musik des Evangelischen Gottesdienstes.* Kassel: Johannes Strauda Verlag, 1961.

Prieberg, Fred K. *Musik im NS-Staat.* Frankfurt am Main: Fischer Taschenbuch, 1982.

Prolingheuer, Hans. *Wir sind in die Irre gegangen. Die Schuld der Kirche unterm Hakenkreuz nach dem Bekenntnis des "Darmstadter Wortes" von 1947.* Cologne: Pahl-Rugenstein, 1987.

———. "Die judenreine deutsche evangelische Kirchenmusik." *Junge Kirche* (11/1981, 3/1982, 5-6/1983, 6/1986).

Routley, Erik. *The Music of Christian Hymnody.* London: Independent Press, 1957.

Scholder, Klaus. *The Churches and the Third Reich.* 2 vols. Trans. John Bowden. Philadelphia: Fortress, 1987–88.

Schuberth, Dietrich, ed. *Kirchenmusik im Nationalsozialismus: Zehn Vorträge.* Berlin: Merseburger, 1995.

Wulf, Joseph. *Musik im Dritten Reich: Eine Dokumentation.* Gütersloh: Sigbert Mohn Verlag, 1963.

National and Universal: Thomas Mann and the Paradox of "German" Music

For a nation such as ours . . . the psychological element is always primary, the essential motivating factor; political action is of secondary importance, a reflex, an expression, an instrument.
—Thomas Mann, *Doctor Faustus*

Warum das ganze Spiel?—Wenn das nicht wäre, Was wäre dann?— Warum das ganze Spiel?

[Why this game?—If not for this, what would there be? Why this game?]
—Hans Pfitzner, *Palestrina*

Owing to his singularly passionate and articulate engagement with music and Germany in general, and with Wagner in particular, Thomas Mann is indispensable in any attempt to come to grips with the issue of music and German national identity. What is the place of music in his work? How does music figure in his imaginings of nationhood? How did he react to the political instrumentalization of Wagner in the Third Reich? And how did these issues shape the book, *Doctor Faustus*, that many would agree represents Mann's most sustained effort to elucidate the hidden nexus of German history and music? These are the fundamental questions that I attempt to address in this essay.

Let it be clear at the outset that, today more than ever, the debate about German culture and German identity is overshadowed by the Holocaust. As Saul Friedländer recently observed, the "centrality" of the Holocaust "in present day historical consciousness seems much greater than it was some decades ago."[1] The ramifications of this situation have been particularly far-reaching in the field of German Studies, where one can detect a widespread tendency to construct Holocaust-centered models of German culture. The rationale of such constructions seems plausible enough: if the Holocaust is deemed central to our historical consciousness, as it clearly

---

1. Saul Friedländer, *Nazi Germany and the Jews*, vol. 1, *The Years of Persecution, 1933–1939* (New York: HarperCollins, 1997), 1.

is, it must also be "the central event" in German history.[2] The problem
with such apocalyptic historiography is that it relies on what Michael A.
Bernstein has termed "backshadowing," that is, "a kind of retroactive fore-
shadowing in which the shared knowledge of the outcome of a series of
events . . . is used to judge the participants in those events as though they
should have known what was to come."[3] Backshadowing leads the historian to the usual suspects, such as antisemitism, xenophobia, authoritarianism, and nationalism. But what if the origin of the German catastrophe
was not some obvious evil but rather some generally esteemed good? Or
something that, like Jekyll and Hyde, was both good and evil? Thomas
Mann, a particularly well-placed witness—first as an insider, later as an
outsider—suspected this was in fact the case. "There are *not* two Germanys," he argued in a speech at the Library of Congress in May of 1945, "a
good one and a bad one, but only one, whose best turned into evil through
devilish cunning. Wicked Germany is merely good Germany gone astray"
(A, 64). Mann's point is clear: what happened in Germany cannot be attributed to an evil essence endemic to German culture but must rather be
viewed as the result of a process of perversion. He believed that it was music, the "best" that German culture has to offer, that made Germany susceptible to the sort of political and moral regression that he, along with the
entire civilized world, had been witnessing in horror and disbelief.

The special, possibly crucial role that "the most German of the arts"[4]
has played in German history is still not as widely acknowledged as it
ought to be. Considerable evidence in support of this claim may be found
in the Germans' own imaginings of nationhood both before and after 1871.
As Celia Applegate has pointed out in a seminal essay, "music was of central importance to the spread of German national feeling in the nineteenth
century, quite possibly of more importance than German literature."[5]
Mann would have agreed. In his Washington address of May 1945, "Germany and the Germans," he assured his audience that "not a word" of all

2. See Sander L. Gilman in his much quoted article "Why and How I Study the German,"
German Quarterly 62 (spring 1989): 192–204. "The Holocaust remains and must remain for
me, and, I hope, for my students the central event of modern German culture, the event toward which every text, every moment in German history and, yes, culture moved inexorably"
(200f.).

3. Michael André Bernstein, *Foregone Conclusions: Against Apocalyptic History* (Berkeley: University of California Press, 1994), 16.

4. Thomas Mann, *The Story of a Novel: The Genesis of "Doctor Faustus,"* trans. Richard
and Clara Winston (New York: Knopf, 1961), 123.

5. Celia Applegate, "What is German Music? Reflections on the Role of Art in the Creation of the Nation," *German Studies Review* 15 (winter 1992): 21–32, here 24.

he was saying about the pivotal importance of music in German history "came out of alien, cool, objective knowledge, it is all within me, I have been through it all" (A, 64f.). And indeed, there is no writer who had a more involved relationship with music than Mann.

Thomas Mann "always thought" that the peculiar talent he possessed was "a kind of displaced musicianship" (L, 186). His ambition was to write "good scores" (R, 232). By that he meant Wagnerian scores—seamless, cleverly woven webs of motifs displaying an infinite wealth of internal correspondences. As far as he was concerned, the art of narration reached its apogee in Wagner's most inspired achievements: "a veritable feast of associations, a whole universe of brilliant and profound allusions, a structure of musical remembrance so magnificent and moving," such that nothing else could compare with it (PCW, 188). To the young Thomas Mann, the mature Wagner represented a challenge to the conventions of nineteenth-century realism. He resolved to meet this challenge, encouraged and legitimated in this endeavor by Nietzsche's assessment of modernity in 1888: "Wagner sums up modernity. There is no way out, one must first become a Wagnerian." [6] Mann was sincere when, in a letter to Theodore W. Adorno in 1952, he confessed: "I have imitated Wagner a great deal, 'remembered' him often." [7]

Like Nietzsche, he greatly admired the "shifting perspective" in Wagner's work—its power to stun the uninitiated and, at the same time, to satisfy the sophisticates.[8] And he never ceased wistfully to ponder the fabulous global success of Wagner's work. What he desired most, however, was that exceptional status of "representativeness" within German culture that only two other figures before him had achieved: Goethe and Wagner. In the end, Mann did achieve such an exceptional status, but only at the cost of turning against Germany. For him, there was no question that Goethe was a more trustworthy spiritual guide and "national hero than that snuffling gnome from Saxony with his colossal talent and shabby personality" (PCW, 50). Nonetheless, he remained more deeply fascinated by Wagner than by Goethe, whom he admired and loved, but in a relatively uncomplicated way. As an explanation of his relationship to Wagner, a sentence from *Doctor Faustus* seems particularly apt: "The highest passion is spent on what is absolutely suspect" (DF, 257).

6. Friedrich Nietzsche, *The Birth of Tragedy* and *The Case of Wagner*, trans. (with commentary) Walter Kaufmann (New York: Vintage Books, 1967), 156.

7. *Im Schatten Wagners: Thomas Mann über Richard Wagner. Texte und Zeugnisse, 1895–1955*, ausgewählt, kommentiert und mit einem Essay von Hans Rudolf Vaget (Frankfurt am Main: Fischer Taschenbuch Verlag, 1999), 220.

8. Letter to Hermann Hesse, 1 April 1910, ibid., 40.

Mann was fully aware of, and sometimes extolled, the eminently German character of Wagner's work, but what he admired even more was its
broad appeal on a European scale. Like everyone else at the time, he accepted
uncritically Wagner's own pretense to universality as well as that of the
German discourse on Wagner. The international success of Wagner's music
was ample proof, so it seemed, that "German" music was indeed an art form
that spoke to all mankind and rose above nationalist partisanship. Mann,
too, aspired to transcend the boundaries of the national, the "merely" German, but he had to do so under very different historical circumstances. In
the end, however, Mann has come to stand before us as a tragic German patriot—tragic in that his passionate engagement with that "explosive reve-
lation" of "Germanness" (R, 53) that was Wagner led him inescapably to
indict the very culture that he had helped define and of which he was perhaps the most distinguished exemplar in the twentieth century.

Mann's work is not only shaped by music, it also speaks of music—
again and again. Beginning with *Little Herr Friedemann,* his breakthrough
story of 1897, the encounter with music is dramatized as the return of the
repressed dionysian. It is always fateful, often deadly. Thus the decline of
the Buddenbrooks is hastened by the introduction of Wagner into the
strained psychological economy of the family. Gustav Aschenbach, too,
meets his fate in his encounter with the dionysian—in Venice, the very
site of Wagner's own death. And the motley world of *The Magic Mountain,*
moribund to the core, but merrily killing time until the arrival, thunder-
bolt-like, of the Great War, falls victim, in the last analysis, to the magic of
music, the irresistible *Seelenzauber* of romantic music from Schubert to
Wagner. There is, then, a growing realization in Mann's work that the private and the public spheres are correlated, however obliquely, and that the
music-induced spiritual adventures of the individual may presage the more
calamitous social adventures of the collective.

Mann's sense of the political consequences of both the individual and
collective infatuation with music becomes explicit in *Doctor Faustus.* Music is the crucial factor in the ambitious design of this great novel, which
attempts nothing less than to trace, on a large historical scale, Germany's
slide into catastrophe. In the immediate aftermath of World War II, the
book was misread as a wholesale condemnation of Germany and of German
culture. One of its detractors was Hans Pfitzner, in the first decades of the
century the figurehead of a proudly "reactionary" philosophy of "German"
music and an ardent nationalist.[9] Today, however, the phantom question of

9. See Michael Kater's essay included in this volume.

collective guilt no longer occupies center stage in the criticism of the novel; other issues, specifically questions about the validity of Mann's construction of German culture, keep being raised.[10] As a result, *Doctor Faustus* has remained Mann's most controversial novel. Nothing in it has proven more contentious than the implication that Germany's fateful turn to Nazism happened, not despite its idolatry of music, as the naively humanistic cliché would have it, but rather because of it.

In order to make this startling point, Mann chose to apply the Faust myth to a psychohistorical interpretation of German history and to transform the figure of Faust into a composer. It is "a grave error" on the part of the myth, he observed, "not to connect Faust with music," for "if Faust is to be a representative of the German soul, he must be musical" (A, 51). Goethe and, before him, the author of the sixteenth-century *Faustbuch* could hardly have conceived of Faust as a musician since in their times the status of music in German culture was unexceptional. But beginning with romanticism, music began to gain ascendancy and continued to do so throughout the nineteenth century. Having been born into a culture in which music was firmly established at the top of the hierarchy of the arts, Mann felt not only entitled but virtually compelled to reconceptualize Faust as a musical genius. As Zeitblom, the narrator of *Doctor Faustus*, points out: "In Germany music enjoys that respect among the people which in France is given to literature" (DF, 127). To Mann this constituted the decisive difference between Germany and the other European countries—a difference that, from *Reflections of a Nonpolitical Man* to *Doctor Faustus*, remained at the center of all his thoughts on national identity.

In *Reflections*, his massive, often brilliant wartime essay, "German" music and national identity constitute the heart of the matter. Part intellectual autobiography, part analysis of German culture, this book was intended as a defense of the German cause. He grounded it in the uniqueness of Germany's music-centered culture. This war, he argued, was being waged for Germany's right to be different from the Western democracies and to maintain a culture in which music, not politics, would rule. Nothing in the book better highlights its music-inspired nationalism than his cryptic aside that war had broken out between "the spirit of the *Lohengrin* prelude and international elegance" (R, 55). Mann leaves no doubt about his abiding love for the *Lohengrin* prelude and for Wagner's work in general when he authenticates it through the recollection of a musical experience twenty

10. For a succinct critical survey of this debate, see John F. Fetzer, *Changing Perceptions of Thomas Mann's "Doctor Faustus": Criticism 1947–1992* (Columbia, S.C.: Camden House, 1996).

years earlier, in Rome, that had moved him to tears and filled him with patriotic pride. The *Banda municipale di Roma* was playing at the Piazza
Colonna before a partisan crowd divided between those who sided with
Alessandro Vesella, a champion of Wagner's music, and those who preferred
"local music." The latter were determined to turn the occasion into a noisy
"national protest." The funeral music for Siegfried was played and duly
greeted with applause and protest. Defiantly, Vesella repeated his favorite
piece, which was then whistled down and booed even while the performance was in progress. What happened next was firmly engraved in Mann's
memory:

> But I will never forget how under *evvivas* and *abassos* the *Nothung* mo-
> tif appeared for the second time; how it developed its powerful rhythms
> above the struggle of opinions in the street, and how, at its climax, at that
> penetrating, shattering dissonance before the double C-major chords,
> shouts of triumph broke out that irresistibly enveloped the shaken op-
> position, forced its retreat, and for a long time reduced it to confused
> silence. (R, 56)

In 1915, that distant musical experience marked for him the birth of
his patriotism. The message seems clear enough: his—and by implication
German—nationalism is, at bottom, harmless, nonaggressive; it is inspired
by nothing more than the love of music, a music that is saturated with a
transnational spirit of universal appeal. If Wagner can triumph in Rome,
then his music must have a quality that is universal. It is a telling detail in
the fictitious biography of Adrian Leverkühn that he, too, attends the open-
air concerts at Rome's Piazza Colonna (DF, 234).

Mann, along with the great majority of German intellectuals, deceived
himself about the aggressive character of Germany's "sacred" war of self-
defense. The author of *Reflections* was as yet unable to see what the author
of *Doctor Faustus* would come to realize slowly and painfully: that his patriotic pride in the triumph of Wagner in Rome masked a broadly shared
pretense to cultural hegemony that turned out to be the harbinger of hegemonic designs on quite a different scale.

Yet common to both *Reflections* and *Doctor Faustus* is Mann's firm belief in the centrality of music to German identity. Music, he wrote in 1917,
is "Germany's national art"; more than other forces, "more than literature
and politics, it has the power to bind and unite."[11] To substantiate this
claim he invoked *Die Winterreise* and *Der Ring des Nibelungen*. Evidently,

11. *Im Schatten Wagners*, 63.

it was Mann's belief that the common love of Schubert, of Wagner, and of the entire musical culture they represented provided the secret bond that would hold together the national community at a time of crisis and upheaval. In the chaos situation of post–World War I Munich, which served Hitler as a launching pad, the appeal to culture as a unifying bond was, of course, a common theme. Thus in an address honoring Hans Pfitzner on his fiftieth birthday in 1919, Mann declared that art which had drunk from the sources of national life, as Pfitzner's music had, was the most needed and in fact the most modern. Taking his cue from *Palestrina*, he argued that chaos would reign if Germany and "German" music failed to meet the test of the historical moment. In a similar vein, in 1920, Mann concluded an essay with a somewhat cryptic rumination on the mystic relationship between the Germans and their music. Looking again at Germany as a cultural entity only, he glorified the nation as the "self-realization of its music" (als Verwirklichung seiner Musik). He likened German culture to a masterly fugue in which voice after voice interacts with its predecessor and serves to bring about "a sublime wholeness."[12] A fleeting utopian dream of harmony, generated no doubt by the anxieties of political upheaval, this vision of Germany illustrates once again how in Mann's mind the notion of Germanness coalesced around music, the highest cultural achievement of the Germans.

Mann's use of music as metaphor for the nation was by no means a novel conceit. Already in 1859, the music historian J. M. Fischer argued that the development of German national character was intrinsically related to the aesthetic achievements of German music.[13] More likely, Mann took his cue from Nietzsche, who, in *Beyond Good and Evil*, famously described the Prelude to *Die Meistersinger* as the true emblem of the German soul. From Mann's post–World War I notions of Germany as the self-realization of its music to *Doctor Faustus* was, conceptually, only a small step. However, when Mann began to reflect in earnest about the novel in which his thinking about music and national identity was to culminate, the positive, utopian aspects of the conceit had been blown away by history and given way to a much darker vision of the fateful bond between Germany and its music.

How did this shift of perspective come about? Put simply, from two concurrent but sharply divergent developments in the aftermath of World War I. As Mann distanced himself from his earlier nationalism and embraced a

12. Thomas Mann, "Brief an Hermann Grafen Keyserling," *Gesammelte Werke in dreizehn Bänden* [hereafter GW] (Frankfurt am Main: S. Fischer, 1990), XII, 603.

13. See Applegate, "What is German Music?," 29.

more liberal political outlook, Germany simultaneously reverted to an extreme form of nationalism that culminated in National Socialism. On both sides, the subject of music was a crucial consideration. While National Socialism used the German musical heritage to legitimize its political designs,[14] Mann now considered it his responsibility to caution against the cult of music and warn against its political exploitation. The inevitable clash of these two positions occurred in 1933 and resulted in Mann's national "excommunication" (PCW, 166). How telling, and how ironic, that he was driven from Germany on account of his insufficiently "German" views of Wagner!

When Mann, in September of 1922, lent his support to the embattled Weimar Republic, he, in effect, broke with his former ideological allies. In their eyes, the Weimar Republic promoted the bastardization of German culture through modernism and jazz. This was the historical moment at which Hans Pfitzner emerged as the standard-bearer of musical conservatism. In 1917, after the successful first performance of *Palestrina* under Bruno Walter, Mann penned a glowing appreciation, unmatched still today, of this unabashedly Wagnerian "musical legend," extolling Pfitzner as living proof of the vitality of German culture (R, 297–312). But after Mann's landmark speech in defense of the "German Republic," Pfitzner regarded Mann as an apostate, his political reorientation an unpardonable sin. And Pfitzner was not one who would easily forget.

Even more ominous were the unmistakable signs of a liaison between Bayreuth and the budding Hitler movement. In the fall of 1923, Hitler was welcomed with open arms at Wahnfried, whereupon Houston Stewart Chamberlain and Winifred Wagner proclaimed him the future savior of Germany.[15] The following year, after a hiatus of ten years, the Bayreuth Festival reopened and turned into a lovefest for the right-wing enemies of the Weimar Republic. Hitler, then imprisoned, was unable to attend, but starting in 1925 he was a regular visitor to Bayreuth. Once he was in power he turned Wagner's Festspielhaus into the court theater of the Third Reich, to the jubilant acclaim of most Wagnerians. Here, then, was forged and consummated an unholy alliance between a flagship institution of German musical culture and the forces of evil.

Mann reacted to these developments with anger and alarm. In 1924, he publicly stated that "Bayreuth, as it presents itself today, does not interest

14. On this subject, see especially Michael H. Kater, *The Twisted Muse: Musicians and Their Music in the Third Reich* (New York: Oxford University Press, 1997).

15. Cf. Frederic Spotts, *Bayreuth: A History of the Wagner Festival* (New Haven: Yale University Press, 1944), 140–42.

me at all, nor, should I think, the rest of the world." [16] The following year he protested for the first time the misappropriation of Wagner by the Nazis and their sympathizers, who were turning the creator of *Lohengrin* and *Tristan*—admired by Baudelaire and Nietzsche!—into "the patron saint of a troglodyte Teutonism." [17] Also in 1925, Pfitzner—an early admirer of Hitler—formally terminated his friendship with Mann, citing the widening political gulf between them as the reason. His "revenge" for Mann's "betrayal" came in 1933. As a cruelly ironic fate would have it, the fiftieth anniversary of Wagner's death coincided with Hitler's ascension to the chancellorship. For Mann, this coincidence spelled doom. On February 10, he paid tribute to Wagner at the University of Munich. The lecture, culled from his magisterial essay "The Sorrows and Grandeur of Richard Wagner" (PCW, 91–148), was received respectfully and without incident. However, when he repeated the lecture abroad—in Amsterdam, Brussels, and Paris—his enemies used the occasion as pretext for a vicious attack. On April 16, the *Münchner Neueste Nachrichten* carried a piece entitled "Protest from Richard Wagner's Own City of Munich," signed by over forty prominent figures on Munich's cultural scene, including a handful of local Nazi officials. In it, Mann was accused of having disparaged and defamed "our great German musical genius" (PCW, 149f.). Perhaps the most revealing of the "charges"—all of them based on distortion and incomprehension—concerned Mann's invocation of Freud for the interpretation of Wagner's work. This appears to have triggered downright chimerical fears: the most German of composers subjected to the authority of a Jew!

For a long time, the identity of the perpetrators of the "Protest" was said to be a mystery. Today, there is incontrovertible proof that this opportunistic denunciation of Mann was initiated not by the Nazis, as was long asserted, but by Munich's cultural establishment, specifically Hans Knappertsbusch, director of the Bavarian State Opera, and by his chief coconspirator Hans Pfitzner.[18] Knappertsbusch apparently wanted to demonstrate that he was an uncompromising guardian of the Wagnerian flame; he thereby hoped to recommend himself to the new rulers for more prestigious tasks. As it turned out, he did so in vain, for Hitler preferred Clemens Krauss as a conductor.[19] Nor had Knappertsbusch forgotten that Mann had supported and befriended his predecessor at the helm of the Munich Opera, Bruno Walter, a Jew. Pfitzner, for his part, never forgave Mann for abandoning "his

16. *Im Schatten Wagners*, 69.
17. Ibid., 73.
18. Ibid., 231, 261.
19. Cf. Kater, *The Twisted Muse*, 98f.

one-time national sentiments," as the "Protest" put it quite bluntly (PCW, 149). What was at stake for Pfitzner was the Germanness of Wagner, which he thought Mann had questioned and undermined.

The considerable political implications of this question were made clear in the pointed reference to the recent "uprising of Germany." This was tantamount to an invocation of Hitler, the supreme Wagnerian and protector of German music, and constituted a mortal danger. Mann wisely decided not to return to Munich from his lecture tour, for, as we now know, had he done so he would have been taken to Dachau.[20] Mann's expulsion from Munich by his fellow Wagnerians turned into a separation from Germany that was permanent. When in 1952, as an American citizen, he returned to Europe, he refused to settle in Germany. He preferred to die in Switzerland.

Mann scholarship has been slow to acknowledge the relevance of these events to the conception of *Doctor Faustus*. If politically unwelcome views on Wagner could lead to the loss of home and homeland, then music and the guardianship of Germany's musical heritage, too, could be hijacked by a reprehensible ideology. To Mann, the events surrounding his "national excommunication"—as he put it in his response to Pfitzner (PCW, 166)—were merely the tip of the iceberg. They pointed to a deeper, more far-reaching concatenation of music, politics, and German identity that decisively shaped his understanding of the prehistory of the Third Reich. Moreover, he himself was implicated in the growing politicization of music, even though in 1933 he had become one of the victims of that process. Mann was by no means the only victim, of course, for many Jewish musicians, among them Bruno Walter, were driven from their positions in German musical life. Against this background, the idea of writing a novel in which Germany would be conceptualized as the "self-realization of its music" in almost all the sinister consequences that recent historical experience had brought to light acquired considerable plausibility, even urgency. Strangely, Bruno Walter's fate, and the deep-seated hostility toward Jews in most branches of musical life in Germany, did not significantly shape that conceptualization, as Mann proved slow in recognizing the seriousness and the ramifications of antisemitism. Still, *Doctor Faustus* demanded to be written. The time for an unsparing reckoning, historical as well as autobiographical, had come. Mann had just concluded his four-part

20. Cf. *Im Schatten Wagners*, 328; Paul Egon Hübinger, "Thomas Mann und Reinhard Heydrich in den Akten des Reichsstatthalters v. Epp," *Vierteljahrshefte für Zeitgeschichte* 28 (1980): 111–143.

cycle of novels, *Joseph and His Brothers,* and was weighing various projects when, early in 1943, history tipped the scale decisively in favor of *Doctor Faustus.* In January of 1943, at Casablanca, the Western Allies agreed on the unconditional surrender of Germany as their ultimate goal, and in February, at Stalingrad, the war turned finally and decisively against Nazi Germany. Visible to all, the writing on the wall spelled "finis Germaniae."

Here, a word of caution is perhaps called for. By reconstructing the conceptual genealogy of *Doctor Faustus* I do not mean to suggest that the novel allegorizes Hitler and the Third Reich. Readers who approach the novel in this frame of mind will inevitably be confused and frustrated by the "constraints of allegorical exactitude."[21] No parallel can be drawn between Leverkühn and Hitler, or between Leverkühn's music and National Socialism. Nor is there any basis for the suspicion, first expressed by Ludwig Marcuse, that in *Doctor Faustus* some of Leverkühn's genius inadvertently rubs off on Nazi Germany. The critical category that truly illuminates the novel's design is not that of symbolic equivalence, but that of anticipation. Put simply, the spiritual and intellectual climate of Leverkühn's Germany anticipates Germany's turn to barbarism; the spirit in which some of Leverkühn's compositions are conceived anticipates the spirit of fascist Germany. The crucial trope here is that of seed and harvest. Mann introduces it early in the novel: "he who sows wind shall reap whirlwind" (DF, 38). The life of Leverkühn is therefore set in the era that precedes the advent of the Third Reich—in terms of music history, the post-Wagnerian era. Not incidentally, it is also the situation that Mann was confronted with as the literary heir to Wagner.

Doctor Faustus is often read as a "Deutschland-Roman," and rightly so. It might even be seen as Mann's attempt to answer the vexing question posed by Wagner: "What is German?" Chapter 14 of the novel, set in 1905, presents an interminable discussion of this subject among students at the University of Halle, young Leverkühn among them. The students bear *echt deutsch*–sounding names: one is called Deutschlin, another Teutleben. As they jump from one woolly profundity to another, what emerges from their nocturnal disquisition is a diffuse but strong sense of German cultural superiority. Other nations, Deutschlin declares, "have a much easier and more comfortable time intellectually," adding sententiously: "The Russians have profundity but no form. In the West they have form but no profundity. Only we Germans have both" (DF, 123). The earnest, but ignorant, idealism of these *Wandervogel*-type students betrays a striking intellectual

21. Fetzer, *Changing Perceptions,* 101.

arrogance. As it turns out, the entire atmosphere in which Leverkühn's socialization occurs is saturated with arrogance and pride in the cultural and musical achievements of Germany. What we find at the core of the Leverkühn figure, then, is the traditional cardinal sin of *superbia*. It caused the downfall of Doctor Faustus in the sixteenth-century chapbook; it also motivates Mann's Faustian artist to turn to the devil when he reaches the much-discussed creative impasse of post-Wagnerian music, which he believes can be overcome only with demonic aid.

Despite this strong affinity between Leverkühn and the hero of the German national myth, critics continue to question Mann's decision to use the sixteenth-century Faust myth as a metaphor for Germany. One wonders, though, whether they would persist with their reservations if they admitted that Mann's use of the myth by no means implies some ultimate condemnation of Germany. The Faustian subtext of the novel is actually woven from strands that connect it both to the *Faustbuch* and to Goethe's Faust.[22] Negotiating the traditional condemnation and the Goethean redemption of Faust, Mann deliberately keeps open the possibility of grace and redemption for Leverkühn as well as for his "fatherland."[23]

The historical weight of Mann's figure is further enhanced by several oblique links to the tragic life of Friedrich Nietzsche. Mann himself pointed out certain parallels: the visit to the brothel, the possibly deliberate infection with syphilis, the mental collapse at roughly the same stage in their lives. Furthermore, the date of Leverkühn's death, August 25, is identical to the date of Nietzsche's. Leverkühn's birthdate, on the other hand, rather recalls Mann's own: June 6.

More than by any literary association, the Germanness of Leverkühn is defined by his place of origin: Kaisersaschern. Again and again, his compositions are described as "music of Kaisersaschern" (DF, 92). Mann was obviously aware of the ideologically compromising implications of such a notion of art since he made a point of placing the chief advocate of the theory that all art bears the imprint of its place of origin—a certain Professor Georg Vogler—squarely among the fascist intellectuals of Munich (DF,

22. For a complete inventory of the Goethean elements in Mann's novel, see Günther Mahal, "Das 'hohe g.' Der Versuch, einem Konsonanten in Thomas Manns 'Doktor Faustus' auf die Spur zu kommen," in *Faust: Untersuchungen zu einem zeitlosen Thema* (Neuried: Ars Una, 1998), 623–60.

23. For a more complete discussion of this point, see my "Amazing Grace: Thomas Mann, Adorno, and the Faust Myth," in *Our Faust? Roots and Ramifications of a Modern German Myth*, ed. Reinhold Grimm and Jost Hermand (Madison: University of Wisconsin Press, 1987), 168–89.

383).[24] But even though Mann has Zeitblom repudiate that philosophy, we see the narrator remain a captive of it, as he keeps advertising Leverkühn's music as "music of Kaisersaschern." To some extent, Mann implicates himself as well. It was he who famously declared in 1938 that "Where I am, there is Germany."[25] Doctor Faustus echoes this proud statement: "Where I am, there is Kaisersaschern" (DF, 242). All attempts to grasp the specifically German character of Leverkühn's music, as imagined by Mann, must therefore be based upon a close look at Kaisersaschern itself. We know that Mann constructed his imagined community with great care in order to make certain that it could serve as an emblem of Germanness.[26] What, then, are its spiritual and cultural components? And how do they play out in Leverkühn's career?

At one point, Kaisersaschern is referred to as the "town of witches and eccentrics, with its stockpile of instruments and a Kaiser's tomb in its cathedral" (DF, 92). The town's eccentrics are explained as an indication of a latent collective neurosis, part of its late medieval atmosphere and heritage. This hereditary neurosis predisposes its inhabitants to commit irrational acts, when the occasion arises, such as the burning of books or similar atavisms. Steeped as it is in superstition, Leverkühn's decision to seek an enhancement of his creative powers by way of a syphilitic infection is perhaps the most extreme manifestation of his "hereditary" proneness to regression.

Appropriately, this typical German hometown has a predominantly Protestant population with a sizable Catholic minority. Zeitblom is Catholic, Leverkühn Protestant; each partakes, to changing degrees, of the national and universal spirit of his religious affiliation. Although no mention is made of it, Kaisersaschern must also be home to a Jewish community, since we are introduced to "the town's rabbi, Dr. Carlebach," who is described, stereotypically, as short, long-bearded, and—ominously—as "Talmudic" (DF, 10) in appearance. Is there a recognition of antisemitism in Leverkühn's hometown? We cannot tell; Zeitblom does not broach the matter. This, too, sets a pattern for the entire novel. For if we were to trust Zeitblom, we would have to conclude that there was no antisemitism in Germany—not at the universities, not in pre–World War I Munich, not in the various institutions of German musical life.

24. The easily recognizable real-life model for Vogler was Josef Nadler, author of the *Literaturgeschichte der deutschen Stämme und Landschaften* (1914 ff.).

25. Thomas Mann, *Essays*, vol. 4, *Achtung, Europa! 1933–1938*, ed. Hermann Kurzke and Stephan Stachorski (Frankfurt am Main: S. Fischer, 1995), 440.

26. Cf. Lieselote Voss, *Die Entstehung von Thomas Manns "Doktor Faustus"* (Tübingen: Max Niemeyer Verlag, 1955), 47–55.

Inevitably, Kaisersaschern is the site of Leverkühn's fated first encounter with music. This occurs, ominously enough, in the book's seventh
chapter, which features his uncle's magnificent warehouse for musical
instruments. It is described as a magical, "culturally bewitching" (DF, 44)
place, apt to stimulate the visitor's "acoustic fantasy." Also at his uncle's
house, young Leverkühn hears for the first time the string quartets of Haydn
and Mozart, and he begins himself to experiment with harmonic progres-
sions. The outlines of a distinctly "German" idea of music are discernible
already here when the precocious youth speaks about music as "ambiguity
as a system. . . . It's all relationship. . . . Order is everything" (DF, 43 f.). Despite the provincial character of the town, the atmosphere in Nikolaus
Leverkühn's house is anything but confining. His assistant is an Italian,
who lives as a boarder with Leverkühn; the warehouse attracts visitors
from near and far; there are business contacts with music centers as far
away as New York. For provincial Kaisersaschern, music is the only con-
duit to the world. Music is presented as having two sides: one provincial,
one cosmopolitan. These contradictory associations turn out to be fundamental to the way in which history and music are linked in the novel as a
whole; their nexus marks its philosophical nerve center.

The two-faced nature of all manifestations of Germanness found its
most significant articulation in the shadowy figure of the kaiser whose
ashes rest in the town's cathedral. This is Otto III, a hapless ruler whose
short life, from 980 to 1002, stands in opposite relation to his historical importance. Mann chose to bury Otto not in his actual resting place, which is
Aix-la-Chapelle, but in Kaisersaschern—an obviously significant "correction" of the historical record, comparable to the decision to transform
Faust into a musician. What is more, these two "adjustments" are linked, as
we gather from the rather pointed observation by the narrator that "[i]t was
not for nothing that [Leverkühn] was a son of the town in which Otto III lay
buried" (DF, 175). In other words, to the extent that Leverkühn composes
"music of Kaisersaschern," his music also reflects something of that shadowy figure from the past. Otto III does not occupy a particularly distinguished place in the collective memory of the Germans; he does, however,
in the source on which Mann relied in this matter: Erich Kahler's *Der
deutsche Charakter in der Geschichte Europas* (1937). Kahler portrays
Otto III as a key figure.[27] Put simply, Kahler's Otto III is the embodiment of
two conflicting tendencies within the German character: the desire both to

27. For a more thorough discussion of Mann and Kahler, see my "Erich Kahler, Thomas
Mann und Deutschland," in *Ethik und Ästhetik: Festschrift für Wolfgang Wittkowski*, ed.
Richard Fisher (Frankfurt am Main: Peter Lang, 1995), 509–18.

be German and something other than German. A Saxon on the throne of the Holy Roman Empire of the German Nation, Otto III wanted to be a Roman, or a Greek; this appeared to be an exemplary case of German "self-contempt" (DF, 39).

For Mann, as for Kahler, Otto III exemplified what was to become a tragic pattern in the Germans' relationship to the world. That relationship is awry in a fundamental way, resulting in the repeated failure of Germany to interact with its European neighbors in a nonaggressive, mutually beneficial way. The pendulum of German history keeps swinging between "a European Germany" and "a German Europe" (DF, 183). Universalism thus can take a benign and a noxious form; it, too, harbors contradictory possibilities. By connecting Leverkühn to Otto III, Mann reinforced the sense of ambiguity that attaches to Leverkühn's music: it is both German and universal, capable of pathological internalization and aggressive externalization. Conceptualized in these terms, the history of German music could indeed serve as a paradigm of German history.

Initially, the course of Leverkühn's development points in the direction of a benign form of universalism. First of all, his music tutor, Wendell Kretzschmar, is an American. Second, having immersed himself in Debussy and Ravel, Leverkühn turns to stylistic models that are "as un-Wagnerian as possible" (DF, 174). Further, among his early compositions are settings of Dante, Blake, and Verlaine. His first opera, Love's Labour's Lost, uses Shakespeare's English rather than a German translation. It is an opera buffa written in the international idiom of neoclassicism. His second opera, for a puppet theater, is on the subject of the "great sinner" Pope Gregory, and bears an unmistakable resemblance to Igor Stravinsky's L'Histoire du soldat. Judging by his early work, then, Leverkühn hardly seems fit to serve as a standard-bearer of German music.

Obviously, these early "cosmopolitan" compositions represent but one side of Leverkühn's creative potential. Quite a different side is first envisaged in chapter 22, the theoretical centerpiece of Doctor Faustus. Leverkühn has reached a crossroads: the compositional possibilities of the inherited musical idioms have lost their novelty and allure. Repetition and parody seem to be the only options left. The specter of sterility looms large and with it a general impasse of the entire culture that has come to look to music as its flagship. The fear that the great musical tradition of Germany may have exhausted itself was widespread. Leverkühn shares that fear. Unlimited creative freedom is thought to spell sterility and the eventual death of German culture. Paradoxically, it is self-imposed order that promises new creative freedom. If regression and barbarism are the only way out of the impasse, he is ready to "dare a barbarism" (DF, 259).

The narrator theorizes Leverkühn's regression as a "dialectic reversal" (DF, 203), true to the Hegelianism of Mann's musical advisor, Theodor W. Adorno. But Mann was a more astute psychologist than either Adorno or Hegel. Behind the narrator's back, as it were, he interprets Leverkühn's decision as an act of withdrawal—inward and backward. Leverkühn leaves Munich and moves to Pfeiffering to live and work in monastic isolation. He withdraws into his Germanness. Tellingly, when he travels to Italy he carries with him even more "Kaisersaschern" than usual. Facing the impending impasse, he turns his thoughts to the great German tradition of absolute music. What made it great and gave it its universal appeal? It was Beethoven's decision, he reasons, to elevate the development section of the sonata form to the central event of musical discourse. Brahms continued and extended this practice; he subjected the organization of musical material to the principle of variation, which Leverkühn considers to be "archaic," a "residue" (DF, 204) of earlier musical practice. This way an unheard-of freedom of subjective expression was gained. Self-imposed order and limitation yielded a new dimension of freedom; most importantly, it brought Germany musical hegemony. What Leverkühn concludes from this does not lack a certain grim logic: reestablishing the principle of order, and radicalizing it, appears to be the most promising way out. The "archaic" ideal of the "strict style," he determines, must therefore be extended to comprise the entire composition: there shall be no "free" note any longer; music will be cleansed of all ornamentation and convention. There shall be "complete organization" (ibid.) of every note. In chapter 22, Leverkühn is already well on his way. He has come to realize that dissonances must be left unresolved; and he has begun to experiment, in the manner of Hector Berlioz, Robert Schumann, and Alban Berg, with secretly coded musical figures that permeate the entire composition. Thus, in his setting of Brentano poems, he employs a short five-note figure—h–e–a–e–es (in English notation: B–E–A–E–E-flat)—which denotes the prostitute (hetaera) Esmeralda. One of the poems ("O lieb Mädel") is in fact addressed to a prostitute who has transmitted to the poet the syphilitic "poison." Here, then, for the first time, the strictly regulated permutations of a musical figure determine the inner organization of the composition. By that time, Leverkühn already carries the disease; the demonic boost to his creativity is showing its efficacy.

Whether Zeitblom's representation of Leverkühn's thought processes in chapter 22 may be considered a fair summary of the steps that led Arnold Schoenberg, the principal model for Mann's hero, to his invention of a new compositional system—the so-called twelve-tone technique—remains an open question. Some music historians view this whole proposi-

tion with skepticism.[28] Not so Schoenberg himself, of course, who protested Mann's use of his "intellectual property" for a "diabolical" purpose.
Schoenberg's overreaction may have had another, hidden cause, for he had
only limited confidence in the philosophical interpretation of the new music by Mann's musical prompter, Adorno.[29] It took years before Schoenberg
could be soothed, and, although he did eventually come to a reconciliation
with Mann, he was unable to make this public before his death in 1951.[30]

We need not further pursue the notorious Schoenberg matter since it
does not affect the crucial question posed by Mann's novel: Does Leverkühn's career in any way illuminate the road Germany took in the twentieth century? This question may now be answered in the affirmative even
though we must bear in mind that Germany is represented in this novel
not only by Leverkühn but also by his loquacious narrator. Zeitblom's
overt nationalism seems to set him apart from his composer friend. On a
deeper level, however, Zeitblom's and Leverkühn's Germanness comple-
ment each other. Leverkühn, to be sure, does not emerge as the emphatically *deutsche Tonsetzer* (German composer) that the subtitle of the novel
advertises until chapter 22. The choice of the word *Tonsetzer* is significant
in that it signals a kinship with certain nationalist purists that made a
point of substituting *Tonsetzer* for *Komponist*, and *Tonkunst* for *Musik*.[31]
As Leverkühn withdraws from the world and becomes preoccupied with
the German musical heritage, he seems to reflect larger collective trends,
such as Germany's political isolation and growing nationalism prior to
1914. His withdrawal has a very specific purpose, namely, to collect himself
and prepare the great "breakthrough" that will project his music—German

28. For a recent, somewhat skeptical gloss of the matter, see Volker Scherliess, "Zur
Musik im 'Doktor Faustus,'" in *"und was werden die Deutschen sagen??" Thomas Manns
Roman "Doktor Faustus,"* ed. Hans Wisskirchen and Thomas Sprecher (Lübeck: Verlag
Dräger, 1997), 113–152.

29. Jan Maegaard, the Danish Schoenberg scholar, reports that Schoenberg refused to endorse Adorno's *Philosophie der neuen Musik* and left instructions to ban Adorno from access
to his papers; see his "Zu Theodor W. Adornos Rolle im Mann/Schönberg Streit," in *Gedenk-
schrift für Thomas Mann,* ed. Rolf Wiecker (Copenhagen: Verlag Text & Kontext, 1975), 215–22.

30. For a full documentation of the Mann–Schoenberg matter, see Bernhold Schmid,
"Neues zum 'Doktor Faustus'—Streit zwischen Arnold Schoenberg und Thomas Mann," in
Augsburger Jahrbuch für Musikwissenschaft 6 (1989): 149–79; 7 (1990): 177–92. Cf. also
Patrick Carnegy, *Faust as Musician: A Study of Thomas Mann's Novel "Doctor Faustus"*
(New York: New Directions, 1973), 37–54.

31. Pfitzner favored this terminology. As for Mann, he was the cofounder in 1918 of the
"Hans Pfitzner-Verein für deutsche Tonkunst" and usually referred to the creator of *Palestrina* as *Tonsetzer* and *Tondichter* (GW X, 417–22; XII, 423–26).

music—onto the rest of the world. The collective mind-set of Germany in
1914 might very well be described in similarly expansionist terms. Germany, too, as the author of the *Reflections* came to realize, strove for a
breakthrough, for "a place in the sun." It desired the status of a world power
commensurate with its cultural achievements. "Kaisersaschern wants to
become a world city" (DF, 324) is Leverkühn's cryptic comment about the
outbreak of war in 1914. The unmistakable note of skepticism in this comment cannot conceal the fact that, as an artist, he is pursuing similar goals
of musical hegemony. Furthermore, much of what we are told about the motivation behind Leverkühn's striving resonates uncomfortably with later
developments in Germany. His desire to eliminate from the musical work
any and all elements that cannot be considered "thematic" in order to realize his ideal of total organization does make it sound as though Leverkühn's music is being viewed as a staging ground for certain excesses of organization and control of a much more concrete and sinister kind.

Chapter 25, the dialogue with the devil, is famous for its rhetorical
fireworks and theological-philosophical sophistication. In the ongoing discourse on music, however, this chapter breaks no new ground; its function
is to summarize and clarify what has gone before. The hourglass is set; the
fine, red sand is running. The devil appears not for the purpose of proposing,
but merely of ratifying the demonic pact into which Leverkühn entered
when, having sought out Esmeralda in Bratislava, he insisted on the con-
summation of his desire despite her warning him that her body was infected.

What is being clarified here are the context and motivation of Leverkühn's Faustian pact. Musical composition has indeed become so difficult
that the creative impulse seems paralyzed, and the artist rendered impo-
tent. The survival of the entire culture as Leverkühn knows it seems at
stake. Turning to demonic powers has become not only tempting, but, given
his Faustian arrogance, totally irresistible. While Leverkühn may think
that he is concerned only with the future of music, it is made clear that
other, less innocuous desires are driving him on. The inner voice he thinks
of as the devil spells it out quite unambiguously: "you will lead, you will
set the march for the future" (DF, 258). Once he has broken through, the
ardently desired musical hegemony will be his. It seems fair to assume, here,
that Mann knew—perhaps from Adorno—Schoenberg's much quoted remark to Josef Rufer that the dodecaphonic method of composition would
ensure the domination of German music "for another hundred years."[32]

32. Willi Reich, *Arnold Schönberg der konservative Revolutionär* (Munich: DTV, 1974),
139; Alexander L. Ringer, *Arnold Schoenberg: The Composer as Jew* (Oxford: Oxford University Press, 1990), 18, 165.

However that may be, we have arrived at the most advanced point in Mann's thinking about the ambiguities inherent in the notion of German music.[33] In his *Reflections*, and for some time thereafter, Mann held an uncritical view of what had become a commonplace: that great music produced by German composers was universal; that German music spoke to all the world ("diesen Kuß der ganzen Welt") and was appreciated by everyone. The work of Wagner was the most recent and perhaps strongest proof of this seemingly obvious truth. By the time of *Doctor Faustus*, however, history had taught Mann that the pretense to universality, however innocuous and inoffensive it may initially have been, harbored a potentially aggressive mentality. In due course, this nationalistic habit of mind induced most Germans to believe that the perceived hegemony of German music somehow justified and, in the last analysis, legitimized Germany's push for comparable political hegemony. This sort of reasoning found its most infuential articulation in the work of Houston Stewart Chamberlain and was fundamental to Nazi *Weltanschauung*.

It is a testimony to the lasting impact of the Wagner affair of 1933 that Mann wrote his two most prominent detractors into the musical discourse of the novel. Works by Pfitzner and Richard Strauss serve as signposts on Leverkühn's road to his pact with the devil.[34] Strauss was by no means the fanatical nationalist that Pfitzner was, even though he served the Nazis for two years as president of the Reich Music Chamber.[35] Nonetheless, his historical role is cast in ambiguity. *Salome* is paid some equivocal compliments; more significantly Leverkühn's trip in chapter 19 to the fabled Austrian premiere of Strauss's "hit" opera (DF, 166) in Graz turns out to have been the pretext for continuing on to his fateful encounter with Esmeralda.

Pfitzner is implicated in an even more covert manner.[36] When the devil promises Leverkühn fabulous spells of inspiration, Pfitzner's theory

33. For a discussion of the history of dodecaphonic music after Schoenberg, see Klaus Kropfinger, "'Schönberg est mort?'—Rückfragen an ein Paradigma," in Klaus Kropfinger, *Über Musik im Bilde: Schriften zur Analyse, Ästhetik und Rezeption in Musik und Bildender Kunst*, ed. Bodo Bischoff et al. (Köln-Rheinkassel: Verlag Christoph Dohr, 1995), 535–54.

34. For a more detailed discussion, see my "'Salome' und 'Palestrina' als historische Chiffren: Zur musikgeschichtlichen Codierung in Thomas Manns 'Doktor Faustus,'" in *Wagner—Nietzsche—Thomas Mann: Festschrift für Eckhard Heftrich*, ed. Heinz Gockel et al. (Frankfurt am Main: Vittorio Klostermann, 1993), 69–82.

35. For a balanced assessment of Strauss's role in the Third Reich, see Michael H. Kater, "Richard Strauss: Jupiter Compromised," in his *Composers of the Nazi Era: Eight Portraits* (New York: Oxford University Press, 2000), 211–63.

36. On Mann and Pfitzner, see my "The Rivalry for Wagner's Mantle: Strauss, Pfitzner, Mann," in *Re-Reading Wagner*, ed. Reinhold Grimm and Jost Hermand (Madison: University

of inspiration, his famous *Einfallslehre*, serves as the theoretical backdrop to their disquisitions on the problem of musical inspiration.[37] Leverkühn is assured that truly great musical ideas will come to him as in a divine dictation—as *"seliges Diktat"* (DF, 317). This is precisely the metaphor Pfitzner used in act I of his "musical legend" for the magical moment when Palestrina, his alter ego, receives the musical idea for the "Kyrie" from angels on high. With the great Mass thus conceived, Palestrina will become the legendary "savior" of music—a fantasy that obsessed not only Pfitzner but Schoenberg as well. It also energizes Leverkühn's Faustian ambition. What would happen—we might imagine his reasoning to have been—if there were no more great music? The answer is unthinkable but clear: the end of German culture—chaos! But music, "Kultur,"—"das ganze Spiel," as Palestrina puts it so succinctly, is deemed an absolute, unquestionable necessity. The mere thought of the possibility of its disappearance apparently triggered chimerical, apocalyptic fears that could easily be transformed into deadly hostility toward all imagined threats to "holy German art": the Jews, the Bolsheviks, the "Asiatic" hordes.

Given the hegemonic designs of Leverkühn's project, should we not be able to perceive a growing nationalism in his compositions? No such development is discernable. If the *Apocalypsis* and the *The Lamentation of Doctor Faustus*, the two culminating compositions, were intended to be read as preludes to the German catastrophe, Mann would have had to bend the trajectory of Leverkühn's oeuvre more clearly in the direction of the cultural agenda of National Socialism. This is not the case. On the contrary, there can be no doubt that the Nazis would have labeled Leverkühn's music degenerate, an example of "cultural Bolshevism" (DF, 409); they would have banned his work and silenced his voice. How, then, can Leverkühn's work be taken as the prefiguration of Germany's road to barbarism if his work is diametrically opposed to all Nazi notions of "healthy" German music?

---

of Wisconsin Press, 1993), 136–58; and "'Der gute, alte Antisemitismus.' Hans Pfitzner, Bruno Walter und der Holocaust," *Bruckner-Probleme: Internationales Kolloquium, 7.–9. Oktober 1996 Berlin*, ed. Albrecht Riethmüller (Stuttgart: Franz Steiner Verlag, 1999), 215–28. See also Michael H. Kater, "Hans Pfitzner: Magister Teutonicus Miser," in *Composers of the Nazi Era*, 144–82.

37. For a subtle analysis of the opera's discourse on inspiration, see Ulrich Weisstein, "'Die letzte Häutung.' Two German 'Künstleropern' of the Twentieth Century: Hans Pfitzner's 'Palestrina' and Paul Hindemith's 'Mathis der Maler,'" in *German Literature and Music: An Aesthetic Fusion: 1890–1989*, ed. Klaus Reschke and Howard Pollack (Munich: Wilhelm Fink Verlag, 1992), 193–236.

We must bear in mind here that Leverkühn's early work was conceived in a distinctly cosmopolitan spirit and that this cosmopolitan potential is just as much part of Kaisersaschern as its demonic dimension. It is important to note that his Faustian ambition to revolutionize music entails a renunciation of his earlier benign universalism. At the same time it represents the perversion of universalism since it aims at domination and cultural hegemony. Leverkühn is well aware of this deformation of his heritage— "Kaisersaschern wants to become a world city"—and begins to strive for a nonhegemonic universality that would be suggestive of a European Germany, rather than a Germanized Europe. To be sure, his culminating works are drawn from two eminently German subjects: the apocalyptic oratorio is based on a series of engravings by Albrecht Dürer, his Faust cantata on the sixteenth-century chapbook. And yet both these compositions rise above any narrow notions of Germanness. The oratorio is the setting of biblical texts. The cantata is "stylistically linked to Monteverdi" (DF, 513); Faust is made to appear as the brother of Orpheus; and "Faust's descent into hell" (DF, 513) evokes "La course à l'abîme" in Hector Berlioz's dramatic legend on the same subject. It is on account of this transnational spirit, wishing to subvert and to revoke the nationalism of his Faustian striving, that Leverkühn's last work can be viewed as "a work of liberation" (DF, 510). Music is to be liberated from its latent nationalism. It is to become a spiritually less burdened, psychologically less tortured form of art—an art that will again be "on a first-name basis with humanity" (DF, 339).

This reading of Leverkühn's work stands in accord with Mann's comment on German nationalism in a speech he gave in October 1943, soon after he had begun to write the novel. The "monstrous German attempt at world domination," he observed, "is nothing but a distorted and unfortunate expression of a 'universalism' that is innate in the German character." In its uncorrupted, "purer" and "nobler" form it had "won the sympathy and admiration of the world." It was the desire for power and domination that "corrupted this universalism and turned it into evil." And looking beyond Hitler's Reich, he expressed his "trust that German universalism will again find a way to its old place of honor" and contribute to "the spiritual enrichment of the world" (A, 35). Leverkühn's trajectory by and large exemplifies this triadic schema.

Mann, however, did not subscribe to the notion of a dialectical progression that is crucial to Adorno's philosophy, with its implications of inevitability and of a higher, eventually redeeming purpose. Adorno did help Mann to imagine Leverkühn's late works, but the novel's overall vision of German history, of music, and of their entanglement, is entirely Mann's own.[38] In the last analysis, the paradox on which *Doctor Faustus* is constructed remains unresolved: music is both national and universal.

On the crucial question of agency—what ultimately determines the history of music—Mann clearly leaned in the direction of human agency. His conception of history may be characterized, in current terminology, as intentionalist, whereas Adorno's was structuralist. In Adorno's *Philosophy of New Music*, the progress of music is deduced from the dynamics inherent in the "musical material" itself. At any given point in time, "certain things are no longer possible" (DF, 256) because they have lost their validity. Hence the inexorable progress "in the historical movement of the musical material" (ibid.); hence the prohibitive difficulties of composing—as Pfitzner's Palestrina is painfully aware—"at the end of a great era" in musical culture. For Mann, on the other hand, the notion of an individual human being making choices under desperate circumstances and with far-reaching moral and political implications was indispensable, all the more so since any rewriting of the Faust myth entails questions of sin and guilt, damnation, and salvation. In this regard, as with the question of German culture as a whole, the book offers a resolution that is neither damning nor exculpatory. The paradox of music turns out to be paradigmatic of the larger "religious paradox" (DF, 515) of "hope beyond hopelessness." Overtly Mann's novel appears to end in a condemnation of Faust, of Leverkühn, of Germany. Covertly, however, through a subtly interwoven subtext on grace, the possibility of redemption is maintained—most hauntingly in Leverkühn's last composition, through the final "high G of a cello" (ibid.), which may well be taken to signify grace.

As a novel about German history, *Doctor Faustus* reveals, in the light of present historical consciousness, one serious flaw: it portrays Germany as a country in which there is no antisemitism.[39] In a book that attempts a psychohistorical reading of German history, this blind spot constitutes a serious and problematic misrepresentation, especially when the focus is on "the most German of the arts" and when the antisemitism in the country's musical culture was, by 1943, a matter of historical record. But as an imaginative exploration of the role of music in German culture, as a probing, unsparing, and challenging examination of the nexus between German his-

---

38. This is the gist of the argument presented by the chief editor of the works of Adorno, Rolf Tiedemann, "'Mitdichtende Einfühlung.' Adornos Beiträge zum 'Doktor Faustus,'" in *Frankfurter Adorno Blätter* 1 (1992): 9–33.

    39. For a comprehensive discussion of this matter, see Ruth Kluger, "Jewish Characters in Thomas Mann's Fiction," in *Horizonte: Festschrift für Herbert Lehnert*, ed. Hannelore Mundt et al. (Tübingen: Max Niemeyer Verlag, 1990), 161–72.

tory and its most highly prized cultural commodity, Mann's *Doctor Faustus* is unrivaled.

Guide to Further Reading

Applegate, Celia. "What is German Music? Reflections on the Role of Art in the Creation of the Nation." *German Studies Review* 15 (winter 1992): 21–32.

Carnegy, Patrick. *Faust as Musician: A Study of Thomas Mann's Novel "Doctor Faustus."* New York: New Directions, 1973.

Fetzer, John. *Changing Perceptions of Thomas Mann's "Doctor Faustus": Criticism 1947–1992.* Columbia, S.C.: Camden House, 1996.

Friedländer, Saul. *Nazi Germany and the Jews.* Vol. I. *The Years of Persecution, 1933–1939.* New York: HarperCollins, 1997.

Kater, Michael H. *Composers of the Nazi Era: Eight Portraits.* New York: Oxford University Press, 2000.

———. *The Twisted Muse: Musicians and Their Music in the Third Reich.* New York: Oxford University Press, 1997.

Mann, Thomas. *Addresses Delivered at the Library of Congress, 1942–49.* Washington, D.C.: Library of Congress, 1963.

———. *Doctor Faustus.* Trans. John E. Woods. New York: Knopf, 1997.

———. *Letters of Thomas Mann, 1889–1955.* Ed. and trans. Richard and Clara Winston. New York: Knopf, 1971.

———. *Pro and Contra Wagner.* Trans. Allan Blunden. Chicago: University of Chicago Press, 1985.

———. *The Story of a Novel: The Genesis of "Doctor Faustus."* Trans. Richard and Clara Winston. New York: Knopf, 1961.

Nietzsche, Friedrich. *The Birth of Tragedy* and *The Case of Wagner.* Ed. and trans. Walter Kaufmann. New York: Vintage Books, 1967.

Vaget, Hans Rudolf. "Amazing Grace: Thomas Mann, Adorno, and the Faust Myth." In *Our Faust? Roots and Ramifications of a Modern German Myth.* Ed. Reinhold Grimm and Jost Hermand. Madison: University of Wisconsin Press, 1987.

Vaget, Hans Rudolf, ed. *Im Schatten Wagners: Thomas Mann über Richard Wagner: Texte und Zeugnisse 1895–1955.* Frankfurt am Main: Fischer Taschenbuch Verlag, 1999.

Culture, Society, and Politics in the Cosmos of "Hans Pfitzner the German"

MICHAEL H. KATER

For Hans Mommsen on His Seventieth Birthday

It is a truism that the hypernationalism on the part of right-wing Germans after 1918 grew out of a hypersensitivity to Germany's defeat in World War I. Yet this nationalism also had roots in the superpatriotism of those who had dreamed of Germany's international "place in the sun" before the outbreak of war in 1914. One such patriot-turned-nationalist might have been the composer Hans Pfitzner, even though his extreme nationalism can be documented only for the post–World War I period. Music in particular, as the most lofty facet of German *Kultur*, had played a central role in shaping German identity. Internationally, too, a consensus prevailed regarding the superiority of the German in all music.[1] Richard Wagner bore more than just a fair share of responsibility for this universal belief. But after Wagner, it was Pfitzner who consciously redefined this superiority in much more militant terms than even Wagner would have intended.

The possible sources of Pfitzner's specific brand of nationalism become clear after a look at his life history. First, he was a German born in 1869 in czarist Russia. (Like Hitler, several prominent Nazis were born outside Germany: Rudolf Hess in Egypt, for instance, and Walter Richard Darré in Argentina.) Although he was only two years old when his family moved to Frankfurt, Pfitzner's self-awareness as a "foreigner" probably was deep-

---

1. Celia Applegate, "What Is German Music? Reflections on the Role of Art in the Creation of the German Nation," *German Studies Review* 15 (winter 1992): 21–32; Albrecht Rieth-müller, "Ferruccio Busoni und die Hegemonie der Deutschen Musik," in *Nationaler Stil und europäische Dimension in der Musik der Jahrhundertwende*, ed. Helga de la Motte-Haber (Darmstadt: Wissenschaftliche Buchgesellschaft, 1991), 65.

seated and drove him to seek especially close bonds with the home of his forefathers. Pfitzner enjoyed only moderate success as a musician until he was almost forty, when in 1908 he was offered the position of opera director and head of the conservatory in Strasbourg in the German *Reichsland* of Alsace-Lorraine. This high-profile appointment in what was then considered an imperialist western outpost of the Wilhelmine Empire against the French surely must have shaped Pfitzner's national consciousness in the face of allegedly inferior outsiders.

All the greater, then, was his disappointment when he had to depart from Strasbourg after Germany's defeat in 1918. First, he had to abandon virtually all of his material possessions. Second, he lost a respectable position that could have served as a platform for further advancement. And third, he gave up a ready identification with a German bastion of cultural imperialism, which had served to strengthen his sense of belonging with the Kaiser's subjects. This three-fold disaster was exacerbated by the circumstances of his relocation within the national heartland: impoverished, he required the help of friends to settle himself in the small Bavarian town of Schondorf and secure his livelihood as composer, conductor, and teacher. That the most important of these friends was Jewish—the wealthy right-wing publicist Paul Nikolaus Cossmann—may have instilled in him the belief, rampant among German patriots who felt cheated out of victory, that the Jews had stabbed Germany in the back and now held all Germans in their merciless grip.

Endowed with a sharp perception of human character, an original wit, and superior intelligence, Pfitzner, perhaps spurred by the lack of success in his early professional life, had always rationalized that he was part of an invisible cultural elite upholding the traditional German values of fealty, honesty, bravery, and the ability to concentrate on spiritual essence. That last quality especially was one that Pfitzner and many like-minded Germans believed to be utterly lacking in non-Germans and, indeed, was something that only Germans could possess or reflect upon. Pfitzner expressed this sentiment through his identification with the hero of his opera *Palestrina*, his first artistic success that premiered under Bruno Walter in Munich in 1917.[2] Set to Pfitzner's own libretto, this stage work was largely autobiographical. Its protagonist was a gloomily contemplative composer of church

2. Such sentiments at that time found expression in other ephemeral German ideas such as that of the *Bund* or a secret *Reich*. See, e.g., Friedrich Hielscher, *Das Reich* (Berlin: Das Reich, 1931); for a critcal assessment, see Kurt Sontheimer, *Antidemokratisches Denken in der Weimarer Republik: Die politischen Ideen des deutschen Nationalismus zwischen 1918 und 1933*, 4th ed. (Munich: Nymphenburger Verlags-Handlung, 1962), esp. 280–306.

music who braved the Council of Trent in the mid-sixteenth century, just as Pfitzner saw himself as standing up to an ignorant mediocrity. The work reflects Pfitzner's grievances during the Weimar Republic, feeling unappreciated and unrecognized by the cultural establishment and sharing in the larger, national impotence and shame following the "undeserved" military collapse.

Pfitzner's compositions may be said to have a German quality on two counts. First, they were virtually all in the postromantic vein that was the currency primarily of German composers (Pfitzner was influenced by Schumann and Brahms, but also Wagner). Second, they favored German subjects of an often brooding and contemplative nature. Apart from *Palestrina*, other examples were Pfitzner's earlier opera *Der arme Heinrich* (1891–93), the libretto of which was patterned on the epos of the German minnesinger Hermann von der Aue. In his opera *Die Rose vom Liebesgarten* (1897–1900), Pfitzner employed motifs by the German romantic painter Hans Thoma; as in *Der arme Heinrich*, Wagner's influence was audible, as was that of Carl Maria von Weber. Nonoperatic successes included the cantata *Von deutscher Seele* (1921), which used texts by the German romantic poet Joseph Freiherr von Eichendorff, and the Piano Concerto in E-flat Major, completed in 1922. This work, with its opening marked "pompous, with force and verve" and featuring a rhapsodic solo in strong contradistinction to what sounds like a march in the orchestra, still impresses some listeners as "typically German" in its "contemplative intricacy."[3]

Pfitzner surrounded himself with a circle of admirers who appreciated his postromantic style as well as his brand of cultural pessimism, patterned after Schopenhauer and eschewing all the political, ideological, and cultural modernism that the Weimar Republic came to stand for. As a reactionary harking back to imperial days, the Reformation, and the Middle Ages, Pfitzner spurned any flowers of the Enlightenment that had now come to full bloom in the Weimar Republic, especially the "Western"-influenced parliamentary democracy that he traced to France and the United States. Anything American was anathema to him, particularly in the 1920s, when modernist German composers—some of them enjoying commercial success—gravitated toward Americanisms: Kurt Weill with his use of jazz in stage works like *Die Dreigroschenoper;* or Paul Hindemith with similar inclinations and an affinity for radio and film; or Ernst Krenek, whose hugely popular work *Jonny spielt auf* featured a black jazz violinist posing as a se-

3. See Ingo Harden's liner notes for the compact disc recording of the concerto, Marco Polo 8.223162, performed by the Slovak Radio Symphony Orchestra of Bratislava, conducted by Herbert Beissel, with soloist Wolf Harden.

ducer of white women. Their harmonic boldness also offended Pfitzner's sense of musical tradition, but not as much as Schoenberg and the Second Viennese School's twelve-tone method, which represented an even worse perversion.

Everything that Pfitzner subsumed under the rubric of "Weimar gutter culture" came under attack in his three-volume *Collected Writings* published between 1926 and 1929.[4] The most acrid of these writings included his "Futurist Danger" (against Ferruccio Busoni, Weill's teacher) and "The New Aesthetics of Musical Impotence" (originally published in 1920 as an attack against Paul Bekker, the prominent Frankfurt music critic who, as a Jew, offended conservatives such as Pfitzner by daring to write about Beethoven). Anything negative that did not readily fit his label of Western degeneracy, Pfitzner ascribed to Eastern Bolshevism, a category more convenient for condemning political phenomena than strictly cultural categories.

The crude polarization between anything good, which was German, and anything bad, which was alien (from either East or West), made up the persona of "Pfitzner the German," a warrior against the perpetrators of the current state of corrosion and destruction: the Jews. Pfitzner the German was supported by his cultist followers, who attributed to his credo a ready-made solution to many endemic ills. In Pfitzner's Manichean worldview, the Jew was the opposite of the German. The November Revolution of 1918 had been a "Jewish-Bolshevik Revolution"; Weimar was therefore a "Jewish Republic." He accused Jewish music critics like Bekker and Alfred Einstein of rationalizing everything instead of listening to their hearts, and he charged his assistant conductor in Strasbourg, Otto Klemperer, with constantly hatching plots to unseat him. Pfitzner was able to tolerate his Jewish friend Cossmann only because he, as a convert to Catholicism, was filled with Jewish self-hatred and fierce antisemitism. Likewise, Pfitzner's friend Bruno Walter, another Jewish convert to Catholicism, did not share in the glorification of Weimar modernism and had been kind enough to premiere Pfitzner's *Palestrina*. Significantly, though, even during the last years of the republic and into the Third Reich, Pfitzner's relationship with both Cossmann and Walter began to deteriorate, although he later tried, out of a sense of Teutonic loyalty, to save Cossmann from the Nazi concentration camps.

Would all this have placed Pfitzner close to the National Socialist movement, even before its Führer Adolf Hitler assumed power on 30 January 1933? Pfitzner certainly would appear to have been predestined to join

4. Hans Pfitzner, *Gesammelte Schriften*, 3 vols. (Augsburg: Filser, 1926–29).

the Nazi movement, but because he had such a high opinion of himself, he wanted something in return. Indeed, his extreme elitism became an obstacle to a closer relationship with the Nazi movement right from the beginning, when Hitler visited Pfitzner in a Munich hospital early in 1923 as he lay recovering from a gallbladder operation.

They had been introduced by Hitler's aide, a mutual friend who, like many ultranationalists, admired Pfitzner's music. Pfitzner was already nationally known, while Hitler was known only in the Bavarian heartland. The two men talked mainly about the curse of Jewry, but the politician departed in anger, for Pfitzner had tried to intellectualize his antisemitism, whereas Hitler relied on raw emotions. The haughty composer must have attempted to impress Hitler with his air of superiority. Essentially, this was a meeting of two forceful egos, one on his way to power as the other battled against an army of real or imagined enemies. Ironically, and sadly for Pfitzner, Hitler walked away from that meeting convinced that the composer must be part Jewish, noting his "rabbi's beard" and his arcane and abstract mode of argumentation.

Pfitzner never joined the Nazi Party, though nevertheless expected it to regard him as the official composer of the Nazi movement. By 1933 he thought he deserved this, having failed to prosper in the "Jewish Republic." Always in the shadow of Richard Strauss, five years his senior and widely regarded as the quintessentially German postromantic composer, Pfitzner met with little national success after *Palestrina* beyond his coterie of cultist followers. His only other opera after that, *Das Herz* of 1931, set sentimental music to a maudlin medieval love story in which the purity of the soul wins against the forces of the devil. Its libretto was written by a former crime-fiction author, and, like all of Pfitzner's stage works, it highlighted the "Germanic" concept of salvation as its central theme.

After January 1933 Pfitzner joined the circles surrounding Nazi Party philosopher Alfred Rosenberg in hopes of being rewarded with an official cultural post. He was still a permanent guest conductor at the Bavarian State Opera, but he had difficulty getting along with resident conductor Hans Knappertsbusch, himself unquestionably loyal to the new regime. When the position of Generalintendant of the Berlin municipal opera opened that summer, Joseph Goebbels, the Gauleiter of Berlin and new propaganda minister, apparently heeded Hitler's suspicions and never even considered him. Although friend and foe would agree that as a composer Pfitzner ranked second only to Strauss, he suffered other setbacks which he himself, as the self-appointed cultural guardian of Germanness, had never expected. He was, for instance, pressured not to attend the Salzburg Festival later that summer, reportedly because of bad relations between Berlin and Vienna, but most likely because of personal chicanery (since, as he duly noted, his nemesis Strauss suffered no such impediments). He was also pensioned from his post as a professor of the Munich conservatory in May 1934, ostensibly because he had reached the mandatory retirement age of sixty-five. Pfitzner, however, knew that exceptions to this rule were always possible, and therefore considered his forced retirement as a punishment for unknown transgressions. Worse, his pension was fixed at a very low level, which deeply humiliated him. Finally, although Pfitzner had been appointed to the presidial council of the newly formed Reich Music Chamber under Strauss, he felt that his works were being passed over for official performances and that he was constantly overlooked for cultural posts.

Pfitzner was prominent and impertinent enough to complain to Prussian prime minister Hermann Göring in early 1935, but the politician and head of the Berlin State Opera told him: "We have saved Germany, and whether you write a couple of operas more or less is irrelevant." Pfitzner audaciously countered: "I did not just compose music, but I also worked on behalf of Germany wherever and whenever I was able to. Please open this volume of my collected works!"[5] Although Göring then promised to pay more attention to Pfitzner's oeuvre in his opera house, Hitler continued to snub the composer, failing to consider him as conductor for the annual Nuremberg Nazi Party rallies in favor of musicians like Wilhelm Furtwängler, and avoiding meeting with him even when they were both in the same town. Therein lies the tragicomic irony of Pfitzner's fate in the Third Reich. Until the end of Nazi rule, Pfitzner, widely acclaimed as the most German of all composers, hoped for a meeting of the minds with the Führer of the Greater German Reich. Hitler, however, refused to believe that Pfitzner was wholly "Aryan." In June 1943 Goebbels noted in his diary that the Führer was "strongly opposed to Pfitzner. He thinks him to be a half-Jew, which, according to his personal records, he certainly is not."[6]

Nevertheless, Pfitzner never gave up his claim to official recognition as *the* German composer of the Third Reich. If he could not attain his goal through the good graces of the highest echelons, perhaps he could succeed with lesser leaders. He faced two important obstacles in this quest. First, he had to contend with the Nazi leaders' utter cultural philistinism and ignorance of his earlier success. By 1933 Pfitzner's musical successes may have paled in comparison with that of Strauss, but in the 1920s and even

5. Pfitzner protocol, 9 February 1935, Österreichische National-Bibliothek, Vienna, Musiksammlung, F [henceforth OW] 68/Pfitzner.

6. *Die Tagebücher von Joseph Goebbels*, Part 2, *Diktate, 1941–1945*, 16 vols., ed. Elke Fröhlich (Munich: Saur, 1993–96), 8:448.

184   MICHAEL H. KATER

earlier he could lay claim to more than mere national recognition.[7] The
leadership of the regime was foolish not to see this and make use of it in the
characteristic manner of totalitarian dictatorships. The second obstacle
was his own personality. After endless personal affronts, Pfitzner emerged
neither politically naive nor, worse, opportunistic (however one interprets
the facts) but rather conceited, even narcissistic, identifying himself and his
entire art with the stream of national cultural history. The moniker "Pfitzner the German" meant, quite simply, that Pfitzner was as German as was
music itself. More, his music was the *most* German in the tradition of Beethoven or Wagner, whom he regarded as equals. This was not just a personal quirk of a supreme egotist. In regarding himself and "German" music this way, Pfitzner, albeit as an extreme example, joined an established
German tradition of nationalist hubris.[8]

Because Hans Pfitzner could not interest Hitler, Goebbels, or Göring in
his work or in his personal situation, he tried to make inroads among their
underlings. Beginning with Rosenberg's cohorts in 1933, he shamelessly offered his services as composer or conductor to any number of party or state-
sponsored events operating on a secondary or tertiary level. This kept him
from having to join the Nazi Party or any of its affiliate organizations. The
lesser leaders, on the other hand, were flattered by the attention from the
composer and were often inclined to exploit him. Thus Pfitzner made appearances as a musician and speaker at functions for Nazi student organizations in the mid-1930s, and by 1944 they in turn sponsored full-fledged
Pfitzner programs. On the occasion of Pfitzner's birthday on 5 May, the composer who otherwise complained that the official Germany was neglecting
him reaped homage at the annual "Pfitzner Weeks" run by Rosenberg's sub-
ordinates from 1935 on. At a Pfitzner Week organized by the Brunswick-
area branch of the German Labor Front in late 1941, Pfitzner was put in
charge of the program, choosing the soloists and assuming major conduct-
ing responsibilities. When Pfitzner did not get his way, he would sulk or
play the tyrant, convincing these lower-ranking party functionaries that
his self-serving gestures were all for the good of the new Germany.

On a few occasions Pfitzner met his match in conflicts with equally

7. See John Williamson, *The Music of Hans Pfitzner* (Oxford: Oxford University Press,
1992).

8. Albrecht Riethmüller, "Stationen des Begriffs Musik," in *Ideen zu einer Geschichte
der Musiktheorie: Einleitung in das Gesamtwerk*, ed. Frieder Zaminer et al. (Darmstadt: Wissenschaftliche Buchgesellschaft, 1985), 59–95; idem, "German Music from the Perspective of
German Musicology after 1933," *Journal of Musicological Research* 11 (1991): 177–87; idem,
Die Walhalla und ihre Musiker (Laaber: Laaber Verlag, 1993).

self-serving party functionaries. In Saxony, the stubborn, boorish Gauleiter Martin Mutschmann opposed the performance of Pfitzner's Christmas opera *Das Christelflein* (first staged in 1906) at the Saxon State Opera in Dresden, ostensibly because of its Christian symbolism (although Pfitzner was not a practicing Christian), but in reality because Pfitzner had once repudiated Mutschmann's crude pro-Saxon propaganda. From then on the composer claimed that his music was being banned from Dresden; more accurately, the Dresden conductors Karl Böhm and Karl Elmendorff simply happened not to like his music.

Nevertheless when the Saxon town of Zwickau received Mutschmann's blessings to found a Robert Schumann Society and organize a Schumann festival in 1943, Pfitzner seemed likely to be included. He deeply admired Schumann for his love of his fatherland and of Richard Wagner, as well as for his alleged suspicion of Jews. Despite some difficulties, the Schumann festival of June 1943 was dubbed a "Pfitzner–Schumann" event. Pfitzner was musical director and showcased his own works next to Schumann's. The thoroughly politicized festival was repeated in the following year, with Pfitzner assisted by the opportunistic young soprano and Nazi Party member Elisabeth Schwarzkopf.

Many of Pfitzner's cultural exploits after September 1939 were buoyed by a new imperialistic war, which placed him once again in the position of cultural defender, a role he had previously played in German-annexed Strasbourg after 1908. In November 1940 he even reappeared in Strasbourg, once again under German domination, to inspire the conquered region with "new German cultural life" at the Upper Rhenish Culture Days.[9] One newspaper reported the event as a personal triumph for the composer. With the help of the Munich Philharmonic and German, not French, soloists, he conducted six works, one of Beethoven and five of his own.[10]

A year later Pfitzner officiated at a similar, politically charged event in The Hague, in Nazi-occupied Holland: a combined "Pfitzner Commemoration" and "Pfitzner Festival" at the Nazi-controlled Dutch Broadcasting System. Festivities in Posen and Cracow, in annexed and occupied Poland, followed a few months later. In Posen, capital of the annexed "Warthegau," concert pianist Maria Greiser, the wife of the Warthegau's Gauleiter Arthur Greiser, played Pfitzner's Piano Concerto in E-flat in November 1941. In September 1942 Pfitzner was asked to appear at the "Posen Music Week." The advertised purpose of the event was to infuse the education system of

9. Reichspropagandaamt Baden to Pfitzner, 3 October 1940, OW, 245/Pfitzner.

10. Walter Dirks, "Hans Pfitzner in Strassburg: Die Oberrheinischen Kulturtage," *Frankfurter Zeitung,* 17 November 1940.

the newly conquered lands with German cultural values and eradicate allegedly inferior Polish traditions. To secure Pfitzner's participation, Gauleiter Greiser offered a higher honorarium than he had asked for. The music week, an unprecedented admixture of Nazi propaganda with the Pfitzner cult, earned Pfitzner additional monetary perks. He lent his name to a newly established music scholarship, and a street in Posen was named after him.

Even more reprehensible than this self-serving collaboration with Greiser was Pfitzner's association with known murderous functionaries of the Third Reich, particularly the Governor-General of Occupied Poland, Hans Frank. Frank, formerly Hitler's personal lawyer, was a high-ranking member of the SS. He resided in Cracow, only a few miles from Auschwitz, and although he had no official responsibility for the camp, he was still a butcher of Jews and Poles in his own right. In September 1941, when Frank heard that Pfitzner was going to perform in a concert for Germans living in Cracow, he thanked him for this "tremendous cultural-political favor, in the service of the fight for Germandom in the East."[11]

Frank was one of the more truly cultured leaders of the Nazi movement: he was fluent in Italian and loved art and music. He had taken great care to establish a Cracow Symphony Orchestra, whose many conductors had more recently included Rudolf Hindemith, Paul Hindemith's younger brother and formerly the cellist of the disbanded Amar Quartet. He had already welcomed to Cracow such soloists as pianists Wilhelm Kempff and Elly Ney, cellist Ludwig Hoelscher, and soprano Tiana Lemnitz. From early 1942 on, Frank not only saw to it that Pfitzner's compositions were performed, but he also invited the composer-conductor to make personal appearances in Cracow. He offered him his own limousine (Pfitzner was then residing in Munich), or a special coach on a scheduled train.

On Pfitzner's first visit in November 1942, he conducted a predictable program of Schumann, Wagner, and his own works. In June 1943, when operations in nearby Auschwitz were in full swing, Pfitzner made plans to have his neglected opera of love and redemption, *Das Herz*, staged in Cracow. When these fell through, Pfitzner and the Cracow Intendant Friedrichfranz Stampe prepared *Das Christelflein* for Christmas. This performance also failed to materialize, because in autumn of 1943 Pfitzner's Munich villa was bombed, leaving him temporarily homeless. Pfitzner sent his regrets to the Governor-General and thanked him for the "large Christmas bird and the sausage" he had sent. He would gladly come in the spring, wrote Pfitzner,

11. Frank to Pfitzner, 27 September 1941, OW, 220/Pfitzner.

and could he, again, travel in the government coach?[12] The composer did not arrive in Cracow again until July 1944, when he stayed for several days to lead the local symphony and perform some of his own songs.

Pfitzner and the governor corresponded until March 1945, with the end almost near. During the Nuremberg Trials, Hans Frank received a death sentence, and Pfitzner sent him one last telegram bearing the words: "Take this heartfelt greeting as a token of sympathy in difficult times."[13] On Wednesday, 16 October 1946, he punctiliously recorded Frank's execution in his pocket calendar. The Poles had already hanged Arthur Greiser.

After the Third Reich's collapse Pfitzner was hauled before the courts for denazification. The reason for his interrogation, ironically, was his nominal appointment by Goebbels as a Reich Culture Senator in 1936. Most denazification trials in postwar Germany were a sham, and certainly in this particular case the composer was indicted for the wrong reason. Pfitzner's crime was not, in fact, his having been formally a Nazi. We should regard him instead as an intellectual perpetrator, and such an offense could not be purged in a court of law.

The actual trial, from which Pfitzner, because of ill health, was absent, proved farcical. As in so many similar cases, the judges, attorneys, and jurors had access only to false or corrupted information and managed only to confuse the few bits of accurate information available. At the end of March 1948, the hearings for the composer were suspended, and he was free to go on a technical acquittal. Conductor Hans Rosbaud's judgment regarding Pfitzner's "unequivocal opposition to National Socialist thought and method" was as obviously false as his assertions about the "slights he had suffered especially at the hands of the National Socialists." They were, however, typical of the quid-pro-quo defenses of Nazis and half-Nazis among themselves, and they effectively set the tone of the entire trial.[14]

With the trial on his mind, Pfitzner set down his reflections on the reasons for the existence of Hitler and the Third Reich and concluded that Hitler was not only an unacceptable "proletarian" but was also evil by virtue of the terror he had caused (Pfitzner was probably alluding to the concentration camps that had killed worthy men like Cossmann). This evil could not, however, in any way be associated with the German people as a whole. On the other hand, after the humiliating treatment of Germany by the

12. Pfitzner to Frank, 18 December 1943, OW, 65/Pfitzner.

13. Pfitzner quoted in Bernhard Adamy, *Hans Pfitzner: Literatur, Philosophie und Zeitgeschehen in seinem Weltbild und Werk* (Tutzing: Schneider, 1980), 338.

14. Rosbaud declaration, 27 December 1947, Amtsgericht München, Registratur S, Schwurgerichtsakten Pfitzner.

Western Allies in 1918, Hitler's mission had been a just one. World War II
had also been a just war, if for no other reason than to expose the hypocrisy
of Germany's enemies, especially the uncultured United States.[15]

Regarding Hitler and the Jews, Pfitzner arrived at the unsavory rationalization that "World Jewry" had been a "racial problem" as well as an
"ideological problem," and that genocide was nothing new: the Americans
had practiced it on their native Indian population with impunity. In this respect, then, Hitler was exonerated by international precedent. *How* he had
eliminated the Jews may have been a different matter, and excesses certainly were inexcusable, but only insofar as they could be truly verified.
Concentration camp cruelty as such was hardly noteworthy, wrote Pfitzner
in his notebook, since excesses were known to occur during any revolution. Why, then, did Hitler engage Germany in World War II? "With respect
to this question I still believe in Hitler's honesty and good will. He wanted
to rejuvenate and liberate his fatherland and, beyond that, render a great
service to *Europe* by driving out the Jews—if necessary, eliminate them by
radical means. For in *World Jewry* he realized the singular danger for the
fortunes of all peoples, and the one reason for all the malignancy in the
world, in fact for just about *everything*."[16]

These statements constituted not only a rationalization of doubts Pfitzner may have had about the Third Reich, Hitler, and his own relationship to
him, but also a scarcely altered reassertion of the chauvinistic, xenopho-
bic, and misanthropic sentiments he had published in his *Collected Writings* in the mid-1920s. Particularly disturbing in these postwar musings is
Pfitzner's reasoning that the unworthiness of Jews could lead to the extreme
of physical extinction, thus granting his moral approval to Hitler's implementation of the Holocaust. What is most frightening is the constancy of
Pfitzner's fully developed hypernationalism from the time of World War I
to the post–World War II era. Despite personal setbacks, he continued to
adore a universally destructive German Führer beyond his death and con-
doned that Führer's most heinous deed, the genocide of Jews, which Pfitzner rationalized with the mainstream antisemitism dating back to the dying days of the Empire.

The fact that he could not rise above primitive mass instincts of ni-
hilism essentially trivializes any of his claim to elitism, personally, politically, and artistically, and betrays his association with what he always regarded as German music. So while there is no denying that Hans Pfitzner

15. Pfitzner, "Glosse zum zweiten Weltkrieg" (typed version, 1946–47), OW, 431/
Pfitzner.
16. Ibid.

was part of the German music tradition, politicized as it was in the course of its national development, German music as an art form had nobler, morally less compromised representatives to its credit.

Guide to Further Reading

Herf, Jeffrey. *Reactionary Modernism: Technology, Culture, and Politics in Weimar and the Third Reich.* Cambridge: Cambridge University Press, 1984.

Kater, Michael H. *Composers of the Nazi Era: Eight Portraits.* New York: Oxford University Press, 2000.

———. *The Twisted Muse: Musicians and Their Music in the Third Reich.* New York: Oxford University Press, 1997.

Potter, Pamela M. *Most German of the Arts: Musicology and Society from the Weimar Republic to the End Hitler's Reich.* New Haven: Yale University Press, 1998.

Steinweis, Alan E. *Art, Ideology, and Economics in Nazi Germany: The Reich Chambers of Music, Theater, and the Visual Arts.* Chapel Hill: University of North Carolina Press, 1993.

Willett, John. *Art and Politics in the Weimar Republic: The New Sobriety, 1917– 1933.* New York: Pantheon, 1978.

Williamson, John. *The Music of Hans Pfitzner.* Oxford: Oxford University Press, 1992.

"Für eine neue deutsche Nationaloper": Opera in the Discourses of Unification and Legitimation in the German Democratic Republic

JOY HASLAM CALICO

The German *Volk* rightly await from their composers the results of that great task which is of crucial importance in our struggle for national unity and independence: the creation of a German national opera. . . . A German national opera that comes from the emotions of the German and speaks to him will doubtless ring in all patriotic sides of the soul of the German *Volk*, and help awaken in him that noble enthusiasm for the struggle for peaceful unity of the German fatherland, which is necessary to resolve this historical question.

To which moment of national disunity is the author referring? A reasonable guess might locate this call to musical arms in the period preceding 1871 and the birth of the unified German nation; one might even guess that Richard Wagner is the author. In fact, the essay, entitled "For a New German *Nationaloper*," appeared in 1952 in the journal *Neues Deutschland*, the official organ of the Central Committee of the SED (Socialist Unity Party) in the German Democratic Republic (GDR).[1] Despite the fact that Germany had been occupied by the four Allied Powers after the war and then politically divided into two countries since 1949, the cultural-political agenda in East Germany remained one of cultural, if not political, unification. If Germans could not live under a single government at this time, at least their shared identity as "Germans," whether east or west, could be preserved through one national culture that transcended artificially imposed political boundaries. Carl Weber has noted that the GDR saw itself as the custodian of German culture until such time as the political split would be re-

1. "Für eine neue deutsche Nationaloper," *Neues Deutschland* (1 November 1952). All translations are my own unless otherwise indicated. Research for this essay was made possible by funding from Duke University, the Deutscher Akademischer Austauschdienst (DAAD), and the Berlin Program for Advanced German and European Studies of the Freie Universität Berlin and the Social Sciences Research Council. The conclusions and opinions in this publication are the author's and not necessarily those of the sponsoring institutions.

solved and the nation reunified as a single socialist state.[2] For the SED, opera was used to achieve a two-fold agenda: the composition of a new *Nationaloper* in the GDR would preserve a unified German national culture, and, at the same time, proclaim the GDR as the custodians of true German culture. Such claims were intended to bolster the position of East Germany as a legitimate nation-state at a time when most countries did not recognize it as such. The SED sought not only to unify East and West Germany, but also to liberate West Germany from the imperialist Western Allies, particularly the United States. According to the SED in the early 1950s, a unified Germany would be, by definition, a socialist Germany. Until that goal was achieved, East Germany would tend the home fires of German culture.

But why was opera so important in the project for German cultural unity and, by extension, GDR national legitimacy in the early 1950s? One answer can be traced to a role opera has traditionally played in cultural politics, that of "[giving] shape to a symbolic landscape by producing and contributing to myths of national authenticity and legitimacy."[3] Operatic spectacle has symbolized the power, wealth, and sophistication of the nations of Western Europe since the court of Louis XIV. Beginning with the various comic genres in the eighteenth century, opera remained primarily national in character even when a single musical language appeared to dominate instrumental music. Serious opera became infused with popular elements of comic opera, national traits among them, and governments reaped the abstract yet significant benefits of its patronage: grand opera is a symbol at home and abroad that a nation is affluent and educated, and thus powerful. As such, it can inspire patriotism at home and engender respect abroad. These sentiments are echoed in the SED Central Committee statement that "opera has a definitive significance for the formation and consolidation of a national culture."[4] In this case, the primacy of opera in the SED's agenda was the result of the convergence of several interrelated political and historical factors, each of which was preconfigured with a relationship to opera that was peculiar to Germany. The combination of these factors produced an environment in which the opera genre was highly charged with political meaning.

2. Carl Weber, "Periods of Precarious Adjustment: Some Notes on the Theater's Situation at the Beginning and after the End of the Socialist German State," *Contemporary Theatre Review* 4, no. 2 (1995): 25.

3. Richard Dellamora and Daniel Fischlin, eds., *The Work of Opera: Genre, Nationhood, and Sexual Difference* (New York: Columbia University Press, 1997), 3.

4. "Zu den Aufgaben der Deutschen Staatsoper," *Neues Deutschland* (19 December 1952).

The SED's emphasis on opera arose from the GDR's relationship to the
Soviet Union, the contributions of interested intellectuals, and a deeply
rooted German tradition of linking opera to political causes. Soviet socialist realism, which was both an aesthetic theory of the arts in the socialist
state and a political tool for the management of intellectual life, placed
substantial emphasis on opera (an aspect of this policy that has gone unre-
marked in studies of Soviet cultural politics). When East Germany adopted
the Soviet model for its own cultural-political agenda, it naturally gravitated toward this emphasis. Further support for the SED's agenda came
from the circle of prominent intellectuals surrounding the playwright
Bertolt Brecht. Although theories about the role of theater and music in socialist society espoused by Brecht and composers Paul Dessau and Hanns
Eisler sometimes placed them in conflict with the SED Central Committee and its agenda of socialist realism, they too were proponents of opera
during this period. Most of all, a preexisting German penchant for associating opera with nationalist politics gave rise to the distinctly German
term *Nationaloper*. The appropriation of opera in the Third Reich had imbued the art form with certain nationalist meanings that could be exploited for the purposes of German national unity in the postwar period.
Compounded by similarities between Nazi naturalism and Soviet socialist
realism, including a common emphasis on the role of opera in cultural politics, this continuity was one of many that characterized opera in the GDR
in the early 1950s.

In 1934, Stalin had mandated the "creation of cultures national in
form and socialist in content."[5] This would become the motto of socialist
realism, although translating it into actual cultural production proved
difficult. What, exactly, *is* socialist realist art? According to Stalin, Soviet
socialist realist culture was superior to all bourgeois cultures because of its
unique combination of Russian classics with Soviet Communism, but the
party offered little practical guidance to artists regarding the implementation of this theory. Apparently it was easier for the party to identify what
was *not* socialist realist art. When artists failed to meet the elusive requirements of socialist realism, as they often did, they were accused of its
equally vague antithesis, formalism. Understood by Soviet Communism to
be the dominant characteristic of decadent Western modernism, formalism was officially defined as "a separation of form from content" with the

    5. Quoted in Marina Frolova-Walker, "'National in Form, Socialist in Content': Musical
Nation-Building in the Soviet Republics," *Journal of the American Musicological Society* 51,
no. 2 (summer 1998): 331.

emphasis on technique or form. Proponents of socialist realism saw modernism not as something new but as reactionary and clichéd, while the return to classical models in socialist realism was "new" because the content was new. The terms "socialist realism" and "formalism" had more to do with politics than with aesthetics and art.

Socialist realism was an effective means of controlling culture, not because its definition was so rigid, but because it was amorphous and mutable, and therefore produced an unstable climate in cultural politics. It was impossible for artists to consistently anticipate the next incarnation of socialist realism, yet the political climate was such that they could ill afford not to try. Vague official definitions allowed the parameters to be interpreted and reinterpreted at the whims of politicians and official institutions, endowing the Communist Party with maximum powers of destabilization.

Socialist realism and formalism were particularly slippery concepts when applied to music, the "meaning" of which resists translation to the verbal. In practice, acceptable music usually combined nineteenth-century models of musical form and language with appropriate socialist messages. By and large, formalism in music would be synonymous with modernism, the last gasp of bourgeois capitalist decadence by Soviet standards. Soviet officials eschewed some of the difficulties inherent in defining musical style by emphasizing texted genres, especially opera, which could be more easily monitored for socialist realism. As a result, the most significant official pronouncements concerning socialist realism and music in the Soviet Union took the form of negative responses to two operas. In 1936, Stalin reportedly saw *Lady Macbeth of Mtensk* by Dmitri Shostakovich and found it inconsistent with his criteria for Soviet opera, after which *Pravda* published a statement deriding the work. The war brought a temporary respite from artistic censorship, but in 1945 the party resumed strict control over cultural production. In 1948 Andrei Zhdanov, perpetrator of the infamous cultural purges of 1946–48, issued the resolution "On the Opera *The Great Friendship* by V. Muradeli." This statement established the criteria for socialist realism and formalism in music that would change cultural politics throughout the Soviet bloc.

The emphasis on opera as a national art form for the socialist state may strike the outside observer as odd; certainly the contradictions inherent in promoting opera for a workers' state are hard to overlook. A genre traditionally associated with upper-class audiences and virtuosic performers, opera is nevertheless consistent with other tenets of socialist realism. Thomas Lahusen has noted that socialist realism tended to privilege large-scale forms in all the arts, such as the novel over the short story, and opera would be the musical equivalent of the novel in size and scope.[6] Opera also has the advantage of being staged with costumes, props, and spectacle, all elements that appeal to audiences and facilitate the didactic use of the genre. Entertainment that presented Soviet values and history onstage could be a valuable educational tool.

In East Germany, the Soviet-influenced leadership advocated the theory of socialist realism in its own cultural politics because it was made up of former members of the German Communist Party (KPD) who had escaped the Third Reich and lived in exile in Moscow. Even after the KPD was officially combined with the Social Democratic Party (SPD) in 1946 to form the SED, former KPD members maintained control of cultural and political institutions, and they remained in favor with the Soviet Military Administration in Germany (SMAD). The significance of culture in their plans for German renewal became apparent immediately. One of the first official organizations created by the Soviets and the KPD in the occupied zone was the Cultural League for the Democratic Renewal of Germany, which was established in 1945. While basic city services and provisions remained scarce, SMAD saw to it that some semblance of cultural life resumed immediately in the Soviet-occupied zone. Theater and concert performances and radio broadcasts resumed as early as May 1945. The former German State Opera in Berlin reopened in its temporary home in the Admiralspalast on Friedrichstrasse in August, and by July 1946 the City Opera could already boast 142 opera performances, 78 concerts, 67 ballet performances, and 16 concerts by the Berlin Philharmonic.

The year 1948 was a turning point for occupied Germany, however, as the Soviet zone began to feel the ripple effect of the Zhdanovite purges emanating from the USSR. The SED responded with a series of resolutions that applied Zhdanov's policies to all cultural life in the new German Democratic Republic and culminated in the resolution of 17 March 1951, entitled "The Struggle against Formalism in Art and Literature for a Progressive German Culture." This is one of the most important documents in SED *Kulturpolitik* (cultural policy), and its tenets remained the essential principles of cultural politics in East Germany until its demise. Among other things, this edict attempted to establish guidelines for identifying musical formalism.[7]

6. Thomas Lahusen, "Socialist Realism in Search of Its Shores: Some Historical Remarks on the 'Historically Open Aesthetic System of the Truthful Representation of Life,'" *South Atlantic Quarterly* 94, no. 3 (1995): 677.

7. "Der Kampf gegen den Formalismus in der Kunst," reprinted in *Dokumente zur Kunst-, Literatur- und Kulturpolitik der SED 1946–1971*, ed. Elimar Schubbe (Stuttgart: Seewald Verlag, 1972), 181.

Although this resolution was not prompted by a specific opera and did not yet call for a new German *Nationaloper,* it did single out two operas for rebuke. The first was *Antigonae* by the West German composer Carl Orff, which had been the token example of musical formalism in official resolutions since 1949. The second was *Das Verhör des Lukullus* (*The Trial of Lucullus*) by Bertolt Brecht and Paul Dessau, and the judgement was unequivocal: "The music for the opera *The Trial of Lucullus* is also formalist." In the speech version of this resolution, Hans Lauter noted that "the percussion makes the work most inharmonious, and likewise produces distortion of taste. . . . Through such music, which cannot be tied to our classical cultural heritage, one can obviously not develop our new democratic culture."[8] The first public performance of *Lucullus* was supposed to have taken place on the very day of this address but had been abruptly cancelled, and only an invited audience of party representatives was allowed to attend the premiere. Thus no one had even seen the opera when the speech was given, but based upon reports from functionaries who had attended rehearsals, the Central Committee was convinced that the opera did not conform to the tenets of socialist realism.

The opera's main character is based on the historical figure Lucullus, a Roman field general in the first century B.C. as renowned for his ruthlessness on the battlefield as for his opulent banquets at home (the term "lucullan," meaning luxurious, is derived from his name). The plot begins with his funeral procession, after which Lucullus finds himself on trial in Hades. He must justify his mortal life, and, with his eternal fate hanging in the balance, presents the funerary frieze commemorating his victories as evidence of his accomplishments. The court calls the figures on the frieze as witnesses. Dead soldiers, grieving mothers, widows, slaughtered children, and conquered foes, all intended to attest to the general's prowess as a leader, are instead revealed to be victims of senseless war. Dessau's musical setting, cited as a negative example in the resolution against formalism,[9] is calculated to underscore the imbalance of power between characters and to problematize the opera genre.

8. "Auszüge aus dem Referat des Genossen Hans Lauter auf der 5. Tagung des ZK," in *Neues Deutschland* (23 March 1951), reprinted in *Das Verhör in der Oper: Die Debatte um die Aufführung 'Das Verhör des Lukullus' von Bertolt Brecht und Paul Dessau,* ed. Joachim Lucchesi (Berlin: Basisdruck, 1993), 193.

9. There is speculation that this was intended to deflect attention from the real problem, Brecht's libretto, since the regime was particularly keen to retain his support. See Gerhard Müller, "Zeitgeschichtliche Aspekte der 'Lukullus-Debatte,'" in *Paul Dessau: Von Geschichte gezeichnet—Symposium Paul Dessau Hamburg,* ed. Klaus Angermann (Hofheim: Wolke, 1995), 144–51.

The resolution in which Dessau was taken to task foregrounded the fundamental disagreements between those committed Communists who had been exiled in the West and those who had spent the war years in Moscow. Former leaders of the KPD returning from the Soviet Union subscribed to the theory of socialist realism and believed that art should use the best of bourgeois culture from throughout history as models for the new socialist German culture. By contrast, Brecht, Dessau, and Eisler spent the majority of their years in exile in the United States, returning to East Germany in the late 1940s. They believed bourgeois forms, however timeless or universal they may seem, could not be adopted uncritically by the new society because they represented and reproduced a social order that was incompatible with the aims of socialism. According to this view, the socialist state needed new art forms and genres, and Brecht, Dessau, and Eisler attempted to recast opera as something pertinent to socialism. In addition to these theoretical differences, there was already a certain antagonism between the SED and Brecht in particular. Because he was arguably the most famous cultural figure in East Germany, the Central Committee needed the world-renowned playwright to lend his support to the government for purposes of international legitimation, but at the same time his fame and ties to the West bred resentment.

Dessau considered opera the most powerful genre with which to artistically highlight the social problems of our time, and Brecht found in him a like-minded composer willing to follow the playwright's theatrical theories through to their musical conclusions. But their vision of opera in East Germany was not consistent with the socialist realist agenda for opera, which was based on nineteenth-century models of harmonic language, instrumentation, melody, and characterization, and this conflict placed them in opposition to the larger Soviet political agenda. Musical style was interpreted as a symbol of political orientation, and composers who did not adhere to the socialist realist musical style were said to be under the influence of the cosmopolitan West. Dissonance was the musical element most often cited as a sign of formalism, and Dessau's musical language was often dissonant. His unconventional instrumentation emphasized percussion or nontraditional orchestra instruments such as the accordion, prepared pianos, and trautonium[10] instead of strings, and this was also suspect (there are no violins in the orchestra for *Lucullus*). Finally, his method of

10. The trautonium was an electronic instrument developed in 1930 by Friedrich Trautwein. The performer controlled the pitch by varying the point at which a wire pressed against a metal bar. It produced one pitch at a time, and the timbre could be manipulated by the performer. Richard Strauss, Paul Hindemith, and Dessau composed works for this instrument.

using melodic style for characterization proved unacceptable to the authorities. He composed simple melodies for the working-class characters and elaborate, virtuosic arias for the war-mongering field general Lucullus. The songs symbolized the honest, noble nature of the workers, while Dessau exploited the full range of operatic clichés (extremely high tessitura for the tenor voice, excessive coloratura, melismatic text setting, text repetitions) to present Lucullus as a pompous member of the ruling class. Dessau's sophisticated use of musical style, in which the hallmarks of traditional opera were appropriated as symbols of imperialism and assigned to the villain, was meant to demonstrate that the bourgeois opera tradition had no place in the antifascist German socialist state.

After the private premiere on 17 March 1951 (which was a rousing success), Brecht and Dessau were called to meet with the East German president because of official concerns about the music. Dessau was later required to confer with a contingent of Soviet composers to discuss the opera's formalist elements. He and Brecht agreed to revisions (including a new title— Die Verurteilung des Lukullus [The Judgement of Lucullus]) so that the work could receive its public premiere in October. Apparently satisfied with their willingness to cooperate, officials did not closely monitor the final version. Dessau's changes were minor, and the "revised" version performed in October is musically almost identical to that which was performed in March. Perhaps Brecht and Dessau's radical vision of what opera in a socialist state should be led the party to adopt the more traditional Nationaloper model.

Lucullus brought about the first cultural-political crisis in music in the GDR, and Eisler's Johann Faustus occasioned the second. Eisler wrote the libretto himself and published the text without music in October 1952, but a debate ensued shortly thereafter, and he never completed the musical setting. He had begun and abandoned numerous opera projects throughout his career, yet he took up the task of writing an opera in the GDR with particular zeal. The genre had always held great appeal for him, and he had written in 1935 that the new social function of opera should be "social criticism, [and] the portrayal of tradition with the destruction of conventional operatic effects."[11] Unlike Brecht and Dessau, Eisler planned to use "accessible" text and music (that is, tonal musical language); he would include folk songs and other traditional German cultural references; and he would

---

11. "Gesellschaftliche Umfunktionierung der Musik," in *Musik und Politik: Schriften 1948–1962*, ser. 3, vol. 1 of Hanns Eisler, *Gesammelte Werke*, ed. Günter Mayer (Leipzig: VEB Deutscher Verlag für Musik, 1973), 374.

employ some classical models, steering clear of the shock value associated with Brecht's stage works. Surviving musical sketches confirm this, since Eisler completed a stylized version of the German folk song "If I were a little bird (Wenn ich ein Vöglein wär)" for the secondary character Gretel. A passage of accompanied recitative for her and Hanswurst also survives, but there is no evidence that he got beyond the most preliminary stages of composing music for the main characters, Faust and Mephisto. Given the politics of style, perhaps he had not yet determined how he would characterize them musically.

On 22 April 1952, Eisler gave a lecture at the Academy of the Arts in Berlin entitled "What Can the Opera Composer Learn from Richard Wagner?" He expressed an opinion similar to Dessau's when he said: "In present times, opera, as opposed to concert music, is the most democratic of major musical forms since it is more readily accessible to listeners of widely differing degrees of musical education."[12] Eisler drew an explicit connection between the contemporary division of Germany and the role opera might play in rectifying that situation when he said of Wagner: "He postulated the popular opera as national artwork against the stupidity of a disunited Germany."[13] Yet despite his earnest musical and political intentions, he never completed *Johann Faustus*. He may appear to have anticipated the SED's call for a new German *Nationaloper* in December 1952, but in fact he was stymied by the unexpected and overwhelmingly negative response to his libretto. Party functionaries and other intellectuals accused him of misusing Goethe's masterpiece *Faust*, even though it was apparent that Eisler had in fact taken much earlier versions of the old German legend as his models. In Eisler's version, Johann Faustus is an intellectual during the Peasants' War of 1525 who suffers terrible guilt for failing to act on behalf of the lower classes, even though he himself was the son of a peasant. Despite all the furor about Goethe, GDR intellectuals ultimately took offense because they interpreted Eisler's treatment of this traditional German legend as an indictment of their own actions under the Third Reich.

While Brecht, Dessau, and Eisler were opposed to socialist realism for theoretical reasons, artists and intellectuals who had lived under the Third Reich found the requirements eerily familiar. In many ways, socialist realism in the GDR in the early 1950s is remarkably similar to the Nazi cultural aesthetic. Maintaining the purity of the cultural heritage and preserving the

12. Ibid., 231.
13. Ibid., 233.

German national culture had been central to the Nazis' cultural-political agenda, and these tenets once again dominated cultural debate in the early years of the GDR. This suggests a curious continuity running through World War II and into the postwar period, as well as a surprising link between Soviet-style Communists and Nazis. Arch enemies on every front, they nevertheless set similar goals for the role of the arts in their respective societies. Socialist realism and Nazi naturalism share an antimodern bias that treats modernism as cliché and "old-fashioned," an appeal to nineteenth-century bourgeois taste and repertoire, an exploitation of historical links to the past, the promotion of a pure national rather than international or cosmopolitan culture, and a connection to the *Volk*.

For music, a crucial distinction between Nazi naturalism and Soviet socialist realism is that the Communists were primarily worried about musical style, whereas the Nazis were concerned with the racial purity of the composer. While the Third Reich did display a general preference for the mass appeal of tonal music, the regime also promoted the music of certain modern composers. Again, the primary concern for the Nazis was that the composer not be Jewish. In contrast, cultural authorities in East Germany did not exclude Jewish artists from the pantheon. We should not, however, interpret this as a sign that antisemitism was not present in East Germany.[14] Communists carried out their own violent purges of Jews in the 1950s in a series of show trials, murders, and detentions throughout the Soviet bloc. They leveled the coded, antisemitic accusation of "cosmopolitanism" at many of their victims, yet antisemitism remained peripheral to socialist realist cultural politics.

A more significant continuity from the cultural politics of the Third Reich to those of the SED was the emphasis on opera. Under Hitler, Alfred Rosenberg had overseen a bureau (Amt Rosenberg) that monitored cultural events for infractions against the Nazi edicts of pure German culture. His primary means of influence was through the press, and his corps of editors and writers at numerous influential publications rebuked perceived offenders in print. The musicologist Herbert Gerigk ran the music division of the Rosenberg Bureau, and he aggressively promoted the ideal of *Volksoper* in a new musical style. This was primarily characterized as the absence of undesirable characteristics, such as late romanticism on the one hand and

---

14. For a thorough account of the different ways in which East and West Germany dealt with the aftermath of the Holocaust, see Jeffrey Herf, *Divided Memory: The Nazi Past in the Two Germanys* (Cambridge: Harvard University Press, 1997). An undercurrent of antisemitism may be traced in the debates surrounding Dessau and Eisler, both of whom were Jewish.

atonality, dissonance, and polytonality on the other. In other words, he advocated a complete break with the style of the late nineteenth century *and* a break with the styles of the 1920s, but did not provide an alternative model. Such a negative definition is reminiscent of the vagaries of the Soviet socialist realist aesthetic. Rosenberg lacked the clout and actual authority to enforce the new *Volksoper* ideal, but his ideas received considerable publicity in print and represented another skirmish in his ongoing power struggle with Joseph Goebbels.

As minister of propaganda and head of cultural affairs (which oversaw the Reich Music Chamber, the Reichsmusikkammer), Goebbels challenged Rosenberg's authority. While Rosenberg was a philosopher, Goebbels was a pragmatist. Opera was not central to his agenda because a genre that had always been associated with upper- and middle-class patrons did not reach his target audience as well as the mass media of film and popular music did. For Goebbels, operetta outranked serious opera because it was more popular, and served a purpose by entertaining and refreshing the population. He never intended to create or promote a new National Socialist opera; in fact, he went so far in 1940 as to craft an agenda focused on the reworking of established masterpieces. When he did concern himself with opera, he favored romantic operas by Ludwig Spohr, Carl Maria von Weber, and Albert Lortzing because they were popular, and he promoted new operas in that style because they would presumably also meet with audience approval. Operas in other styles, such as the works of Carl Orff and Werner Egk, were also deemed acceptable if they proved popular with audiences.

Goebbels did, however, appreciate the symbolic significance of opera for the nation and did not want Germany to be perceived as uncultured and reactionary. In this realm of image politics, opera played an important role for the Third Reich. Young Adolf Hitler had been greatly influenced by Wagner's music, as well as by his virulent nationalism and antisemitism. His personal relationship with the Wagner family has been well documented. Although the number of public performances of Wagner's operas continued a decline that had begun in the 1920s, the Nazis began officially supporting the Bayreuth Festival in 1933 and used it as a public spectacle to honor not only Wagner, but Hitler and the Reich as well. The frequency with which Wagner's operas were staged as part of official government events greatly distorted the total number of performances given in Germany each year. His operas were not a central part of the public opera-going experience, but the prominence of Wagner's music in official functions indicates that establishing a link between Hitler and Wagner was a public relations priority. Because of his status as an undisputed master of German music who also happened to share much of Hitler's worldview, the cultural authorities in the Nazi era appropriated Wagner to legitimate the Nazi regime.[15]

In contrast to the dominant discourse of the Nazi era, the development of a new operatic genre for the GDR was foremost on the agenda for East German cultural politics in the early 1950s. The essay "For a New German *Nationaloper*" in *Neues Deutschland* was greeted enthusiastically by the journal *Musik und Gesellschaft* (*Music and Society*). One month after the resolution appeared, its editors responded: "[N]ow that the organ of the SED Central Committee has published a lead article about the necessity of creating a German national opera, we cannot estimate the significance of this fact highly enough."[16] Beethoven's *Fidelio* was held up as a model, and librettists were advised to seek subject matter in events from German history, such as the Peasants' War, the Revolution of 1848, and the battle against fascism. Toward that end, the Central Committee recommended that the composition process include not only a composer and a librettist but also a historian to advise on matters of historical accuracy. On 19 December 1952, *Neues Deutschland* followed up with an article entitled "The Tasks of the German State Opera," in which the role of the flagship opera house in the development of a national opera was specified, and the primacy of opera in the national project reaffirmed:

> The opera belongs as an inseparable component to the national culture
> of a people. During the period of development of the nation, the unity of
> poetry, music, theater, acting, dance and staging made this art genre like
> a point of crystallization of the artistic life of the nation. The creation
> of opera during the emerging epoch of our nation was the focal point of
> cultural life. . . . For the German people currently leading the fight for
> the survival of the German nation, the creation of a central leading in-
> stitution of German operatic art is an historical necessity. . . .[17]

Not surprisingly, the article singles out Russian *Nationaloper* as the best model for GDR composers. Use of the word *Nationaloper* in this discourse when the term did not figure prominently in Nazi discussions of opera was

---

15. See Thomas Grey's essay included in this volume.

16. "Für eine neue deutsche Nationaloper," *Musik und Gesellschaft* 2, no. 12 (December 1952): 1.

17. "Zu den Aufgaben der Deutschen Staatsoper," *Neues Deutschland* (19 December 1952). Reprinted in *Dokumente zur Kunst*, ed. Schubbe, 259.

a deliberate attempt to tie the emerging East German state to a tradition of nineteenth-century nationalism. Wulf Konold noted that the term *Nationaloper* is vague, but generally refers to nineteenth-century operas written in regions in which a sense of nation was just developing. As these regions developed a national consciousness, often coupled with freedom from foreign occupation, they also shook off the dominance of Italian opera to produce works based on local folk tales in the vernacular language. Ultimately, according to Konold, whether or not a work qualifies as a *Nationaloper* depends upon the intentions of the composer and librettist, or upon the interpretation of later audiences whose perspectives may be determined by their own sociopolitical situations.[18] GDR music historian Horst Seeger has written that it is not an artistic concept, but rather a cultural-political abstraction.[19] As such, *Nationaloper* was a fitting nomenclature for the GDR opera project. It describes opera that bears a specific, new national identity, one that is the result of recent liberation from "foreign" domination. The political rhetoric of East Germany always held that the Germans had been liberated from the Third Reich by the Soviets. The term and the concept of *Nationaloper* thus circumvent the Nazi era and its appropriation of nineteenth-century opera, and forge direct historical and cultural links between the GDR and the unified Germany that emerged in the late nineteenth century.

The cultural-political concept of *Nationaloper* was well suited to the aims of the SED, yet the term has generally served to retroactively characterize nineteenth-century opera through the prism of twentieth-century ideas of nationhood. To prescribe the composition of *new* German *Nationaloper* is something else again. The *Lucullus* debate, which focused on the music, and the *Johann Faustus* debate, focused on the libretto, indicate that intellectuals as well as political functionaries were convinced of the significance of opera in establishing the antifascist German democratic socialist state. As Dellamora and Fischlin have noted, opera has traditionally helped to shape the symbolic national landscape by contributing to myths of authenticity and legitimacy. Eisler and Dessau were politically committed composers dedicated to the project of building the German socialist state and to creating appropriate new music for that state. They chose to inaugurate their GDR careers with opera not only for its didactic potential,

18. Wulf Konold, "Nationale Bewegungen und Nationalopern im 19. Jahrhundert: Versuch einer Definition, was eine Nationaloper ausmacht," *Der Schöne Abglanz: Stationen der Operngeschichte* (Berlin: Dietrich Reimer Verlag, 1992), 111–28.

19. Horst Seeger, "Zum Begriff 'Nationaloper' und seiner Anwendung auf Weber," *Oper Heute: Ein Almanach der Musikbühne* 11 (Berlin: Henschelverlag, 1988), 235.

but also because opera is symbolic of established European national cultures. In East Germany, a new operatic genre was expected to accomplish what could not be achieved through conventional channels of diplomacy.

It is useful to remember that the Iron Curtain had not yet fully descended in the early 1950s. During the occupation and at least until the East German uprising of 17 June 1953, the borders within Berlin were still fairly permeable. For many, the division of Germany into two separate states may not have seemed permanent or even real. Under these circumstances, many East German intellectuals believed that culture could provide the impetus for reunifying a nation whose division seemed arbitrary and perhaps even only temporary. In the end, of course, it did not. The fall of the Berlin Wall was precipitated not by a *Nationaloper* but by the crumbling Soviet economic infrastructure. Nevertheless, the cultural politics of the early GDR reveal yet another continuity in the history of Germany. Since the nineteenth century, German intellectuals and leaders have turned repeatedly to music as a hallmark of national identity and to opera in particular as a symbol of national unity and power. As early as 1803, music critic Friedrich Rochlitz noted in the *Allgemeine musikalische Zeitung* that the development of German opera was at a distinct disadvantage because Germany lacked a capital city that could act as a true artistic center. The coalescence of a nation would facilitate the emergence of opera, which would in turn be a symbol that the nation was viable and sovereign. The rebelliousness Wagner cultivated after 1848 was not motivated by national politics as much as it was driven by the composer's sense that his artistic ideals could not be implemented without social revolution. He later represented music drama as a national work of art in order to capitalize on national pride that emerged with the foundation of the German Empire in 1871. Opera and nationalism thus became inextricably intertwined in a single symbol of German power, which was then masterfully exploited by the Third Reich. Intellectuals in the GDR were the most recent in a long line of Germans to recognize the power of that symbol, and to hope that a nation could be unified around it.

Guide to Further Reading

Bathrick, David. *The Powers of Speech: The Politics of Culture in the GDR*. Lincoln: University of Nebraska Press, 1995.

Betz, Albrecht. *Hanns Eisler: Political Musician*. Trans. Bill Hopkins. Cambridge: Cambridge University Press, 1982.

Blake, David. *Hanns Eisler: A Miscellany*. Contemporary Music Studies 9. New York: Harwood Academic Publishers, 1995.

Bunge, Hans. *Die Debatte um Hanns Eislers "Johann Faustus": Eine Dokumentation.* Brecht-Studien Series 20. Berlin: Auflage, 1991.

Calico, Joy Haslam. "The Politics of Opera in the German Democratic Republic, 1945–1961." Ph.D. diss., Duke University, 1999.

Dümling, Albrecht. *Laßt euch nicht verführen: Brecht und Musik.* Munich: Kindler Verlag, 1985.

Fulbrook, Mary. *Anatomy of a Dictatorship: Inside the GDR, 1949–1989.* New York: Oxford University Press, 1995.

Jäger, Manfred. *Kultur und Politik in der DDR: Ein historischer Abriß.* Köln: Edition Deutschland Archiv, 1995.

Köster, Maren. *Hanns Eisler. 's müßt dem Himmel Höllenangst werden.* Archive zur Musik des 20. Jahrhunderts, vol. 3. Hofheim: Wolke Verlag, 1998.

Lahusen, Thomas, and Evgeny Dobrenko, eds. *Socialist Realism without Shores.* Durham: Duke University Press, 1997.

Naimark, Norman M. *The Russians in Germany: A History of the Soviet Zone of Occupation 1945–1949.* Cambridge: Harvard University Press, Belknap Press, 1995.

Neef, Sigrid and Hermann. *Deutsche Oper im 20. Jahrhundert: DDR, 1949–1989.* Berlin: Peter Lang, 1992.

Reinhold, Daniela, ed. *Paul Dessau 1894–1979: Dokumente zu Leben und Werk.* Berlin: Henschelverlag, 1995.

Schebera, Jürgen. *Hanns Eisler: Eine Biographie in Texten, Bilden und Dokumenten.* Mainz: Schott, 1998.

Darmstadt, Postwar Experimentation, and the West German Search for a New Musical Identity

GESA KORDES

After the German capitulation in 1945, artists' struggle to come to terms with the legacy of the Nazi regime led to a general reevaluation of artistic traditions. This struggle toward finding a new German identity is readily apparent in postwar publications in which writers simultaneously display a reticence to discuss the Nazi past and a strong desire to distance themselves from it. Composers, especially those of the younger generation, also participated in this struggle. Many attempted to distance their work from German music of the Nazi years while catching up with musical developments abroad from which they had been cut off. Composers like Stockhausen, Henze, and others came to the *Darmstädter Ferienkurse* as one of the centers of new music in Western Europe that offered the opportunity to experiment with recent compositional techniques. They focused first on neoclassicism, but soon turned to the twelve-tone method, serialism, and other abstract experiments regarded as forms of musical expression untainted by Nazism. Both the German government and the occupying powers encouraged this trend toward abstract music with politically motivated cultural funding decisions, thus steering German composers toward a new musical identity that distinguished itself from images of the Nazi past.

Although the repair of physical destruction proceeded rapidly after World War II, psychological damage was much more substantial, if more difficult, to measure. Germans, especially intellectuals and artists, were faced with the dual task of coping with past crimes and finding a new foundation for the future. In postwar publications, most references to the practices of the Nazi regime were indirect. When the past was referred to at all, the focus inevitably shifted to the present, often with a reassurance that the future would bring change. Literature on music was utterly evasive on the subjects of the Nazis' ban on Jewish composers, the campaigns against musical modernism, and especially the use of music for propaganda purposes.

The first postwar issue of the *(Neue) Zeitschrift für Musik* (hereafter *ZfM*), which appeared in December 1949, was replete with the type of vocabulary used to veil sensitive subjects. The issue included a series of articles surveying the principal musical developments during the first half of the twentieth century.[1] In his introductory article, the editor, Erich Valentin, proclaimed the general resolve of postwar musicians to discontinue traditions he described as "historically completed"—that is, traditions that were used and abused by the Nazi regime, and had thus outlived their usefulness. He then called for a more flexible use of labels for artistic developments, in contrast to the narrow description of music during the Hitler era:

> We all still live in the illusion of standing at the beginning of the century of which Ludwig Büchner once expected the great reconciliation [of opposing political and artistic concepts]. . . . The fast pace of life, into which fate forced us, blurred the limits and kept us from gaining a distance from things. . . . Most of what lies behind us is already historically completed. . . . Today, we have become more careful, and we refrain from creating premature formal terms to label the styles that define our immediate present. Too much havoc has been created with terms such as "expressionism," "neogothic," "neoclassicism," etc. Therefore, we want to avoid making the same mistake of practically hampering a development . . . by determining it before it reaches its goal.

Valentin went on to describe the general shift in the 1930s from a culture of highly educated amateurs to a musical mass culture that placed new demands on public music education. He was careful, however, to overlook the Nazis' large contributions to such developments.

Other authors in this issue of *ZfM*, particularly those leaning more to the left, also glossed over the past but tended to be more open in suggesting new ideas for the future. Peter Harlan, for example, did not directly mention Nazi ideas in his article on public music education, but he proposed directives that were clearly distant from the Nazis' attempt to control music education as a tool for political indoctrination:

1. The following excerpts are all taken from *ZfM* 111 (1949), in this order: Erich Valentin, "Die letzten fünfzig Jahre," *ZfM* 111 (1949): 1–4; Peter Harlan, "Betrachtete Musikausübung," *ZfM* 111 (1949): 22–25; Friedrich Högner, "Fünfzig Jahre Evangelische Kirchenmusik," *ZfM* 111 (1949): 13–16.

"Directive-makers" are currently not in existence—although many view themselves as such while having only a very limited, local influence. The schools can experiment, i.e. every single music teacher can concentrate on his own hobbyhorses, which is definitely more effective, because he is guided by his own passion. We do not want a uniform "direction." . . . Education is something that shapes human beings, and should not be forced upon them like the branch of a cultivated cherry onto a wild cherry tree. Because in this case the person would not be educated but rather, changed.

Only one article openly confronted and condemned musical events under the Nazis: Friedrich Högner's essay on Protestant church music. Since some components of the Protestant church supported resistance against the regime, Högner felt encouraged to provide a detailed report. He described the struggle of church musicians to maintain their independence from Nazi ideology, and concluded that their music mainly served religion, not ideology. Accordingly, he was the only one of the authors in this issue of *ZfM* who could look back with a certain degree of satisfaction, and not have to propose new directions: "May the reader forgive the author, an active and 'activated' participant, when he concludes gratefully that these fifty years were rich and fulfilled, in spite of several dark appearances; they included sowing and harvest, unrest and fight against satiation."

As with the articles by Valentin and Harlan, Högner's article points to the deep insecurity that pervaded German cultural values after World War II. The writers almost unanimously avoided confrontation with the past while focusing on untainted traditions and attitude changes that would prevent a recurrence of the events of recent history.

Given this evasiveness, the mandate for young composers was not clear. How could composers set out to create something distinct from the music of the Third Reich without confronting what that music really consisted of? A consensus about the attitudes toward music in the Third Reich could be based only on the most blatant proclamations on music by a handful of Nazi ideologues. Accordingly, postwar composers increasingly turned their attention to exploring compositional approaches that had been so virulently attacked by these extremists that they could be regarded as untainted and could serve as a basis for composition in the new Germany. They also hoped to promote the notion that their art would be free of political interference, as a way of distancing themselves from the activities of composers who let themselves be exploited by the Nazis.

It was generally assumed that Nazi cultural administrators made music one of their primary educational priorities, but with a special emphasis on its importance for Germans. Whether it served to unify a social class, a family, or members of the political elite, music provided a communal experience potentially capable of subliminal ideological indoctrination. This view grew out of the romantic notion of music as a medium capable of expressing concepts inexpressible in language, concepts that were therefore closer to the center of the human spirit. In addition, the Nazi regime regarded music as closely linked to racial and national qualities. The musical style associated with the German *Volk* was identified by a leading demagogue, Werner Gerdes, in *Die Musik* in 1942:

> To us, every *Volksgenosse* of healthy stock is sufficiently musical to absorb simple melodic lines, healthy harmony, and vigorous rhythm as phenomena of an inner character. Diatonic scales with harmonic functions, essentially determined by tonic and dominant, are by tradition and experience suitable as our tonal system in the major and minor modes. . . . Thus, the biological prerequisites for a people's musical culture are given. Physically, intellectually, and spiritually, Germans possess the necessary capacities. If inherited traits of all Germans are healthy, then all Germans must be musical.[2]

Both jazz and atonal composition deviated from the Nazis' concept of "healthy music" and thus suffered heavily from censure. Atonality and twelve-tone composition were particularly suspect: the departure from tonality appeared to attack a natural musical hierarchy by destroying the "natural order of notes in the tonal principles of classical music."[3] One of the Nazis' most notorious cultural rhetoricians, Hans Severus Ziegler, likened atonality to "cultural bolshevism":

> Together with a number of leading cultural experts and cultural politicians, I espouse the opinion that *atonality, as a result of the destruction of tonality, signifies "Entartung" [degeneracy] and cultural bolshevism.* . . . It [the music] is finally the object of snobbish adulation or purely intellectual consideration on the part of more or less decadent literary figures and writers. . . .[4]

2. Werner Gerdes in *Die Musik*, as quoted by Michael Meyer, "Assumption and Implementation of Nazi Policy towards Music" (Ph.D. diss., UCLA, 1970), 485.

3. Erik Levi, "Atonality, 12-Tone Music and the Third Reich," *Tempo* 178 (1991): 18.

4. Hans Severus Ziegler, *Entartete Musik—Eine Abrechnung* (Düsseldorf: Völkischer Verlag, 1938), 16, 24; quoted by Bernd Sösemann in "'Eine Erneuerung ist ohne die Musik nicht möglich': Kunst und Musik als Mittel der Propaganda in den 'Wochensprüchen der NSDAP,'"

Twelve-tone composition, too, afforded a degree of abstraction that was regarded as "un-Germanic." In addition, it was invented by a Jew, and several of its main proponents were Jewish. Hence, the denigration of atonality, especially the twelve-tone method, became central to Nazi musical propaganda. After Hitler's downfall in 1945, then, German composers saw this method as one of the few means of writing in musical styles untainted by Nazism. Twelve-tone composition was apparently the only tradition in "serious" music that had not been used by the Nazi government for educational or propaganda purposes; anything associated with its Jewish creator and his school had been shunned as an intellectually "degenerate" (entartet). Furthermore, its concentration on purely musical material offered a degree of abstraction that could discourage misuse by any political group. Accordingly, it would soon hold great appeal for young composers as well as the West German government in their attempts to create a new German musical identity.

At first, the young generation had a burning desire to acquaint themselves with the musical developments that had taken place elsewhere. Owing to the widespread destruction of the country's means of communication, the rebuilding of musical life depended on the establishment of music festivals and concert series that would allow musicians to exchange information face to face. The foundation of the *Darmstädter Ferienkurse* by the musicologist Wolfgang Steinecke in 1946 provided such a forum, and his organizational talent soon transformed Darmstadt into one of the most influential centers of musical renewal in Europe. Bearing the full name of *Ferienkurse für Internationale Neue Musik Darmstadt* (Vacation Courses for International New Music in Darmstadt) for the first two years, it was one of several initiatives in formerly fascist-dominated regions in the early postwar period that took on an international character. Another such festival was Manuel Rosenthal's and Roger Désormière's concert series of works by Stravinsky in Paris, organized immediately after the city's liberation. A third festival originated in 1949, when Milan hosted the first International Congress of Twelve-Tone Music.[5] In all three cases the focus was the same: to enable composers to exchange information with international colleagues and familiarize themselves with compositional techniques and works that had been forbidden by the totalitarian regimes in their respective countries.

in *Neue Musik und Tradition: Festschrift Rudolf Stephan zum 65. Geburtstag,* ed. Josef Kuckertz et al. (Laaber: Laaber Verlag, 1990), 542 (emphasis in original).

    5. Gianmario Borio and Hermann Danuser, eds., *Im Zenit der Moderne: Die Internationalen Ferienkurse für Neue Musik Darmstadt 1946–1966: Geschichte und Dokumentation in vier Bänden,* vol. 1 (Freiburg: Rombach, 1997), 153, 176.

In the following years, the Darmstadt courses underwent two name changes that reflect a gradual change of focus from an overview of international compositional styles to an attempt to enable the young generation to shape their own new musical styles with the help of international discussions and workshops. In 1948, the courses became *Internationale Zeitgenössische Musiktage Darmstadt* (International Contemporary Music Festival in Darmstadt), and finally *Internationale Ferienkurse für Neue Musik Darmstadt* (International Vacation Course for New Music in Darmstadt) in 1964.[6]

In the programs of the first *Ferienkurs* in Kranichstein, one composer figures particularly prominently: the emigrant Paul Hindemith. From 1945 to 1947, Hindemith was expected to give a new impulse to German musical life.[7] His music represented a natural connection to the prewar traditions of tempered modernism. His form of neoclassicism was internationally accepted, and since he had been driven into exile by the Nazi regime, the conservative bent of his ideas on music and education did not come across as politically problematic.[8] In 1948, however, Hindemith's prominence in Darmstadt programs lessened while Arnold Schoenberg's increased.[9] During this year, Hindemith encountered increasing criticism for his lack of musical innovation. The following excerpt from an article by Hans Mayer in the revived progressive journal *Melos* is typical for the tone of criticism brought against Hindemith's works in 1948:

> What Brahms had just imagined as the curse of being a follower [of renowned German composers like Bach and Beethoven, presumably], Hindemith has had to ponder all the more thoroughly in our days! And we will not even begin to talk about those naive followers of the supposedly new German music who are perhaps young in years, but appear to have aged prematurely.[10]

Moreover, attention was increasingly drawn to what was felt to be Hindemith's rather disturbing connection to conservative musical tradi-

6. Ibid., 29–31.
7. Norbert J. Schneider, "Phasen der Hindemith-Rezeption 1945–1955," *Hindemith-Jahrbuch* (hereafter *HJb*) 13 (1984): 140.
8. Rudolf Stephan, "Neue Musik in der Bundesrepublik Deutschland, 1945–1950," *HJb* 11 (1982): 7.
9. Wolfgang Steinecke, "Zwölf Jahre Kranichstein, Chronik 1946–1958," *Darmstädter Beiträge zur Neuen Musik* 1 (1958): 95.
10. Hans Mayer, "Kulturkrise und neue Musik," *Melos* 15 (1948): 278.

tions.[11] The reason for this development lay in the increasing suspicion among the younger generation, in its search for new beginnings, of any system of traditional values spreading through German artistic communities, a suspicion enhanced by the Adenauer government's thoroughly conservative posture.[12] Hindemith's music represented a style not only favored by the conservative public but also showered with high governmental honors. For young composers who wished to create a pure, autonomous art form that shunned popularity and official recognition (and therefore distanced itself from any associations with the Nazis' known political exploitation of music), Hindemith became less desirable as a model, and his music practically disappeared from the Darmstadt concerts after 1950.[13]

Theodor Adorno also helped to publicize the Darmstadt ideas by way of frequent condemnations of Hindemith and his followers. In his radio presentation, "Kritik des Musikanten" (1956), Adorno went as far as to compare Hindemith's musical conservatism, his use of a quasi-tonal system, and his educational ideas to the political use of music as a guided communal experience promoted by the Nazis.[14] By discrediting Hindemith, Adorno contributed to paving the way for the increasing acceptance of serialism as the cutting edge of German musical developments.

The search for a new, untainted musical tradition led inevitably to the Second Viennese School. A politically neutral musical style offering opportunities for further development was discovered in the works of Anton von Webern during the 1949 Darmstadt courses. Webern's impact resulted in part from a "productive misreading": his music was analyzed primarily in terms of its structure as a serialization of different parameters, overlooking its expressive potential. The French composer Olivier Messiaën then used these serial techniques in his Darmstadt piano piece *Mode de valeurs et d'intensités*, which immediately became a model for the new generation. Its significance lies in the fact that its structure is not defined by the expressive properties of melodic themes but by the combination of predetermined series of different parameters. The piece is thus derived from the inherent qualities of the musical material itself, not from any desire to convey personal expression.[15] This "neutrality" had a strong appeal for musicians

11. Schneider, "Phasen der Hindemith-Rezeption," 126.

12. Hermann Danuser, "Tradition und Avantgarde nach 1950," in *Die neue Musik und die Tradition*, ed. Reinhold Brinkmann (Mainz: Schott's Söhne, 1978), 22.

13. Schneider, "Phasen der Hindemith-Rezeption," 132.

14. Andres Brines, "Hindemith und Adornos Kritik des Musikanten," *HJb* 1 (1971): 28–29.

15. Cf. *Die Reihe* 2 (1956), where every author names Webern the point of departure of this development.

who wanted to avoid any romantic notion of expression that had proven to be so easily misused by political powers. Hans Werner Henze described his own music at the time as "a political-ideological vacuum, a societal neutrum, a mystery, not open to rational explanation . . . the only art that is incapable of judging or condemning. . . ."[16] Henze's words clearly illustrate the desire to elude the trauma of political manipulation of the arts by creating a music that was completely self-contained and immune to extramusical influences.

Nevertheless, despite such calls for political neutrality, government support for the musical experiments of these young composers was by no means spurned once the officials showed an interest in it. And the official acceptance of modern experimental trends in composition helped shape Germany's postwar musical identity principally by increasing state support for the serialist avant-garde, channeled through a public institution—radio. Since radio stations could be reactivated relatively quickly after the war and presented the most immediate venue for reaching a large audience, they proved useful during the "denazification" process because the public already was accustomed to relying on radio broadcasts for general information. The Allies decided to make radio their main tool for cultural decentralization and supported seven major regional radio stations established before the Nazi era. After the founding of the Federal Republic in 1949, these institutions continued to be state-funded instruments of Germany's cultural politics. Josef Klingenbeck described their importance as follows:

> The radio is today, more than any other cultural institution, a measure of the deeper values and strengths of a nation. It is a first-rate cultural mirror, in which every single citizen of the country and every interested listener abroad can satisfy himself day after day about the relative worth of the country's individual cultural institutions.[17]

The radio stations' interest in serial music created an unprecedented public support system. Stations not only commissioned pieces from serialist composers, but went to enormous lengths to support their performances in concert and on the air. In a recent discussion with the author, Dr. Peter Molt, a founding member of both the CDU party and the Konrad Adenauer Foundation, pointed out that the postwar decision to lend public support

16. Hans Werner Henze, *Musik und Politik,* ed. Jens Brockmeyer (Munich: Deutscher Taschenbuch Verlag, 1976), 9.
17. Josef Klingenbeck, "Rundfunk und Musikkultur," *ZfM* 111 (1949): 37–38.

to the serialist avant-garde was certainly not prompted by a *conscious* public desire to make up for the Nazis' suppression of this technique. Rather, he credited a general spirit of discovery and experimentation, as well as a desire to establish a new national cultural identity, as motives for the support. Dr. Molt conceded, however, that there was at the same time a general search for untainted artistic traditions and a preference to fund artistic endeavors that were perceived as radically new and intellectual. Serial music fit these criteria in every way and therefore probably won subconscious approval. Ironically, the cultivation of serial music came to depend entirely on the official support of politicians that its composers had initially set out to avoid.

Radio stations further provided the support in the early 1950s for the avant-garde's next stage of abstraction: electronic music. With synthesizers, the quest to define series of musical parameters as precisely as possible took on the intensity of scientific research. Had it not been for the installation of electronic studios at major radio stations (for example, Cologne in 1953), this next step in musical abstraction would have been impossible. At the same time, this development generated a controversy over the political implications of serialism. Avant-garde composers opposed tonality for its hierarchical, totalitarian order—as it had once been described, in fact, by the Nazis. During the mid-1950s, however, the same accusation was raised against electronic music's ostensible aim of imposing total control over musical material by means of predetermined musical operations. The ensuing controversy was one of the factors that prompted Herbert Eimert and Karlheinz Stockhausen to found the journal *Die Reihe* in 1955—to provide a forum for explaining the purposes and techniques of electronic music. In a footnote in the *Reihe* article that defines the serialist's freedom of choice in the selection of his material, Eimert himself reacted vehemently to the accusation of musical totalitarianism:

> At present it is the fashion for empty-headed critics to make out that the systematic "management" of musical material is identical with the terrorist rule-of-force in totalitarian political systems. "Total," "totalitarian,"—here there is room not only for staggeringly ingenious word play, but, if one so desires, for turning upside-down the relationship between a proposition and its necessary precondition. Thus it is possible to produce at will any connection between the apostles of total musical organization and the nihilistic fellow-travelers or propagandists of totalitarian powers. One such "social critic" of music has in fact attributed to the twelve-tone system the power to produce program music whose only suitable counterparts would be concentration camps, machine shops and the

world of Kafka; and logically enough, his next step is to proclaim that the great "human themes" are birth and growing up, love and maturity, age and death—all the oratorio-titles of late romantic liberalism, now converted into the corresponding clichés of official propaganda music.

This is the sort of argument that belongs to the thought control and slogan propagation of the most recent past, in which nothing was more precious than "Nature"; . . . Nature with all its categories—The Race, The People, Blood and Earth. This misuse of the word may be one of the reasons why art can no longer be brought back to the state of nature. It is not reason and order that are the allies of despotism; it is slogans like "Back to Nature": or, to quote Günther Anders, "The rule of terror uses as its favorite word, 'Nature.'" To listen to music in which there is systematic order, and to hear in it the counterpart to political totalitarianism, is just as witless as to appeal to "Nature" when what one really means is textbook harmony.[18]

Eimert here clearly described serialism as a reaction against the politicized music of the Nazi era. The pointedness of his response also illustrates just how political these arguments had become, and how sensitive serialism's advocates were to the accusation of totalitarianism.

Music of "reason and order" as an objectified response to misguided romantic subjectivism—this is also the claim of Germany's leading defender of serialism, the music critic Wolf-Eberhard von Lewinsky. In his opening article for *Die Reihe* 4 (1958), "Young Composers," he linked the avant-garde's struggle for abstraction to its historical background. Quoting Debussy, he even called for a new take on music as a secret science, pure and free of political contamination:

[T]he private gush of feeling, the expression of the composer's feelings in music has become no less suspect than naive nature photography. . . . Debussy said: "music must be a secret science. . . . I should in fact propose to found a society of musical esotericism, instead of attempting to carry art to the public: there ought to be a school of neo-musicians, concerned to preserve the wonderful symbols of music in all their purity— a school at last reestablishing the respect for art that is contaminated by so many people. . . ."

Debussy's words express a wish also cherished by certain young present-day composers, and which graphically illustrates the situation

18. Herbert Eimert, "The Composer's Freedom of Choice," *Die Reihe* 3 (1957): 9 n. 5.

they are in. They are struggling to find a musical language that will meet their inner demands and have intellectual clarity; a survey of recent history would make this fact comprehensible (as a reaction to, and consciousness of, their own tasks and values). . . . [They strive for a] music that is genuinely free of superfluous rites, in a way that is individual but not tied to personality.[19]

Composers of other European countries reacted—consciously or not—in a similar way to their immediate past. Fascist Italy, for example, like Nazi Germany, sought to exploit its musical heritage to promote an ideal of national musical superiority. In his article on Luciano Berio in *Die Reihe* 4, Piero Santi related the postwar struggle of young Italians for an untainted, apolitical, impersonal musical style:

> Everyone's aim is authentic organization of the world of sound, which is finally to be freed from foreign superstructures and external compulsion; accordingly it is generally recognized that one must constantly exercise strict analytical control over both material and language. . . . Thus, in the years after World War II, new Italian music, too, had a part marked out for it. Naturally, it profited from study of hitherto unavailable works, and from insights that had been gained elsewhere; but the natural reaction was against our own most recent past. To put it more bluntly: there was a reaction against "expression at all costs," against rhetoric (veiled to a greater or lesser degree), against sentimentality which no longer dared to express itself melodramatically, unreservedly. . . .[20]

The connection between the emergence of serialism and political events during and after World War II cannot be ignored. During the late 1940s and 1950s, German composers were striving to create a new German musical identity as distant as possible from both postromantic subjectivity and the political manipulation of music under the Nazis. Political appropriation of music had led to an extreme counterreaction: the avoidance of personal musical expression in favor of abstraction. The avant-garde's quest for this abstraction—prompted by a conscious or unconscious response to their own recent history—alienated "serious" contemporary music from general audiences. This music was kept alive in the artificial environment of public radio stations, consciously or unconsciously, for equally political reasons: to compensate for the Nazis' condemnation of

19. Wolf-Eberhard von Lewinsky, "Young Composers," *Die Reihe* 4 (1958): 1–2, 4.
20. Piero Santi, "Luciano Berio," *Die Reihe* 4 (1958): 98.

modern music and to enhance a culturally representative, "untainted" art form. Peter Heyworth pointed out in 1964 that "the mere fact that the Nazis had in effect banned modern music was by a natural process of reaction sufficient to make post-war Germany cultivate it."[21]

Beyond the artistic decisions of postwar composers, the Western Allies profoundly influenced the development of German cultural identity. In this context, the beginning conflict between East and West played a crucial role in cultural funding decisions. Under political pressure from Soviet authorities and the newly founded SED government, East Berlin's Kulturbund and the composers associated with it gradually drifted toward a politically motivated, utilitarian approach to art music during the late 1940s and early 1950s. East German composers increasingly decried abstract music, especially twelve-tone and serialist works, as isolated, esoteric, formalistic, and useless to the envisioned development of a progressive, politically engaged musical culture.[22] The attempt to set off West German culture against its East German counterpart provided the Western Allies and West German cultural institutions with an additionally strong motive for supporting the serialist avant-garde.

These developments in the early postwar years continue to affect decisions about which musical traditions constitute an "official" German musical identity and receive public support. Marching bands, for example, were once a venerated German tradition, central to public music education and musical life of all social classes. Under the Nazis, they became a focal point of the regime's public displays. In Germany today, bands are restricted to church processions and military functions or otherwise merely serve as caricatures of military pomp in carnival processions. Serialist music, however, while never widely popular, still continues to attract enthusiastic support from intellectuals and public institutions, particularly academe.

Guide to Further Reading

Adorno, Theodor W. *Dissonanzen: Musik in der verwalteten Welt,* 5th ed. Göttingen: Vandenhoeck & Ruprecht, 1972.
————. *Philosophy of Modern Music.* Trans. Anne G. Mitchell and Wesley V. Bloomster. New York: Seabury Press, 1973.

21. Peter Heyworth, "The Gilded Cage," *Encounter* 22 (1964): 75–76.
22. Elizabeth Koch Janik, "From Mendelssohn to *Musik und Gesellschaft:* The Search for a Progressive Musical Tradition in East Berlin, 1945–1951" (paper presented at the twenty-third annual meeting of the German Studies Association, Atlanta, 1999).

Borio, Gianmario, and Hermann Danuser, eds. *Im Zenit der Moderne: Die Internationalen Ferienkurse für Neue Musik Darmstadt 1946–66: Geschichte und
Dokumentation in vier Bänden.* 4 vols. Freiburg: Rombach, 1997.

Burgess, Anthony. *Little Wilson and Big God.* Toronto: Stoddart Publishing, 1987.

Fortner, Wolfgang. "Kranichsteiner Aspekte." *Darmstädter Beiträge zur Neuen
Musik* 1 (1958): 22–24.

Griffiths, Paul. *Modern Music: The Avant Garde Since 1945.* London: J. M. Dent &
Sons, 1981.

Helm, Everett. "Wiederaufbau des deutschen Musiklebens nach 1945 und Paul Hindemith." *Hindemith-Jahrbuch* 9 (1980): 130–37.

Henze, Hans W. "Wo stehen wir heute?" *Darmstädter Beiträge zur Neuen Musik* 1
(1958): 82–83.

———. *Musik und Politik.* Munich: Deutscher Taschenbuch Verlag, 1976.

Heyworth, Peter. "The Gilded Cage." *Encounter* 22 (1964): 74–78.

Kneif, Tibor. *Politische Musik?* Vienna: Doblinger, 1977.

Krenek, Ernst. "Den Jüngeren über die Schulter geschaut." *Die Reihe* 1 (1955): 31–33.

Konold, Wulf. "Hindemith, Hartmann und Zillig heute." *Hindemith-Jahrbuch* 8
(1979): 119–37.

Mayer, Hans. "Kulturkrise und Neue Musik." *Melos* 15 (1948): 218–22, 276–82.

Nono, Luigi. "Geschichte und Gegenwart in der Musik von heute." *Darmstädter
Beiträge zur Neuen Musik* 3 (1960): 15–21.

Perris, Arnold. *Music as Propaganda.* Westport, Conn.: Greenwood Press, 1985.

Pousseur, Henri. "Outline of a Method." *Die Reihe* 3 (1957): 44–88.

———. "Theorie und Praxis in der neuesten Musik." *Darmstädter Beiträge zur
Neuen Musik* 2 (1959): 15–29.

Stuckenschmidt, H. H. "Die dritte Epoche: Bemerkungen zur Ästhetik der Elektro-
nenmusik." *Die Reihe* 1 (1955): 17–21.

Vogt, Hans. *Neue Musik seit 1945.* Stuttgart: Philipp Reclam jun., 1972.

Wörner, Karl H. "Neue Musik 1948–1958: Versuch eines historischen Überblicks."
Darmstädter Beiträge zur Neuen Musik 2 (1959): 7–14.

———. *Karlheinz Stockhausen: Werk und Wollen.* Rodenkirchen: P. J. Tonger, 1963.

American Jazz in the German Cold War

UTA G. POIGER

From the 1920s to the 1950s, jazz had many outspoken enemies in Germany. Since musicians first introduced Germans to jazz during the Weimar years, its critics linked the music to feminized men and lascivious women, to racial degeneration, and to commercialism. In the 1920s, conservatives, for example, described jazz as a music created by "niggers," marketed by Jews, and expressing a "primitive sexuality." Such attacks found their culmination in Nazi attempts to prohibit jazz and in the Nazi persecution of jazz fans. When the music experienced a renaissance in both Germanies after 1945, East German authorities repeated the harassment of those devoted to jazz, while critics in West Germany publicly disdained them. Both sides were particularly concerned about dancing jazz enthusiasts and jam sessions in East and West German "Hot Clubs."[1]

By the early 1960s, however, the picture had changed. The West German defense minister Franz-Josef Strauß declared jazz to be a music for the new West German army, and West Berlin adolescents could dance to American music in a state-sponsored club called "Jazz-Saloon." East German authorities, too, allowed jazz concerts, although they continued to be more worried about American music than their West German counterparts. An

---

1. This essay revisits ideas explored in Uta G. Poiger, *Jazz, Rock, and Rebels: Cold War Politics and American Culture in a Divided Germany* (Berkeley: University of California Press, 2000), especially chapter 5 and the epilogue. Quotes from Michael Kater, "The Jazz Experience in Weimar Germany," *German History* 6 (1988): 145–58, 154. On jazz in the Weimar Republic and the Third Reich, see Michael Kater, *Different Drummers: Jazz in the Culture of Nazi Germany* (New York: Oxford University Press, 1992).

important transformation had occurred: in the course of the 1950s, increasing numbers of East and West Germans, including state officials, had come to think of jazz as an acceptable and even respectable musical form.

Assumptions about proper masculinity and femininity and changing views of the culture and history of black Americans underlay the East and West German reevaluations of jazz. Making the music respectable required controlling the behavior of jazz fans and especially the way they danced. Moreover, the proliferation of jazz was linked to narrowing definitions of jazz and to redefining the meaning of individual jazz styles—from Dixieland to bebop. In both Germanies it was only in the second half of the 1950s that narrower definitions of jazz as different from "lighter" popular hits gained widespread currency. Jazz promoters distinguished between "authentic" jazz on the one hand and "commercial" music and dances like boogie-woogie and rock and roll on the other.

The changing place of jazz in the postwar German cultural landscapes was part of the efforts in both states to newly define "Germanness" in the aftermath of National Socialism and in the face of the Cold War. Jazz promoters on both sides of the Iron Curtain were well aware of the political ramifications of their efforts. In West Germany, radio host, writer, and producer Joachim Ernst Berendt became the most influential person to shape positive reevaluations of jazz, while in East Germany, Reginald Rudorf, a social scientist, radio host, and writer, was the leading proponent of the music.

Making Jazz Respectable in West Germany

Joachim Ernst Berendt, in his West German radio broadcasts, publications, and lectures, defined jazz as a serious artistic and philosophical enterprise. Born in 1922, Berendt had seen his father, a Lutheran minister, sent off to a concentration camp in 1938. An avid jazz fan before 1945, the young Berendt became a radio host for jazz programs in the French Occupation Zone after his return from the Russian front and soon began to publish numerous articles and books on jazz. Well aware that racism had driven anti-jazz sentiment in Germany and elsewhere ever since jazz had emerged as a distinct musical idiom in the 1920s, he asked his audiences to put aside their prejudices.[2]

Berendt carefully narrowed the definitions for what he considered "authentic jazz." He asserted emphatically that the popular hits broadcast on

2. For biographical information about Berendt, see Kater, *Different Drummers*, 96, 208–9, and the autobiography, Joachim-Ernst Berendt, *Das Leben—Ein Klang: Wege zwischen Jazz und Nada Brama* (Munich: Drömer Knaur, 1996).

American and European radio stations or played at most concerts were not jazz. According to Berendt, jazz was not a dance music, and true jazz fans did not dance while listening to the music. Berendt thus disassociated jazz from the dance halls that had characterized the arrival of consumer culture in both Europe and the United States since the late nineteenth century. He also discredited those jazz fans who were dancing and romping around at jam sessions in postwar German Hot Clubs and other jazz joints. For Berendt, listening to jazz was an intellectual experience, and he went to great lengths to show that jazz music represented "the essence of the modern age" as well as any twentieth-century philosopher could.[3]

In a 1952 article for the *Frankfurter Hefte*, Berendt used formal analysis to distinguish a sequence of different jazz styles, from the Dixieland and Chicago styles of the 1920s, to the swing of the 1930s, and finally to the bebop and cool jazz of the postwar period. Drawing on the systematic analysis that Frenchman Hugues Panassié had developed in the 1930s, Berendt argued that one jazz style followed the other almost in a logical order. Further, Berendt found parallels between the development of jazz and the trajectory of European music from baroque, to classic, to romantic, and to the recent modernist music of Stravinsky. In so doing, Berendt validated jazz as a serious artistic tradition, but at the same time made European music the standard against which the "progress" of jazz was to be judged.[4]

While Berendt explained that jazz musicians had adopted and adapted European harmonies and instruments, he also emphasized the African elements of jazz and stressed that neither jazz music nor black jazz musicians were "primitive." He explained that European-trained ears had difficulty understanding the African influences, and especially the rhythms of jazz. The New Orleans jazz of the 1920s, for example, did not sound "beautiful according to the sensibility of white man," but it was a truthful and adequate expression of the situation of the oppressed, "for whom music is often the most perfect and only possibility to claim freedom and humanity."[5] Berendt believed that whites had the moral responsibility both to feel compassion toward blacks and to try to understand their music, for, as he stressed, whites had caused the plight of black Americans.

Yet Berendt also claimed jazz as a white music. In his interpretation of the 1920s Chicago jazz, which white musicians had developed after listen-

3. Berendt, *Der Jazz: Eine Zeitkritische Studie* (Stuttgart: DVA, 1950), 7, 90.
4. Joachim Ernst Berendt, "Zum Thema Jazz," *Frankfurter Hefte* 7 (October 1952): 768–79. See also Berendt, *Das Leben—ein Klang*, 318; Hugues Panassié, *Le Jazz Hot* (Paris: R. A. Correa, 1934; English ed., New York: Whitmark, 1936).
5. Berendt, "Zum Thema Jazz," 775–76.

ing to black migrants on Chicago's South Side, Berendt focused mostly on Bix (Leon Bismarck) Beiderbecke and his German ancestry. Berendt alleged that the longing among the Beiderbecke family "for the forests of Pomerania" (most of which had become part of Poland after World War II), for "the lakes of Mecklenburg" (which was part of East Germany after World War II), and "for the Prussia of Bismarck" (which had been distinctly authoritarian) had driven Bix "into a romantic state" "out of which the first important white musician grew who could feel compassion for and reshape the melancholy of black music born out of century-long slavery and oppression." [6] It is hard to say whether Berendt consciously drew parallels between the fate of postwar Germans and African Americans as peoples dispersed and displaced, but he certainly stressed the German roots of a famous jazz musician to make jazz more acceptable to Germans. Perhaps Berendt's interest in Chicago jazz was merely strategic.

Berendt paid relatively little attention to the big bands of the 1930s and 1940s. He applauded the swinging rhythms and technical perfection of the swing musicians of the 1930s, but he did not spend much time on the mostly white swing big bands who, playing in ballrooms and theaters, had brought black dance band music into the popular mainstream. After World War II, the U.S. army had spread these rhythms throughout Germany, and many Germans listened and danced to them enthusiastically.

Berendt's real interest was the intellectual jazz of the years after 1945. He explicitly preferred the more spartan, less danceable music of bebop and cool jazz over earlier styles. Bebop had been developed by black musicians, such as Charlie Parker and Dizzy Gillespie, in Harlem jazz clubs around 1945. The small bebop combos featured the improvisations of solo performers and played a jazz characterized by unusual asymmetric melodies and dense polyrhythms sometimes perceived as nervous. Berendt conceded that it was hard "for the uninitiated" to understand this music.

Bebop musicians, according to Berendt, had tried to lift music to an "absolute sphere" independent of the feelings of the improvising musicians and their audience. In particular, Berendt admired how bebop players—ostensibly breaking their link to their audience/consumers—showed open disdain for their audience. Comparing its "critical relationship to time and causality" to that of modernist literature and music, Berendt located bebop as a logical development in responses to modernity and made it into "high" culture. Cool jazz, which was just emerging as a distinct style as Berendt was writing and which he had heard during a trip to the United States, had

6. Ibid.

taken up certain symphonic effects from European classical music. Berendt did not mention this, but claimed that cool finally had resolved bebop's imbalances and, together with Stravinsky's music, represented "the human concept of a whole era." Bebop and cool jazz, Berendt's favorite jazz styles, however, were the ones least likely to find an appreciative audience among many Germans.[7]

Concluding that jazz represented the "spiritual state of modern man," Berendt stressed that it had gone beyond its African and African American roots to gain a following around the world. He thus made jazz into a universalizing experience. Perhaps it was not by chance that Berendt seemed to like cool jazz even better than bebop. Played by both black and white musicians, and combining "white" and "black" musical styles, cool jazz quickly became the symbol of successful racial integration. Berendt appreciated the theoretical and musical sophistication of bebop musicians, who saw themselves as artists and who sought to reject racial stereotypes of black performers. Yet, by focusing on jazz as a "universal" music, Berendt, like many other critics in the United States and elsewhere, could not appreciate the specific political implications that bebop, for example, had in the context of African American struggles against oppression.[8]

Berendt in fact imagined an entirely different political function for jazz. Claiming that the music "immunized" its followers against totalitarianism, he asserted that jazz and authoritarianism or dictatorships were incompatible. It was not by chance, said Berendt in 1953, that the military was hostile toward jazz, and he reminded West Germans that people in East Germany "for the second time in fifteen years" lived under threats because they liked jazz.[9]

Berendt's validations of jazz as noncommercial, modernist, and antiauthoritarian art music relied on sexual conservatism. He sought to sanitize, desexualize, and decommercialize what he considered true jazz and proper jazz fan behavior. In his 1953 manual for jazz fans, *Jazzbuch*, Berendt described as the emblematic "true" jazz fan a Catholic priest who was lis-

7. On the relationship of swing and bebop, see Scott DeVeaux, *The Birth of Bebop: A Social and Musical History* (Berkeley: University of California Press, 1997).

8. See Joachim-Ernst Berendt, "Americana: Erlebnisse und Gedanken von einer US-Reise," *Melos* 18 (March 1951): 78–82. On the problems of constructing jazz as a universal experience and challenges to this view, see Scott DeVeaux, "Constructing the Jazz Tradition: Jazz Historiography," *Black American Literature Forum* 25 (fall 1991): 525–60; Jon Panish, *The Color of Jazz: Race and Representation in Postwar American Culture* (Jackson: University of Mississippi Press, 1997). The most famous challenge to this position is LeRoi Jones (Amiri Baraka), *Blues People: Negro Music in White America* (New York: Morrow, 1963).

9. Berendt, "Für und wider den Jazz," *Merkur* 7 (1953): 887–90.

tening to jazz in his remote monastery and for whom jazz was compatible with the writings of Augustine. Further, Berendt made a distinction between the "serious" fans and the so-called Swing-Heinis—a term that the Nazis had likewise used in their persecutions of jazz fans. Implying that jazz fans were male, Berendt described Swing-Heinis as youths who, with their striped socks, shorter pants, and longer hair, stood in direct opposition to the soldier ideal. Berendt urged true jazz fans, who he thought were apt to take a dim view of the Swing-Heinis' wild behavior and pursuit of fashion, not to eject them from their circles. Indeed, serious and respectable jazz fans should teach them about the true meaning of the music. These ideas had class implications: Berendt wanted jazz fans to shed styles associated with lower-class culture and to assume a more bourgeois demeanor.[10]

In the aftermath of intense German nationalism and racism prior to 1945 and in the context of West German efforts to erect the Christian West as a cultural and political ideal in the first half of the 1950s, Berendt's stance was in many ways radical. He validated jazz as a serious artistic tradition and insisted that neither jazz nor black jazz musicians were primitive. But at the same time he made European music the standard against which the "progress" of jazz was to be judged. His validations focused on the one hand on improvisation, that is the spontaneity of creation by the jazz performer, and on the other hand on the respectability of "authentic" jazz musicians and their audiences. Berendt made jazz compatible with the bourgeois notion of (high) culture and with a bourgeois gender system.

Clearly, Berendt's ideas were attractive: his 1953 *Jazzbuch* sold seventy-five thousand copies within months. Upon its publication, Berendt became the single most powerful jazz critic in West Germany. Over the next four decades, he would have a deep impact on the European music scene as a writer, producer, and organizer of festivals, promoting not only jazz but also blues and "world music."

The Success of Jazz in West Germany

The image of the intellectual male jazz fan whom Berendt championed differed from the fans actually frequenting the so-called Hot Clubs in large West German cities in the late 1940s and early 1950s. These jazz clubs often ran their own bars with live jazz music and were a place where musicians and fans met, talked, and danced. Particularly popular were the jam sessions. Many of the clubs were members of the West German Jazz Federation,

---

10. Joachim-Ernst Berendt, *Das Jazzbuch: Entwicklung und Bedeutung der Jazzmusik* (Frankfurt am Main: Fischer, 1953).

which published its own journal, *Jazz-Podium*, modeled in many ways on the American *Downbeat*. By the early 1950s, however, club leaders grew increasingly dissatisfied with the quality of the music and the behavior of fans at jam sessions; they were also unhappy about negative reporting in the press. In response, the German Jazz Federation sought to counter the negative image of jazz through its publications and with lectures. Promoting the image of an "intellectual," nondancing jazz fan was part of this effort, and the Jazz Federation accordingly sponsored a series of lectures by Berendt.[11]

These measures proved successful, for by 1955 the new type of jazz fan—more "intellectual," more "serious"—was widely visible in West Germany. For many of them Berendt's *Jazzbuch* became a bible. In West Berlin these "respectable" fans organized the New Jazz Circle Berlin, which made sure that information about jazz concerts was published in the press. Most important, the club organized regular lectures in which the audience listened intently to recordings, which jazz experts—either guest speakers or club members—interpreted. These events at first took place in the basement of a Berlin restaurant, but after the restaurant closed in late 1955, club members found space in the West Berlin American cultural center (Amerikahaus). Like many other American cultural centers in West German cities, it became a meeting place for jazz fans. The club's emphasis on "respectability" and its dedication to an intellectual experience of jazz actually discouraged lower-class and female jazz fans: 90 percent of the audience at lectures were male, and a majority came from the middle and upper classes. Opinion surveys conducted for the U.S. government by West German polling institutes suggested that as narrower definitions of jazz prevailed, jazz became increasingly popular among young people from the West German middle and upper classes.[12]

It was in the context of youth riots and the adolescent consumption of rock and roll that these respectable jazz fans and their music attracted attention after 1955 as a remedy against youthful unruliness. One newspaper article, in juxtaposing the behavior of jazz fans and the fans of rock and roll, maintained that in the latter group, latent adolescent protest turned into anarchy. Accompanying the article was the picture of a girl who was throwing her partner through the air during a rock and roll dance number. Most

11. See Horst Lange, *Jazz in Deutschland: Die deutsche Jazz-Chronik 1900–1960* (Berlin: Colloquium, 1966); Kater, *Different Drummers*; Ralph Willett, *The Americanization of Germany, 1945–1949* (New York: Routledge, 1989), 86–98.

12. See "Drei Jahre NJCB," *Volksblatt*, 27 April 1958; USIA, Office of Research, Public Opinion Barometer Reports, Barometer Surveys XX.9 and XX.11, West Germany, May 1957 and October 1958, RG 306, NA (National Archives).

true jazz fans, the caption claimed, rejected such displays—which clearly connoted gender disarray. The article explained that jazz associations directed adolescent protest into appropriate channels; their work was therefore worthy of state support.[13]

West German bureaucrats began to follow these suggestions. In 1956–57, city officials in West Berlin sponsored ten jazz lectures and one jazz concert as part of their youth protection efforts. Such state-supported events marked the growing broad acceptance of jazz in West Germany. However, this phenomenon was not merely the result of changing attitudes within West Germany. Indeed, it cannot be fully understood without looking at the battles over jazz in East Germany.[14]

"Authentic" Jazz and Politics in East Germany

Around 1950, East German authorities, like their Soviet counterparts, had started an outright campaign against jazz, and jazz remained highly controversial in the following years. Not surprisingly, jazz fans in East Germany found it more difficult than those in West Germany to pursue their interests. Frequently, they smuggled records and Western publications on jazz into the GDR and listened to Western radio stations. Yet some East German voices existed that sought to make jazz officially acceptable.[15]

The most outspoken promoter of jazz music in the GDR was Reginald Rudorf. Born in 1929, Rudorf came from a middle-class family and was a member of the East German SED. By the early 1950s he was teaching social sciences at the University of Leipzig. From 1952 to 1957 Rudorf published articles and gave lectures indicting what he called "unauthentic" jazz and urging East German officials to support the proliferation of "authentic" jazz. Although his definitions of the various types of jazz were somewhat inconsistent, he generally praised blues, Dixieland, and spirituals as authentic and rejected bebop and other forms of modern jazz.[16]

Rudorf's efforts on behalf of jazz were successful, as long as he located his arguments within the official cultural doctrine of the East German SED. In March 1951 the SED's Central Committee had announced the fight against formalism and called for a search for an authentic German national

---

13. H. W. Corten, "Kann der Jazz unserer Jugend schaden?" *Die Welt,* 21 July 1957.

14. Minutes of the 28. Sitzung, Jugendwohlfahrtausschuss, Bezirksamt Kreuzberg, 2 May 1957, Landesarchiv Berlin, Rep. 206, Acc. 3070/3582.

15. See Reginald Rudorf, *Jazz in der Zone* (Cologne: Kiepenheuer and Witsch, 1964).

16. See the autobiography by Reginald Rudorf, *Nie wieder links: Eine deutsche Reportage* (Frankfurt am Main: Ullstein, 1990).

culture. East German officials denounced all cultural expressions that put
more stress on form than content; such art allegedly lost its humanist and
democratic character and was characteristic of the imperialism of late capitalist systems, particularly the United States. Officials leveled accusations
of "decadence," "cosmopolitanism," and "formalism" against, for example,
the literature of Kafka, against abstract painting, and also against undesirable music, such as jazz.[17] In distinguishing between authentic jazz on the
one hand and commercial dance music and modern jazz on the other, Rudorf employed this same language. For example, he indicted swing music
and bebop as "decadent." Further he frowned upon the rhythmic "excesses" of percussionists or the "atonal" lines of swing. At the same time that
he derided certain aspects of jazz, Rudorf stressed that African American
folk music, including some forms of jazz such as blues and Dixieland, could
fruitfully stimulate the development of a new "clean" German dance music. Rudorf followed a logic that jazz fans in the Soviet Union had employed
with varying success since the 1930s.[18]

In his rejection of musical forms like swing and boogie, Rudorf was
prompted by what he perceived as transgressions committed by male and
female fans. "The ecstatic jumps of the deplorable brushheads and their
Amizonen," quipped Rudorf, "are at their worst when the orchestra plays
louder, when a saxophone begins to squeak in a vulgar way or when shrill
trumpet solos ring." By identifying male jazz fans merely by their bouffant
hairstyles and speaking of them derogatorily as "the brushheads" (*Bürsten-
köpfe*), Rudorf associated them with fashion and thus with femininity. By
characterizing their female counterparts as *Amizonen*—a term that played
with "Amazons," "Amis" (Americans), and "American Zone" and that was
used by Germans to denounce women who had sexual relations with U.S.
soldiers—Rudorf portrayed Americanized German women as sexual aggres-
sors and as masculinized.[19] Rudorf thus linked the absence of male and female respectability to threats against proper German national identity.

In his promotion of blues and Dixieland, Rudorf proposed that authentic jazz could help counter the dangerous effects of American commercial
music in East Germany and elsewhere. Just as East Germans could learn

17. See, for example, Günter Erbe, *Die verfemte Moderne: Die Auseinandersetzung mit dem "Modernismus" in Kulturpolitik, Literaturwissenschaft und Literatur der DDR* (Opla-den: Westdeutscher Verlag, 1993); Reginald Rudolf [sic], "Für eine frohe, ausdrucksvolle Tanz-musik," *Musik und Gesellschaft* 2 (August 1952): 247–52; Reginald Rudorf, "Die Tanzmusik muß neue Wege gehen," *Musik und Gesellschaft* 4, part 1 (February 1954): 51–56; part 2 (March 1954): 92–95.
18. Rudolf [sic], "Für eine frohe, ausdrucksvolle Tanzmusik"; Rudorf, "Die Tanzmusik."
19. Rudorf, "Die Tanzmusik."

from the lively music of the Soviet Union and the other people's republics, so too, Rudorf suggested, could they learn from authentic jazz. Rudorf's validation of jazz, like Berendt's in West Germany, rested on distinguishing authentic from commercial music and on separating authentic jazz from any association with decadence or unbridled sexuality.

Yet in spite of similarities in their logic, Berendt and Rudorf came to different conclusions. In contrast to Berendt and many of the West German jazz associations who found bebop and modern jazz most valuable, Rudorf rejected such forms of jazz as "decadent,"especially as an expression of black American decadence. In 1954 Rudorf explained that the oppression of African Americans had induced a crisis in their culture. Some black musicians had sold out to the music industry, he argued, while others, "often disconnected from the struggle of their people," had sought refuge in technical experiments. But while this latter group thought that they were protesting commercialism and artistic oppression, wrote Rudorf, "they were merely making decadence richer by one form of expression." Rudorf criticized black and white bebop musicians who had created their music in recording studios rather than in dance halls. He particularly disliked Charlie Parker's music because Parker revealed "nihilist tendencies" in his "morbid performances." Further, Rudorf explained, the "cult of technical experiments" continued in cool jazz, characterized by atonality and other formal elements "which were adversaries of melody and therefore of music." In modern jazz, he concluded, a unity existed between "decadent form" and "decadent content." Rudorf assured East Germans that such modern jazz was not played in the GDR, but that it existed in West Germany.[20]

Race played a complicated role in East German criticisms of jazz. Rudorf certainly did not draw his distinction between authentic and inauthentic jazz along color lines. Indeed, he saw black musicians as both the greatest traitors of and the greatest hope for jazz; thus he reserved his most scathing critiques for the black bebop musicians and his most celebratory remarks for the black musicians who played spirituals and blues. Yet his indictments of certain forms of jazz dancing as "degenerate" used a vocabulary employed by those who had promoted racial hierarchies that saw (white/"Aryan") Germans as superior to Jews, blacks, and other groups like "Gypsies." The concept of degeneracy evoked this racial logic, and by using it in the context of dances and music that Rudorf saw rooted in African American culture, he also reasserted racial hierarchies between black Americans who allegedly lacked respectability and white Germans. Finally,

20. Ibid. See also Rudorf, *Jazz in der Zone,* 43–44.

in validating authentic jazz, Rudorf used rhetoric that had antisemitic undertones: like other East German officials and intellectuals, he turned
against the "cosmopolitan" culture industry and "cosmopolitan" hits.[21]

Organizing East German Jazz Fans

Rudorf's use of official terminology allowed him to carve out a space for
jazz in East Germany. Within his framework of distinguishing authentic
from commercial and modern "formalist" jazz, Rudorf was able to broaden
the range of officially acceptable tunes, and in 1955 he and his friend Heinz
Lukasz even gained official recognition from the state youth organization,
Free German Youth (FDJ), for an association of Leipzig jazz fans.[22]

Although Rudorf and Lukasz advertised their jazz club as an organization firmly rooted in the political missions of the party and FDJ, their group
was actually not very different from its West German counterparts. Dancing was clearly neither Rudorf's nor the Leipzig club's priority. Almost half
of the members were students, and like many West German jazz clubs, the
group attracted mostly men, who listened intently to jazz recordings.[23]

In spite of Rudorf's rhetorical efforts, however, many East German officials continued to be suspicious of *all* jazz and *all* jazz fans. Squarely linking
jazz to unrespectable expressions of femininity and masculinity, one official
countered Rudorf's suggestion that jazz was the music of the urban prole-
tariat with the assertion that it had emerged from brothels and gangster
hangouts. Officials indicted Rudorf and jazz fans in Germany and abroad as
followers of "cosmopolitan" dance music and "internationalism."[24] They
found their suspicions confirmed when the Leipzig jazz club did not endorse
East German rearmament, and in May 1955 the government dissolved the
group.[25]

Thus, both East German opponents and promoters of jazz relied on the
same concepts—such as decadence and disdain for a capitalist music industry—in arguments for their respective causes. This overlap undoubtedly

---

21. Rudolf [*sic*], "Für eine frohe, ausdrucksvolle Tanzmusik"; Rudorf, "Die Tanzmusik."
See also "Die Arbeitsprinzipien der Interessengemeinschaft," Leipzig, n.d., ca. 1955, Institut
für zeitgeschichtliche Jugendforschung, Jugendarchiv (hereafter JA-IzJ), A392.
22. See Rudorf and Lukasz, letter to the Zentralrat der FDJ, Kulturabteilung, 12 April
1955, JA-IzJ A392; copy of letter from Thomas to Abteilung Kultur, Zentralrat der FDJ, 10 May
1955, JA-IzJ A392; Lange, *Jazz in Deutschland*; Rudorf, *Jazz in der Zone*.
23. Sekretariat, "Abschrift," Leipzig, 26 January 1956, JA-IzJ A392.
24. "Jazzdiskussion," Berlin, 7 April 1955, JA-IzJ A392.
25. Copy of letter from Thomas to Abteilung Kultur, Zentralrat der FDJ, 10 May 1955;
also Kurt Knoblauch, FDJ Bezirksleitung Leipzig, to FDJ-Zentralrat, 3 August 1955, JA-IzJ A392.

contributed to the confusion that characterized official East German attitudes toward jazz in the years after 1955. While many officials sought to root
out jazz, others tried to use it to attract young people to the socialist cause.
FDJ and Culture Ministry officials had rejected Rudorf's vindication of jazz
in the spring and summer of 1955; they prohibited the Leipzig jazz club and
stopped Rudorf's and Lukasz's radio programs. In February 1956, however,
the FDJ Central Council included a defense of jazz in its manifesto *An Euch
Alle* (*To All of You*), and a period of greater leniency followed.

   This renewed tolerance of jazz in East Germany occurred in the context
of the "thaw" in the Soviet orbit. After the Twentieth Party Congress, the
organizing committee for the Sixth World Youth Festival decided to hold it
in Moscow during the summer of 1957 and to demonstrate Soviet openness,
among other things, by including a competition for Soviet and foreign jazz
groups. In the spring of 1957, East German authorities held their own contest
to determine who would represent the GDR in Moscow. The winner was the
Jazz-Band Halle, a Dixieland orchestra led by Alfons Zschockelt, but bands
oriented toward cool and West Coast jazz were also allowed to participate.[26]

   Despite this greater openness, SED officials, like their Soviet counterparts, continued to be suspicious of the activities of jazz fans. In 1957 officials increasingly clamped down on jazz clubs, and Rudorf stretched the
limits too far when he organized jazz concerts in Protestant churches and
gave lectures in West Germany. In March of 1957 he was arrested and later
that year was sentenced to two years in prison for slandering the FDJ and
the SED in front of Leipzig and Munich audiences and for having used jazz
as a cover for political crimes. In this repressive climate, numerous jazz
musicians and jazz club members—among them Zschockelt and, after his
release, Rudorf—left for West Germany.[27]

Jazz as a Cold War Weapon

In the meantime, the press and officials in West Germany and the United
States were closely watching developments in East Germany.[28] The suppression of jazz in East Germany and other countries of the Warsaw Pact

   26. Karl-Heinz Drechsel, insert for *Jazz in Deutschland: Aus dem Amiga-Archiv 1947–
65*, 4th CD (Berlin, n.d.).
   27. See Rudorf, *Jazz in der Zone*, 116–25; "Die Tätigkeit des Ministeriums für Kultur, ins-
besondere der HA Musik auf dem Gebiete des Jazz," n.d., ca. September 1957, Bundesarchiv
Abteilungen Potsdam, DR1 Nr. 243.
   28. "Gefahr für den Stehgeiger," *Der Spiegel*, 26 October 1955; "Zonen-Jazzexperte in
Ungnade," *Der Tag*, 24 February 1957; "Prügel für Jazzanhänger," *SBZ-Archiv* 8, 25 April
1957; U.S. Mission Berlin, Dispatch 983, 7 May 1957, RG 59, 762b.00/5-757; Dispatch 388,

made the music into an attractive messenger for American and West German democracy. After many requests from the field and positive press
reports about respectable European fans, jazz became an official part of
the cultural programs that the U.S. Information Agency (USIA) sponsored
after 1956.[29]

West Germans, for their part, used jazz against youthful rebelliousness
at home and to distinguish themselves from both the Nazi past and the
Cold War enemies to the east. This multiple function of jazz—as an alleged tamer of young rebels and as a representative of Western democracy—contributed to its astounding proliferation through books, festivals,
and radio and television shows in West Germany in the second half of the
1950s. Jazz never appealed to a majority of Germans, but in 1957 an opinion survey conducted for the USIA found that West Germans appreciated
jazz more than did their European neighbors in France, England, or Italy.[30]

Jazz became the appropriate cultural expression for the "end of ideologies" that American, West European, and German intellectuals were pos-
tulating in the late 1950s. One West German expert interpreted jazz as a
music that, when performed perfectly, "carried its meaning and affirmation
in itself."[31] In this logic, jazz ideally had nothing to do with politics, and
yet, through its "apolitical" privileged place, it could become a political
weapon of the West.

Some West German officials certainly grasped this potential. In August 1958 Defense Minister Franz-Josef Strauß voiced his support for jazz
in response to an inquiry Berendt had made on behalf of the West German
Jazz Federation: "the community-building powers" of jazz converged with
the efforts of the West German army. Strauß stressed that he was thinking
of "pure jazz" (*Jazz in Reinkultur*), not of "pseudo-jazz," and he suggested
forming a "Head Jazz Band" (*Leit-Jazz-Kapelle*) that would be made up of
especially qualified musicians and would lead others in the proper direction. Strauß explicitly used jazz to show that West Germany and the West
German army differed from both its German Cold War enemy to the east
and from the Third Reich. He criticized the suppression of jazz in totalitarian regimes and explained that with its improvisations and its freedom

16 December 1957, RG 59, 762.00/12-1657; Dispatch 489, 31 January 1958, RG 59, 762b.00/
1-3158; Dispatch 575, 10 March 1958, RG 59, 762.00/3-1058, NA.

29. See Charles A. Thomson and Walter H. C. Leaves, *Cultural Relations and U.S. Foreign Policy* (Bloomington: Indiana University Press, 1963), 123.

30. Poiger, *Jazz, Rock and Rebels*, ch 5. USIA, Office of Research, PMS-18, "West European Reactions to Jazz," 1957, RG 306, NA.

31. Dietrich Schulz-Köhn, "Der Jazz—Marotte oder Musik," *Kölnische Rundschau*,
14 December 1958.

to have many forms, jazz did not fit into the picture, "according to which the dictatorships of the world want to change the world through brutal force." The expression of these views by the defense minister was widely reported and received with some astonishment. Most baffled was perhaps Berendt himself, who in response reiterated that jazz and the military were incompatible. Berendt's intentions of constructing a respectable, antiauthoritarian jazz audience certainly ran counter to those of Strauß. And yet Berendt's efforts in many ways had made it possible that jazz could be put to political uses by the West German state.[32]

By the late 1950s, as the Adenauer Era was slowly coming to an end, jazz came to symbolize the new pluralist, postfascist, and antitotalitarian society increasingly espoused by West German politicians. This logic cut across party lines. Thus Willy Brandt, the mayor of Berlin and emerging national leader of the opposition Social Democrats, used the new image of jazz to portray himself as a modern and liberal politician. Brandt had himself photographed with Louis Armstrong by his side—with Armstrong eating bratwurst.[33] And by 1964 the government-funded West German Goethe Institute—designed to represent German culture abroad—was sending West German jazz bands to several Asian countries. American and West German authorities tried to avoid any association with the negative stereotypes of consumer culture, even as they made consumption increasingly into a Cold War weapon. In this context jazz appeared as an ideal vehicle in the cultural and political battles of the Cold War.

Another example of the new function of jazz as a messenger for West German democracy was the state-sponsored West Berlin youth club called "Jazz-Saloon," which opened in 1960. The West Berlin minister of youth affairs Ella Kay herself served nonalcoholic drinks and beer in the club. Two additional clubs soon followed. Their explicit purpose was to turn adolescents into sensible consumers. Pictures in the press showed a respectable audience of young women in skirts and sweaters and young men in suits. One commentator reported that pants for young women and jeans for young men—which had been the fashions for female and male rock and roll fans and rioters—were not "desirable."[34] The music offered was rarely the bebop

32. "Jazz-Begeisterung in der Truppe," *Die Welt*, 9 August 1958; Joachim E. Berendt, "Jazz auf dem Kasernenhof," *Die Welt*, 23 August 1958.

33. See Tamara Domentat, ed., *Coca-Cola, Jazz und AFN: Berlin und die Amerikaner* (Berlin: Schwarzkopf and Schwarzkopf, 1995), 199.

34. See Senator für Jugend und Sport, "Bericht über die Situation der Berliner Jugend," *Der Rundbrief* 10, no. 11/12 (1960): 1–24, especially 5–10; "Ein ganzes Haus für Jugend und Jazz," *Kurier*, 30 April 1960; Horst Sass, "'Jugend Jazz Saloon' überfüllt," *Die Welt*, 2 May 1960; "Berliner Geschichten," *IBZ*, 18 June 1960; "Das haben sie nicht in Paris gelernt," *Blick-*

and cool jazz so much admired by Berendt and his followers, but by using the term "jazz" in the name and in the music offerings of the club, officials tried to show that their club was at once modern, open, and respectable. As one social worker concluded, these clubs educated young people not with "the sledge-hammer, but with the jazz trumpet."[35] They were part of West German efforts to diffuse the 1950s youth rebellion, but also provided West German adolescents with the opportunity to listen to hot, if not too hot, American rhythms. Thus the clubs revealed that West German definitions of acceptable adolescent behavior indeed had widened. And finally, the clubs and their use of jazz also highlighted differences between East and West Germany.

On the other side of the Iron Curtain, East German officials continued to be more repressive. They allowed concerts of traditional jazz, but tried to ensure that bands did not play too much Western music. Never again would they prohibit jazz altogether, but they intervened when jazz fans tried to found formal groups. Official East German suspicions were certainly fostered by American and West German efforts to make the music into a messenger of liberal democracy and a Cold War weapon in the late 1950s.

For East and West German officials, who were trying to make a break with the racist German past, jazz had some attraction because of its roots in African American culture and perhaps also because many white American jazz musicians were Jewish, although that was never an explicit topic. However, tolerance had clear limits. Neither in Strauß's promotion of jazz nor in the West Berlin "Jazz-Saloon" were the African American roots of jazz a conspicuous theme, and jazz promoters stressed that jazz had transcended its African American origins. Jazz, in order to be acceptable, clearly had to be "deracialized" and even "whitened." Further, in the debates over jazz both East and West Germans asserted visions of culture that rendered conservative gender mores and respectable Germanness interdependent. In both countries, jazz also needed to be "desexualized" before it could become respectable.

Nonetheless, important differences emerged: on the defensive against Western imports and commercial culture, East German authorities were far more repressive. In this context jazz fans and officials in East Germany continued to see jazz as a potential vehicle for political resistance, a possibility that West Germans had successfully contained. Numerous inquiries into German–American relations have stressed German hostilities toward

---

punkt 97/98 (July 1960); Reiner Breitfeldt, "Es sind keine 'müden Senatsschuppen,'" *Blick-punkt* 104 (1961).

35. Herbert Rudershausen, "Jugendpflege in der Bar," *Der Rundbrief* 10, no. 9/10 (1960).

America culture, but this essay should make it clear how some American cultural imports did become part of a more liberal West German self-representation that stood in contrast to prevailing East German attitudes. In the second half of the 1950s, the two Cold War Germanies embarked ever more clearly on separate, yet always related paths—in both the realm of politics and of culture.

Guide to Further Reading

Berendt, Joachim Ernst. *Das Leben—ein Klang: Wege zwischen Jazz und Nada Brahma.* Munich: Droemer Knaur, 1996.

DeVeaux, Scott. *The Birth of Bebop: A Social and Musical History.* Berkeley: University of California Press, 1997.

Gabbard, Krin. "The Jazz Canon and Its Consequences." *Annual Review of Jazz Studies* 6 (1993): 65–98.

Kaspar Maase, *Bravo Amerika: Erkundungen zur Jugendkultur der Bundesrepublik in den fünfziger Jahren.* Hamburg: Junius-Verlag, 1992.

Kater, Michael H. *Different Drummers: Jazz in the Culture of Nazi Germany.* New York: Oxford University Press, 1992.

Panish, Jon. *The Color of Jazz: Race and Representation in Postwar American Culture.* Jackson: University of Mississippi Press, 1997.

Poiger, Uta G. *Jazz, Rock, and Rebels: Cold War Politics and American Culture in a Divided Germany.* Berkeley: University of California Press, 2000.

Rauhut, Michael. *Beat in der Grauzone: DDR-Rock 1964 bis 1972—Politik und Alltag.* Berlin: Basisdruck, 1993.

Rudorf, Reginald. *Nie wieder links: Eine deutsche Reportage.* Frankfurt am Main: Ullstein, 1990.

Ryback, Timothy W. *Rock Around the Bloc: A History of Rock Music in Eastern Europe and the Soviet Union.* New York: Oxford University Press, 1990.

Starr, S. Frederick. *Red and Hot: The Fate of Jazz in the Soviet Union.* 2d ed. New York: Limelight Editions, 1994.

Postwar German Popular Music: Americanization, the Cold War, and the Post-Nazi *Heimat*

EDWARD LARKEY

In a recent issue of the periodical *Popular Music* devoted to Germany, editor Simon Frith argued that German popular music "has to be understood differently to popular music elsewhere" in spite of that fact that at the local level the rock scene "is not much different in Germany or Britain, in Australia or Finland, in the USA or Poland." He cited the questionable manner in which "contemporary folk-like" songs (that is, in the *volkstümlich* style, discussed below) "have been used to construct a sense of 'Germanness' which avoids historical reality and responsibility."[1] According to Frith, the problem in delineating "German rock" is rooted ultimately in the definition of "Germanness." I would argue further that defining the "German" of popular music in Germany is also about the desire, on the one hand, to adhere to traditions and the need, on the other, to respond to the pressures of a globally distributed popular music. These conflicting forces offer a new dimension to the problem of defining Germanness through music, and they reveal much about the social, political, and cultural issues among competing factions in postwar Germany.

This essay investigates how the "German" is defined in and through different types of popular music: (1) genres considered traditionally or inherently German, like the Schlager or the commercial *volkstümlich* music that dominated the popular music market for many decades; (2) styles and genres that emulate internationally distributed forms such as rock and roll, rap/hip-hop, and New Wave (*Neue Deutsche Welle*); (3) the musical culture growing up around major figures of the German rock and pop scene such as

1. Simon Frith, editor's introduction to *Popular Music* 17 (1998): v.

Udo Lindenberg and inventing a specific rock-based German popular music distinct from, and perhaps in opposition to, the Schlager genre; and (4) the contributions of bands or vocalists from the former German Democratic Republic, whose "German" identity may be disputed as politically or ideologically tainted.

The German Schlager

Even today, Schlager[2] and *volkstümlich* music are thought of as quintessentially German. The term "Schlager" means "hit" and was originally used not to refer to a particular genre but as an indicator of commercial success. Schlager music itself derived from operetta and dance melodies of the nineteenth and early twentieth centuries, later incorporating popular film tunes from the late 1920s onward. André Port le roi's somewhat idealized view of the genre designates the 1920s as the golden years of the Schlager, when jazz, radio, and sound movies revolutionized the cultural industries, and considers the 1960s and 1970s as a second climax, when Schlager sang the praises of concurrent social and economic developments.[3]

Many Schlager songs are distinguishable from Anglo-American–influenced rock or pop tunes by their cadences, rhythms, harmonies, and instrumentation. The Schlager had thrived during official campaigns against African American and Jewish influences in jazz by conservative forces during both the Weimar Republic and the Nazi period, vilifying such Jewish-led groups as the Weintraub Syncopators and Comedian Harmonists, and swing bands such as Teddy Stauffer's jazz ensembles. Thus the Schlager came to symbolize the conservative cultural values in the post–World War II period. In the 1950s, the Schlager reflected the optimism of the *Wirtschaftswunder* (economic miracle) in Germany by featuring lyrics that sentimentalized the *Heimat* (native land), expressed the wish to travel to exotic places (Italy, the South Seas, or the American West), and extirpated unpleasant thoughts of the Nazi past.[4] These songs shaped the attitudes of those growing up in the 1950s, many of whom equated Schlager with escapist diversion from reality and history, as well as with unbridled consumerism and

2. For a discussion of the historical continuity of the Schlager as the "most German" of all song genres, see Mark Terkessides, "Die Eingeborenen von Schizonesien," in *Mainstream der Minderheiten: Pop in der Kontrollgesellschaft*, ed. Tom Holert and Mark Terkessides (Berlin: Edition ID-Archiv, 1996), 115–38.

3. André Port le roi, *Schlager lügen nicht: Deutscher Schlager und Politik in ihrer Zeit* (Essen: Klartext, 1998), 8.

4. Ibid., 94.

commercialism. Schlager songs employed lyrics in standard German rather than dialect and generally utilized nonsyncopated rhythms until the 1980s. The competition between Schlager writers—who advocated the use of German lyrics and traditional musical structures—and the adherents of Anglo-American-influenced music dominated the Schlager's ongoing struggles for legitimacy and for capturing the German market from the 1950s through the 1980s.

Only with the advent of a new, Anglo-American-influenced German pop—like that of Peter Maffay, singer/songwriter Konstantin Wecker, and others in the 1980s—have the strictly drawn boundaries between Schlager and rock music become indistinct. A recent resurgence in the popularity of the Schlager with vocalist Gildo Horn, Germany's 1998 entry for the Eurovision Song contest, has reignited the debate about the nature of the Schlager and its revival, albeit in a somewhat ironic manner.

As a subset of the Schlager genre, *volkstümlich* music evolved from folkloric roots and today receives much attention in the public broadcasting networks of all German-speaking countries, in highly stylized television spectacles like the *Musikantenstadl,* or in the competition known as the Grand Prix of *Volkstümlich* Music. This music, which derives a mythically constructed regional folk music from all German-speaking regions and incorporates it into the German popular music industry, extends even beyond the borders of the German-speaking countries. A highly successful South Tyrolian group calling itself the Kastelruther Spatzen (The Sparrows of Kastelruth) is rooted in a seemingly "authentic" alpine folk music of the German-speaking minority in that region of Italy.[5] Even the Slovenian folk ensemble of Slavko Avsenik, a band credited with originating the *volkstümlich* genre, sets folk melodies and march music to a highly stylized standard German with a "southern"—albeit artificial—accent. *Volkstümlich* music romanticizes and idealizes a rural way of life unfamiliar to the urbanized majority of German-speaking populations. The breadth of this genre ranges from the drippy songs of Heino (Heinz-Georg Kramm) from Düsseldorf to the currently popular groups like the Wildecker Herzbuben, a two-man vocal duo.

Volkstümlich songs transmit values emphasizing *Heimat,* a love of one's homeland or native soil. They use place names for their groups (sometimes with the word "original" before it to reinforce the image of deeply

5. For a thorough discussion about the constructed nature of the value "authenticity" when applied by folklore scholars to folk music, see Regina Bendix, *In Search of Authenticity* (Madison: University of Wisconsin Press, 1997).

rooted tradition), folk costumes, southern German dialects, folk instruments (such as zither, accordion and guitar), and the simplest of melodies and cadences with stereotypical harmonies.[6] Performances help create a community atmosphere by encouraging audiences to clap their hands and sway to the music and with stage sets stimulating nostalgic associations (for example, modeled after childhood homes and projecting an aura of "tradition and security"[According to Mechtild von Schoenebeck, performance conventions such as marching in formation on and off the sets and folk-like costumes all emphasize "order" and fateful submission to nature. Males play instruments while females sing; song lyrics underscore the woman's role as emotional, spiritual, and ornamental supporter of the male; and national pride, while not explicitly promoted through the *volkstümlich* genre, nevertheless comes through as a subtext. Schoenebeck argued that these songs glorify "everyday life and the world of ordinary people" with "retrospective" and "retrogessive" values in step with the "political programs and ideas of Germany's right-wing parties," expressing the notions that it is better to keep to oneself and that life is best in the beautiful German homeland.[7]

"German" Rock and Roll

Many German observers of the rock and roll scene of the 1950s tend to look down upon their compatriots for having been exploited by the Schlager industry to attract youth dissatisfied with the prudishness and conservatism of the *Wirtschaftswunder* era. Rock and roll was one of the first forms of Anglo-American music to "conquer" Germany after the mid-1950s and reinforce a "quasi-colonial relationship" between (West) Germany and the United States. The popularity of Elvis Presley, who was stationed in Germany between 1958 and 1960 while serving in the U.S. army, produced German clones like Peter Kraus and Ted Herold and teenie star Conny Froboess, and even opened the door for the American singer Connie Francis, who remained popular for many years. These vocal artists sang German cover versions to popular American rock and roll, pop, and doo-wop tunes. "Jailhouse Rock" (which became "Harbor Rock" in the German version) was typical of what became known as the "Teenager-Schlager."

An entry in *Das Lexikon des Deutschen Schlagers* identifies the real

---

6. Mechtild von Schoenebeck, "The New German Folk-Like Song and Its Hidden Messages," *Popular Music* 17 (1998): 287.

7. Ibid., 289–90.

rock and roll enthusiasts as a "minuscule minority" while the "teen-
agers among the target group of 'Schlager friends' had become a market-
dominating consumer potential for recordings."[8] Anglo-American rock
formed a part of what Tibor Kneif derisively called an expression of "an extreme and youthfully ruthless individualism possible only in the late phase
of a culture which has become liberal, or even indifferent to its prior values and convictions."[9] Kneif accused Germans of achieving no comparable
sovereign identity in rock music despite Germany's powerful economy or
political system. Owing to the identity crisis caused by the "shameful
Nazi past," German rock critics generally trivialized original and unique
contributions of German rock, receiving it with either lukewarm praise or
sarcasm.[10]

Rock critic Hermann Haring saw the years of rock and roll (1950s) and
beat (1960s) as a time when the Germans digested their defeat in World
War II.[11] He felt that by 1969 German musicians should have learned enough
from their exposure to Glenn Miller and Frank Sinatra tunes, rock and roll,
skiffle music, beat, and blues to create new music from their own cultural
background. Rock critic Albrecht Koch ridiculed the concept of German
rock as an invention of the dominant Schlager industry,[12] which not only
incorporated musical elements of rock and roll into its production but re-
worked the lyrics of the American original tunes into more harmless variations. While songs like "Tom Dooley" sung by the Kingston Trio were popular both in their German versions as well as in their American originals on
the hit parades in Germany in the 1950s, others underwent curious transformations. For instance, a collection of American tunes on a three-record
set released by Germany's largest popular music recording company in the
1950s, Polydor, included a cover version of Little Richard's "Tutti Frutti"
in a small jazz combo arrangement stylistically closer to the Pat Boone version than to the original. "See you Later Alligator," sung originally by Bill
Haley and the Comets, was rewritten as "Mr. Patton aus Manhattan" and
sung by Renée Franke. The Elvis Presley tune "Heartbreak Hotel" became
"Hotel zur Einsamkeit" ("Hotel Loneliness") when sung by Werner Over-

8. Matthias Bardong, Hermann Demmler, and Christian Pfarr, eds., *Das Lexikon des
deutschen Schlagers* (Mainz: Schott; Munich: Piper, 1993), 29.

9. Tibor Kneif, *Rock-Musik: Ein Handbuch zum kritischen Verständnis* (Reinbek bei
Hamburg: Rowohlt Taschenbuchverlag, 1982), 214.

10. Ibid., 299–300.

11. Hermann Haring, *Rock aus Deutschland West: Von den Rattles bis Nena: Zwei
Jahrzehnte Heimatklang* (Reinbek bei Hamburg: Rowohlt Taschenbuchverlag, 1984), 12.

12. Albrecht Koch, *Angriff auf's Schlaraffenland: 20 Jahre deutschsprachige Popmusik*
(Frankfurt am Main: Ullstein, 1987), 11 ff.

heidt to lyrics rewritten by Hans Bradtke. The Big Bopper's tune "Chantilly Lace" was transformed into an outrageous mixture of English and German sung by vocalist Rudi Büttner as *Ich liebe You.*" The set also contains "Charley Brown," a tune popularized by the Coasters in the United States. While the original is sung by a male vocal group, the German version is sung by women, with the exception of the baritone refrain "Charley Brown hat immer nur Unsinn im Sinn" ("Charley Brown can only think of nonsense"). The English version, by contrast, dwells on Charley Brown's complaint of self-pity at getting caught doing pranks in the classroom ("Why's everybody always pickin' on me?").

American influence even went beyond rock and penetrated the more "authentically German" Schlager. Former British or U.S. servicemen like Chris Howland, Bill Ramsey, and Gus Backus remained in the country to become famous vocalists (much like other foreign contemporaries in the Schlager industry such as Caterina Valente from France, Siw Malmquist from Sweden, and Vico Torriani from Switzerland). A further device employed by the record companies both to parody the use of American English in German popular music and at the same time to "modernize" the Schlager genre was the use of words like "baby," "darling," "I love you," "girls," "boyfriend," "teenager," and so on. Many Schlager vocalists used English and American stage names to enhance their images: Freddy Quinn was the pseudonym for Manfred Nidl-Petz; Bruce Low was a Surinam-born singer with the name of Ernst Bjelke; Harald Schubring called himself Ted Herold; Roy Black was the stage name of Gerd Höllcrich; and Herbert Anton Hilger still goes by the name of Tony Marshall. Language purists were appalled by these developments, and East German authorities in particular polemicized against Americanizing tendencies in the West German recording industry. Cultural conservatives in both the East and the West considered the use of English and the decline of the German language evident in the American-derived rock and pop music to be a further example of the cultural demise engendered by the American-dominated recording industry.

Neue Deutsche Welle

The Neue Deutsche Welle (NDW), or "new German wave," is the commercial outgrowth of the British and American punk movement in German-speaking countries in the late 1970s, in which British groups like the Clash and the Sex Pistols and American bands like the Dead Kennedys and Ramones were at the forefront. The evolution from punk to NDW came about with the popularity of both Nina Hagen and Udo Lindenberg. While Lindenberg was one of the early pioneers of realistic, laid-back jargon in rock lyrics, employing ironic plays on words and fostering a self-effacing yet playful relationship with his audiences, Hagen became something of an *enfant terrible* in German rock music after moving to the West from East Berlin in 1976, with her blunt feminist lyrics and a commercially tested backup group (members of the political rock band Lokomotive Kreuzberg, which later became the New Wave band Spliff).

According to Longerich, the term "Neue Deutsche Welle" was first used by Alfred Hilsberg, chief editor of the music periodical *Sounds*, to refer to punk-derived music played by German groups using mainly German lyrics. Longerich credited NDW musicians with creating "an authentic German rock music" by returning to the German language, which had long been missing from the German rock music of the 1960s and 1970s. German lyrics enabled musicians to "express their individual life experiences exclusively in lyrics of their mother tongue, offering their listeners multiple association possibilities full of semantic directness." Longerich further asserted that the NDW allowed German rock musicians to free themselves from Anglo-American rock traditions and ally themselves with their own subculture. Contrary to English punks, however, with their more proletarian roots, German New Wavers came from a fairly well-off German middle class. This meant that their songs and music manifested "the boredom and indifference of youths whose parents provided for their financial security and who did not know what to do with themselves." [13]

Longerich's generalization about NDW's innovative use of the German language needs to be qualified, however, because a number of politically oriented, rock-based groups coming out of the student protest subculture in the 1960s and 1970s (groups such as Lokomotive Kreuzberg, Ton Steine Scherben, Floh de Cologne, and the Austrian band Schmetterlinge) were already writing their lyrics in German. Still, the use of the German language is at the center of the rejuvenation of German popular music initiated by the NDW. Prior to that, German was typically relegated to *volkstümlich* or Schlager productions, while the view predominated among pop music fans and musicians alike that English was the prime language of pop music. The political rock groups of the 1960s and 1970s were among the first to attempt to use serious German rock lyrics, while dialect came into fashion for Austrian, Swiss, and southern German groups [Nina Hagen, Udo Lindenberg, and the NDW bands that followed them took the use of German lyrics one step further by bridging the gap between political rock and Schlager] Neue

13. Winfried Longerich, *"Da Da Da": Zur Standortbestimmung der Neuen Deutschen Welle* (Pfaffenweiler: Centaurus, 1989), 64–65.

Deutsche Welle reintroduced colloquial speech and subcultural idioms into lyrics, thus affording bands the opportunity to sing about genuine personal feelings or frustrations, distinguishing them from their Schlager cousins in their openness, anxiety, and sensitivity, as well as their irony, parody, and satire. NDW was also instrumental in overcoming the dichotomy between the sentiments of political rock and the "unpolitical" problems and tribulations of personal daily interactions and issues generally confined to the realm of the Schlager. This development has sometimes been pejoratively described as the emergence of the "new" German Schlager.

One of the most representative songs of this genre is "Eiszeit" by the band Ideal,[14] whose female vocalist, Anette Humpe, went on to become one of Germany's more successful producers. "Eiszeit" creates an image of an extremely isolated yet chillingly defensive individual without hope: "The telephone, still for years / no one I want to speak to / I see my face in the mirror / nothing has weight anymore." Another strophe declares: "In my film I am the star / I only can deal with myself / Armored safe of diamonds / unknown combination." The refrain of the song—"Ice-Age / within me the Ice-Age begins / in the labyrinth of the Ice-Age / minus 90 degrees"—directs attention to an individualized (and female) subject responding to an abstractly determined, ominous, and intimidating social reality.

This depiction of social reality as an emotional "big freeze," ice age, or emotionally barren landscape is a metaphorical device typical of other NDW songs as well. The Swiss band Grauzone produced a hit in the late 1970s, "Eisbär," in which the male protagonist proclaims, "I would like to be a polar bear / in the cold polar north / If I were a polar bear / I would not need to cry / Polar bears don't have to cry."[15] Another song by Ideal, "Sex in the Desert,"[16] conveys an image of a climate inimical to any kind of sexual pleasure, normally the topic of choice among youths in pop music: "The horizon moves closer / and what no one knows / everyone thinks of one thing / but it is too hot for that / Sex—sex in the desert." On the same album, the song "Monotonie"[17] continues the mood of boredom and listlessness: "Monotony / in the South Seas / Melancholy at 30 degrees [Celsius] / Monotony under palm trees / Campari on Tahiti / Bitter Lemon on Hawaii."

Such lyrics as these reveal the roots of the socially critical, politically

14. Ideal, *Der Ernst des Lebens*, 1981, WEA/Elite Imperial, track 1, side 1.

15. Heide Buhmann and Hanspeter Haeseler, *Zeitzeichen: Liederbuch der Rock- und Songpoesie* (Schlüchtern: Verlag Buhmann and Haeseler, 1993), 2:136.

16. *Der Ernst des Lebens*, track 3, side 1.

17. Ibid., track 2, side 2.

involved student movement active between 1967 and 1976, but whose (largely Marxist) utopian goals were increasingly suspect to its adherents and society as a whole. NDW lyrics reflect the disillusionment with abstract political goals by conveying a new subjectivity and insecurity.

Udo Lindenberg

Udo Lindenberg was originally a drummer with a north German dance band in the late 1960s and early 1970s. After his first English-language album flopped in 1971, he started to write his own German-language songs with rock and other musical elements. His first LP success was "Alles Klar auf der Andrea Doria" (1973), which set the tone for further projects and was the basis for his undisputed popularity throughout the 1970s. Not only was Lindenberg one of the first German rock artists to sign a long-term deal with a major recording company, Teldec, but he also helped establish the primacy of the Hamburg rock scene in the 1970s.[18] According to Albrecht Koch,

> it was Goodtime-Music which could be played in the bars of Hamburg as well as in the pubs of London or the clubs on the East Coast [of the United States]. It was standard rock, interspersed with quotes like aural images . . . , female choruses . . . , opera arias . . . , comical instrumentation or special effects and was not supposed to be intellectually challenging.[19]

Lindenberg had a certain appeal as an anti-star, with his receding hair line and unspectacular vocal style. He utilized the daily jargon of pub-goers, musicians, youths, and outcasts to tell stories of different people and figures, like "Rudi Ratlos," "Johnny Controlletti," "Elli Pirelli," elderly pensioners ("Nichts haut einen Seeman um"), or youthful escapists ("Er wollte nach London"). He adapted his nasal singing style "to the phrasing and emphasis of rock rhythms" and avoided clear melodic lines and Schlager phrasing.[20] His lyrics were more verbose and less rhythmically coordinated to the music than Schlager lyrics, utilizing his own version of a provocative and disarmingly down-to-earth language to sing about daily issues and experiences of younger as well as older generations. According to the rock

18. Haring, *Rock aus Deutschland West*, 80.
19. Koch, *Angriff auf's Schlaraffenland*, 66.
20. Ibid., 67.

critic Hermann Haring, Lindenberg's success was due to the combination of the "fat, powerful rock music" of his band Panikorchester with "a smooth and appropriate slang."[21]

His lyrics broke through Schlager conventions and taboos in their topics as well. Lindenberg gained notoriety with his continued efforts to perform in East Germany. Not only did various songs speak directly to audiences in the East—for example, "Wir wollen doch einfach nur zusammen sein," "Hallo DDR," "Vopo," or "Mädchen von Ostberlin"—but Lindenberg wrote a song about the East German Communist Party chief Erich Honecker to the tune of "Chattanooga Choo-Choo," in which he directly requested permission to perform in the German Democratic Republic: The "Sonderzug nach Pankow" ("Special Train to Pankow") epitomized his unconventional and direct manner of communication:

Excuse me, is this the Special Train to Pankow? / I must be on my way there, onto East Berlin. / I have to clear something up with your chief Indian. / I am a yodeling talent and want to play there with my band. / I have a bottle of Cognac with me and it tastes very good, / I could sip it quite easily with Erich Honecker, / and I say: Hey, Honey, I'll sing for little money / in the Palace of the Republic / if you let me. / All the stupid Schlager clowns are allowed to sing there / are allowed to sing their schlock there, / only little Udo, only little Udo / he is not allowed to and we don't understand why. / I know that I have many friends / in the GDR, and with each hour there are more. / Oh Erich, are you really such an obstinate pig-head? / Why don't you let me sing in your Workers and Peasants' State?[22]

Lindenberg flaunted an irreverent, ironic, and disarmingly deconstructive attitude toward serious political issues and broke through many cultural and political conventions. In addition to songs about homo- and bisexuality, Lindenberg ridiculed the closed-minded stereotypes of the Cold War. One of his songs seemed to exaggerate the fears of conservative Germans with the words: "In 15 Minutes, the Russians will be at the Kurfürstendamm," implying that Russian troops would be invading the Western part of Berlin, but actually referring to Russian soldiers' desire to go on a shopping spree.

21. Haring, *Rock aus Deutschland West*, 78.
22. Koch, *Angriff auf's Schlaraffenland*, 70.

Rap and Hip-Hop Music

German youths' first encounter with rap and hip-hop imports from the United States came about with the release of the films *Wild Style* in 1982 and Harry Belafonte's *Beat Street* in 1984. West German centers for rap and hip-hop then emerged in Cologne, Dortmund, Kiel, West Berlin, Braunschweig, and Heidelberg, and East German rap and hip-hop evolved in Dresden and East Berlin. The fall of the Berlin Wall at the end of 1989 further fueled development of a German rap and hip-hop scene. One of the first significant German hip-hop productions was the 1991 album *Krauts with Attitude* on the Bombastic label, which featured three cuts in German, eleven in English, and one in French.[23] The album title was derived from the American rap group Niggaz with Attitude (NWA) and was also the title of an article in the West German music periodical *Spex*. In Dietmar Elflein's view, the *Krauts with Attitude* production initiated a transformation of rap into Deutscher Hip-Hop and Deutscher Sprechgesang (German speechsong), which "grafted an adopted music style onto a national identity." Yet at the same time it excluded immigrant and particularly Turkish youths from participating, even though their subculture resembled the playful exhibition of virility and defense of honor typical of African American ghetto youth.[24] As a result, the German hip-hop scene has diverged into two distinct genres of Neuer Deutscher Sprechgesang and Oriental hip-hop.[25]

While several groups modeled their peculiar style of chanting/singing after American performers like Public Enemy, the Beastie Boys, LL Cool J, and others, locating mythic roots in black American ghetto culture while also distancing themselves from the American models to a certain degree, German rappers were almost always burdened with justifying their image and productions in the face of their middle class and nonghetto upbringing. The Fantastische Vier, for example, chose to propagate a "good time" (*gute Laune*) through German lyrics, which seemed to "be more truthful."[26]

23. Dietmar Elflein, "From Krauts with Attitudes to Turks with Attitudes: Some Aspects of Hip-Hop History in Germany," *Popular Music* 17 (1998): 256–58.

24. Ibid., 261.

25. Oriental hip-hop was launched with the success of the *Cartel* project, which tried to unite disparate sectors of the immigrant hip-hop community into a mythical "Turkish" ethnic group, but which in reality included many other nationalities of immigrants in Germany. This can be seen particularly in productions of Da Crime Posse, with two Turkish members, one German, and one Cuban. Oriental hip-hop consists of "hip hop beats enriched by reminiscences of ragamuffin, samples of Turkish folk or Pop Muzik and mostly Turkish raps" (ibid., 260).

26. Andrea Müller, *Die Fantastischen Vier: Die Megastars des deutschen Rap* (Düsseldorf: Econ Taschenbuchverlag, 1996), 51.

According to one biographer, Andrea Müller, black rap music came from the ghettos and spoke of social problems. The Fantastische Vier, however, wanted to avoid a potentially absurd "back-alley image" (*Gossenimage*) that was alien to their upbringing (and "unauthentic") and avoided the usual contents of black rap music. Müller asserted that the band, which started out in 1989 as the first German hip-hop group to obtain a contract with an international recording company, created this contemporary German chant-style to be suitable for parties and for promoting "positive feelings."[27]

The first successful CD of the Fantastische Vier, *Vier Gewinnt* (*Four Wins*),[28] shows the group's efforts to situate itself within the spectrum of German and international rap and hip hop. The title track "Vier Gewinnt" co-opts the self-assertive and self-congratulatory conventions employed by African American rap artists, in which the artists each introduce themselves and describe their particular strengths. In the most programmatic track on the CD, "Hip Hop Musik," the group seeks to refute the usual clichés and assert its own brand of German hip-hop, while fully conscious of the ambivalent nature of the genre and the need to adapt some of the clichés in order to create something new: "I can't hide behind rap clichés / but without them we will not succeed / to get a hip hop jam going in Germania."[29] The group then explains its own German adaptations of African American slang: "I say 'raise your hand high' instead of 'put your hand in the air' / I say 'hey people, what's going on' instead of 'say ho' and 'motherfucker.'" In a jab at the generation of aging 68ers who now make up the establishment in the 1990s, the group also distances itself from the so-called critical songmaker tradition in the late 1960s and early 1970s stimulated by American and British folk singers like Bob Dylan, Donovan, and Pete Seeger: "German *Liedermacherbrauchtum* I believe we have conquered / we speak as we always do otherwise and make / hip hop music."[30] The lyrics continue by renouncing any imitation of the image, the ideas, and the language of the "gold-chain motherfuckers" who represent "too much kitsch," advocating instead "German *Sprechgesang*," which some find *supergeil* (approx. "damn good") and other consider a *rotes Tuch* (that is, they "see red"). They reject any attention to skin color and state their unwillingness

27. Ibid., 52, 54–57.

28. Col 472263 2, Sony Music Corp., 1992.

29. "denn ich kann mich ja jetzt gar nicht hinter rap-klischees verstecken / dennoch wird es einem ohne diese nie gelingen / in germanien nin hip hop jam in schwung zu bringen," ibid., track 11.

30. "deutsches liedermacherbrauchtum ham wir glaube ich besiegt / wir sprechen wie wir das sonst auch tun und machen /—hip hop musik," ibid.

to limit themselves stylistically, but demand "respect," recognizing and honoring the origins of hip-hop while expanding the "rap family." In the last strophe, they emphasize that rap expresses their "feeling for life" (*Lebensgefühl*), in spite of the fact that European hip-hop "is only a laboratory creation" (*kommt aus der Retorte*). The Fantastische Vier propose that "only in the mother tongue can the play on words function / only then can you accentuate the sense of the words / linguistic self-confidence is the principle / liberate yourself from prejudices and enjoy / this hip-hop music."[31]

GDR Rock Music and Cold War Competition

Early political strategies of the communist SED party leadership in the 1950s aimed at setting up an alternative to the capitalist Schlager industry of the West. However, with the passage of time, the popularity of the Beatles and the Rolling Stones and pressure on the SED to compete with Western culture in order to win over young East Germans forced the party to tolerate Western music, gradually leading to increasing commercialization and privatization in the period preceding unification.

In 1958, the so-called 60:40 rule was decreed, mandating that no more than 40 percent of the repertoire of GDR bands and vocalists or of the programming of radio and television shows be from capitalist countries; at least 60 percent had to be from socialist countries. Certain songs with lyrics deemed harmful to youth and seemingly promoting criminal or antisocial behavior were banned outright from the airwaves and repertoires. This included the song "Tom Dooley" and many Rolling Stones tunes, which remained banned until 1978. Control was also exerted by censoring lyrics, as bands were required to apply for annual performance licenses to play in front of live audiences. First they had to submit their lyrics to an "editorial board" (*Lektorat*) comprised of members of the cultural commission of their city or county district. Only after approval of the lyrics, the band's physical appearance, and its music was it possible for the band to audition. Band members were also obliged to prove that they were involved in music instruction at an approved music school, in which not only music but also Marxism-Leninism were taught and a modicum of political control was exercised.

After a 1965 crackdown against Western-style rock bands exhibiting be-

31. "Nur in der muttersprache kann der spass am wortspiel funktionieren / nur so kannst du den sinn der worte gut akzentuieren / sprachliches selbstbewußtsein das ist das prinzip / mach dich frei von vorurteilen und geniesse diese—hip hop musik," ibid.

havior considered unbecoming of socialist society, all groups with English-language names like the Butlers or the Diana Show Band were required to change their names to German ones, and English lyrics were also proscribed. Furthermore, rock music originating in the West was considered a security risk and a potential ideological threat. The state security apparatus was constantly on the lookout for "special incidents," for example, disturbances at rock concerts that had the potential for publicity in the Western press, thus becoming "ideologically diversionary" and potentially "subversive" and constituting a "threat to security and order." Bands who resisted the ideological and political prescriptions of the SED were considered "unreliable" and could be refused a performance license, a recording contract, radio station airplay, or travel visas to the West. As of 1984, only five GDR rock bands were considered "travel capable" (a special term applied to those allowed to travel to the West).

In addition to these measures, a special terminology was employed in the press and the popular music industry to create ideological and cultural distance between the music of the West—which was accessible through Western radio and television stations—and GDR music. Thus the term "rock" music was avoided until the early 1980s, replaced by "youth" or "dance" music; bands were called "combos," "dance" ensembles, or "dance" orchestras; and music was not "popular" but "youth-effective" (jugendwirksam), implying a mechanism for popularity that was imposed from the top down, rather than one oriented toward the audience that was allowed to develop from the bottom up. GDR institutions refrained from using the term "disk jockey" until the mid-1980s as well, employing the ridiculously complicated German term "Schallplattenunterhalter" ("record entertainer"). Instead of using the term "Neue Deutsche Welle" which would signal the direct influence of a recent trend in the West, cultural bureaucrats at the Amiga recording company and the radio stations used the term "Neue Tanzmusik" (new dance music).

The dependence on the few state recording studios and its engineers, as well as the musical prejudices of their inhouse music producers and "editors" until the mid-1980s, meant that GDR rock musicians had to try to accommodate an institutionalized Schlager-like aesthetic with the forces of Western trends. But with the rapid increase in the number of discotheques in the GDR in the mid-1970s, GDR music all but disappeared from the dance floors because sound engineers could not turn up the bass lines. This prompted curious calls for "danceable" "dance music" from cultural bureaucrats who were alarmed at the sudden decrease in popularity of GDR music. In response, engineers attempted to maintain the balance of rhythm, harmony, and melody while also heeding the imperative that the lyrics be comprehensible in the aural reproduction of the music, resulting in a hopelessly outdated sound and what many today see as a characteristic "tinniness" of GDR rock music of the 1970s and 1980s. At the same time, punk and New Wave music was not only rejected on political or ideological grounds, but also because New Wave music ran counter to the aesthetics and sense of propriety of many in the GDR media and cultural institutions.

In the postunification period some of the bigger names on the GDR rock scene have persisted. Very few bands were able, like the Prinzen, to ally themselves with West German producers in the first half of the 1990s and become commercially successful all over Germany. Most others touting a peculiar East German identity have almost no appreciable following in West Germany. West Germans tend to pigeonhole the popularity of East German bands as part of the desire to return to conditions prior to unification, an attitude denounced as *Ostalgie* or nostalgia for the East. East German bands complain that the airwaves of West German radio stations are inaccessible to them and that audiences are prejudiced against them without even hearing their music.

Conclusion: A New National Popular Music in Postwar Germany?

In the 1950s and 1960s, English lyrics, syncopated rhythms, and imitations of Anglo-American models signaled solidarity with the social, political, and cultural innovations underway in postwar West Germany as it became integrated into the anticommunist alliance dominated by the United States. This spread of American and later British music of the Beatles, Rolling Stones and other groups represented an acceptance of the promises of a consumer utopia rising out of the spiritual and physical ruins of Nazi Germany and a willingness to adopt a new identity while submerging issues of culpability for the past. The music of this period also reveals an ambivalence, however: on the one hand, the widespread Americanization manifested in German popular music in the immediate postwar period indicated a break with the musical and historical heritage of the Nazi past associated with the traditional Schlager and folk genres; on the other hand, the continued popularity of these traditional genres throughout the 1950s and 1960s allowed emotional ties with the past implicitly to persist into the present.

Ultimately, a fusion of the two trends proved to be most successful. The accommodation of Anglo-American musical trends with German traditions was gradually introduced by an avant-garde cultural minority—jazz fans in the 1940s, rock and roll fans in the 1950s, beat fans and hippies

in the 1960s, and punk culture in the 1970s and 1980s—who paved the way
for new aesthetic and commercial successes in the popular music industry.
Each new attempt at fusion managed to compete successfully with both
the U.S. and British models as well as the older, firmly entrenched Schlager
industry, ultimately laying the groundwork for Udo Lindenberg (and later
others like the Tote Hosen, Herbert Grönemeyer, and the Cologne-based
band BAP, to name a few) to establish a strong rock-based, postwar tradition
of German popular music. By the 1980s and 1990s, this inventive revival
of German lyrics was even capable of influencing Schlager-based models
like those of Peter Maffay to shape what became known as the New German
Schlager or New German Pop. The fusion of German language lyrics with
Anglo-American-influenced music helped establish a new German musical identity by using language to help distinguish Germanic music from the
English-based. The switch to German lyrics has transformed globally distributed music like hip-hop, punk, rock and roll, and other Anglo-American
styles into something socially, ethnically, and territorially German.

By contrast, the *volkstümlich* and Schlager styles needed no additional
delineation as "German." As traditional German genres, these imply the
territorial association with intimacy and *Heimat*. *Volkstümlich* music already bears the territorial imprint of the German countryside and is thus
sufficiently "naturalized" as a Germanic tradition. Its musical components
signify German *Heimat* and social context, and it is typically associated
with nationalistic exclusion, ethnic-national defensiveness, and regres-
sively romantic delusions about the natural and social environment.

The Schlager, with its distinctively "Germanic" rhythms, harmonies,
and language, is distinguished from "Italo-Pop" or the French chanson. Its
long tradition posits it squarely within the German historical and cultural
context. Against the backdrop of the global music industry it may signify
musical obsolescence and conservatism as it competes for legitimacy. The
current Schlager revival underway since the mid-1990s in Germany traces
its lineage to traditions in the Weimar Republic in which Jewish vocalists,
composers, and lyricists like those in the Comedian Harmonists figured
prominently. The ambiguously ironic undertones of this revival reveals a
characteristic uncertainty and insecurity about the rediscovery of this tradition in postunification Germany, as it struggles to situate its own traditions in the context of globalizing influences.

Guide to Further Reading

Bardong, Matthias, Hermann Demmler, and Christian Pfarr, eds. *Das Lexikon des
deutschen Schlagers*. Mainz: Schott; Munich: Piper, 1993.

Elflein, Dietmar. "From Krauts with Attitudes to Turks with Attitudes: Some Aspects of Hip-Hop History in Germany." *Popular Music* 17 (1998). Pp. 255–66.

Frith, Simon. Editor's introduction. *Popular Music* 17 (1998): v–vi.

Haring, Hermann. *Rock aus Deutschland West: Von den Rattles bis Nena: Zwei Jahrzehnte Heimatklang.* Reinbek bei Hamburg: Rowohlt Taschenbuchverlag, 1984.

Kneif, Tibor. *Rock-Musik: Ein Handbuch zum kritischen Verständnis.* Reinbek bei Hamburg: Rowohlt Taschenbuchverlag, 1982.

Koch, Albrecht. *Angriff auf's Schlaraffenland: 20 Jahre deutschsprachige Popmusik.* Frankfurt am Main: Ullstein, 1987.

Lindenberg, Udo. *Highlige Schriften: Alle Songtexte—auch englische—von '46 bis '84.* Reinbeck bei Hamburg: Rowohlt, 1984.

Longerich, Winfried. *"Da Da Da": Zur Standortbestimmung der Neuen Deutschen Welle.* Musikwissenschaftliche Studien 9. Pfaffenweiler: Centaurus, 1989.

Müller, Andrea. *Die Fantastischen Vier: Die Megastars des deutschen Rap.* Düsseldorf: Econ Taschenbuchverlag, 1996.

Port le roi, André. *Schlager lügen nicht: Deutscher Schlager und Politik in ihrer Zeit.* Essen: Klartext, 1998.

von Schoenebeck, Mechtild. "The New German Folk-Like Song and Its Hidden Messages." *Popular Music* 17 (1998): 279–92.

On the History of the "Deutschlandlied"

JOST HERMAND

Deutschland, Deutschland über alles,
Über alles in der Welt,
Wenn es stets zu Schutz und Trutze
Brüderlich zusammenhält,
Von der Maas bis an die Memel,
Von der Etsch bis an den Belt—
Deutschland, Deutschland über alles,
Über alles in der Welt!

Deutsche Frauen, deutsche Treue,
Deutscher Wein und deutscher Sang
Sollen in der Welt behalten
Ihren alten schönen Klang,
Uns zu edler Tat begeistern
Unser ganzes Leben lang—
Deutsche Frauen, deutsche Treue,
Deutscher Wein und deutscher Sang!

Einigkeit und Recht und Freiheit
Für das deutsche Vaterland!
Danach laßt uns alle streben
Brüderlich mit Herz und Hand!
Einigkeit und Recht und Freiheit
Sind des Glückes Unterpfand—
Blüh im Glanze dieses Glückes,
Blühe deutsches Vaterland!

[Germany, Germany above all
Above everything in the world
When, always, for protection and defense
Brothers stand together.
From the Maas to the Memel
From the Etsch to the Belt,
Germany, Germany above all
Above all in the world.

German women, German loyalty,
German wine and German song,
Shall retain, throughout the world,
Their old respected fame,
To inspire us to noble deeds
For the length of our lives.
German women, German loyalty,
German wine and German song.

Unity and justice and freedom
For the German Fatherland
For this let us all strive
Brotherly, with heart and hand.
Unity and justice and freedom
Are the pledge of fortune.
Flower in the splendor of this happiness,
Flower, German Fatherland!]

National anthems are always precarious—especially the old ones, which gush with an unconcealed chauvinism about the greatest king, the chosen people, death for the Fatherland, or even the global destiny of one's own nation. Yet because such songs are so deeply rooted in tradition, it requires nearly superhuman efforts to replace them with newer, more up-to-date national anthems. Entire nations are thus overwhelmed time and time again by clichéd sentimentalities at ceremonial occasions, and with softened hearts and moistened eyes, simply belt them out. Among the most infamous of these songs is the notorious "Lied der Deutschen," which has served as the official national anthem under every German government except the GDR since the Weimar Republic.

This particular song, however, was not actually ill conceived. Seen historically, it belongs to the broad current of *Vormärz* poetry that voiced a desire for national unity. Such desire had its first high point during the Wars of Liberation and was rekindled by the Rhine Crisis of 1840.[1] Among those so inflamed was August Heinrich Hoffmann von Fallersleben, a medievalist, collector of folk songs, and author of widely known children's songs—for example, "Alle Vögel sind schon da" ("All the Birds Are Already Here") and "Kuckkuck, Kuckkuck ruft's aus dem Wald" ("Cuckoo, Cuckoo Comes

---

1. See Jost Hermand, *Old Dreams of a New Reich: Volkish Utopias and National Socialism* (Bloomington: Indiana University Press, 1992), 21f.

from the Forest"). There are really no bloodcurdling stories to be told about him, only that by 1830 the devoted follower of Jacob Grimm and favorite of the reactionary minister Karl zum Altenstein had become a professor of German language and literature at the university in Breslau, where he developed into a respectable Germanist, collector, and editor.

Inspired by the events of the Rhine Crisis and the hopes raised by the accession to the throne of Friedrich Wilhelm IV, Hoffmann von Fallersleben took to composing rousing verses, the first volume of which appeared with the consciously satirical title *Unpolitische Gedichte (Apolitical Poems)*, published in late July of 1840 by Hoffmann and Campe in Hamburg. In line with the then widespread longing for national unity, these poems took up arms against German particularism *(Kleinstaaterei)*, obsequiousness and hypocrisy, and similar objects of *Vormärz* criticism. In keeping with the old fraternity tradition, the work is also rife with anti-French and anti-Napoleonic sentiments. Later, in the winter semester of 1840–41, Hoffmann von Fallersleben held the first German lecture on the folk song, and, suddenly famous, went on to write the second volume of his *Unpolitische Gedichte.* As in the first volume, he again resorted to well-known melodies in order to give the whole work a consciously popular note. While this volume was being published in Hamburg in August of 1841, Hoffmann von Fallersleben briefly retreated to the British island Helgoland, where on 26 August he wrote the "Lied der Deutschen" in the style of a German folk or popular song and set it to the melody of Haydn's hymn to the emperor ("God Save Franz, the Kaiser") of 1796. Julius Campe, his liberal publisher, visited him in Helgoland and was immediately impressed by the poem, thinking that it promised to be as remarkably successful as Nikolaus Becker's "Rheinlied" ("Sie sollen ihn nicht haben" ["They shall not have it"]) of 1840. He therefore laid four gold coins on the author's table, sailed immediately back to Hamburg, and had the text and melody published as early as September 1.

The "Lied der Deutschen" referred back historically at least as far as the Wars of Liberation and Ernst Moritz Arndt's famous question "Was ist des Deutschen Vaterland?" ("What is the German's fatherland?"). In wording and conviction, Hoffmann von Fallersleben's text resonated with much of what came before it, for example, Heinrich Joseph von Collin's song "Österreich über alles" of 1809, as well as the adaptation of this song in 1813 to "Deutschland über alles" by Johann Daniel Runge, the brother of Philipp Otto Runge. The phrase "Einigkeit und Recht und Freiheit" ("unity and justice and freedom") was also already well known, as Johann Gottfried Seume had used this formulation as early as 1810. At the same time, Arndt used the words "Freiheit, Vaterland und Recht." In Ferdinand Freiligrath's work this conviction then culminated in the refrain "Deutschland und Freiheit über alles" ("Germany and freedom above all").[2] Even the ominous verses "Von der Maas bis an die Memel, / von der Etsch bis an den Belt" ("From the Maas to the Memel, from the Etsch to the Belt") did not represent anything substantially new. Philipp Jakob Siebenpfeiffer had already declared in 1832 at the liberal-national Hambach Festival that he was addressing all Germans from the "Alps to the North Sea." Georg Herwegh did the same in his poem "Die deutsche Flotte" ("The German Fleet"), published in 1841 during his exile in Zurich, in which he designated the Germans as the people "vom Po bis zum Sunde" ("from the Po to the Sund"). Compared with this, Hoffmann von Fallersleben's text almost sounded modest. Even the mention of the Maas was at that time not meant as an expression of imperialism, since the Dutch part of Limburg on both sides of the Maas had belonged to the German Confederation since 1839.

Seen in this context, the "Lied der Deutschen" is clearly tied to the hopes of those old patriots among the veterans of the Wars of Liberation, fraternity brothers, and political romantics, all of whom sought a Germany that was above all a unified language community rather than a conglomerate of the diverse, dynastic states. These groups readily granted all Poles, Czechs, and Hungarians living within the borders of the German Confederation their own nationality, but in exchange they did want to include the German-speaking Austrians in a reunited German Reich. Considered representatives of the greater German (großdeutsch) solution, these circles were usually more democratic than the Prussians and their supporters, who supported the lesser German (kleindeutsch) solution. This latter group wished for the leadership of the Hohenzollerns in Germany, and wanted to exclude the Catholic Habsburgs from the German nation they envisioned. That Hoffmann von Fallersleben used the melody of the old Austrian imperial anthem for his "Lied der Deutschen" was a clear affront against efforts toward a lesser German solution and was understood as such by its defenders.

But it was not only the representatives of the lesser German solution who took offense at and attempted to suppress this poem, which to their regret contained neither dynastic piety toward the Hohenzollerns nor a sufficiently chauvinistic-militaristic flavor. So too did the politically rebellious Left Hegelians, who had little use for the "Lied der Deutschen," for they clung to a dream of the 1789 revolution and acknowledged as their

2. Further details can be found in Heinrich Gerstenberg, *Deutschland, Deutschland über alles: Ein Lebensbild des Dichters Hoffmann von Fallersleben* (Munich: C. H. Beck, 1916), 38f., 61ff.

true fatherland only a state with unfettered individual liberty. Likewise, in 1844 the prologue to Heinrich Heine's *Deutschland—Ein Wintermärchen* (*Germany—A Winter's Tale*) confronted the German national ideology of the "lackeys in the black-red-gold livery" with concepts such as universalism, humanism, and cosmopolitanism. Then there were of course Karl Marx and Friedrich Engels, who in these years had already begun to see their true homeland in international socialism.

Still, the most vigorous opponents of Hoffmann von Fallersleben's "Lied der Deutschen" were not Heine and Marx, but the Prussian authorities, who in their allegiance to the Hohenzollerns immediately branded such expressions of German national sentiments as a threat to their state. After the publication of this song, they therefore began an official investigation, if not a witch-hunt, against Hoffmann von Fallersleben, barring him in April 1842 from any further practice of his academic activities. Finally, in December of the same year, he was banned from the university because of serious offenses against the "existing order" and even banished from Prussia altogether. Subsequently, he was chased from state to state, though he still managed to meet with friends—among them such figures as Karl Gutzkow, Ferdinand Freiligrath, Adolf Glaßbrenner, Georg Herwegh, and Fritz Reuter. He also continued work, undaunted, in the publishing house of Zürcher Literarisches Comptoir on several volumes with highly "political" poems, such as *Deutsche Lieder aus der Schweiz* (*German Songs from Switzerland*, 1842) and *Deutsche Gassenlieder* (*German Street Songs*, 1843). In these works he argued for active self-sacrifice, and against all who fell into line, all conformists, careerist students, and residents of the ivory tower—in short, against all the petty philistines who too willingly subjected themselves to state authority. In these volumes, he continued to rework old, familiar songs to make his lyrics accessible to as many people as possible.

As for the content of his works, Hoffmann von Fallersleben always proceeded from the perspective of the people, whom he tried to mobilize against the ruling monarchs in the spirit of "unity and justice and freedom." He belonged therefore to the few who recognized immediately that enterprises like the Valhalla monument near Regensburg or the restoration of the Cologne cathedral were flawed in their attempts to use authoritarian means to achieve unity. Wherever he appeared and performed his songs, liberals passionately celebrated Hoffmann von Fallersleben, but the police viewed him with such suspicion that he was sometimes arrested. As a result, he briefly considered emigration to the United States in 1844, but one year later finally found asylum on an estate in Mecklenburg, where a friend had arranged for a work permit for him, thus allowing him to live there legally. From this time on, he became more withdrawn politically and limited his work to collecting and publishing literary works, primarily folk songs. He even observed the 1848 revolution from afar, and he declined to cast a vote for the Paulskirche parliament. He still hoped for reconciliation with Prussia and thus a reinstatement of his professorship. Eventually the Berlin authorities acknowledged his loyalty—though in the shabbiest way. Beginning in 1849 they paid him a part-time stipend of 375 talers a year, but they never rehired him, leaving Hoffmann von Fallersleben to spend the remainder of his days as a librarian for the Duke of Ratibor in the Corvey monastery, where he continued his zealous collecting and editing.

But back to the "Lied der Deutschen." It was first sung publicly on 5 October 1841 by the Hamburger *Turnerschaft* (patriotic gymnastic society) during a torch-lit procession in honor of the liberal professor Karl Theodor Welcker. In 1842 it appeared in *Deutsche Lieder aus der Schweiz*, after which it gradually became more well known and was also included in students' songbooks. It did not, however, have the kind of success Campe had hoped for.[3] Especially after the failure of the 1848 revolution and the suppression of all democratic and populist tendencies, it was sung less and less. And when German unification finally arrived in 1871, it was not the kind for which the old national democrats had hoped, that is, one coming from the people, but was instead unification from the top down. Hoffmann von Fallersleben, who had turned seventy-three in 1871, welcomed this unification in verses such as "Und endlich wird beschieden / mir diese große Zeit / ein einig Reich voll Frieden / voll Glück und Herrlichkeit" ("And finally it is granted / to me in this great age / a unified Reich full of peace / full of happiness and splendor"). Still, the earlier enthusiasm was just not there. Rather than a strong democratic national spirit, the hatred of the French and the cult around the Hohenzollerns held this together. Not surprisingly, then, the anthems of the Wilhelminian age became songs such as Max Schneckenburger's "Die Wacht am Rhein" ("The Watch on the Rhine"), as well as "Es braust ein Ruf wie Donnerhall" ("A Call Roars like a Thunderclap") of 1840 and the still more unfortunate "Kaiserhymne" ("Heil Dir im Siegerkranz" ["Hail to You, O Laureled Victor"]). The Hoffmann and Campe publishing house still had hundreds of copies of the "Lied der Deutschen" in stock around 1900, which remained unsold and eventually crumbled into dust.

3. Even less successful were the songs "Deutschland über alles" by Robert Zimmermann und "Deutschland über alles" by Karl Simrock, which were published in 1848. See Helmut Lamprecht, *Deutschland, Deutschland: Politische Gedichte vom Vormärz bis zur Gegenwart* (Bremen: Schünemann, 1969), 101.

And so it remained until 1914. Even the "new course" under Wilhelm II really did not benefit the "Lied der Deutschen," since it was a banner that could be carried neither by the Hohenzollern loyalists nor by the anti-French. Germany did not have an actual national anthem at all during this time. For instance, the 1908 booklet *Die Nationalhymnen der europäischen Völker* (*The National Anthems of the European Peoples*) made no mention of Germany, but only of Prussia, which was represented by the 1834 song "Ich bin ein Preuße! Kennt ihr meine Farben?" ("I am a Prussian! Do you know my colors?") by Bernhard Thiersch. Indeed, by 1908 many had never even heard of Hoffmann von Fallersleben. That the "Lied der Deutschen" had come from him was no more commonly known than that he had written the song "Alle Vögel sind schon da." While the latter had long since become an anonymous popular song, the former became ever more obscure, thanks to its "democratic" sentiments. Such a song was simply not acceptable at court. Heinrich Gerstenberg, probably the most important Hoffmann von Fallersleben scholar of that era, wrote that as late as 1914 court libraries kept Hoffmann von Fallersleben's *Unpolitische Gedichte* under lock and key, and that he himself had been advised that too strong an interest in Fallersleben could endanger his career.[4]

The chauvinistic Pan-German League was equally harsh in its rejection of the "Lied der Deutschen." They also found it too "democratic," but in addition considered the poem's restriction to Central Europe much too modest—that is, not adequately imperialistic. For instance, Arthur von Wallpach wrote the following verse around 1900, in a clear attack on Hoffmann von Fallersleben's "Lied der Deutschen":

> Wohlan, ein Gott, ein Volk, ein Reich,
> von Kapland bis zum Friesendeich,
> von Argentiniens Weizenflur
> bis in die Wolganiederung nur!
> Ein Deutschland ohne Schranken![5]

> [Hail to one God, one people, one Reich,
> from Capetown to Friesland,
> from Argentina's fields of wheat
> to the Volga lowlands!
> A Germany without bounds!]

4. Gerstenberg, *Lebensbild Hoffmann von Fallersleben*, 5.
5. Cited in Lamprecht, *Politische Gedichte*, 223.

Max Schneidewin declared in 1899—in his booklet *In Sachen des Nationalliedes* (*Concerning the National Anthem*)—that the recent political and economic developments destined Germany to assume a "dominant position" among the "peoples of the globe." Therefore, the harmless "Lied der Deutschen" by Hoffmann von Fallersleben should under no circumstances become the German national anthem. Instead of "wine and song," Schneidewin called for "blood and iron"; instead of "justice and freedom," the will to power; and instead of "black-red-gold" sentimentalities, he expressed a "black-white-red" greed for conquest.[6]

The "Lied der Deutschen" was only truly popular during these years with students, who still harked back to a nationalism derived from Klopstock and the poetry of the Wars of Liberation. Still, in order not to come under suspicion of being too soft or too Epicurean, they often replaced the lines "German women, German loyalty / German wine and German song" with "German custom, German loyalty / German courage and German song." And that change in tone helped the "Lied der Deutschen," in August of 1914, achieve its first national breakthrough—alongside the "Kaiserhymne" and "Die Wacht am Rhein." Also crucially important was the famous report of a battle on 11 November 1914, during which a young volunteer regiment overran enemy lines near Langemarck, reportedly singing "Deutschland, Deutschland über alles."

From this time on, the foreign press began to take note of the "Lied der Deutschen" and to attack it as a shameless expression of German imperialism. This is apparent even in the various translations of the song. The American version, for instance, begins with the lines "Deutschland, Deutschland, first of nations," while the French translation renders the next two lines as "Si, pour se défendre et attaquer, / Elle s'unit fraternellement" ("When, to defend and to attack / The nation unites as brothers").[7] As early as 1916, Gerstenberg, in his book marking the seventy-fifth anniversary of the "Lied der Deutschen," attacked the "foreign attempt at defamation" that ascribed to the song "a greed for world domination." However, he then went on to speak of "Germany's global mission" and concluded: "As a poet of German culture Hoffmann [von Fallersleben] will be unforgettable, as long as German song resounds in the greater Germany we now seek in the war."[8]

The song thus finally expanded across a substantially broader horizon and could be used for the most diverse purposes: democratic, nationalistic,

6. Max Schneidewin, *In Sachen des Nationalliedes* (Hameln: Fuendeling, 1899), 12, 29 ff.

7. See *Politische Dichtung*, ed. Robert F. Arnold, vol. 3 of *Deutsche Literatur in Entwicklungsreihen* (Leipzig: Reclam, 1936), 299.

8. Gerstenberg, *Lebensbild Hoffmann von Fallersleben*, 61, 89.

chauvinistic, imperialistic, and even racist. The defeated German troops sang it when they marched back into the Reich in November 1918. The German national assembly sang it on 12 May 1919 in response to the announcement of the Western powers' harsh conditions in the peace treaty of Versailles. The reactionary right-wing Ehrhardt Brigade also sang it during the Kapp Putsch of March 1920, as they marched through the Brandenburg Gate and pressed on toward the heart of Berlin. Reich president and social democrat Friedrich Ebert, in his efforts to promote a policy of cooperation and reconciliation among all political factions, officially declared the song the German national anthem in 1922. During a celebration of the constitution on 11 August of that same year, he made a clear reference to the third stanza of Hoffmann von Fallersleben's song when he stated that "the song of unity and justice and freedom should serve as the ceremonial expression of our patriotic feelings."[9] Thus the Weimar Republic finally had a national anthem—and the SPD, which had long been known as the party of the "comrades without a homeland," finally acquired some national credentials.[10]

Leftists were naturally quite embittered by the decision. Kurt Tucholsky saw in it the final proof that the Germans had learned nothing from war and defeat. In 1929 he gave his sharpest criticism of the Weimar Republic the provocative title "Deutschland, Deutschland über alles," in allusion to the "foolish verses" of that "loud-mouthed poem," which a "republic deserted by all noble spirits" had adopted as its national anthem.[11] Naturally, such a strong reaction made nationalist and *völkisch* circles even more enthusiastic about the decision. Ernst Feise, for instance, had by 1923 already worked the new national anthem into his "Lied der Auslandsdeutschen" ("Song of the Germans Abroad"): "Traute Heimat, deine Söhne" ("Beloved Homeland, your Sons").[12] When the Bayreuth Festival resumed in 1924 after

9. See Max Preitz, "Hoffmann von Fallersleben und sein Deutschlandlied," *Jahrbuch des Freien Deutschen Hochstifts* (1926): 299.

10. Around the turn of the century, the SPD was still parodying the song. In its magazine *Der Wahre Jacob* there appeared on 9 October 1900 a "new German national anthem" that attacked the imperialism of the Wilhelminian ruling elite and closed with the verse: "Deutsches Recht und deutsche Freiheit, / Ach, was schert uns solcher Tand; / Drüber lachen wir die neuen / Deutschen mit der Eisenhand. / Nein, im Glanze der Kanonen / Blühe künftig nur die Welt, / Bis All-Deutschland mächtig krachend / Einst in Schutt und Trümmer fällt" ("German justice, German freedom / Ah, what do we care for these trifles / we new Germans of the iron hand / laugh at such things. / No, in the splendor of the canons / may the world henceforth flourish / until Germany tumbles with a mighty crash / and falls one day into ruins.").

11. Kurt Tucholsky, *Deutschland, Deutschland über alles!* (Berlin: Neuer Deutscher Verlag, 1929), 230, 12.

12. See Heinrich Gerstenberg, *Deutschland, Deutschland über alles! Vom Sinn und Werden der deutschen Nationalhymne* (Munich: C. H. Beck, 1933), 96.

a ten-year interruption, the entire public rose after the concluding chorus of the *Meistersinger* and spontaneously sang "Deutschland, Deutschland über alles." Consequently, Max Preitz, a bourgeois-*völkisch* Germanist, could assert as early as 1926 in the *Jahrbuch des Freien Deutschen Hochstifts* that with the battle of Langemarck the "Lied der Deutschen" had become entwined "for all eternity" with "German destiny."[13]

In the spring of 1933, the new National Socialist regime acknowledged this anthem of the despised November Republic as the German national anthem, together with the Horst-Wessel-Lied ("Die Fahne hoch" ["Raise the Flag on High"]). On 1 August 1937, in Breslau, Adolf Hitler called it the anthem "that seems the holiest to us Germans."[14] And with that, there was little else to be said for the next several years. Not only at every party rally but practically everywhere else as well, it was sung, if not roared: in schools, churches, barracks, theaters, even on the radio, where it signaled the end of every broadcast day. Given the song's status in the new Reich, the industrious Heinrich Gerstenberg quickly brought out a new book in 1933 about the *"deutsche Volkshymne,"* as he now called it, in order to immediately cast himself in a favorable light with the new regime. As was to be expected, the anthem took on ever-stronger imperialistic and racist overtones. Indeed, following 1933 every part of the song was emphasized in the crassest way— be it German loyalty, German unity, or Germany's position "über alles in der Welt." Even the song of praise to "German women"—after centuries of "Christian humility" on the part of the other sex—suddenly became understood as a conscious return to the older "Germanic respect for women."[15] The only element that caused some difficulty was the praise of "German wine" because, as explained in a Nazi pamphlet, "we" have recognized alcohol as "harmful to reproduction."[16]

The National Socialists' enthusiasm for the "Lied der Deutschen" reached its high point in 1941, with the song's one-hundredth anniversary, at a time when the German troops were still triumphing "über alles in der Welt." Homage was paid to the author of "our immortal national anthem" in five books marking the occasion: Adolf Moll's *Deutschland, Deutschland über alles* (1940), Rudolf Alexander Moißl's *Das Lied der Deutschen* (1941), Kurt Eggers' *August Heinrich Hoffmann von Fallersleben in seinen Liedern* (1941), Wilhelm Marquard's *Heinrich Hoffmann von Fallersleben*

13. Preitz, "Hoffmann von Fallersleben," 327.
14. Cited in Ernst Hauck, *Das Deutschlandlied: Aus dem Kampf um unsere Einheit* (Dortmund: Stalling, 1942), 59.
15. Ibid., 36.
16. Ibid., 37.

(1942), and Ernst Hauck's *Das Deutschlandlied: Aus dem Kampf um unsere Einheit* (1942). The fact that Ebert was the first to help it achieve this fame was always suppressed. Most simply mentioned Hindenburg instead.

A situation that might have given rise to a new national anthem did not come about until 8 May 1945. But what came of the opportunity? In the Soviet zone of occupation, authorities immediately banned the "Lied der Deutschen," and on 5 November 1949, after the founding of the German Democratic Republic, the song "Auferstanden aus Ruinen" ("Risen from the Ruins"), by Johannes R. Becher and Hanns Eisler, became the national anthem of the new state. This marked a clear break from tradition.[17] In the Western sectors, however, there was much less interest in such ruptures with the past.[18] When the Federal Republic of Germany was founded in the fall of 1949, the national colors were declared to be the black, red, and gold of the revolution of 1848, but the question about a new national anthem was at first left undecided. Most felt it was too soon to keep singing "Deutschland, Deutschland über alles." In September 1949, the Bundestag considered a proposal to declare the "Deutschlandlied" (as it was known since World War I) the national anthem, because it stemmed from a "natural, self-evident popular sentiment" (to quote the text of the right-wing conservative making the proposal). A majority vote rejected the proposal. A brochure, "Das Deutschlandlied," which was written in support of the proposal by Friedrich Kochwasser in 1949 in Nürtingen and sold some fifteen thousand copies, could not sway the decision.

According to the constitution, the right to decide such questions fell to the president, Theodor Heuss. Heuss was clearly against the "Deutschlandlied," while Konrad Adenauer, the first chancellor of the Federal Republic, was just as strongly for it. This led to an unusual battle over the anthem. With Heuss hesitating to decide the question, Adenauer seized the opportunity. At the conclusion of a rally on 12 April 1950, in the Titania-Palast in West Berlin, he "spontaneously" began singing the third stanza of the "Deutschlandlied" in order to give a sounder ideological foundation to his claim to sole representation and to his reunification policy. Most SPD members thereupon left the hall, while the three Allied military commanders representing West Berlin stared at each other in amazement and remained seated.[19] When Kurt Schumacher, the SPD faction leader, labeled

---

17. See Sabine Schutte, "Nationalhymnen und ihre Verarbeitung," *Hanns Eisler*, special edition of *Das Argument: Berliner Hefte für Politik und Kultur* 5 (1975): 208–17.

18. Only the British military government outlawed public singing of the "Deutschlandlied" in its sector on 18 August 1945.

19. See *Der Spiegel* 4, 17 April 1950, 4.

this action "unwise" two days later in the *Neue Zeitung*, the CDU immediately launched a counterattack. Ludwig Erhard wrote that by singing the
"Deutschlandlied" during a political rally only "a few kilometers from the
sector border," Adenauer had wanted to emphasize the express "desire of
the Federal Republic's government" to "establish liberty and justice for
all Germans."[20] The clearly negative reaction of many East Berliners to
Adenauer's appearance at the rally is evidenced, among other things, by
Bertolt Brecht's "Kinderhymne" ("Childrens' Anthem"), which he wrote a
few months after the event in an attempt to develop a nonchauvinistic
conception of the German nation. To take one brief excerpt, it reads:[21]

> Und nicht über und nicht unter
> Andern Völkern wolln wir sein
> Von der See bis zu den Alpen
> Von der Oder bis zum Rhein.
> Und weil wir dies Land verbessern
> Lieben und beschirmen wir's
> Und das Liebste mag's uns scheinen
> So wie andern Völkern ihrs.

> [And not above and not below
> Other nations do we want to stand,
> From the ocean to the Alps
> And from the Oder to the Rhine.
> And because we are making this land better,
> We love and protect it.
> May it appear to us to be the best
> Just as others consider theirs to be.]

Theodor Heuss, however, would not admit defeat after this surprise attack and fought on for a clear break from tradition. He concluded his official
radio address to the West German citizenry on New Year's Eve 1950 with
the "Hymne an Deutschland" ("Land des Glaubens, deutsches Land! Land
der Väter und der Erben" ["Land of conviction, German land! Land of the
fathers and of their heirs"]) by the poet Rudolf Alexander Schröder in an
arrangement by Hermann Reutter. While Heuss hoped to establish the song
as the new national anthem, the reaction was lukewarm. The same applies

---

20. *Neue Zeitung*, 24 April 1950.
21. Bertolt Brecht, *Gesammelte Werke*, 20 vols. (Frankfurt am Main: Suhrkamp, 1968),
10:977.

to the attempt by the Norddeutscher Rundfunk (Northern German Broad-casting) to usher in the song "Ich hab' mich ergeben" ("I surrendered") as the new national anthem. Similar efforts to replace the "Deutschland-lied" at ceremonial occasions, such as the 1950 Winter Olympic Games in Oslo, with Schiller's "Ode to Joy" and music by Beethoven, met with the same end.

In the course of the general restoration of the economic and social sys-tem, those on the Right continued to push for their point of view. A good indication is the brochure *Um das Deutschlandlied,* published in 1951 by the Hoffmann von Fallersleben Society, founded in 1936. In the brochure, Erwin Guido Kolbenheyer, Will Vesper, Hans Grimm, Heinz Steguweit, Edwin Erich Dwinger, Wilhelm Furtwängler, and Hans Knappertsbusch all argued for retaining the "Deutschlandlied." The text was presented to the Bundestag for approval in October of the same year, but Heuss stood firm. Not until Adenauer pressured him in a letter dated 29 April 1952 did Heuss yield, and finally, on 6 May 1952, he declared the "Deutschlandlied" the official (West) German national anthem. He recommended, however, that only the third stanza be sung at ceremonial occasions. In his reply to Adenauer, Heuss explicitly restated that he had hoped for "a clear turning point in the history of the German people and the German state," but ad-mitted that he had underestimated the "traditionalism and persistence" of the German people.[22]

Almost without exception, the foreign press reacted negatively to this decision. Particularly in France there was a feeling—on both the Right and the Left—of having been duped. "Such an attitude," wrote *Le Matin,* "leaves us to fear the worst." "The national anthem of the Third Reich has become the national anthem of Bonn," wrote *Figaro. Le Monde* called Heuss's surrender a "victory for reactionary thinking." *Humanité* spoke of a "rapid retreat to militarism."[23] The West German press, however, was nearly unanimous in its praise for Heuss. "This decision," wrote the *Frank-furter Allgemeine* on 6 May 1952, will "be welcomed by the people, no matter what class, as something quite natural and a matter of course." On the same day the West Berlin *Tagesspiegel* commented even more frankly: "When one thinks of our oppressed compatriots in the East, one sees the 'Deutschlandlied' less as a renewal of tradition and more as a responsibility for the future." Two days later in *Christ und Welt* it almost sounded like

22. This correspondence is collected in Gerhardt Seiffert, *Das ganze Deutschlandlied ist unsere Nationalhymne* (Fallersleben: Hoffmann von Fallersleben-Gesellschaft, 1964), 16 ff.

23. See *Der Spiegel* 6, 14 May 1952, 11.

there had never even been a Hitler or a Third Reich at all: "We believe that in siding with the 'Deutschlandlied' the Federal Republic is turning to the great and honorable strengths of our past."

And with that the "anthem battle" was settled in the FRG for the time being—and the status quo had triumphed once again. The West German public accepted this outcome without opposition, and some even greeted it enthusiastically. When the "Deutschlandlied" was played on the occasion of the West German soccer team's victory in the world championship in Bern in July 1954, West German fans did not sing the lines "Einigkeit und Recht und Freiheit," but instead simply "Deutschland, Deutschland über alles in der Welt." West German historians and literary scholars were generally just as affirmative when addressing this question in the 1950s and 1960s. For instance, Fritz Sandmann wrote in 1962 in *Geschichte in Wissenschaft und Unterricht (History in Scholarship and Pedagogy)* that he hoped "that this song will again be sung by the entire German people as an expression of true love for the fatherland."[24] Ulrich Günther, in his 1966 work *Studien zur Geschichte und Didaktik der deutschen Nationalhymne (Studies on the History and Didactics of the German National Anthem)*, also welcomed the decision of 1952 as a decision in the spirit of "genuine tradition."[25] Hermann Wendelbourg and Anneliese Gerbert were equally supportive in the epilogue for their edition of Hoffmann von Fallersleben's *Lieder und Gedichte,* published in 1974 by Hoffmann and Campe. According to them, it was precisely the "Deutschlandlied" that "during that time of disorder" (that is, during the Third Reich) provided many Germans with the proper standard for their civic thinking and thereby lent them an "inner support"—an effect they thought the song could still have today.[26]

Actual strains of an unredeemed past surfaced in the provincial press and the old German national writers' societies. For example, the following additional stanzas appeared on 7 January 1956 in *Reichsruf: Wochenzeitung für das nationale Deutschland (Call of the Reich: A Weekly for the German Nation)*, which was published by the West German Reichspartei and the tone of which was set by former SS leaders such as Peter Kleist and Erich Kernmayer:

24. Fritz Sandmann, "Das Deutschlandlied und der Nationalismus," *Geschichte in Wissenschaft und Unterricht* 13 (1962): 655.

25. Ulrich Günther, *Über alles in der Welt? Studien zur Geschichte und Didaktik der deutschen Nationalhymne* (Neuwied a. Rhein: Luchterhand, 1966), 118.

26. See August Heinrich Hoffmann von Fallersleben, *Lieder und Gedichte* (Hamburg: Hoffmann and Campe, 1974), 247f.

Deutschland, Deutschland über alles
Und im Unglück nun erst recht.
Nur im Unglück kann die Treue
zeigen, ob sie wahr und echt,
und so soll es weiter klingen
von Geschlechte zu Geschlecht:
Deutschland, Deutschland über alles
und im Unglück: Nun erst recht!
Über Länder, Grenzen, Zonen
hallt ein Ruf, ein Wille nur,
überall wo Deutsche wohnen,
zu den Sternen hallt der Schwur:
Niemals werden wir uns beugen,
nie Gewalt für Recht anseh'n,
Deutschland, Deutschland über alles
Und das Reich wird neu ersteh'n!

[Germany, Germany above all
Especially now in this time of misery.
Only in misery can loyalty
show if it is true and genuine.
And so it shall resound far and wide
from one generation to the next:
Germany, Germany above all
and especially now in misery!
Over nations, borders, zones
echoes a call, the simple will.
Everywhere where Germans live,
the oath resounds to the heavens:
Never will we bend,
Never take force as justice,
Germany, Germany above all
And the Reich will rise again!]

Ernst Hauck, who had established his Nazi credentials prior to 1945 with books such as *Welcher Rasse hat Jesus angehört?* (*To Which Race did Jesus Belong?*, 1934) and *Das Deutschlandlied: Aus dem Kampf um unsere Einheit* (*The Deutschlandlied: Out of the Struggle for Our Unity*, 1942), could also not resist beating his old chauvinistic drum in the *Coburger Tageblatt* on 17 August 1962. Indeed, some of these West German authors adhered to a militant anticommunism, much as they had already done back in the 1930s, and attempted to mobilize Hoffmann von Fallersleben's legacy for the people on the other side of the Iron Curtain. As Fritz Andrée wrote in 1959: "The division of the people has again become a matter of destiny for us Germans. Hoffmann [von Fallersleben]'s longing for unity is also our longing. He certainly could not have imagined that so close to his home town a border would split the country open like a bleeding wound and that no more trains could roll over the Weser Bridge near Corvey, past his final resting place, and into the eastern half of Germany."[27] With similar words, Gerhardt Seiffert declared in 1964 that he was pleased that "healthy popular sentiment" had decided in favor of the song. This allowed, he thought, for the possibility that someday a "unity" would extend beyond the sector borders.[28] Whether explicitly or covertly, all of these positions somehow embraced the Hallstein Doctrine, an international legal condemnation of the GDR.

Only this can explain the move as early as the 1970s of Bavarian Governor Alfons Goppel and the governor of Baden-Württemberg, Hans Filbinger, acting in the CDU–CSU coalition, to take up once again the first stanza of the "Deutschlandlied" and proudly sing "Deutschland, Deutschland über alles."[29] Both state governments arranged for a phonograph recording of the complete song, featuring the pop singer Heino, to be distributed in all schools within their states. In the same vein, Hans Jürgen Hansen published a nostalgic picture book in the spring of 1978, with the title *Heil Dir im Siegerkranz: Die Hymnen der Deutschen* (*Hail to You, oh Laureled Victor: The Anthems of the Germans*). Toward the conclusion of the work he observed with remarkable frankness: "A generation after Hitler, a sovereign federal government in Bonn could, in accordance with black-red-gold democratic tradition, again confidently declare the entire text of 'Deutschland über alles' as the national anthem."[30]

Opposition to such tendencies has not coalesced. Admittedly, some SPD parliamentarians and trade unionists protested repeatedly against the use of the first verse during official ceremonies. The *Deutsche Volkszeitung* also came out strongly against the "Deutschlandlied."[31] Otherwise, the

27. Fritz Andrée, *Wirkungs- und Erinnerungsstätten des Dichters Hoffmann von Fallersleben* (Fallersleben: Hoffmann von Fallersleben-Gesellschaft, 1959), 6.

28. Seiffert, *Das ganze Deutschlandlied*, 15, 34. The title of his brochure translates into English as *The Entire Deutschlandlied Is Our National Anthem*.

29. See *Der Stern* 13 (1978): 17.

30. Hans Jürgen Hansen, *Heil Dir im Siegerkranz: Die Hymnen der Deutschen* (Oldenburg: Stalling, 1978), 77.

31. *Deutsche Volkszeitung* 25 (1972): 5.

West German Left limited itself primarily to setting straight later falsifications of the song. But in this case, such limited responses do not adequately acknowledge the entire cultural history of the song and therefore the full implications of its use in contemporary Germany. Much as one might wish it to be so, the history of the "Lied der Deutschen" consists of more than its democratic past. The reception of the song necessarily reminds us of the darkest moments of Germany's past. After 1914, the nationalist Right twisted it so strongly to their imperialistic intentions that its liberal origins have been rendered unrecognizable—perhaps permanently. The beauty of its melody and the democratic meaning of a number of its verses notwithstanding, the song will always evoke democracy's tragic failure in Germany.

It was therefore correct, though not very wise, when West German leftists in the 1970s pictured Hoffmann von Fallersleben next to Marx and Heine on a poster with the heading: "They'd be blacklisted today."[32] More astute, it seems to me, were those dissident groups, who, in reference to a book by Bert Engelmann, sang the words "Einig gegen Recht und Freiheit" ("united against justice and freedom") in protests against the CDU–CSU establishment. Indeed, a number of people at such actions sang in rebellion: "Einig gegen dumme Frechheit" ("united against stupid insolence"). Many found such word games cynical, yet others saw it as a further step in the process of *Vergangenheitsbewältigung* (overcoming the past)—a step, moreover, that had too long been absent.[33]

Guide to Further Reading

Andrée, Fritz. *Wirkungs- und Erinnerungsstätten des Dichters Hoffmann von Fallersleben*. Fallersleben: Just & Seiffert, 1960.

Busch, Otto. *125 Jahre "Deutschland, Deutschland über alles."* Munich: Bassermann, 1967.

Enzensberger, Ulrich. *Auferstanden über alles*. Berlin: Rotbuch-Verlag, 1986.

Günther, Ulrich. *Über alles in der Welt? Studien zur Geschichte und Didaktik der deutschen Nationalhymne*. Neuwied am Rhein: Luchterhand, 1966.

Hansen, Hans Jürgen. *Heil Dir im Siegerkranz: Die Hymnen der Deutschen*. Oldenburg: Stalling, 1978.

32. See Wolfgang Beutin and Thomas Metscher, *Berufsverbot: Ein bundesdeutsches Lesebuch* (Fischerhude: Fischerhude Texte, 1977).

33. Recent feminist criticism has joined in the criticism of the song, calling it "from beginning to end an anthem for a men's singing society," as Luise F. Pusch wrote in 1990. Cited in Benjamin Ortmeyer, *Argumente gegen das Deutschlandlied: Geschichte und Gegenwart eines Lobliedes auf die deutsche Nation* (Cologne: Bund-Verlag, 1991), 115.

Hermand, Jost. *Old Dreams of a New Reich: Volkish Utopias and National Social-ism.* Bloomington: Indiana University Press, 1992.

Kurzke, Hermann. *Hymnen und Lieder der Deutschen.* Mainz: Dieterich, 1990.

Mosse, George L. "National Anthems: The Nation Militant. " In *From Ode to An-them: Problems of Lyric Poetry.* Ed. Reinhold Grimm and Jost Hermand. Madi-son: University of Wisconsin Press, 1989. Pp. 86–99.

Ortmeyer, Benjamin. *Argumente gegen das Deutschlandlied: Geschichte und Gegen-wart eines Lobliedes auf die deutsche Nation.* Cologne: Bund-Verlag, 1991.

Preitz, Max. "Hoffmann von Fallersleben und sein Deutschlandlied," *Jahrbuch des Freien Deutschen Hochstifts* (1926): 299–326.

Reisenbichler, Elke. *Das Deutschlandlied.* Munich: Verlag Hohe Warte, 1986.

Sandmann, Fritz. "Das Deutschlandlied und der Nationalismus." *Geschichte in Wis-senschaft und Unterricht* 13 (1962): 653–72.

Schutte, Sabine. "Nationalhymnen und ihre Verarbeitung." In *Hanns Eisler,* special edition of *Das Argument: Berliner Hefte für Politik und Kultur* 5 (1975): 208–17.

Tümmler, Hans. *Deutschland, Deutschland über alles.* Cologne: Böhlau, 1979.

Ethnicity and Musical Identity in the Czech Lands: A Group of Vignettes

BRUNO NETTL

This essay considers the musical culture of Germans—ethnic Germans whose principal language was German—living in the lands that now encompass the Czech Republic. From the fifteenth century to 1945, the German-speaking inhabitants of Bohemia and Moravia, and particularly of Prague, were participants in German and Austro-German society. But their culture was unique because of its consistent interaction with the culture of the Slavic-speaking Czechs, with that of the large and ancient community of Bohemian Jews, and more distantly the Rom or Gypsies. It is these interrelationships, illustrated by a group of vignettes, that are the principal subject here.

The Conservatory of Europe: Germans, Czechs, Jews and Music

Within Europe, the Czech lands have been widely regarded as "music country." Czechs, Germans, Jews, and Rom have all seen themselves (and been seen by others) collectively as particularly musical, as masters not only of their own but also of other peoples' music. And music has often been used to negotiate the political, social, and economic differences among them. Let me briefly sketch the characters of this interethnic drama.

In nineteenth- and twentieth-century Europe, Germans have often laid special claims to music, and they have been accepted as the quintessential masters of art music by connoisseurs from many nations, even in the relativistic late twentieth century.[1] But it has not always been so; the admission

---

1. Albrecht Riethmüller, *Die Walhalla und ihre Musiker* (Laaber: Laaber Verlag, 1993).

of Germans to what some people think is the world's most musical peoples is relatively recent. In 1776, in his *General History of Music*, the English scholar and writer Charles Burney apologized for having earlier accused Germany of "want of genius. " But he stops short of claiming German superiority in music, asserting only that "to pronounce that an empire . . . whose inhabitants amount to a seventh part of the people [of Europe] should be deficient in genius, was not only unjust but inconsistent and absurd."[2]

Yet in the early twenty-first century, ethnic Germans dominate the world's standard art music repertory. In North America, the names engraved on music buildings are largely German. In the concert halls and music schools of Germany, Britain, and many other European countries, "normal" music is by German and Austrian composers, which sometimes includes Bohemian or explicitly Czech composers as a German subtype. This is a view that has also infiltrated scholarship, which has been analyzed by Pamela Potter in *Most German of the Arts* and by the Czech-born musicologist Vladimír Karbusický, who in his book *Wie deutsch ist das Abendland?* accuses German musicologists of having privileged German music by relegating Slavic and Latin traditions to merely local importance and calling the greats of other nations *Kleinmeister*.[3] The ethnic Germans living in the Czech lands, those whose mother tongue was German, are difficult to identify as a separate group through much of history, as individuals and families and entire localities moved between German and Czech orientations; but in the pre-Nazi period of Czechoslovakia, they amounted to some 2–3 million living largely at the borderlands of Bohemia and Moravia, and in Prague.

Second, take the Czechs, speakers of a West Slavic language, the majority population of Bohemia and Moravia since the early Middle Ages. Throughout their history, they have been beset economically, politically, and culturally by Germans. At times they succumbed, as many of them took German as their first language and became culturally German. But mostly they fought back, striving to maintain their Czech ethnicity, and they did this in considerable measure by using music as a weapon, promulgating their music and also becoming excellent musicians in general, to the extent that the neighboring Germans came to stereotype them as quin-

2. Charles Burney, *A General History of Music*, 2 vols. (1776–82; reprint, New York: Dover Publications, 1935), 2:393.

3. Pamela Potter, *Most German of the Arts: Musicology and Society from the Weimer Republic to the End of Hitler's Reich* (New Haven: Yale University Press, 1998); Vladimír Karbusický, *Wie deutsch ist das Abendland? Geschichtliches Selbstbewusstsein im Spiegel der Musik* (Hamburg: Von Bockel, 1995).

tessential musicians, a stereotype they were in time to adopt themselves. They sometimes told this joke: When a Czech boy is born, he is presented with a bag of money and a fiddle. If he reaches for the money, he will become a thief; if for the fiddle, a musician.

Prague from the late Middle Ages on had one of the largest Jewish populations of any European city.[4] Jewish participation in music seems for centuries to have been significant everywhere in Europe and was so in Bohemia. Indeed, in the seventeenth century the Prague community produced such an excess of musicians that policies to restrict their number by forbidding musicians to teach music to more than two of their children were instituted. More recently, before the Holocaust, the population of Jews in the Czech lands amounted to only about 1 percent; but a count of prominent twentieth-century composers turns out to comprise about 25 percent Jews. To the secular Jewish community in the 1930s, musicality was a badge of ethnic identity.

As for the musical interaction of the Rom with other ethnic groups in the Czech lands, they are a significant group—some two hundred thousand within the total of 10 million—who have rarely been duly respected or given equal treatment. Romantic figures in folklore, they make significant appearances in works of artists in the other ethnic groups, for example, the folk-song arrangements by Dvořák and in *The Diary of One Who Vanished* by Janáček. But doesn't everyone think of them too as a society of paradigmatic musicians?

It's definitely "music country." It was again Burney, over two hundred years ago, who described the musical reputation of Bohemians (we're not sure which Bohemians) as "the most musical people of Germany, or, perhaps, of all Europe . . . and that if they enjoyed the same advantages as the Italians, they would excel them."[5] Apocryphally (though I dare say correctly), Burney is also said to have described Bohemia as the "conservatory

4. According to various estimates, the Jewish population of pre–World War II Czechoslovakia was approximately 350,000, roughly 2.5 percent; and in Bohemia and Moravia alone there were about 120,000 Jews, less than 2 percent of the population. In Prague, the Jewish population appears to have been approximately 10 percent in the late eighteenth century, and five percent in 1900 and 1939. See *Encyclopedic Dictionary of Judaica* (New York: L. Amiel Publishers, 1974), 146, 488; Gary B. Cohen, *The Politics of Ethnic Survival: Germans in Prague, 1861–1914* (Princeton: Princeton University Press, 1981), 86–102; Livia Rothkirchen, "The Jews of Bohemia and Moravia: 1938–1945," in *The Jews of Czechoslovakia*, 3 vols. (Philadelphia: Jewish Publication Society of America, 1968–84), 3:13.

5. Charles Burney, *The Present State of Music in Germany, the Netherlands, and United Provinces* (London: T. Becket, 1775), 131.

of Europe" because many of its musicians had moved away in the eighteenth century, in a virtual diaspora, to populate orchestral chairs and composers' positions throughout Europe.

It is easy to wax enthusiastic about the great accomplishments of Bohemian musicians in the field of art and popular music. But it is important to note that these "musical" peoples—Czechs, Germans, Jews—had for centuries, going back to 1400 and before, found it necessary to engage in struggles for land and economic resources, for political and economic hegemony, but also for cultural recognition and ethnic identity. Welcome neighbors to the Slavs in the Middle Ages, the Germans of the Czech lands proceeded to move to a position of dominance and hegemony, eventually became partners in a benevolent cultural syncretism, were then reduced to the status of a minority, and finally became both perpetrators and victims of the Holocaust, before their remnant departed, turning into a diaspora of exiles and a culture of nostalgia for unredeemed territories.

The Victors of White Mountain: Czech Music under German Hegemony

The era of German cultural dominance started in the seventeenth century. To the Czech-speaking peoples of the last two hundred years, the battle of 1620 at White Mountain, a hill now virtually in the suburbs of Prague, has lived in memory as a devastating defeat, ending two hundred years of conflict between Czechs—who wished for ethnic and a measure of religious freedom and individuality based on the teachings of Jan Hus—and the imperial might symbolized by the traditional Catholic Church and the German language. Using various hegemonic techniques, the victors of White Mountain imposed German language, literature, and culture and denigrated the Czech, making the Czech language into the tongue of the countryside, of peasants and servants, and by stereotype, of fools and illiterates. The Catholic aristocracy, Germans brought from Austria, and Czechs who adhered to the imperial power then went on to make Bohemia into a land that produced magnificent music and great musicians, little concerned with their explicit ethnicity. In the seventeenth and eighteenth centuries, the Austro-German political and religious power tried with considerable success to make Bohemia into a German land. The period from 1618 to 1945 was one of struggle, first of the Czechs to regain the dominant position appropriate to them as the numerical majority, later of the Germans first to maintain their dominant cultural position and then to hold a place as a respected and influential minority.

From the start of this era of German domination, the musical dimensions of identity reveal on the one hand a desire to develop a distinctive German-Bohemian music, and on the other hand to gloss over any distinction between "German" and "Czech." There was a struggle by the Germans of Bohemia to avoid simply becoming an outpost of Germany and Austria, but to maintain, instead, a distinctive German-Bohemian culture. One result was the development, by the seventeenth century, of a particular kind of musical figure, the traveling musician, versatile and usually at home in vernacular as well as cultivated music, with musical and social characteristics unique to the Czech lands.[6] These individuals (termed *Musikant* in German, *muzikant* in Czech, distinguishing them from the more elite-oriented *Musiker* or *hudebník*) evidently lived and worked in a bilingual environment.

A unique, syncretic Czech-German musical culture thus developed—celebrated, incidentally, in Dvořák's opera *Jakobín*. The grand musical culture of the German-speaking aristocrats and courts of Bohemia was based on the tradition in Bohemian villages (also known in German cities) of combining the task of schoolmaster and church organist (with the title of cantor). As a result of this practice, many chamber servants, farm workers, hunters, and herdsmen had some musical competence and populated the local orchestras. However, for a truly stellar career in music one could rarely count on employment in one's home country, especially since the court in Prague shunned local composers and instead brought masters from Italy and Vienna. Thus, most of the seventeenth- and eighteenth-century Bohemian-born musicians familiar to twentieth-century students of music history—such as Biber, Stamitz, Richter, Vanhal, Pichl, Benda, Mysliveček, Gyrowetz, and many more—moved to Vienna, to Germany, Italy, France, England, even to Russia to pursue their careers.

These eighteenth-century masters had an enormous influence on German music history—Biber on violin technique and musical representation, Stamitz in his role in the invention of the classical style, Benda on the melodrama, Mysliveček on Mozart the symphonist, and so on. Curiously, in German musical historiography, when works are subdivided by nation, these Bohemian composers appear at best as a subtype of German composers. Today, in Czech music historiography, they are usually presented as Czechs. In the eighteenth century itself, little attention seems to have been paid to the question of ethnicity. A comprehensive 1787 description and guidebook of Prague that provides a detailed accounting of the geography, culture, and population of the city down to a census by age, gender,

6. Karl Michael Komma, *Das böhmische Musikantentum* (Kassel: Hinenthal), 1960), 81–82.

and religion says not a word about ethnic and linguistic identity—except for separating out the Jewish population.[7] It presumed evidently that the "normal" language of all was German. This work, incidentally, also lists the occupants of chairs at the university, and about half of them have characteristically Czech names.

The ethnic identity of these eighteenth-century Bohemian musicians—how they saw themselves—is an unanswered question. There is little doubt that most of them spoke German, maybe often better than Czech. Yet Burney, in his musical tour of Bohemia, allowed that "it was with much difficulty that I acquired information from the Bohemian musicians, as even the German language is of little use in that kingdom, throughout which the Sclavonian dialect is generally used."[8] Clearly, we don't know whether Stamitz and Pichl and Mysliveček spoke German more than Czech, nor in which language they felt most at home. In the musicians' diaspora they were ordinarily treated as Germans. Were these musicians then Germans whose ancestors had spoken German for generations, but who happened to be inhabiting lands also inhabited by speakers of Czech, or were they descendants of ethnic Czechs who had switched to German as their principal linguistic orientation? Were they really Czechs, by language and culture, who assumed a veneer of German to make it in polite society? Two hundred years ago the issue of national identity may have been less well defined, and in the nineteenth century still the relationship between nationality, ethnicity, and linguistic identity is confusing. Even Smetana, the great nationalist, evidently learned Czech first as a boy but then studied and mainly spoke German, neglecting through middle age the more advanced development of Czech among his language skills.[9] It was not until World War II that the nationality of composers became the critics' and writers' and cultural politicians' currency of musical land-grabbing.

Mich rührt so sehr böhmischen Volkes Weise:
Folk Music in German and Czech Cultures

For most of the nineteenth century, German and Czech folk music negotiated a balance, as Czech folk music emerged as a distinctive and respected body of music, and art music remained essentially "German." From the eighteenth century on, Czech society used music to reestablish its culture,

---

7. *Vollständige Beschreibung der königlichen Haupt- und Residenzstadt Prag . . .*
Besonders für Fremde und Reisende bearbeitet, 2 vols. (Prague: Schönfeld, 1987), 1:218–23.
   8. Burney, *The Present State of Music,* 134.
   9. Brian Large, *Smetana* (New York: Praeger, 1970), 122–24, 148.

by collecting and nurturing folk music and using its styles as national markers in art music and by developing icons to represent musically the struggle for political identity. These icons included the Hussite hymn "We Who are Warriors of God," which was used by Bedřich Smetana, Karel Husa, and Viktor Ullmann to represent that struggle and was widely understood as a freedom-fighting anthem; folk and national dances such as the polka and the furiant; and ethnic and culturally significant themes that furnish the plots of the most significant operas and tone poems. An important trope here is the claim to excellence of "Czech" music, and to the excellence of Czechs in music and as musicians generally. As part of this essay's focus on the role of music in the ethnically German population, it is important to recognize that what distinguished the musical culture and musical identity of the German-speaking Bohemians is the constant interaction with the Czechs. The ambivalent role of the Bohemian Germans in the imagination of Czech people even in the twentieth century goes back to the defeat at White Mountain and the subsequent—and for some two centuries unremitting—desire to make the Czechs into Germans of a sort. But this role also reflected the recognition of the contribution of Bohemian musicians to the glories of German music. To the Germans, Czech music was folk music, the music of the versatile vernacular musician.

The complicated interaction between Germans and Czechs is symbolized, for example, in the words of Czech and German songs, like this one ridiculing a small town near the border:

Žadnij neví co jsou Domažlice
Žadnij neví co je to Taus.
Taus je to německý, Domažlice český
Žadnij neví co je to Taus.

[No one knows what is Domažlice,
No one knows what is Taus.
It's Taus in German, Domažlice in Czech,
No one knows what is Taus.]

A German song from the German side of the western border, near Regensburg, makes a similar juxtaposition in linguistic and culinary terms, and contrasts the Czech dumplings with the German cabbage and sausage:

A bissl böhmisch und a bissl deutsch
Und a Trum Knödl und a gselchts Fleisch

Und a Packl Kraut und a Stückl Wurscht,
Des geht fürn Hunger, aber net fürn Durscht.[10]

[A bit of Czech and a bit of German,
a bunch of dumplings and some smoked meat,
And a package of Kraut and a piece of sausage,
That's good for hunger, but not for thirst.]

But despite stylistic similarity, some overlapping of tunes and texts, and some bicultural references in the texts, these are distinct folk music repertories. Also, as symbols of identity and ethnicity, they and their cultural contexts played quite different roles in their—and in each other's—respective societies. Thus, to the Bohemian Germans, Czech music was quintessentially "folk," as befits a people whose culture was relegated to rural and working-class status. When Prague Germans thought of folk music, they thought of the Czech; the fine thing about Czech music was its rich folk music, and if Czech art music was good, this was due to its use of folk material. To eastern Slavs, Czech folk music sounded very German; but to Germans, it had its exotic aspects. Rilke, the German poet born in Prague, said it clearly:

Mich rührt so sehr
Böhmischen Volkes Weise;
Schleicht sie ins Herz sich leise,
Macht sie es schwer.[11]

[I am so moved
By the sound of Czech folk song;
Gently it enters your heart
And makes it heavy.]

When it came to the use of folk songs and folk music styles in the world of art music of the Czech lands, it seems that German-speaking composers rarely turned to German folk songs but, instead, like Viktor Ullmann, often resorted to Czech folk songs. At the same time, Czech composers—even the more or less German-oriented Zdeněk Fibich—seem

10. Liner notes to the LP record, *Wer da niat ka* [*Whoever can't do that*] Colosseum SM 3014, ca. 1974.
11. From Rainer Maria Rilke, *Larenopfer* (1896).

hardly ever to have availed themselves of the German folk music within their borders. The use of elements of Czech folk music and participation in the collecting and editing of Czech folk songs became, from Smetana on, virtually a professional obligation of Czech composers, who participated in the publication of hundreds of songs with piano accompaniment (in styles inspired by German composers such as Brahms) in dozens of anthologies. So, indeed, it would seem that German musical identity in twentieth-century Prague was bound up with the concept of Czech folk song.

The Prague Casino and the Realm of Rübezahl: Germans as a Minority Culture

In the late nineteenth century, and even more with the establishment of the Czechoslovak Republic in 1918, the German presence took on the identity of a minority and thus played itself out musically in the creation of an ethnic German folk culture. In the course of the nineteenth century, I have suggested, the Czech intellectual establishment cooperated with the German in stereotyping Czechs as the makers of folk music par excellence, as being the great vernacular musicians of Bohemia. True, early in the nineteenth century, German folk songs too began to be collected and recorded, but only in the late nineteenth century, seeing the establishment of Czech hegemony, did the Germans of Bohemia take a serious interest in folk music. Indeed, the notion that Sudeten-Germans had a distinct culture that needed to be nurtured and protected came into its own with the founding of the Czechoslovak Republic. But already before that, changes in the cultural and linguistic orientation of the population, particularly of Prague, could be noted. According to Gary Cohen, the 15 percent of Prague residents who were primarily German-speaking in 1880 had, by 1910, been reduced to 7 percent.[12] This was due largely to the influx of Czech industrial workers from the countryside, as well as the successes of the Czechs in the struggle for revitalizing their culture and changing orientations within the large Jewish population—73 percent German-oriented in 1890, but only 45 percent by 1900.[13]

Reactions to this decline in German culture in Prague include the development in the 1860s of the Prague Casino (which provided a library,

12. Cohen, *Politics of Ethnic Survival*, 93–94. See also Stanley Buchholz Kimball, *Czech Nationalism: A Study of the National Theatre Movement, 1845–83* (Urbana: University of Illinois Press, 1964).

13. Cohen, *Politics of Ethnic Survival*, 102.

adult education classes, lectures, and forums for discussion), and of other
cultural organizations with a German agenda. While the German-speaking
population of Bohemia had, in the eighteenth and early nineteenth centuries, been culturally unified, the twentieth century brought about a significant split between the German-speaking community of Prague and that of
the Sudeten-German outskirts. Prague's German culture was syncretic; it
maintained itself as a major sector of cultural life by joining Jewish and
Czech scholars, artists, and intellectuals, nurturing a cosmopolitan character, and taking an interest in Czech folk music. The Sudetenland had an
almost entirely German-oriented art music culture and a body of vernacular and folk music that began to be nurtured separately. By the twentieth
century it is easy to see a division between the German culture of Prague
and of the border regions.

Actually, the concept of "Sudetenland" came into its own when the
Germans of Bohemia ceased being a part of the dominant society of the dual
monarchy and became a minority in Czechoslovakia. After 1918, Sudeten-
Germans began to establish themselves as a separate population, with a
distinctive culture. This was illustrated by a volume of biographies published in 1926, *Sudetendeutsche Lebensbilder*[14] (*Sudenten-German Lives*),
the purpose of which was to demonstrate the power of German culture. It
did this by providing biographies of arguably German intellectuals and
artists, including the musicians Hammerschmiedt, Gluck, Biber, Stamitz,
and Hanslick. But it also provided biographies of Germanic royalty and nobility who ruled in Bohemia from ca. 8 A.D. to the eighth century, and even
of Germanic women who married into the royalty of the Czech Přemysl dynasty. Characteristically German cover and title-page designs underscored
the book's agenda.

Folk music, too, played a role in the increasing nationalism of the
Sudeten-Germans during the 1930s. This was whipped up by the political
activist Conrad Henlein, who was supported by the musicologist Gustav
Becking, among whose activities was the direction of a student chorus that
entertained Sudeten-German populations with folk and patriotic songs
during academic vacation periods. The concept of a distinctive Sudeten-
German culture was balanced, however, by the notion of Sudeten-Germans
as "unredeemed" Germans soon to return to the fatherland. Scholarly and
practical collections of German folk songs appeared in some quantity between 1918 and 1939, but the most characteristic is one *Die Volkslieder*

---

14. Erich Gierach, ed., *Sudetendeutsche Lebensbilder* (Reichenberg: Stiepel, 1926).

der Sudetendeutschen,[15] from the end of this period (after the annexation), whose history poignantly reflects the story of the Sudeten-Germans and the decline of their culture. No longer is one shown the Germanness of Bohemian culture, with its center in Prague. Rather, the emphasis is on the unique musical character of the Sudeten country and, in the second instance, its closeness to that of Germany proper.

Edited by Gustav Jungbauer and Herbert Horntrich and published in installments, *Die Volkslieder* is a superbly documented collection of songs from many sources. Although originally intended to be three times its eventual size, its one volume contains seven hundred melodies that are well indexed and classified by function; there is also an index of informants (with occupations) that suggests that these songs were current among the upper middle class and the intelligentsia of the small towns of outer Bohemia. Despite the suggestion that Sudeten-German culture is distinct, the collection includes many songs also found in collections made in Germany proper and among other German-speaking populations; a few, however, have tunes also found in Czech repertories.

The preface by Gustav Jungbauer from 1938 provides the history of this and other Sudeten-German folksong collections, and concludes, "May this edition, which is intended to bring new life to folk music, accomplish its purpose for the benefit of our Sudeten-German community and of the entire German nation."[16] But an afterword from 1940 reports that "the inhabitants of . . . Bohemia, Moravia, Silesia have returned home to the greater German empire" and suggests that this collection no longer had the function it may once have had.[17] Apologizing for delays, the publishers prepared an appendix of twenty-seven songs collected from Sudeten-Germans who had been living in Poland but had returned.

Die Volkslieder der Sudetendeutschen seems to me to symbolize the decline of German culture and its music in Bohemia. In its final form, it abandoned the distinctiveness of Bohemian-German culture for emphasis on its relationship to the German fatherland, and presaged the devastation of war and the subsequent migration of the great majority of Sudeten-Germans to nearby parts of West Germany. The German Folk-Song Archive in Freiburg continued some collecting of the folk songs of Sudeten-Germans after 1950.

---

15. Gustav Jungbauer and Herbert Horntrich, eds., *Die Volkslieder der Sudeten-deutschen* (Kassel: Bärenreiter, 1938).

16. Ibid., 5.

17. Ibid., 714.

After the war, the Sudeten-Germans immigrants to West Germany and some of their descendants maintained for a long time a quixotic political movement urging recapture of the homeland, a movement not built with emphasis on music but rather on the physical beauty of nature and architecture. Thus the most significant artistic symbols are collections of photographs (with emotional literary text) of the mountainous parts of northern Bohemia, such as *Heimatland Riesengebirge,* subtitled *Ein Heimatbuch aus dem unvergesslichen Reiche Rübezahls* (*A Book of the Homeland, From the Unforgettable Realm of Rübezahl*).[18] In a gesture mildly reminiscent of Barbarossa—or of the legendary Czech Hussite warriors, defeated in 1422 and asleep in the mountain Blaník until their fatherland needs them— Rübezahl, the legendary old man of the Krkonoše mountains, becomes the guardian in whose care the Sudeten-Germans leave their homeland until they can return.

One may speculate about the reasons for the relative neglect of their music among the Sudeten-Germans after 1945. Driven from their homes and living in Munich and Stuttgart, they concentrated more on the memory of towns, architecture, and visual art because these, with their fixed locations in the lost lands, are better able to support the effort to return than music, which can be heard anywhere. Possibly, also, the recognition of Bohemian-German music as a product of both Czechs and Germans may have discouraged its use as a weapon of Sudeten-German nationalism. *Die Volkslieder der Sudetendeutschen* contains no songs about Rübezahl.

18. Joseph Renner, ed., *Heimatland Riesengebirge: Ein Heimatbuch aus dem unvergesslichen Reiche Rübezahls,* 2d ed. (Kempten/Allgäu: M. Renner, 1959). On p. 3, under a photograph, a short unascribed poem ends:

Riesengebirge, deutsches Gebirge,
meine liebe Heimat du!

[Giant Mountains, you German mountains,
You, my dearest homeland.]

And on p. 5, a preface by Othmar Fiebiger begins with his short verse:

Seitdem wir sie verloren,
nun ist's uns allen klar:
wie schön, wie reich, wie gottvoll
doch unsere Heimat war.

[Since we have lost it,
It has become clear to us,
How beautiful, how rich, how divine
Was our homeland.]

*The Victims of Theresienstadt: Jewish Contributions
to Bohemian Musical Culture*

Paul Nettl (1889–1972), my father, born in Vrchlabí (or Hohenelbe) in the Riesengebirge or Krkonoše mountains, is among the scholars who, in publications of the 1920s and 1930s, most emphatically celebrated the German character of Prague. But his earliest works in this line concern the musical life of the Jewish community of Prague in the sixteenth and seventeenth centuries.[19] This was a large community—in 1787, over 10 percent of the Prague population was Jewish—with a vigorous musical life, which spoke German and, probably, *Mauscheldeutsch*, a local Jewish-German dialect distinct from Yiddish (*Mauscheldeutsch* = *"Moischele-Deutsch"* = "Moses German").[20] Three centuries ago the Jewish community evidently provided much of the secular and vernacular music entertainment of the Prague bourgeoisie, a practice no doubt diffused as the nineteenth century wore on. But in the twentieth century, Jewish musicians, teachers, writers, and scholars were again carrying much of the musical life of the German community of Prague; and their patrons were often Jews as well. No wonder, perhaps, that many of the Jewish musicians of twentieth-century Prague considered themselves ethnic Germans in the most definitive sense. Paul Nettl, living in North America after the Holocaust, said in regard to his continued adherence to the German language, "mir ist der Schnabel deutsch gewachsen" ("I grew a German beak").

But the German-speaking Jews of Prague—as I experienced their culture in the 1930s, culturally German—also made special concessions to the Czech environment and, naturally, to aspects of Jewish culture. Many members of this Jewish community had no interest in religion or in Jewish ethnic traditions; and yet they identified themselves as Jews and maintained an ethnic identity that they defined mainly by personality and behavioral traits, including strong emotional expression and a special musicality—an almost automatic understanding of music. While they participated in a musical culture that emphasized European art music and the central classical and romantic repertory, their approach to this repertory seemed to me to have a particular slant; they privileged a characteristic configuration of the common musical culture. In my experience (and I stress that this is my personal perception), the music that this culture group most regarded as its

19. Among Paul Nettl's principal publications on the subject are *Beiträge zur böhmischen und mährischen Musikgeschichte* (Brno: Rohrer, 1927); *Altprager Almanach 1927* (Prague: Bücherstube, 1927;) and *Mozart in Böhmen* (Prague: Bücherstube, 1938).

20. Fritz Mauthner, *Erinnerungen I: Prager Jugendjahre* (Munich: G. Müller, 1918), 33 ff.

own featured the Viennese classicists—but most of all Mozart and Schubert; the great Czech romantics, Smetana and Dvořák; Gustav Mahler and
the Second Viennese school (Schoenberg and Berg); the lieder of Schubert
and certain others by Schumann; and Czech folk songs with piano accom-
paniments in the style of nineteenth-century classical music. A fine repertory, but the list may illustrate the conception of the German culture as the
great classics from the center of the Austrian empire; the Czech, as the association with nationalism and folk music; and the Jewish component in
Mahler, Schoenberg, and Heine's poetry for Schumann's songs. Bach, Beethoven, Brahms, Chopin, Verdi, Wagner—unquestionably great composers
too, but not as close to the heart.

The significance of European music—especially German-Austrian-
Czech nineteenth-century music—in the construction of cultural identity
of central European immigrants in Israel has been well described by Philip
Bohlman.[21] In Prague of the 1930s, too, we may see a particular configuration of a generally known repertory as a symbol of society and subculture.
In the case of Paul Nettl, whose publications about the music history of the
German speakers of Bohemia from the Sudeten country of Biber to Prague
at the time of Mozart constitute his principal scholarly legacy, the notion of
a musical culture that combined Czech and German and distinctively Jewish traditions was fully compatible with a German cultural orientation.[22]

In one way, German musical culture of Bohemia died with the departure of the Sudeten-Germans after 1945 and the execution of many Germans in Prague, including the Nazi-oriented musicologist Gustav Becking.[23] But more significantly, it also came to an end with the eradication of
the Jewish population of Prague. It is probably fair to say that a large pro-
portion of the composers of art music in Czechoslovakia of the 1930s were
of Jewish background. A survey of prominent composers in 1938 would have
included the distinguished Czech elder statesmen—Viteslav Novák, Alois
Hába, Josef Suk—but also, importantly, a group of Jewish composers whose

21. Philip V. Bohlman, The Land Where Two Streams Flow (Urbana: University of Illinois Press, 1989).

22. Paul Nettl, "Music," in The Jews of Czechoslovakia, 3:539–58.

23. Becking, during his years as a professor in Prague (1930–45), devoted himself
substantially to the agenda of proving the German identity of composers and folk music being
claimed by Czech scholars and publicists. A conflict with the Czech historian Vladimír Hel-
fert (in 1936) revolved about the true biological and musical ancestries of Stamitz, Biber,
Benda, Schobert, and surprisingly even Franz Schubert. From 1935 on, he was one of the leading figures in the culture wars between Sudeten-Germans and Czechs. See Kurt Stangl, "In
Memoriam Gustav Becking," Musikforschung 2 (1949): 126–31.

linguistic orientation was German, but who also knew Czech—Victor Ullmann, Hans Krása, Pavel Haas, Erwin Schulhoff, and Gideon Klein. Schulhoff spent much of his life studying and playing in Germany, though he
eventually moved to Russia but was caught and executed in Germany. The
other four, finding themselves in Prague after the German invasion of
March 1939, also lost their lives as victims of the Holocaust.[24]

In the 1930s, these Jewish composers were the chief representatives of
German-oriented art music culture in Prague, though in their lives and
works they seem to have toggled between Czech and German. Thus Ullmann wrote *Der Kaiser von Atlantis* (in German), but also variations on a
Moravian folk song. The German-speaking Krása, son of a Czech-speaking
father and a German-speaking mother, wrote in Czech a young people's
opera about children's getting the better of a domineering organ-grinder,
Brundibár (later performed frequently in the Theresienstadt camp). Klein
and Haas wrote songs to German as well as Czech texts.

It is well known that all five of these composers met their deaths at the
hands of the Nazis. All but Schulhoff were held in the camp at Theresienstadt (Terezín), and all of them were taken to Auschwitz on the same day,
16 October 1944, where presumably shortly thereafter they died.[25] Did
they think of themselves as principally German, or Czech, or Jewish composers after their internment? It seems likely that in their early days, they
did not see themselves simply as Jews, but rather as Czechoslovakians who
happened to speak German and happened to be Jewish. There may have
been subtle changes in attitude. Thus probably the most significant compositions of Victor Ullmann, the student of Arnold Schoenberg, were his
six piano sonatas, and he liked to use the theme-and-variations form for
one movement. In Sonata no. 2 (1938), there are variations on a Moravian
folk song, and in no. 3 (1939) variations on a theme by Mozart. But by 1944,
Ullmann's last work, the Sonata no. 7, contains variations on a "Hebrew
folk song."

Zerging in Dunst: After 1945

The last German empire disappeared. With its music? Wagner has Hans
Sachs predict very clearly:[26]

---

24. Joža Karas, *Music in Terezín 1941–1945* (New York: Beaufort Books, 1985).

25. *Terezínská pamětní kniha* (*Terezin Memorial Book*), 2 vols. (Prague: Melantrich,
1995).

26. The last lines of *Die Meistersinger von Nürnberg*.

Zerging in Dunst
Das heil'ge röm'sche Reich,
Uns bliebe gleich
Die heil'ge deutsche Kunst!

[Were it to disappear into thin air,
The Holy Roman Empire,
We would still have
Our sacred German art.]

After 1945 in Czechoslovakia, the identification of Bohemian culture as partly of German heritage naturally declined and even virtually disappeared. Dual place-names such as Vrchlabí/Hohenelbe and Jihlava/Iglau dropped their German forms, Kafka as a German author was replaced with Kafka the Czech who was obliged to write in German, and eighteenth-century composers with variant name spellings took on the Slavic versions—Stamitz (once Steinmetz) to Stamec, Filz to Fils, Dussek to Dušik, Reicha to Rejcha—restoring them to the realm of Czech culture. The communist cultural establishment encouraged dissociation with the "Western" Germans in order to forge closer ties with the Slavic East. Only as the spirit of the Velvet Revolution of 1989 moved closer, and with it the greater openness to the West, was the German heritage in composition and scholarship again gradually acknowledged. Meanwhile, across the border in West German cities, musicologists played a major part in emphasizing and sometimes exaggerating the German contribution to Bohemian music history, largely assigning a less important role to Czechs and Czech music.

An influential and yet curious post–World War II book, *Die Musik der deutschen Stämme* (*The Music of the German Tribes*) by Hans Joachim Moser, included "Deutschböhmen" as a tribal area and emphasized the many definitely German composers and scholars born there. Claiming the area to be essentially, and in its background, German, he asserted that "the secular art music of the Czechs arose late, as is appropriate to a primarily peasant society."[27] Indeed, in his widely used music dictionary, Moser says of Smetana: "Leader of [Czech society's] growing ethnic identity, he is nevertheless, according to the standards of the great musical nations, only a minor master." Of Dvořák he wrote, "[I]n his creativity we feel, on account of the constantly erupting vernacular musicianship, an absence of true depth and concentration."[28] Both Czech and German Bohemians rec-

---

27. Hans Joachim Moser, *Die Musik der deutschen Stämme* (Stuttgart: Wancura, 1957), 528.

28. Hans Joachim Moser, *Musik Lexikon*, 4th ed. (Hamburg: Sikorski, 1956), 1195, 303.

ognized the character of their musicians as *Musikanten* rather than *Musiker*, suggesting facility, flexibility, a vernacular orientation, a certain lack of seriousness. The concept plays a role in the German literature on Bohemian musical culture. The significance of professional musicianship even in villages has been widely praised and claimed to be a major factor in the widespread development of art music culture for several centuries. Various scholars have touched on the question of whether it is primarily a Czech trait or a German one or syncretic. Helmut Boese's sympathetic dual biography of Smetana and Dvořák is significantly titled *Zwei Urmusikanten*.[29] The very even-handed treatment of ethnic Germans and Czechs in Michael Komma's work, *Das böhmische Musikantentum*, suggests that what sets apart the Bohemian German musicians is their contact with Czech vernacular culture.[30] Rudolf Quoika, in *Die Musik der deutschen in Böhmen und Mähren*, a work of solid scholarship that nevertheless shows some irredentist emotion, emphasized the uniqueness of the Bohemian "Spielmann" among German and indeed European musicians from the Middle Ages on.[31]

Cultural appropriation may work both ways—and each direction has its share of irony. German scholars and music lovers have all along counted the Stamitzes, Myslivečeks, and Bendas—and even to an extent the likes of Smetana, Dvořák, and Fibich—as part of their heritage. And Czech scholars such as Jan Racek have described as part of the history of "Czech music" all of the events that occurred in what is now within the boundaries of the Czech Republic.[32] Indeed, if there is a unique German-Bohemian musical culture, its uniqueness rests on the interaction of Czech and German cultural and stylistic elements.[33] The sacred German empire, in its lethal twentieth-century manifestation, did disappear into thin air in 1945, and with it, there also disappeared the distinctively Czech-German musical culture, wiped out by the greed and murderousness of the Nazi obsessions.

While always a part of culture and politics, art nevertheless also has a

---

29. Helmut Boese, *Zwei Urmusikanten: Smetana-Dvořák* (Zürich: Amalthea-Verlag, 1955).

30. Komma, *Das böhmische Musikantentum.*

31. Rudolf Quoika, *Die Musik der Deutschen in Böhmen und Mähren* (Berlin: Merseberger, 1956).

32. Jan Racek, *Česká hudba* (Prague: Panton, 1958), identified all of the music of the Czech lands to 1800 as "Czech music."

33. According to Komma writing around 1959: "It is a fact—explained by the abiding strength of the German-Czech symbiosis—that German musicians in particular understand more clearly the character of Czech musical culture in the diaspora than before, acknowledge it, and even miss it as something once part of their neighborhood" (*Das böhmische Musikantentum*, 17).

life of its own and can adapt, change its symbolic function, retain its existence. In my most recent visits to Prague, the culture heroes of musical life
were, naturally, Smetana and Dvořák. But above them, head of a kind of tri-
umvirate, towered the figure of Mozart, the Austrian composer whom the
Bohemians claimed to have understood best—and who thought he had been
best understood in Prague.[34] Never mind who these eighteenth-century
Mozart fans were, or what their language and their loyalties were. Informal
counts of concert and opera repertories show Mozart to be the composer
most heard in Prague even now. And so Wagner's Hans Sachs may have it
right in ways he might have found surprising: the German Casino building
is still there on Příkopy avenue, clearly marked, but now housing the popular TGI Friday restaurant. And in the Jewish cemetery rests Franz Kafka,
the quintessential Prague-German author, in an honored grave that lies in
the shadow of one of Prague's preeminent tourist havens, the huge, pink,
palatial Hotel Don Giovanni.

Guide to Further Reading

Cohen, Gary B. *The Politics of Ethnic Survival: Germans in Prague, 1861–1945.*
    Princeton: Princeton University Press, 1981.
Demetz, Peter. *Prague in Black and Gold: Scenes in the Life of a European City.*
    New York: Hill & Wang, 1997.
Gay, Peter. *Mozart.* New York: Viking, 1999.
The Jews of Czechoslovakia. 3 vols. Philadelphia: The Jewish Publication Society of
    America, 1968–84.
Jungbauer, Gustav, and Herbert Horntrich, eds. *Die Volkslieder der Sudeten-
    deutschen.* Kassel: Bärenreiter, 1938.
Karas, Joža. *Music in Terezín 1941–1945.* New York: Beaufort Books, 1985.
Kimball, Stanley. *Czech Nationalism: A Study of the National Theatre Movement,
    1845–83.* Urbana: University of Illinois Press, 1964.
Komma, Karl Michael. *Das böhmische Musikantentum.* Kassel: Hinenthal, 1960.
Large, Brian. *Smetana.* New York: Praeger, 1970.

34. The towering figure of Mozart reigning over the musical life of Prague is part of both
the Czech and the German traditions. Numerous collections of essays about the history of
Prague feature something on Mozart. See, e.g., Rudolph, Freiherr Prochazka, *Das romantische
Musik-Prag: Charakterbilder* (Saaz: Erben, 1914), which begins with an essay, "Mozart Nach-
klänge" (1–20); Paul Nettl, ed., *Hundert Türme, ein Buch vom alten Prag* (Prague: Bücherstube,
1929), which includes an essay by the editor titled "Mozart und Casanova, eine Erzählung"
(102–13). By the same token, a Mozart society of the Czech Republic publishes a periodical
titled *Bertramka: Věstník Mozartový Obce v ČR,* its contents devoted largely
to the association of Mozart with Bohemia, Prague, and the Czechs.

Nettl, Paul. *Mozart in Böhmen*. Prague, 1938.

Newmarch, Rosa. *The Music of Czechoslovakia*. Rev. ed. Oxford: Oxford University Press, 1969.

Payzant, Geoffrey. *Eduard Hanslick and Ritter Berlioz in Prague: A Documentary Narrative*. Calgary: University of Calgary Press, 1991.

Quoika, Rudolf. *Die Musik der Deutschen in Böhmen und Mähren*. Berlin: Merseberger, 1956.

Rice, Timothy, James Porter, and Chris Goertzen, eds. *Europe*. Garland Encyclopedia of World Music 8. New York: Garland, 2000.

Sayer, Derek. *The Coasts of Bohemia: A Czech History*. Princeton: Princeton University Press, 1998.

Solomon, Maynard. *Mozart, A Life*. New York: HarperCollins, 1995.

"Is That Not Something for *Simplicissimus*?!" The Belief in Musical Superiority

ALBRECHT RIETHMÜLLER

For the monarch's birthday on 12 February 1797, Haydn composed a simple song set to the text "God save Franz the Kaiser." Its similarity to the English "God save great George our King" did not escape the notice of the knowledgeable Charles Burney, who promptly shared his observation with the composer.[1] Haydn immediately penned an orchestral version designated "song of the people" (*Volck's-Lied*). Guided by years of experience and an unerring instinct for calculating the success of a composition, he may have anticipated that this birthday tribute would become well known throughout the land, even perhaps the national hymn of the Habsburg monarchy. What he certainly could not foresee was the complicated history that was to unfold in many countries around this nascent genre, the national anthem. For with every political change, not to mention a new type of state, texts can be revised and melodies replaced. Haydn could no more have envisioned that the melody of "God Save the King" would one day be used by a democratic United States than he could have foretold that his own melody would one day grace a text that begins "Germany, Germany above everything, above everything in the world" ("Deutschland, Deutschland über alles, über alles in der Welt").

Hoffmann von Fallersleben wrote his "Song of the Germans" ("Lied der Deutschen") in 1841 with the wish that it be sung in Germany to Haydn's melody. It took some time for this wish to become a reality. From its in-

---

1. Joseph Haydn, *Gesammelte Briefe und Aufzeichnungen*, ed. Dénes Bartha (Kassel: Bärenreiter, 1965), 335.

ception in 1871, the German Empire took no particular liking to a text whose author had in the meantime remained politically suspect. What Hoffmann von Fallersleben and his comrades had yearned for—the unity of Germany—had, in a sense, become reality, but the republican conviction that inspired his text made the song unusable for the imperial state. The empire's solution was to set the melody of "God Save the King" to the words of the Prussian hymn, "Hail to thee in the victor's laurels" ("Heil dir im Siegerkranz"). With the collapse of the central European monarchies at the end of World War I, it was revised; the remnants of the Habsburg monarchy that constituted the new Austrian Republic renounced its old kaiser hymn and with it Haydn's melody. Conversely, Germany now used Haydn's composition, placing it in the service of the new democratic state. Under Friedrich Ebert, the first president of the Weimar Republic, Hoffmann's wish was finally fulfilled. And by 1933, the freshly installed Third Reich had no particular aversion to the "democratic" song, in contrast to the empire after 1871; the text was all too adaptable to the ideology that now ruled. In order to give validity to the claims of the brownshirts who had brought the new ideology to power, a party refrain, the "Horst Wessel Song," was added. In 1949, the first chancellor of the German Federal Republic, Konrad Adenauer, succeeded in sidestepping parliament to retain Hoffmann–Haydn's "Deutschlandlied" (with its "Deutschland, Deutschland über alles") as the national anthem. In the aftermath of the Holocaust and the devastating destruction of World War II, it was clear that the world would shudder upon hearing these words, thus the limitation was adopted that "on official occasions the third stanza is to be sung."[2]

Before achieving his aim, Chancellor Adenauer first had to quell the resistance of the liberal-democratic president of the republic, Theodor Heuss, who considered Hoffmann's lyrics anachronistic and the anthem's association with the "Horst Wessel Song" highly unfortunate (the Nazi song, now all but forgotten, was still a vivid memory in 1950). Heuss was by no means the first to object to the anthem. In 1884, in a thoroughly different historical context, Nietzsche deemed the line "Deutschland, Deutschland über alles" as "perhaps the most imbecilic saying ever to be formulated."[3] Nietzsche's remark has often been read as antidemocratic, but former journalist

2. Bulletin 51 of the Presse- und Informationsamtes der Bundesregierung, Bonn (6 May 1952), 537. The third stanza begins with "Einigkeit und Recht und Freiheit." For further discussion of the *Deutschlandlied* as well as the full text of the poem, see the essay by Jost Hermand included in this volume.

3. Friedrich Nietzsche, *Kritische Studienausgabe*, ed. Giorgio Colli and Mazzino Montinari, 11 vols. (Munich: Deutscher Taschenbuch Verlag, 1988), 11:77.

Heuss and former philologist Nietzsche may have interpreted the motto literally and were therefore repelled by its unmistakable moral and illogical message: "you are above all others in the world."

Keepers of the Sacred Flame

Sharing the same rights as citizens of other nations, Germans are entitled to express patriotic pride in their rich cultural, and above all, musical heritage. Beyond this, however, is the question of how such sentiments are instrumentalized for the maintenance of cultural dominance. With a certain indifference to existing realities, the notion that one's own country—if not geopolitically then at least culturally—is superior to other nations has been a widespread assumption in Germany, one that has time and again fallen on sympathetic ears. Whether the bearers of this message were politicians or artists, journalists or scholars is immaterial. For the idea itself is an illusion (*Einbildung*, with its multiple meanings of imagination, imprint, fantasy, and conceit) that stems from a feeling, is based on a belief, and belongs to the realm of opinions and convictions. The specific channels that propagate this idea are of less concern than the fact that it circulates and becomes anchored in people's consciousness. Found less in theoretical, prescriptive contexts, or even scholarly treatises, it resides in informal, everyday conversation, where it operates as both text and subtext. All media that communicate the subject of music disseminate this message, whether in lecture halls, concert programs, music textbooks, newspapers, radio broadcasts, the Internet, or scholarly musicological studies, whereby the fundamental distinctions among these forms are negligible. The belief in this superiority exists independently of political conviction or ideological orientation, let alone musical experience. It can be observed across the political spectrum from the Right to the Left, among professional musicians as well as amateurs.

Any attempt to prove the superiority of what one regards as "German music" by theoretical means would resemble the accomplished physicist Philipp Lenard's attempts to counter Einstein's theory by proclaiming the existence of "German physics," draping ideology—in this case antisemitism—in a cloak of scientific respectability. This essay does not question the meaning of the phrase "the German in music" but is concerned solely with the illusion of superiority in matters of music, an illusion that the following series of quotations illustrates.

1817: In the introduction to his *Lectures on the History of Philosophy*, Hegel inoculated his readers with a serum that, in effect, was to prevent generations of Germans, not just Hegelians, from granting equal status to foreign ideas. He informed the reader that in other European countries philosophy had "disappeared and dissolved itself into recollection and foreboding" while "it has been preserved in the German nation as a particularity. We have received nature's higher calling to be the keepers of this sacred flame."[4] Hegel's "we" no doubt referred first and foremost to himself as another bearer of the Olympic torch once carried by Plato and Aristotle in the course of history. At the same time, he propagated the notion of national superiority; in so doing, his allusion to the call of nature to justify historical developments relies on one of the oldest tactics of the power of suggestion. A century later, Hans Pfitzner offered a linear, nationally centered interpretation of the history of music by comparing music's development in modern times to a baby initially in the care of a Dutch nanny, who after a season at an Italian boarding school made his home in Germany from the mid-eighteenth century on as a "beautiful, strong youth."[5] Even in recent years a similar attitude has been mirrored in German musical historiography—the journey from land to land is remodeled into a string of pearls with Schütz and Bach through Beethoven, Schumann, Wagner, and Brahms to Schoenberg and Webern, and depending on one's disposition, to Stockhausen (as it progresses toward the present, the development is regarded either as an ascent or descent). At best, foreign composers are found along the margins of this one, truly legitimate history of music, which alone preserves and guarantees Germany's authentic musical tradition. Hegel's added term "sacred" was a particularly popular concept during those years of widespread secularization, and indeed music was deemed sacred almost by nature, not only in the field of church music but equally so in its secular form. The notion of "the sacred art of music" at the heart of proclivities and convictions that support the concept of art religion has remained a specialty of German-speaking countries up to today. Such an attitude is encountered far less, if at all, in European cultures more to the west and south. The devotion (by necessity pseudo-religious) bestowed on music through the rituals of art religion not only reflects a bourgeois approach to music but serves to requisition the domain of music for Germany, just as Hegel's arguments did for philosophy.

1846: Touching on the topic of music in his examination of the sixteenth century, the historian Johann Gustav Droysen maintained that in

4. "Wir haben den höheren Beruf von der Natur erhalten, die Bewahrer dieses heiligen Feuers zu sein." Georg Wilhelm Friedrich Hegel, *Werke in 20 Bänden* (Frankfurt am Main: Suhrkamp, 1971), 18:12.

5. Hans Pfitzner, "Futuristengefahr," in *Gesammelte Schriften* (Augsburg: Benno Filser, 1926), 1:193.

Catholic Italy "the old, false dualism of the sacred and secular has been renewed," whereas "in Germany, the Reformation initially introduced folk melody into the church, and the congregational chorale became the trunk of the tree on which the art of German music or the most German art clambered like a vine."[6] It would be a misrepresentation of Droysen to assume he meant "music is the most German art"—a phrase as foolhardy as it is foolish, which became popular in the first half of the twentieth century.[7] His issue rather was that the Protestant hymn, based on folk music, became the point of reference and support for art music. Far from declaring music as the most German art, he explicitly stated that the origins of a national art can be found in the Protestant hymn, the linchpin for the "art of German music," even the "most German art" (in the manner of rhetorical amplification). Religious considerations, or those linked to a subjective need, rather than musical considerations most likely motivated the Protestant historian's interpretation. Furthermore, the paradigm of deriving art music from the lied, whether folk song or hymn, was common in his day.[8] Luther, also responsible for the German translation of the Bible, figured here as the key figure in the Germanizing of music. That certain rambling quality of Droysen's emphatic style was to become common in subsequent chauvinistic discourses, as well as his disdainful view of Italy: as in Goethe's time, one still traveled with enthusiasm to Italy to revel in its art, but these were

---

6. ". . . führte in Deutschland die Reformation vor Allem das Volkslied in die Kirchen ein und der Choral der Gemeinde ward der Stamm, an dem sich die Kunst der deutschen Musik, die deutscheste Kunst emporrankte." Johann Gustav Droysen, *Vorlesungen über die Freiheitskriege* (Kiel: Universitäts-Buchhandlung, 1846), 1:112.

7. Thomas Mann gave voice to this idea in *The Story of a Novel: The Genesis of "Doctor Faustus,"* published in 1949, but with conflicting emotions. Having once believed in the myth, together with countless others, he found it difficult to alter his thinking. Pamela Potter used the slogan as the title for her study of German musicology in the twentieth century, *Most German of the Arts: Musicology and Society from the Weimar Republic to the End of Hitler's Reich* (New Haven: Yale University Press, 1998); and somewhat differently punctuated, it serves as title again in my article "Musik: die 'deutscheste' Kunst," in *Verfemte Musik: Komponisten in den Diktaturen unseres Jahrhunderts,* ed. J. Braun et al. (Frankfurt am Main: Peter Lang, 1995), 91–103. Celia Applegate seems to have responded to the phrase with the essay "How German Is It? Nationalism and the Idea of Serious Music in the Nineteenth Century," *19th-Century Music* 21 (spring 1998): 274–98. See also Vladimír Karbusický, *Wie Deutsch ist das Abendland? Geschichtliches Sendungsbewusstsein im Spiegel der Musik* (Hamburg: von Bockel, 1995), in which he denounces Hans H. Eggebrecht's *Musik im Abendland* (Munich: Piper, 1991).

8. The botanical imagery embellishing Droysen's thought is, however, ambivalent. One could read into it—certainly counter to the author's intentions—that art music is not an outgrowth of the musical tree but a parasitic plant clinging to it.

journeys into the past. That one doubted one's own cultural superiority also became a thing of the past, especially where music was concerned.

1851: In his *History of Music in Italy, Germany and France,* first published in 1851, the influential music journalist Franz Brendel offered a potpourri of arbitrary assumptions, audacious judgments, and conspicuous violations of the mandates of intellect and reason—in short, all of the ingredients for a myopic, nationalistic rhetoric. "With *Beethoven,* Germany's art returns to the mind (*Geist*), thus to patriotism as well, in the narrower sense." Brendel summed up Beethoven's general position in history by focusing on "the national": "now it comes to life, elevated by *Mozart's* achievements and strengthened through this point of transition, as the only prevailing and legitimate power."⁹ Beethoven is thereby crowned as the nationalist, and it is "the national" alone, categorically stressed, that justifies the phenomenon Beethoven. These claims referred not only to Beethoven in a social context but to his compositions as well—the undeniable reason why his name is remembered. In the end it was Beethoven, not Bach or the ever-controversial Wagner, who prevailed as the cherished prima donna on the national theater's stage of musical preeminence.

1907: In a letter to his wife Gerda, Ferruccio Busoni related the experience of his friend and student, the twenty-six-year-old pianist Egon Petri:

> As Egon crossed the German border, he was carrying Beethoven's sonatas in his suitcase, which were pulled out and inspected in the customs office. "What is that?" asks the officer. "They are scores. Beethoven's sonatas." "Ah, *those* are Beethoven's sonatas," replies the officer as he leafs through them. "To understand them is the most difficult thing of all," he says, handing back the volume. "And," he adds, taking Egon for an Englishman, "a *foreigner* is incapable of it; for that you have to be German." Is that not something for *Simplicissimus*?!¹⁰

The milieu of a customs office is hardly the podium on which Beethoven sonatas are usually presented, nor are civil servants their typical arbiters. The officer in charge was convinced these sonatas belonged to the most

---

9. "Deutschlands Kunst nimmt in *Beethoven* die Rückwendung zum Geist, damit zugleich zum Vaterländischen im engeren Sinne. . . . jetzt tritt es [das Nationale] auf, gehoben durch die Errungenschaften *Mozart's,* gesteigert durch diesen Durchgangspunct, als das Allein Herrschende und Berechtigte." Franz Brendel, *Geschichte der Musik in Italien, Deutschland und Frankreich* (Leipzig: Heinrich Matthes, 1875), 299.

10. Ferruccio Busoni, *Briefe an seine Frau,* ed. Friedrich Schnapp (Zurich: Rotapfel, 1935), 136.

challenging works for listeners to grasp (inherent, too, the possibility that they could be *too* challenging), yet he legitimized their singularity not on the efforts but on the nationality of the performer. Busoni's allusion to the satirical journal *Simplicissimus* refers to the most appropriate venue where such an episode belongs. Later, in another context regarding Beethoven, Busoni referred to these musically inclined officers as the "German music police." Along with ignorance, narrow-mindedness belongs to the indispensable arsenal of nationalists or, in equal measure, racial supremacists.

1935: "Richard Wagner's music conquered the world because it was consciously German and strove to be nothing else." After 1933, the nazified journal *Die Musik* occasionally printed such rhetoric of the new wardens of power in the bold-typed, full-page format commonly associated with advertisements. This particular declaration is attributed to the minister for propaganda, Joseph Goebbels,[11] who in this statement was presumably less concerned with Wagner's music than with the political intentions of his Führer. The remark, intended to assure himself and others of the momentousness of national identity, embodies a dilemma that all supremacists face, one which should be kept in mind in any search for identity. While his reasoning is grounded in self-centered isolationism and the fulfillment of domestic success, it is equally dependent on international triumphs— whereby the rest of the world can choose whether to submit to the dictates voluntarily or by force. The familiar maxim "the German essence will rejuvenate the world" ("am deutschen Wesen soll die Welt genesen") expresses the same way of thinking in different words and is a key component of the conscious and unconscious trappings of cultural dominance. But by the time that mendacious orator began his twelve-year tenure, the "global triumph of German music" had already passed, according to the once prominent music critic Paul Bekker. He maintained that the international preoccupation with nationalism in music reached its peak before World War I, at which time the capacity for "the mediating effect of music among peoples" was temporarily suspended.[12] Bekker published these words—an unusually astute diagnosis of the historical juncture in 1918—in 1920. Of course he could not have known that in little more than a decade the situation would further disintegrate or that the German government would chase him out of his homeland.

1991: Scanning the arts section of a prestigious German newspaper, my eyes happened to fall on a review of a recording of piano sonatas by

---

11. *Die Musik* 28 (1935–36): 721.

12. Paul Bekker, *Die Weltgeltung der deutschen Musik* (Berlin: Schuster & Loeffler, 1920), 38.

Aaron Copland, Charles Ives, Elliott Carter, and Samuel Barber. Generously laced with condescending barbs, it decried the "surfeit of musical emptiness and display of sheer technical fireworks" in Carter's work and labeled Barber's op. 26 a "late romantic epigon." But the crux of the evaluation was in the following sentence: "Despite these objections, the recording remains an exceptionally useful document of American composers' ultimately futile search for their own identity in a form that is foreign to them."[13] The recording's single contribution, then, is to illustrate a purported failure. How removed from reality, how thoroughly blinded by ideology and deep-seated prejudice must one be to presume, at the end of the twentieth century, that the sonata form is more foreign to a New Yorker or Bostonian than to someone from Sondershausen or Donaueschingen? Before 1945, the German press was full of claims that this or that essential musical substance was foreign to Jewish composers; in 1945, following the events that had just taken place, the enemy seems to have simply donned another hat (that many American composers are Jewish makes this all the more ticklish). Refraining from the crude Germany versus America dichotomy, this critic reflects a prevalent European stance when he surmises at the outset that "American composers are not and have never been particularly successful with the traditional forms and compositional principles of European music." Whether individual national chauvinism will fuse into a new Euro-chauvinism remains to be seen. Far from new, in any event, is the verbal tactic of hiding behind Europe (or the West) when what one is actually referring to is one's own country, region, or city.[14]

The preceding review, like the other examples, is isolated and has been chosen arbitrarily. It is typical nonetheless of standardized opinions about music that have circulated in print and discourse during the last several decades. Language is as effective in shaping our conscious thoughts about music as the music itself. Passing observations or mere intimations often contain the coded messages; even if only occasionally repeated, they take root without further discussion. That they remain unanalyzed is also symptomatic. They simply exist, unreflected, fueled by the weight of consensus.

13. "Trotz der Vorbehalte bleibt die Einspielung als Dokument der letztlich vergeblichen Suche nach der eigenen Identität amerikanischer Komponisten in einer ihnen fremden Form äußerst verdienstvoll." Signed "zul.," "Unterwegs. Klaviersonaten aus Amerika," *Frankfurter Allgemeine Zeitung*, 8 August 1991.

14. West as in Occident (*Abendland*). Before leaving for an extended stay in North America in 2000, I bade farewell to a German conductor and music historian in his mid-sixties. He expressed the wish that we resume contact as soon as I returned home to the *Abendland* and was baffled when I reminded him that I was not actually leaving it.

Success and Circumscription

The domain of music, though pivotal, is not the only sphere where hegemonic inclinations reside. Already in the nineteenth century, David Friedrich Strauss speculated that the nation that prided itself as the land of poets
and thinkers cultivated its literary history more as compensation for a lack
of political success (in comparison to England or France) than out of an interest in literature for its own sake.[15] Reinforced by the arduous process of
Germany's unification in the nineteenth century and the disastrous events
in the first half of the twentieth century, the need arose once again to coun-
terbalance political failure. National feelings, battered by total defeat and
political dependency, could look to such surrogates as "Made in Germany,"
the Deutschmark, and the Mercedes star. As a guarantee for retaining cultural authority, music remained unsuspecting and stalwart. In other artistic fields, the attempt to stage hierarchies and rivalries had long existed (in
comparisons with French literature, for example), but claims of preeminence here were impossible to formulate without appearing unconvincing,
if not absurdly pertinacious. By contrast, the notion of dominance with respect to music, the art form of feeling, was able to be preserved internally.

The exceptional achievements of German musicians, particularly composers since the time of J. S. Bach, are universally recognized; what they have
attained cannot be minimized. There have been occasional attacks against
German or Teutonic music to be sure, most audibly in France around the
time of World War I. Debussy was certainly not free of disparagement. But
censure remained marginal, undermining neither the music's success nor its
status. The solidification of the worldwide prestige of music from German
composers coincides roughly with two historical developments: the rise of
ardent nationalism in the middle of the nineteenth century and the crystal-
lization of a canon of musical works, more present in the symphonic literature than in the operatic repertory.[16] Whereas opera in Germany remained
international in its scope, the concert repertory favored a preponderance of
works by native composers, although noticeably less so after 1945. Even
though one acknowledges in theory that music is a universally understood
"language," one would certainly agree that the communication is not in Es-
peranto. *La musique—elle parle allemande.* If not, its level of importance,

---

15. Cf. preface of *Christian Friedrich Daniel Schubart's Leben in seinen Briefen,* 2d ed.,
ed. Eduard Zeller (Bonn: Emil Strauss, 1878), xiii.

16. Cf. Anselm Gerhard, "Kanon in der Musikgeschichtsschreibung. Nationalistische
Gewohnheiten nach der nationalistischen Epoche," *Archiv für Musikwissenschaft* 57 (2000):
18–30.

its value, may be doubted. It is striking that even after 1945, connoisseurs and the intellectual elite in Germany appeared to cling to the idea of the qualitative superiority of their own music far more tenaciously than did the public at large. On listeners' request radio programs, audiences wanted to hear *Capriccio italien* just as often as the overture to *Euryanthe*. The ethically rigorous specialists were the ones who drew a thick line of demarcation between what they decided was tasteful or tasteless. Even in recent decades, textbooks and reference sources in Germany deal with nineteenth-century music in terms of "national schools." One cannot help but notice that as a rule the German school is missing, leading readers to conclude that on the one hand there is music and on the other, such foreign, national schools.

A constellation of nationalism, international dissemination, and canonization contributed to the development of hegemonic beliefs, yet this alone does not fully explain the phenomenon. Given the prejudices pervading the field under discussion, individual observations tend to invite hastily constructed theories and lead to endless debates about what is German—a long-standing, familiar enterprise in Germany, but not only there. I am unable and unwilling to take part in these discussions (whether anthropological or musical in nature), nor am I interested in speculating about the role inferiority plays in the complex of superiority. I prefer to proceed with epideictical means, to simply observe and illustrate.

But one is hard pressed to find reliable answers for even the simplest questions. For instance, where do feelings of superiority historically and objectively begin and how far back in history with regard to music do they extend? It would perhaps be wise to suspend judgment in this case in order not to fall victim to the contemporary temptation to pinpoint the origins of twentieth-century ideologies, primarily Nazi ones, as far back in time as possible. What can be said with assurance is that the belief in musical dominance was fully developed by the middle of the nineteenth century.

The communication and spread of this belief relies on language, which in this case employs nebulous and indefinable categories that are more effective the more ambiguous they are. Indeterminacy, beginning with the word "German" itself, persists. The terminological lattice includes such terms and expressions as the symphonic (or symphony), the spiritual (*Geistiges*), musical logic, thematic work, counterpoint/polyphony, seriousness, depth, *Innerlichkeit*, pure music, absolute music, and others—all of which pose as national traits (which of course they are not) and are taken to be near synonymous with German music. Together they form a plexus that suggests musical superiority, which in turn helps sustain the belief that music is the "most German art," that the Occident finds its musical fulfillment in German compositions, and so on. The complementary side of this argument, with the obvious implication that foreign music inherently lacks these essential traits, should not be overlooked. With the aid of a second terminological network, descriptions of music lacking "Germanness" (be it foreign or not) have since the mid-nineteenth century included such words as slick, clever, lacking in ideas, sentimental, and full of kitsch. Though in and of themselves not antisemitic, these labels have often reinforced or figured as antisemitic clichés, whether blatant or covert.[17]

The endless and futile pursuit to determine the indeterminable in music is occasionally pervaded by the idea of a German style. Unlike its Italian or French counterparts, the German gout is mixed.[18] The associations with this category that may have surfaced in the eighteenth century are one thing; the estimations and intentions that arose in connection with it later (which are not necessarily the same) are another. The salient point here is to be aware of the opposition between mixture and purity, which, in the paradigm of wine mingled with water, sparked the attention of philosophers as early as Plato, who highlighted the philosophical side of the problem. In a time when the ideal of purity was a determining factor (not only in a musical context, but also for blood and race), "mixed style" may have sounded suspect. The only way to neutralize the association with impurity was to view something "mixed" as a synthesis that transcended its constituent elements. Even academic music historiography did not shy away from inventing the necessary explanations, as the following passage on Beethoven illustrates: "Only a German composer was capable of such a synthesis of styles, as it appears in the Allegretto of the Seventh Symphony: sonata form, obbligato accompaniment, and elements of fugue and passacaglia are melted into an indissoluble unit; here the great masters of two centuries of German instrumental music are conjured up."[19] The second sentence even hints that this composite is in and of itself explicitly German, that in the central issue no hybridization occurs.

At this point one is maneuvering in a zone that is very much preoccupied with the psychology and strategies of language and very little with mu-

---

17. The aversion to placing Mendelssohn on equal footing with Schumann may well be a delayed manifestation of both of these complexes.

18. For a discussion of the idea of a mixed style characterizing the "German" in music, see Bernd Sponheuer's essay included in this volume.

19. "Nur ein deutscher Musiker war zu einer solchen Synthese der Stile fähig, wie sie sich im Allegretto der Siebenten zeigt: Sonatenform, obligates Accompagnement, Fugen- und Passacaglienelemente werden miteinander zu einer unauflöslichen Einheit verschmolzen; die großen Geister zweier Jahrhunderte deutscher Instrumentalmusik werden hier heraufbeschworen." Arnold Schmitz, Beethoven (Bonn: Buchgemeinde, 1927), 105.

sic or the tones themselves. Blatant *völkisch*-nationalist writings, including those having to do with music, are in this respect far less interesting, since it goes without saying that their *raison d'être* was "the German." This applies even more to the writings of music functionaries of the Nazi regime. Their publications were obviously effective, but more subtle manifestations were equally so, as in such a passage in which Beethoven is declared the German summation of various styles. In order for non-German readers to grasp the full impact of certain words and understand how they were used, it is often necessary to reconstruct their meaning in specific contexts.

One section of Horkheimer's and Adorno's *Dialectic of Enlightenment* (published first in 1944 in New York and in German, and then in 1947 in Amsterdam) bears the title "The Culture Industry." At the outset, Adorno mentions that he was able to fall back on such established English terms as "movie industry."[20] The book's impact, initially modest, rose to cult status among Western European students and scholars in the late 1960s. The catch-phrase "culture industry" designated on the one hand an antipode of culture under commercial capitalism, and on the other an American counterpart to indigenous German or European culture and the arts. To speak of industry in connection with art, especially music, was still a sacrilege in Germany in the early 1970s; the transplantation of the term culture industry into a German context was surely part of Adorno's calculated provocation. He may have been bemused over the fact that it took twenty years for the powder keg to ignite. The critique of the culture industry, "preceded by the critique of 'Americanism' during the Weimar era,"[21] gained momentum in a climate in which other battle slogans like "imperialism" and "capitalism" were in vogue (adopted from the communist East). Such concepts also found their way into serious discussions on music. If the terms "capitalism" and "culture industry" elicited disgust through their juxtaposition of the selfless, impecunious pursuit of making music (amidst a small elite who earned millions) and the lowly realm of greed and commerce, the castigation of "imperialism" in a musical context was far more abstruse. Here one criticized foreign politics in the context of art and music while simultaneously harboring hegemonic leanings.

20. Cf. Max Horkheimer and Theodor W. Adorno, *Dialectic of Enlightenment*, trans. John Cumming (New York: Herder & Herder, 1969), 121. In this translation of the Frankfurt 1969 edition, the chapter's full title reads "The Culture Industry: Enlightenment as Mass Deception."

21. Giselher Schubert, "'Amerikanismus' und 'Americanism': Hindemith und die neue Welt," *HJb* 27 (1998): 83.

"In the past few years, the German culture industry has been analyzed sector by sector, from film . . . to classical music."[22] When North American readers encounter such an unassuming comment in a current article on the one-hundredth anniversary of Richard Strauss's birth, they are unlikely to comprehend the emotions associated with the verbal weapon "culture industry" in Germany during the early 1970s. Indeed, the German music industry, with all its efficiency, was both the forerunner of and the model for the culture industry. The maintenance of a multitude of orchestras and opera houses (state subsidized money is still money) is one component; more crucial, however, is the music publishing industry, which during the course of the nineteenth century burgeoned into an enormously powerful and prosperous motor. Internationally positioned for success, benefiting from protectionist practices, energized by both domestic creative potential and rampant nationalism, and eager to contribute to national prestige—for instance, the historical editions of the complete works of Bach, which began in 1851, and Handel, in 1858—this music trust left its competition behind. In contrast to literary houses hampered by the troublesome aspect of translations, music publishers had unencumbered access to the international market through their affiliated firms. Their ability to establish "German" as the prestigious trademark for classical music stands in sharp contrast to their lack of international success in popular music, which was not only far more modest from the start but seems to have sunk into further insignificance during the twentieth century.

To the diversified ammunition employed to create the feeling of musical preeminence belongs not only a high assessment of the domestic but a devaluation of the foreign. The following depicts a rough assessment of the German perspective during the first half of the twentieth century. Scandinavia is still considered as little more than an outpost of the Leipzig Conservatory; Sibelius is suspected of composing third-rate symphonies at best; it is debated whether Slavic music deserves to be considered European at all; Bartók would be acceptable if not for the folk elements in his music; Puccini finally succeeded in transforming Italian music into kitsch; apparently Spain is missing from the map altogether; Baudelaire and Valéry are preferable to Debussy and Ravel in France; the study of English music is a waste of time; and finally, the criticism of jazz in America (another skin color complicates matters) is warranted in any case. This catalog of dismissive judgments is purely fictitious (not even a reflection of the symphonic

---

22. Robert Everett Green, "Musical God or Monster?," *Globe and Daily Mail*, 4 September 1999.

composers with only one thing in common: they were all German. It contained nothing composed after World War I, nothing foreign (Slavic or otherwise), and not one work by a Jewish composer. One may have expected to find such an assortment in a *völkisch* training camp prior to 1914, but in a private academy grooming the German intellectual elite for the twenty-first century, it is bizarre. Significant here is the principal's or music teacher's robust and resilient chauvinism, which may perhaps be presumed, together with the harrowing pedagogical neglect in failing to promote any music of the twentieth century.

A few miles away on the other side of the border, the tourist industry has been advertising Austria as the "land of music" for some time now (modesty is never a virtue of the propaganda we now call advertising). Unwittingly one is reminded of the opposite slogan "land without music" that once circulated in England, whether as an understatement or melancholy slur. Musical dominance, shining like a star across the globe, once again compensates for deficits in political and economic power in the second Austrian Republic. Musicologists have also recently begun establishing a strictly Austrian musical identity distinct from and even opposed to a German one, to reset the jewels of music history in a new national setting. This effort demonstrates how distant a European musical identity is, in spite of the fact that music circles are continually preoccupied with conjuring up their allegiance to the Occident (*Abendland*)—an odd notion seldom encountered in other fields, artistic or otherwise. But this phenomenon applies not only to Austria, where memories of the Turkish siege and the ensuing acquaintance with cultural and religious boundaries have remained vivid up to the present day.

The progression from the "most German art" to Austria as the "land of music" is a comfortable step, especially owing to the common language. The refashioned identity ascribed to music represents an involuntary response to Austria's political self-image. By obscuring its own historical tradition, the Austrian People's Party has helped forge a new Austrian identity by fabricating one that is "far removed from the pan-Germanism" that flourished before and after 1938.[26] As distinct as the musical differences between various regions may be, even from one valley to the next, efforts to derive national musical characteristics from the music itself ordinarily produce only nebulous results. There are three main reasons why music is so often invoked in nationalistic, patriotic, and chauvinistic discourse: (1)

26. Michael H. Kater, "Paul Celans Todesfuge und die Paradigmen der Kontinuität in Deutschland und Österreich," in *Unverloren. Trotz allem. Paul Celan Symposion Wien 2000*, ed. H. Gaisbauer, B. Hain, and E. Schuster (Vienna: Mandelbaum, 2000).

national characteristics pasted onto music are arbitrary; (2) arguments consist mainly of clichés that can neither be proven nor disproven; and (3) above all, these arguments are often confused with the qualities of music and its sounds. Even more astounding is the uncanny transformation of national identities. The Viennese classical music that could not be German enough yesterday is now Austrian today.

Things were quite different in 1891. The Austrian Bruckner specialist August Göllerich wrote a keynote address for a convention in Vienna dedicated to that composer now regarded as being particularly Austrian. In the tortured German prose once prevalent in panegyrics, soon to become standard fare in nationalistic eulogies, Göllerich exclaimed: "In that field of most German activity, in the kingdom of music, [Bruckner] strove and achieved, a fortifier of the most proper German feeling, an evangelist of the truest German faith, who evermore proclaims to the world that the noble and beautiful is not created for the sake of fame or privilege, but that it is German to do a thing for its own sake and for the joy one receives from it."[27] When Göllerich's widow wrote to thank the Bavarian governor for inviting her to attend the unveiling of Bruckner's bust in Valhalla near Regensburg in 1937, she added "Heil Hitler!" to her signature.[28] This was by no means a compulsory act, since she was writing from the still independent Austrian Republic, from whence the suggestion to include Bruckner's bust in the German temple of honor originally came.

One may have presumed that the new Austrian identity would rest on a multi-ethnic vision incorporating its inherited musical diversity rather than on the transfigured, purest form of the fulfillment of the "most German art." All conjecture aside, the ease with which national identities can be transferred highlights the arbitrariness of such endeavors in the first place and calls into question the credibility of any country's attempts to establish its national identity through music. "Austrians, it is said, have convinced themselves that Hitler was a German and Beethoven was an Austrian."[29] The illusions live on.

27. "Auf dem Felde deutschester Bethätigung, im Reiche der Musik, hat er gerungen und erreicht, ein Befestiger eigenst deutschen Fühlens, ein Prediger echtest deutschen Glaubens, der immerdar der Welt verkündet, daß das Edle, Schöne nicht um des Ruhmes und Vortheiles wegen in die Welt tritt, sondern daß es deutsch sei, eine Sache, die man treibt um ihrer selbst willen und aus Freude an ihr zu treiben." *Deutsches Volksblatt* (Vienna), 13 December 1891, front page. Printed in boldface type at the bottom of each page in this edition of the *Volksblatt* was the tag, "Buy only from Christians!" (*"Kauft nur bei Christen!"*). Cf. Christa Brüstle, "Musik für Verehrer: Ein Beitrag zur Geschichte der frühen Bruckner-Rezeption," *Österreichische Musikzeitung* 51 (1996): 33.

28. Bayerisches Hauptstaatsarchiv (Munich), StK 107476.

29. Roger Cohen, "A Haider in Their Future," *New York Times Magazine*, 28 April 2000.

Contributors

CELIA APPLEGATE (associate professor of history, University of Rochester) has concentrated her research on the political culture of modern Germany, with a particular interest in the history of German nationalism and national identity. She is the author of *A Nation of Provincials: The German Idea of Heimat* (Berkeley, 1990), and has published extensively on localist ideologies, German national identity, and music's role in identity formation in the eighteenth, nineteenth, and twentieth centuries.

DORIS L. BERGEN (associate professor of history, University of Notre Dame) is the author of *Twisted Cross: The "German Christian" Movement in the Third Reich* (Chapel Hill, 1996), and is currently completing a study of German military chaplains in World War II and a project on the *Volksdeutschen* (ethnic Germans) of Eastern Europe in the 1930s and 1940s. Bergen has published essays on the German churches in the Nazi era, Christian antisemitism, the Wehrmacht chaplains, religion and the Holocaust, and gender and genocide.

PHILIP V. BOHLMAN (professor of music and Jewish studies, University of Chicago) has coedited several important studies on historical and ethnomusicology, has prepared editions of Jewish folk music, and serves as series editor for Recent Researches in the Oral Traditions of Music and for Chicago Studies in Ethnomusicology, the latter published by the University of Chicago Press. His most recent books include *World Music: A Very Short Introduction* (Oxford, 2002) and *"Jüdische Volksmusik"—Eine mitteleuropäische Geistesgeschichte* (Vienna, in press).

JOY HASLAM CALICO (assistant professor, Illinois Wesleyan University) has delivered papers at national and international conferences and at several universities and has published in American, German, and international venues, including *Fontes Artis Musicae* and *Chorus America*. Her research areas include nineteenth- and twentieth-century art song, the Second Viennese School, and especially East German opera and cultural politics. She is currently working on a study of Brecht and opera.

BRUCE CAMPBELL (assistant professor of German studies, College of William and Mary) is the author of *The SA Generals and the Rise of Nazism* (Lexington, Ky., 1998), and coeditor with Arthur Brenner of *Death Squads in Global Perspective: Murder with Deniability* (New York, 2000). He has published on a variety of subjects on right-wing culture in the Weimar and Nazi periods, and is currently preparing a biography of Gerhard Roßbach and a comparative history of amateur radio and modernity in Germany and the United States.

JOHN DAVERIO (professor of musicology, Boston University) has published widely in American and international musicological journals and has contributed essays to major studies on Beethoven, Schumann, Brahms, nineteenth-century German song, and nineteenth-century piano music. He is the author of *Nineteenth-Century Music and the German Romantic Ideology* (New York, 1993), *Robert Schumann: Herald of a "New Poetic Age"* (Oxford, 1997), and, most recently, *Crossing Paths: Schubert, Schumann, and Brahms* (Oxford, forthcoming).

THOMAS S. GREY (associate professor of musicology, Stanford University), has published extensively on Wagner's writings and music dramas, music aesthetics, and criticism in the eighteenth and nineteenth centuries, nineteenth-century opera, Beethoven, Mendelssohn, and music and the visual arts. He is the author of *Wagner's Musical Prose: Texts and Contexts* (Cambridge, 1995) and the editor of *Richard Wagner: Der fliegende Holländer* (Cambridge Opera Handbook series, 2000) and *The Cambridge History of Opera* (Cambridge, forthcoming).

JOST HERMAND (William F. Vilas Research Professor, University of Wisconsin, Madison) has authored more than thirty books on topics including German culture from 1750 to the present, German-Jewish history, and the methodology of cultural studies; has edited approximately sixty works in German literature and culture; and serves as series editor of German Life and Civilization (16 vols., New York, 1987–present). His most recent publications include *Judentum und Deutsche Kultur* (Cologne, 1996), and *Die deutschen Dichterbunde* (Cologne, 1998).

MICHAEL H. KATER (Distinguished Research Professor of History and Social and Political Thought, Canadian Centre for German and European Studies at York University) has published widely on Weimar and Nazi Germany in the areas of politics, society, and culture. His most recent works include *The Twisted Muse: Musicians and Their Music in the Third Reich* (Oxford, 1997), and *Composers of the Nazi Era: Eight Portraits* (Oxford, 2000).

GESA KORDES (Ph.D. candidate in musicology and lecturer in baroque violin, Indiana University) has presented papers in the United States, Canada, and France and has published articles on J. S. Bach, Ernest Reyer, and Richard Wagner in both American and foreign journals.

EDWARD LARKEY (associate professor of German, University of Maryland, Baltimore County) has published articles on popular music in East and West Germany and is the author of *Pungent Sounds: Constructing Identity with Popular Music in Austria* (New York, 1993). He is currently investigating rock music in the pre- and postunification eras in East Germany.

BRUNO NETTL (emeritus professor of musicology and anthropology, University of Illinois, Urbana-Champaign) has published widely on the nature of the discipline and the music of Iran, India, and the Blackfoot Indians. His works have been translated into six languages, and his most recent works include *Heartland Excursions: Ethnomusicological Perspectives on Schools of Music* (Urbana, 1995), and *In the Course of Performance: Studies in the World of Musical Improvisation*, coedited with Melinda Russell (Chicago, 1998).

UTA G. POIGER (assistant professor of history, University of Washington, Seattle) has published on postwar culture and gender issues in East and West Germany. She is the author of *Jazz, Rock, and Rebels: Cold War Politics and American Culture in a Divided Germany* (Berkeley, 2000), and is coeditor with Heide Fehrenbach of *Transactions, Transgressions, Transformations: American Culture in Western Europe and Japan* (New York, 2000).

PAMELA POTTER (associate professor of musicology and German, University of Wisconsin, Madison) has published on music and musicology in the Weimar Republic, the Third Reich, and the GDR, the life and works of Richard Strauss, and German influence in American music and scholarship. She is the author of *Most German of the Arts: Musicology and Society from the Weimar Republic to the End of Hitler's Reich* (New Haven, 1998; German ed., Stuttgart, 2000).

ALBRECHT RIETHMÜLLER (professor of musicology, Freie Universität Berlin) has published on music in antiquity and the eighteenth through the twentieth centuries, the history of music aesthetics and music theory, and the relationship between music and politics. He is the author of *Ferruccio Busonis Poetik* (Mainz, 1988) and *Gedichte über Musik: Quellen ästhetischer Einsicht* (Laaber, 1996) and has edited studies on Beethoven, Johann Strauss, Bruckner, and Brecht's composers. He currently serves as the editor of the *Archiv für Musikwissenschaft* and the *Handwörterbuch der musikalischen Terminologie.*

BERND SPONHEUER (professor of musicology, Christian-Albrechts-Universität zu Kiel) has published extensively on the music of Gustav Mahler, German music and music aesthetics of the eighteenth and nineteenth centuries, Hanns Eisler, and music in the Third Reich. He is the author of *Musik als Kunst und Nicht-Kunst: Untersuchungen zur Dichotomie von "hoher" und "niederer" Musik im musikästhetischen Denken zwischen Kant und Hanslick* (Kassel, 1987), an investigation of the intellectual underpinnings of musicological research. He is also co-editor of *Rezeption als Innovation: Untersuchungen zu einem Grundmodell der europäischen Kompositionsgeschichte* (Kassel, 2001).

HANS RUDOLF VAGET (Helen and Laura Shedd Professor of German Studies and Comparative Literature, Smith College) has published extensively on the writings of Goethe, Wagner, and Thomas Mann as well as subjects in music history and film, and is one of the chief editors of the new edition of the works, letters, and diaries of Thomas Mann. His recent publications include *Im Schatten Wagners. Thomas Mann über Richard Wagner. Texte und Zeugnisse 1895–1955* (Frankfurt, 1999) and a number of major essays on Hitler and Wagner.

Index

absolute music, 13, 29, 41, 48, 51–54, 90, 221, 297
Adenauer, Konrad, 261–62, 263, 289
Adler, Guido, 19, 90
Adorno, Theodor, 37–38, 170–72, 175–76, 301; *Dialectic of Enlightenment*, 299; *Introduction to the Sociology of Music*, 41n. 14; on serialism, 211; on Wagner, 97n. 32, 99n. 34, 101–2
Agricola, Johann Friedrich, 45n. 25
Allgemeine Musikalische Zeitung (journal), 4–5
Altenstein, Karl zum, 253
amateur music, 10, 18, 21, 23, 32, 128, 131
Andrée, Fritz, 266
antisemitism, 174, 176, 298; in German Christian movement, 146–51; and jazz, 218, 227–28; in music scholarship, 22; in Nazi ideology and policy, 24, 141, 145–54, 163, 199–200, 206, 209; of Pfitzner, 20, 179, 181–83, 185, 188; and Wagner, 83–84, 87n. 14, 97–100
Applegate, Celia, 156, 292n. 7
Arent, Benno von, 95, 96
Armstrong, Louis, 29, 231
Arndt, Ernst Moritz, 142, 253
Arnim, Achim von, 109
Association of German Folklore Societies

(Verband deutscher Vereine für Volkskunde), 106, 110
atonal music, 26–27, 208–9, 301
Auschwitz, 186, 283
Austrian People's Party, 303

Bach, Johann Sebastian: in German musical canon, 1, 31, 86, 91, 132, 210, 291, 296, 302; in outer space, 1; political use of, 23, 131, 145; reception of, 41, 46, 48–54, 145, 282; sacred music of, 142; scholarship on, 5, 14, 300; *St. Matthew Passion*, 9–10, 51; Wagner's reference to, 100
Bach Gesellschaft, 14, 60
Backus, Gus, 239
BAP, 249
Barber, Samuel, 295
Barenboim, Daniel, 30–31n. 55
Bartók, Béla, 300
Baudelaire, Charles, 163, 300
Bauer, Wilhelm, 150
Bayreuth, 12, 24, 93–96, 101, 139, 162–63, 200, 259–60
Beastie Boys, 244
Beatles, 246, 248
Becher, Johannes R., 261
Becker, Nikolaus, 65, 253
Becking, Gustav, 278, 282

Spielschar Ekkehard, 23, 128–39
Spitta, Philip, 19
Spliff, 240
Spohr, Ludwig, 200
Spotts, Frederic, 96
SS-Ahnenerbe, 25–26
Stalin, Josef, 192
Stamitz, Johann (Jan Stamec), 273–74, 278, 284, 285
Stampe, Friedrichfranz, 186
Stauffer, Teddy, 235
Steguweit, Heinz, 263
Steinecke, Wolfgang, 209
St. Matthew Passion (Bach), 9–10, 51
Stock, Richard Wilhelm, 96–97
Stockhausen, Karlheinz, 205, 213, 291
Storn, Theodor, 134
Story of a Novel, The (Mann), 292n. 7
St. Paul (Mendelssohn), 9
Strasbourg Conservatory, 179
Strauss, David Friedrich, 296
Strauss, Franz Joseph, 29, 218, 230–31
Strauss, Richard, 30, 196n, 300; as conductor, 18; *Feuersnot*, 17; *Guntram*, 17; in Mann's *Doktor Faustus*, 173; nationalism of, 2, 21; Pfitzner's view of, 182–84; role in Nazi regime, 25, 182–84; *Salome*, 19, 173
Stravinsky, Igor, 209, 220, 222
Sudetenland, 277–80
Suk, Josef, 282
Sulzer, Johann Georg, 38
Swafford, Jan, 11

Tannhäuser (Wagner), 79
Tchaikovsky, Peter Ilyich, 301
Theresienstadt camp, 153, 283
Thiersch, Bernhard, 257
Thoma, Hans, 180
Tiersot, Julien, 89, 91, 93
Ton Steine Scherben, 240
Torriani, Vico, 239
Toscanini, Arturo, 37
Tote Hosen, 249
Treitschke, Heinrich von, 16
Trial of Lucullus, The (Brecht and Dessau), 195, 196–97, 202
Triest, Johann Karl Friedrich, 4–5, 44, 47, 52–55

Tristan und Isolde (Wagner), 88
Tucholsky, Kurt, 259
twelve-tone music, 27, 170, 181, 205, 209, 216

Uhland, Ludwig, 63, 75, 110, 134
Ullmann, Viktor, 275, 276, 283
Ulrich, Titus, 66
United States Information Agency (USIA), 230
University of Göttingen, 5
University of Vienna, 18

Valentin, Erich, 207–8
Valéry, Paul, 300
Valhalla, 7, 255, 304
Vanhal, Jan, 273
Verdi, Guiseppe, 153, 282
Vesella, Alessandro, 160
Vierteljahrsschrift für Musikwissenschaft, 19
Volksdeutschen (ethnic Germans), 143–44, 269–86

Wagenseil, Johann Christoph, 92
Wagner, Cosima, 83, 87n. 14
Wagner, Richard: in German musical canon, 11–12, 30, 31, 32, 141, 184, 282, 291, 293; on Germanness, 2, 32, 41, 178, 203; impact of death of, 17, 165; Mann's view of, 155, 157–60, 162–63, 165, 173; as music critic, 14, 18; Nazi view of, 2, 93–102, 155, 162–64, 200–201, 294; Pfitzner's view of, 180, 184, 185, 186; politics of, 60, 203; in postwar Germanies, 198. Works: *Der fliegende Holländer*, 92, 302; "German Art and German Policy," 41, 83, 85, 100; "Judaism in Music," 87n. 14; *Lohengrin*, 159; *Die Meistersinger von Nürnberg*, 12, 42, 78–102, 161, 283–84, 286; *Opera and Drama*, 84; *Parsifal*, 88; *Der Ring des Nibelungen*, 87, 88, 160; *Siegfried Idyll*, 30n. 55; *Tannhäuser*, 79; *Tristan und Isolde*, 30n. 55, 88; "What Is German?" 12, 33, 78, 83, 85, 100, 165
Wagner, Siegfried, 95, 101, 132n. 15
Wagner, Winifred, 93, 101, 162
Wagnerism, 12, 85–87, 88–91, 162–63
Walente, Caterina, 239